AF608042

Competing for Capital

Competing for Capital

Europe and North America in a Global Era

Kenneth P. Thomas

Georgetown University Press/Washington, D.C.

Georgetown University Press, Washington, D.C.

Printed in the United States of America.

10 9 8 7 6 5 4 3 2 1 2000

This volume is printed on acid-free offset book paper.

Library of Congress Cataloging-in-Publication Data

Thomas, Kenneth P.

Competing for capital: Europe and North America in a global era / Kenneth P. Thomas
p. cm.–Georgetown Series on Public Policy in a Global Economy
Includes bibliographical references and index.
ISBN 0-87840-808-8 (cloth : alk. paper)
1. Capital movements—European Union countries. 2. Capital movements—North America. 3. Investments, Foreign—European Union Union countries. 4. Investments, Foreign—North America. 5. Competition, International. 6. European Union countries—Foreign economic relations—North America. 7. North America—Foreign economic relations—European Union countries. I. Title. II. Series.
HG5422.T467 2000
332'.042—dc21 00-027156

To my wife, Carroll, with all my love.

Contents

Preface

The study of capital mobility and its effects has exploded over the past few years—a welcome if overdue occurrence. Several studies have documented the constraints placed on economic policy, social policy, and regulatory policy. Capital mobility has been implicated in greater income inequality, tax burden shifting, and fiscal crisis. This volume, by contrast, is one of the first efforts to focus on ways to *control* the effects of capital mobility. It analyzes the phenomenon of competition for investment—a process that could not take place in the absence of capital mobility. Through the mediation of this competition, the mobility of capital is translated into subsidies to capital and races to the bottom in terms of regulation or taxes.

Investment competition is half of what Stephen Guisinger has called "the market for investment," which poses collective action problems for both buyers and sellers of capital. In Chapter 2 of this volume, I argue that there are good reasons to expect that the sellers of capital have an easier time solving their collective action problem than do the buyers of capital—that is, governments. Controlling the effects of rising capital mobility then reduces to finding effective strategies for governments to cooperatively regulate their behavior. This analysis harkens back to Richard Cooper's early analysis of interdependence, which has influenced my thinking greatly.

In *Capital Beyond Borders: States and Firms in the Auto Industry, 1960–94*, I showed the decreasing bargaining power of host governments in relation to multinational corporations in the auto industry over the thirty-five-year period of the title. Interestingly, this decrease in government bargaining power was far more pronounced in the United States and Canada than in the United Kingdom, despite the fact that each host faced rising capital mobility. Solving that partial anomaly gave birth to this volume. I was aware even then that the European Union (EU) had rules governing the subsidies (generally referred to there as "state aid") given to firms. Because these rules do not exist in North America, an obvious hypothesis was that the EU's state aid regime accounted for some of the difference in the outcomes I found in *Capital Beyond Borders*.

Konstantine Gatsios and Paul Seabright argue that EU state aid rules represent member states' attempt to solve their collective action problem through the delegation of enforcement powers to the European Commission—a line of analysis pursued more recently by Mitchell Smith. Because the EU provides the world's only significant attempt to comprehensively control subsidies, this volume is largely an assessment of the EU's success in doing so. To improve the usefulness of this volume for EU as well as international relations specialists, I include an extensive analysis of the state aid rules and their historical development before moving on to a wide-ranging evaluation.

My reading of the evidence is that the EU's efforts have led to a reduction in subsidies and competition for investment. This situation provides a useful example for controlling the effects of capital mobility in other geographical areas within or between U.S. states, within the North American Free Trade Agreement, and within the World Trade Organization. I hope to encourage cross-fertilization of ideas about ways to control capital mobility in these and other areas, in practice as well as theory.

Acknowledgments

This project is the largest I have ever undertaken—and the most rewarding. It could not have taken place without an incredible amount of support from many quarters.

My wife, Carroll Thomas, provided intellectual and moral support throughout this project.

In Brussels, Akis Hadjisotiriou and Ann Martin found an apartment for us, provided much hospitality during our visits, and sent timely research material to me over the years. Their children, Sophie and George, were a source of delight.

Frank Plastria and Arille Tassin at the Vrije Universiteit Brussel helped me get established and connected during my first research trip to Brussels.

Maureen Molot provided a hospitable research environment at the Norman Paterson School of International Affairs of Carleton University when we were in Ottawa.

Douglas Yuill and Fiona Wishlade hosted my stay at the European Policies Research Centre at the University of Strathclyde and helped me further by providing copies of the Centre's annual publication, *European Regional Incentives*.

Michelle Cini, Barbara Jenkins, and Fiona Wishlade read and commented on the entire manuscript. Their advice over the years has helped me immensely.

Michelle Cini and David Buchholz provided me with copies of their dissertations, and Robert O'Brien gave me a copy of the page proofs of his book, *Subsidy Regulation and State Transformation*, all of which were invaluable resources.

Greg LeRoy of Good Jobs First! and author of *No More Candy Store* provided incredible support for all manner of information relating to local fights against subsidy abuses, many of which he was involved in, and left a substantial mark on Chapter 5.

Janice Shields, formerly of Essential Information, and Sandra Hinson of the Grassroots Policy Project dramatically expanded my connections among U.S. activists involved in subsidy accountability. Sandra provided almost the entire listing in Appendix 4.

Mike LaFaive at the Mackinac Center and Jeff Horner of the Citizens Research Council of Michigan helped me piece together an especially important but difficult case to estimate.

My deepest debt is to Reinhard Walther of Directorate General IV, Inventory and Analysis Unit, who helped me wade through the vast amounts of statistical information that he and his staff generate, answered numerous questions, and commented on much of the manuscript. I literally couldn't have done this work without his help. I also received substantial assistance from the DG IV Information Office, most notably from Panagiotis Alevantis.

Udo Pretschker of the Organisation for Economic Co-operation and Development and Jesse Kreier of the World Trade Organization advised me about their respective organizations' work in the area of subsidies, provided a number of their publications, and commented on parts of Chapter 7.

The theoretical argument of this book was presented at the Program for International Politics, Economics, and Security at the University of Chicago.

Charles Lipson started me on the path to this book when he innocently suggested, not long after I defended my dissertation, that I should expand my limited coverage there of the European Union's state aid policy into a journal article. Little did he suspect that this idea would produce not just a journal article, but a book and numerous book chapters, as well as a research agenda that is by no means complete even now.

Duncan Snidal provided me with suggestions on the game theory in the appendix to Chapter 2. Any errors remaining there are definitely my fault.

Other people who commented on different parts of the book included Tom Ottervanger, Mark Ronayne, Kary Moss, Laura Macdonald, David Buchholz, Michaela Dabringhausen, Michael Hulshoff, Sandra Hinson, Leigh Hancher, Inda Bevis, Mitchell Smith, Bronwyn Dylla, Michael Webb, Claudio Radaelli, Nikos Zahariadis, Dennis Judd, Michele Hoyman, and Marty Rochester. I would also like to thank the numerous people who agreed to be interviewed.

I know I'm still leaving people out; my apologies to all of them. Despite all of this help, without doubt errors remain. These errors are my own responsibility.

The University of Missouri Research Board and the University of Missouri–St. Louis Research Awards program, the department of political science, and the Center for International Studies at the University of Missouri–St. Louis provided financial support for this research.

A very early version of my argument in this book appeared as "EU Regulation of State Aid to Industry: Lessons for North America" in *Economic Integration in the Americas*, edited by Christos C. Paraskevopoulos, Ricardo Grinspun, and George E. Eaton (Cheltenham, England: Edward Elgar, 1996). The basic "Rising n-Person Prisoners' Dilemma" model of Chapter 2 appeared earlier in *Capital Beyond Borders: States and Firms in the Auto Industry, 1960–94* (London: Macmillan, 1997). Parts of Chapter 5 appeared in " 'Corporate Welfare' Campaigns in North America" in *New Political Economy* (1997), and parts of Chapter 7 appeared in "International Control and Discipline of Subsidies: The EU and WTO Surveillance Exercises," *STI Review* 21 (1998).

I would especially like to thank John Samples at Georgetown University Press, who took the time to see the possibilities in a conference paper I was scheduled to present and invited me to keep him in mind when my book publishing plans became firmer. Two anonymous reviewers at the Press made very valuable suggestions on my manuscript.

Finally, I want to thank my parents, Kenneth W. and Mary Thomas, who made it all possible.

Abbreviations

AA	Alabama Arise
ACORN	Association of Community Organizations for Reform Now
ACTWU	Amalgamated Clothing and Textile Workers Union
AFSCME	American Federation of State, County, and Municipal Employees
AIT	Agreement on Internal Trade
CAMI	Canadian-American Motors, Inc.
CAP	Common Agricultural Policy
CBI	Confederation of British Industry
CBO	Congressional Budget Office
CBPP	Center on Budget and Policy Priorities
CDBG	Community Development Block Grant
CEC	Commission of the European Communities
CEE	Central and Eastern European
CFED	Corporation for Enterprise Development
CFI	Court of First Instance
CII	Compagnie International pour l'Information (France)
CPI	consumer price index
CRAs	credit rating agencies
CTJ	Citizens for Tax Justice
CTF	Canadian Taxpayers Federation
DG	Directorate General
DM	Deutsche Marks
DOJ	Department of Justice (United States)
E	Euros
EAGGF	European Agricultural Guidance and Guarantee Fund
EC	European Community
ECJ	European Court of Justice
ECOFIN	economic and finance
ECSC	European Coal and Steel Community
ECU	European Currency Units
EDA	Economic Development Administration
EEC	European Economic Community

ERDF	European Regional Development Fund
ESF	European Social Fund
ESR	export sales relief
EU	European Union
FF	French francs
FIFG	Funding Instrument for Fisheries Guidance
FoE	Friends of the Earth
GATT	General Agreement on Tariffs and Trade
GDP	gross domestic product
GGE	gross grant equivalent
IDA	Industrial Development Authority (Ireland)
IMF	International Monetary Fund
IMI	Instituto Mobiliare Italiano (Italy)
JIT	just-in-time
JTPA	Job Training Partnership Act
LDCs	less-developed countries
MAPA	Minnesota Alliance for Progressive Action
MNC	multinational corporation
MFA	Multi-Fiber Agreement
NAFTA	North American Free Trade Agreement
NDP	New Democratic Party (Canada)
NGA	National Governors Association
NGE	net grant equivalent
NGO	nongovernmental organization
NUTS	nomenclature of territorial statistical units
OCAW	Oil, Chemical, and Atomic Workers Union
OECD	Organisation for Economic Cooperation and Development
OPEC	Organization of Petroleum Exporting Countries
PIRG	Public Interest Research Group
PPI	Progressive Policy Institute
PPP	purchasing power parity
R&D	research and development
RICO	Racketeer-Influenced and Corrupt Organizations
RNPD	rising-n-person prisoners' dilemma
SBA	Small Business Association
SCM	Subsidies and Countervailing Measures
SWOP	Southwest Organizing Project
TFT	tit-for-tat
TWA	Trans World Airlines

UK	United Kingdom
UNICE	Union of Industrial and Employers Confederation of Europe
UPS	United Parcel Service
US	United States
USTR	U.S. Trade Representative
VW	Volkswagen
WIA	Workforce Investment Act
WTO	World Trade Organization

1

Bidding for Business: An Unclosable Can of Worms?

In 1993, Mercedes-Benz was planning two major investment projects—one on each side of the Atlantic—with the prospect of creating thousands of jobs at each location. What would governments do to attract these huge investments? Superficially, the same process was at work in the United States and in Europe. State governments in the United States, and European national governments, competed with each other using grants, tax breaks, and other subsidies to lure the investment in an auction that only the company could win. No matter how high the inducements to locate in a particular area, the plants would each create a fixed number of jobs that would be located somewhere within the United States and somewhere within Europe regardless of location incentives.

Despite appearances, however, the two auctions were different—and they produced starkly different results. To locate its U.S. plant in Alabama, Mercedes received incentives that various estimates placed at 58 percent to more than 100 percent of the investment's value.[1] In Europe, after an intense search of new sites within the European Union (EU) and in the Czech Republic, the company decided to invest in an existing but practically new factory in western Germany; Mercedes received subsidies amounting to only 40 percent of the investment value.[2]

How was Mercedes able to extract far higher subsidies for its U.S. investment? The answer lies not in the fact that the U.S. plant was new whereas the German facility was not, nor even in the fact that German workers made wage concessions (the Alabama plant was non-union in a low-wage state). Differing policies on aid to business in the United States and the EU are the explanation. The level of incentives provided by Alabama could not be provided to a firm in western Germany—whether new, expanding, or distressed—because EU rules prevent that from happening.

In the United States, by contrast, there are no ground rules to limit the sweeteners that polities can use to induce investment. All fifty states, as well as many counties and cities, act independently to attract investment from foreign and domestic sources—indeed, even tempting established firms to move their operations from one state to another. The use of such programs has proliferated over the past twenty years.[3] Within the EU, fifteen[4] independent countries have ceded some power to control such auctions—slowly and grudgingly but nevertheless surely—to the European Commission, the day-to-day administrative branch of the EU.[5] Over the years, maximum grant levels have been established for the different regions of the EU, and the Commission has secured enforcement mechanisms such as the power to order refunds of investment subsidies given in violation of EU policy. In the United States, by contrast, there has been virtually no attempt at central coordination of government bidding for business, and voluntary regional agreements among state governments in the Midwest and Northeast have been failures.

This state of affairs presents a challenge for theory and policy. Theoretical analysis of cooperation suggests that the easiest way to achieve cooperation among actors (whether they are individuals, governments, or others) who have mutual interests—but would benefit more if they could free-ride on an agreement without sharing its costs[6]—is for a third party to enforce an agreement. For example, although citizens agree that governments have important functions to perform, each citizen would be better off if he or she did not have to pay, as long as government still did its job. If governments relied on voluntary contributions, their revenues would be far lower than they are now; therefore, taxation is a compulsory means to enforce an "agreement" to finance the functions of government.

Similarly in international relations, observers often argue that the global scene is most orderly when a single country has such a preponderance of power that it can enforce agreements among nations. For example, although all countries benefit from free trade, countries that export freely while restricting imports can benefit even more. A single powerful or "hegemonic" country can persuade such countries to open their markets through promises to provide or deny access to its much larger market.

Theoretically, the U.S. government can act as a third party vis-a-vis the states to enforce agreements among them. The federal government has levers on state policy—mainly financial—that allow it to dictate policies that ostensibly are made at the state level. For instance, the federal government in the late 1970s mandated that all state governments raise their drinking age to 21 (usually from 18); the threatened loss of federal highway funds forced states to go along.

One might expect, therefore, that the United States would have an easier time achieving cooperation among its states to rein in auctions for investment than the EU, in which the states are independent nations and the power of the Commission (and the financial resources wielded) is far less than that of the U.S. federal government. Nevertheless, the EU has made genuine progress on this issue, whereas the United States has made little progress.

These issues are not important merely in the abstract. Although very few investments received location incentives in the 1960s, such incentives are extremely common today—and not only for large projects such as Mercedes.[7] Subsidies can be economically distorting and reduce an economy's overall efficiency, and subsidies to capital represent a redistribution away from labor. Combined with broad tax reductions to attract investment, location incentives help shift the tax burden away from corporate income, leaving countries with three problematic responses: increasing personal taxation, running bigger budget deficits, or cutting programs. In addition, interstate competition for foreign investment reduces the overall benefit to the country as a whole from such investment.

When the United States was the world's largest source of foreign investment but host to relatively little, Americans paid little attention to the question of how to get the most social benefit from a new investment. Now that the United States is also the world's largest host for overseas investment, the issue is more salient (although in fact it is just as important when the investor is domestic as when it is foreign).

Clearly, if an investment is going to be made in the United States, the country as a whole will get the same number of jobs no matter where the investor locates. Uncoordinated bidding by states to favor one over all the rest reduces the total benefit to the country by the amount of the subsidy. If one wished to use subsidies to encourage firms to locate in areas of high unemployment, a centrally coordinated regional policy would be better than hoping that states with the highest unemployment rates would be able to make the highest bid for job-creating investments. As we shall see with regard to the work of Timothy Bartik, the empirical evidence in the United States and the

EU suggests that higher-unemployment locales do not offer higher investment incentives.

Moreover, with the approval of the North American Free Trade Agreement (NAFTA), competition for investment is certain to increase, just as it did after the U.S.-Canada Auto Pact[8] and the U.S.-Canada Free Trade Agreement. Therefore, the need for control mechanisms is even more pressing because governments may react to the loss of tariffs as a policy instrument by turning to greater use of location subsidies.

Why Is Bidding for Business Bad?

Not everyone agrees that location subsidies are bad policy. Moreover, some of those who do hold that position have an inadequate appreciation of the dynamics of subsidy wars (see Chapter 2). In fact, there are two distinct lines of criticism of such location incentives, which may be referred to as the efficiency critique and the equity critique, respectively.[9] In this section, I briefly examine these two views, then analyze dissenting positions that deny that location subsidies are necessarily a bad thing.

The efficiency critique is straightforward, especially within the EU context. Economic efficiency is best served by unfettered free markets, as exemplified in the creation of the Single Market. In this view, EU policy should have barriers to neither trade nor capital movements—and location subsidies are simply a disguised barrier to free capital movements. Because such subsidies reduce the market's efficiency, they should be eliminated. This view of subsidies has been very prominent in the Commission's public pronouncements,[10] especially during Sir Leon Brittan's tenure as Competition Commissioner. Indeed, on this view, all subsidies—not just location incentives—should be eliminated; this position (as we shall see) creates one major locus of conflict within the Commission.

The equity critique of investment incentives is based on distributional considerations rather than efficiency criteria. On this view, mobile firms use their bargaining power to extract concessions from jurisdictions, whereas in the past they made investments without expecting or receiving financial inducements. The aggregate effect of this pattern of bargaining over location is to shift income from labor to capital,[11] making the distribution of income within countries less equal.[12] A related way of understanding this point, almost a combination of the two approaches, is to note that if a factor of production is subsidized, it will be oversupplied and therefore rewarded disproportionately—as the Commission itself has argued.[13]

Interestingly, such views are heard far more often from the Left in North America than from the Left in EU countries.[14] The reason is not difficult to understand: Because North America has substantially lower levels of state ownership, the issue of subsidies to state-owned firms—a highly charged issue in the EU context—is almost nonexistent in the United States and relatively minor in Canada. Because the same body of law governs location incentives and subsidies to publicly owned companies in Europe, strengthening control of the former implies greater scrutiny over the latter as well. As the *Economist* has remarked, "This means that governments can no longer run state industries for social and political rather than economic ends. Therein lies the rub. What is the point of state ownership if the state must run its firms as if they were private ones?"[15] As a result, there has been sharp conflict within the European Community (EC) over whether the Commission's targeting of subsidies to state-owned firms has been an attack on the mixed economy *per se*. Moreover, independent of the question of state ownership, the European Left's more interventionist industrial policies require the use of subsidies, and control on state aid reduces the availability of this policy tool.[16]

Despite attacks on location subsidies on efficiency and equity grounds, a few analysts defend them in principle (as opposed to their obvious continued use by policymakers, for which see Chapter 2).[17] Black and Hoyt[18] claim that bidding for investment can itself be efficient when it moves public services from average-cost pricing to marginal-cost pricing. As they admit, however, this result obtains only if firms and governments know the relevant costs of locating at different locations. In fact, companies guard this information jealously, which is another factor that strengthens the firms' hand in this bargaining situation. Moreover, Black and Hoyt's argument addresses only the efficiency issues of location incentives, not the equity critique.

Bartik makes a similar claim, suggesting that the market for investment is itself efficient in the sense that jurisdictions with high unemployment will offer the highest investment subsidies.[19] Yet survey evidence that jurisdictions with higher unemployment "tend to be more active in industrial recruitment and other economic development activities" does not demonstrate that they have the financial and fiscal capacity to offer higher location inducements than richer jurisdictions; evidence from the EU suggests that they do not. Despite the fact that development differentials between the best- and worst-off areas of the EC are greater than they are in the United States,[20] and despite the fact that the worst-off member states can legally provide higher levels of state aid than the richest members, the worst-off areas simply cannot afford to outbid the better-off areas for investments on a consistent basis.[21] Fisher and Peters have found that this situation is true in the United States as well, concluding:

> There is little reason to believe that higher-unemployment states and cities provide the largest standing offers. This suggests that the antecedent conditions for Bartik's argument that incentives may have net national benefits is not true: The spatial pattern of taxes and incentives in America is not likely to promote the redistribution of jobs from places of low unemployment to places of high unemployment.[22]

This analysis implies that instead of relying on uncoordinated bidding for investments to equalize unemployment, countries should rely on a centralized regional agency to provide incentives to minimize the amount spent on them, if they are to be used at all.[23] This approach would be more effective than simply "deplor[ing]," as Bartik does, "economic development policies to increase jobs when they are pursued by low-unemployment areas."[24]

The Wider Consequences of Competition for Investment

Competition for investment includes more than just location subsidies, and it has far-reaching consequences beyond those discussed above. On the financial side, investment competition includes subsidies, tax incentives, and general reductions of corporate tax rates. On the nonfinancial side, governments can make investment more attractive to companies by reducing regulatory costs (pollution control is one example, though the range of possibilities is quite wide, depending on the specific situation) or by reducing the cost of labor (e.g., low or no minimum wages, laws that prevent or weaken unionization, the United Kingdom's opt-out from the Maastricht Agreement's Social Chapter from 1993 to 1997). This situation raises the possibility of "races to the bottom" in these policy areas as countries try to attract investment.

As with location subsidies, resisting races to the bottom also takes the form of a prisoners' dilemma. Doing so successfully requires cooperation from parties who might otherwise be competing for investment. One way to do this is to agree to set floors below which competition cannot go. The EU's Social Charter is one example; minimum wage laws are another. (The latter is another example of federal imposition of "cooperation" on U.S. states.) The alternative is what David Vogel calls the "California effect": A large, rich jurisdiction insists that others meet its standards.[25] In essence, the California effect is equivalent to Mancur Olson's "privileged group," in which a single large actor can benefit from cooperation[26] and action is required to prevent free riding. Although Vogel argues that a California effect of improving standards may be more likely regarding environmental regulations (where costs are insignificant except within a very few industries), he acknowledges that labor costs *are* subject to international competition.[27] Furthermore, a California effect is unlikely in the case of financial competition for investment because the value of incentives is so high (often reaching 100 percent of the investment).

The consequence of financial competition for investment, via general tax rate reductions and special deals for individual investments, has been a long-term reduction in the corporate tax burden.[28] This reduction has been especially pronounced in the United States and Canada, see Table 1-1.

As Table 1-1 shows, this shift in tax burdens has been a worldwide trend. This trend has profound implications for the welfare state. If corporate taxes fall, there are only three possible responses that a government can follow: raise individual taxes, run greater deficits, or reduce spending. In practice, governments have tried to do some of each, though perhaps each of the possibilities has predominated at different times (in the order listed).

Table 1-1 shows that in the United States, for example, the bulk of the corporate tax share decline had occurred by 1975. Personal taxes rose to compensate, fueling the perception that Americans are highly taxed—as illustrated by the "tax revolt" beginning with California's Proposition 13 (reducing property taxes) in 1978.[29] Because of resistance to increased taxes, policymakers moved to increasing budget deficits in the 1980s (a tack taken in many other countries as well). By the end of the decade, however, concern about the allegedly pernicious

Table 1-1 **Corporate Income Tax Share of Total Tax Revenues, 1948–1996 (%)**

	1948	1955	1975	1991	1996
U.S. states	8.6			6.6	
Total U.S.		20.3	11.4		9.6
Canada		17.6	13.6		8.9
Japan		18.4	20.6		16.4
Germany		9.8	4.4		3.8
France		N/A	5.2		3.8
U.K.		17.5	6.2		10.5
Italy		5.5	6.3		9.2
G-7 mean (unweighted)		14.9	9.7		8.9

Sources: For U.S. states, data are from Howard (1994). For G-7 countries, data are from Organisation for Economic Cooperation and Development (OECD), *Revenue Statistics, 1965–1997* (Paris: OECD, 1998); data for 1955 were calculated from Table 130 (OECD, 1998, p. 194); data for 1965–1996 are from Table 13 (OECD, 1998, p. 84).

effects of budget deficits grew,[30] and governments throughout the industrialized world have embarked on efforts to reduce deficits to low figures—such as 3 percent of gross domestic product (GDP), in the EU—or produce a balanced budget (in the United States). Budget reduction is causing policy convergence over a wide range of policies, including social welfare and health care benefits—which have become less generous.[31]

Tax competition has begun to receive substantial attention from policymakers. Important work is being done at the Organisation for Economic Cooperation and Development (OECD), the EU (for both, see Chapter 7), and the International Monetary Fund (IMF). Vito Tanzi of the IMF argues that tax competition has already changed the composition of taxes (lower corporate income taxes, rising consumption taxes, higher personal income taxes on wage income but lower taxes on personal capital income). In addition, he suggests that total tax revenues may eventually fall as a consequence.[32] A late 1999 article in the *Baltimore Sun* suggests that South Carolina may have fallen into fiscal crisis because of its investment-attraction tax policies.[33]

As Sven Steinmo points out, these outcomes are exactly the opposite of what citizens of the industrial democracies wanted. Voters in the United States, the United Kingdom, and Sweden thought the problem with their tax systems was that too little of the burden was placed on the rich and too much was placed on the middle class and poor. "Tax reform" in the 1980s, however, shifted tax burdens downward further.[34] Ultimately, then, competition for investment may tend to undermine democratic governance.

In summary, competition for investment entails many problems. Firm-specific subsidies (i.e., location incentives) may lead to less-efficient uses of capital and represent a shift of income from labor to capital. Beyond these direct consequences, investment competition can reduce socially desirable regulations (e.g., regarding the environment or the workplace), and it has clearly led to a shift in the tax burden from mobile firms to less mobile actors. Not only does this trend fly in the face of voters' preferences, it puts pressure on government budgetary capacity and hence on the welfare state.

The View from the Economic Developer's Desk

The literature on state and local economic development largely accepts the assertion that competition for investment is a poor policy choice, primarily because of the claim that location incentives are not effective in affecting firms' location decisions.[35] Because governments continue to take part in such bidding wars, however, economic development analysts have attempted to explain their seemingly irrational behavior. As Reese remarks, "Scholars have looked at a variety of explanations for such widespread use of supply-side techniques [i.e., investment incentives], including attitudes of economic development professionals, decision-making procedures, state enabling legislation, and local political imperatives."[36]

As Chapter 2 shows in detail, however, this conception of investment competition as simply irrational is wrong: The cost of not offering location subsidies *when other jurisdictions are doing so* is lost investment. Nevertheless, offering investment incentives *is* bad policy. From the standpoint of economic development officials, however, it is important to see if anything can be done about the problem. In other words, can control of bidding for business be successful? This question is important for policymakers, and it is especially timely in the context of NAFTA and as U.S. states and Canadian provinces are beginning to accept the difficulties of continued investment competition.[37] The evidence from the EU suggests that the answer to this question is yes. EU policy benefits member states, their workers, and taxpayers by limiting public subsidies for investment they would receive anyway, and such a policy could be adopted successfully in North America.

This analysis also speaks to other aspects of economic development policy. First, the focus here on comprehensive evaluation of the effects of location incentives means that I take most cost-benefit analysis used by economic development agencies to be beside the point. Even if tax revenues in a given state increase by more than the amount of taxes foregone—a commonly used (and abused)[38] measure in many states—this analysis does not take into account what happens in other states,[39] nor does it consider the appropriate counterfactual (i.e., no incentives being given in a particular place). For example, when a firm relocates from one state to another, if it faces the same tax rates in each state, total tax revenues fall by the amount of the location incentives, even if the state receiving the investment sees a net increase in revenue. Even with a new facility, policymakers must take into account the fact that the aided plant will displace existing facilities. This dynamic has been an obvious problem with the U.S. bidding wars for automotive investments in the 1980s and 1990s because of overcapacity in the industry. Although Honda, Nissan, and other firms coming to the United States brought jobs to their new locations, they were driving older Big Three (General Motors, Ford, and Chrysler) plants out of business in other states, in part because the new plants had younger (and therefore healthier) workers and no retirees to support.[40] Moreover, states fail to consider the proper counterfactual to granting incentives—namely, situations in which no one grants incentives. If that alternative could be made viable, policymakers would immediately recognize that current policies are wrong.

Second, the benefits of discretionary versus automatic types of investment attraction are under studied; some critics of location subsidies often assume away such benefits. Automatic programs,[41] in which investors know in advance exactly what they are eligible for in terms of investment support, are attractive to firms and are easy to administer. As John Bachtler notes, such programs are very easy for firms to take into account at the earliest stages of site selection.[42] They also have the additional advantage (if they are granted throughout the government's territory) that their lack of selectivity means that they do not qualify as subsidies under the General Agreement on Tariffs and Trade (GATT) Agreement on Subsidies and Countervailing Measures (see Chapter 7). On the other hand, automatic subsidies cost much more than support programs in which administrators exercise discretion over the amount of the award and whether a project qualifies at all. Bachtler points out that automatic subsidies cost more than discretionary subsidies because many investment projects would have gone ahead without automatic subsidies or at lower levels of support than those provided by automatic programs; thus, investors often receive "windfall" gains.[43] The European experience since 1980 has demonstrated an inexorable shift from automatic to discretionary programs as a result of the twin pressures of the budget and European Commission opposition to automatic programs.[44]

These tradeoffs are not well understood among some critics of firm-specific location incentives. In particular, conservative critics of targeted subsidies often suggest that we should simply reduce corporate taxes in general instead.[45] In essence, however, such a policy entails a move toward automatic investment subsidies; it ignores the budgetary consequences (let alone the contribution to tax burden shifting, as discussed above). The Mercedes case in Alabama illustrates this point well. After negotiating the deal with Mercedes, the state implemented the policy through legislation that made the investment incentives the firm received generally available. By January 1995—just a little more than a year after Mercedes announced its decision—eighty-seven projects with more than $3 billion in investment had qualified for support under the program.[46] By April of 1995, the state was unable to pay Mercedes $43 million for construction costs that the firm was owed under the agreement. After giving up on using tax revenues pledged to education because of a threatened lawsuit and losing a court battle over using oil and gas tax monies instead, the state borrowed from the state employees pension fund at "virtually a junk-bond rate" of 9 percent.[47] (See Chapter 5 for more details and the similar case in Rio Rancho, New Mexico, involving Intel Corporation.)

The model advanced in Chapter 2 removes the difficulty that the economic development literature has in explaining why development agencies use location subsidies. Rather than regarding such subsidies as irrational or straining to find a tenuous political rationality to them, I argue that this behavior is quite rational given the strategic situation in which governments find themselves. Solving the problem requires changing the strategic situation itself. It also requires us to adopt a comprehensive standpoint for evaluating policies so that externalities are fully taken into account—which locally based cost-benefit analysis does not do. Some solutions are better than others, however. Replacing firm-specific incentives with a general lowering of the corporate tax burden is extremely damaging to governments' tax bases and contributes to what is already a more than forty-year trend of tax burden shifting. Governmental cooperation is key to overcoming the problems of the strategic situation—which is why that issue occupies a central place in the analysis that follows, beginning in Chapter 2.

Plan of the Book

Chapter 2, "The Market for Investment," takes up my theoretical argument in detail. It shows why, in a capitalist economy, nations and subnational units alike must compete for investment. In fact, although bidding wars for investment are irrational from a comprehensive viewpoint (i.e., national versus states or provinces, EU versus individual members), such an approach is quite the opposite from the standpoint of individual governments: It is the best choice available to officials caught in the prisoners' dilemma of investment attraction. We have a situation in which all governments would be better off if they did not offer incentives but each has an individual incentive to do so. A government cannot unilaterally cease to offer incentives if others continue to provide them. Only through cooperation among governments can all achieve better outcomes without paying a price in lost investment. The introduction of the prisoners' dilemma will help to provide a rigorous framework for the conceptual analysis. In addition, because the moral of prisoners' dilemma relates precisely to the difficulty of obtaining cooperation, the reason we have seen so little cooperation on this issue becomes immediately comprehensible. Abstract analysis of cooperation suggests two strategies with chances for success in the real world: enforcement of an agreement by an outside party and learned cooperation through repeated plays of the game. The first strategy characterizes the situation in the United States; the federal government at times has been able to enforce uniform policies on the states through manipulation of financial incentives to the states. The second strategy, which is discussed heavily in international relations "cooperation under anarchy" literature, characterizes the fifteen independent nations of the EU.

Chapter 3, "European Union Control of State Aid," begins the European case study by describing the legal basis for the European Commission's regulation of all kinds of subsidies to business and the institutional arrangements used. It describes the role of state aid policy within competition policy, the increased emphasis it received in context of the Single European Market (the 1992 program), and the relationship of state aid policy to regional development policy. It emphasizes the dual nature (i.e., legal and political) of policies on state aid, considers how important political divisions within the EU over state ownership and intervention affect policies on state aid, and analyzes the Commission's standard views on different types of state aid.

Chapter 4, "Development of the State Aid Regime," examines the development of the Commission's power and policies in this area. It considers European Court of Justice cases that established important legal precedents such as the right to order repayment of illegally paid subsidies, the necessity for the Commission to provide convincing economic analysis, and the requirement that aid has to be necessary to obtain goals enunciated in the treaty ("compensatory justification"). It also examines the important issue of enforcement of Commission decisions, the numerous ways that EU member states have tried to find loopholes or evade the rules over the years, and the Commission's response to improve compliance. Chapter 4 also analyzes numerous Commission policy initiatives (such as regionally differentiated aid maxima), its various industry frameworks, and the campaign against so-called general aid.

Chapter 5, "The North American Nonregimes," contrasts the EU experience with the virtually unregulated investment competition in the United States and Canada. It offers estimates of the levels of business subsidization in both countries. One important finding is that the United States is a much higher subsidizer than it portrays itself in international trade negotiations.[48] Chapter 5 reviews the story of federal regulation of locational subsidies, focusing on 1986 U.S. federal restrictions on industrial revenue bonds and various antipiracy bans for federal programs—as well as the more promising Canadian code of conduct on incentives, which was signed in July 1994. Chapter 5 also chronicles the largely unsuccessful efforts at voluntary state and provincial cooperation to reduce competition for investment, as well as the pressure from nongovernmental organizations (NGOs) to end, reduce, or regulate "corporate welfare."

Chapter 6, "How Much Bang for the Euro?" provides an evaluation of the European Commission's efforts in the state aid field. This chapter represents a return in part to the economic developer's perspective; it explores whether the complex state aid control mechanism actually gets results. I draw on data I gathered in Brussels, Paris, and Glasgow, as well as interviews with Commission and OECD staff, plant location consultants, and other researchers, to conclude that the EU's efforts are indeed paying off, even if they are not completely successful. In particular, the Commission has been able to enforce an overall reduction in total aid and in aid that is potentially available to mobile projects; it has wiped out export subsidies for intra-Community exports and eliminated general aid programs that had no sector or regional specificity and were especially open to abuse. On the other hand, the Commission has not fully solved the problem of unreported aid; moreover, Community funds have offset some of the reductions in national aid, and state aid policy has had only a mixed effect on cohesion. The reunification of Germany has led to a number of problems for Directorate General (DG) IV's control of state aid (e.g., the Bremer Vulkan scandal of aid diversion, a large number of non-notified aids). Finally, the problem of unregulated substitutes for state aid is lessening to some extent as Ireland's 10 percent corporate income tax for manufacturing has been brought under the state aid rules, and the United Kingdom has signed the EU's Social Chapter.

Chapter 7, "Lessons for Theory, Lessons for Policy," draws lessons from the EU experience for North American and international economic policymaking and for international political economy theory. It argues that a central reason for the superior EU results in comparison with the North American (especially U.S.) experience is the existence of an institutionalized monitoring and enforcement body. The European approach is more effective than the historical GATT approach to subsidies, which relied on actions by individual states for monitoring and retaliation through countervailing duties rather than building in possibilities for real enforcement, as in the EU setup. The fact that institutionalized monitoring can be more conducive to states' cooperating with each other than their strict subordination to another government is an important theoretical finding for international political economy. Chapter 7 goes on to argue that the European model for controlling state aid could well be successful in the North American environment. The political difficulties of achieving such a major reform should not be underestimated, however—as the prisoners' dilemma certainly demonstrates. Nonetheless, there is widespread recognition of the problem.

Moreover, conditions may be favorable to a solution that is broader than just the United States. In July 1994, Canada concluded a provincial trade agreement that includes a first-ever legally binding (in part) provincial code of conduct on investment incentives. The signing of the North American Free Trade Agreement may also make it sensible to reach agreement on competition for investment in that context. Finally, the Uruguay Round's Agreement on Subsidies and Countervailing Measures draws heavily on the EU model and applies to subnational as well as national governments. All of these developments increase the likelihood that bidding wars can be brought under some control in the United States.

The book concludes with policy recommendations to help smooth the way toward control of location subsidies. These recommendations include a periodic accounting of state aid in the United States and Canada (such as those now published annually by the EU) and a search for ways to extend the Canadian provincial incentives agreement to the American states. Moreover, both countries (but especially the United States) must stop blocking international subsidy transparency. Both worked to end an OECD project on industrial subsidies, as Chapter 7 notes, and the United States devotes less than one full-time professional to its World Trade Organization (WTO) notification efforts. Domestic constituencies in both countries want to judge subsidy policies but are hampered from doing so because of attempts to gain advantage in international trade.

Note on Data and Sources

One difficulty in writing a work such as this is the vast disparity in data availability between the EU and the United States and Canada. The EU now publishes annual surveys of state aid that compile the amount of aid given in every member state and categorize and analyze aid trends. In North America, by contrast, there is no such systematic data collection, even though in principle U.S. and Canadian subsidy notifications to the WTO (see Chapter 7) should include all subsidies at every level of government. At present, there are substantial drawbacks to both countries' notification efforts; these difficulties have more to do with their relationship with each other than with wider trading relationships.[49] Therefore, the data presented in Chapter 5 should be regarded as preliminary only because they are based on extrapolations from states for which good estimates of subsidies are available. Moreover, these data are less up-to-date than the data provided by the EU (see further discussion in Chapter 5). For the EU, the data in Chapters 3, 4, and 6, by contrast, are based on two 1999 sources: the *Seventh Survey of State Aid* and the *Twenty-Eighth Report on Competition Policy.* Thus, although I have made every effort to have the most up-to-date data possible, readers should understand that data availability is not what it should be. Indeed, one of the most important recommendations of this book is that the United States and Canada should publish comparable subsidy data because we cannot fully judge North American subsidy policy without such data.

Notes

1. Ken Blum with Robert Ginsburg, *The Mercedes Benz Subsidy Package: Whose Benefits? Whose Losses?* (Chicago: Midwest Center for Labor Research, 1995), 1; "The Invaders Are Welcome," *Economist,* 8 January 1994, 32; Eric Patterson, "Behind the Mercedes Move," *Expansion Management* 9 (January/February 1994): 4.
2. Economist Intelligence Unit, "German Labour Costs Continue to Cause Problems," *Business Europe*, 27 December 1993; "East, West—Home's Best," *Financial Times*, 20 December 1993, 13.
3. William Schweke, Carl Rist, and Brian Dabson, *Bidding for Business: Are Cities and States Selling Themselves Short?* (Washington, D.C.: Corporation for Enterprise Development, 1994), 18–20.
4. Austria, Finland, and Sweden became members of the EU in 1995, although they had previously been subject to EU state aid rules through the European Economic Area agreement.
5. This volume does not directly address the debate between (neo)functionalists and intergovernmentalists over the nature of the EU. It assumes that the European Commission and member states have power resources that can be brought to bear in the event of conflicts between them in this issue area and seeks to understand the limits to the power of each. This approach is exemplified by Mitchell P. Smith, "Integration in Small Steps: The European Commission and Member-State Aid to Industry," *West European Politics* 19 (July 1996): 563.
6. Specialists will recognize this situation as the collective action problem, an *n*-person prisoners' dilemma.
7. For example, Tetra Plastics received $263,000 in investment and job creation tax credits and $750,000 in highway infrastructure for making a $24 million, 100-worker expansion in St. Charles County, Missouri. See Fred Faust, "The 'Air' in Nike Stays Here," *St. Louis Post-Dispatch*, 30 September 1994, E1, E7.

8. Kenneth P. Thomas, "Auto Bargaining in Canada, 1965–87," in *Multinational Corporations in a Changing Global Political Economy,* ed. Steve Chan (London: Macmillan, 1995).
9. Another, more restricted, view criticizes subsidies that promote environmentally harmful activities. See Chapter 5 for a discussion of environmental NGOs with such views.
10. Commission of the European Communities (CEC), "Fair Competition in the Internal Market: Community State Aid Policy," *European Economy* 48 (September 1991), 7–114.
11. Presumably, if government had kept the subsidy amount, at least a portion would have gone to uses benefiting labor; when such subsidies are provided to businesses, however, they go entirely to capital.
12. For example, see Ian Robinson, *North American Trade As If Democracy Mattered* (Ottawa: Canadian Centre for Policy Alternatives, 1993), 34–35.
13. CEC, "Fair Competition in the Internal Market," 28. The authors cite a German study that found that eliminating all German subsidies and reducing taxes by the same amount would increase GDP and employment.
14. Besides Robinson, examples include Jerry Jacobs, *Bidding for Business: Corporate Auctions and the 50 Disunited States* (Washington, D.C.: Public Interest Research Group, 1979); Robert Goodman, *The Last Entrepreneurs: America's Regional Wars for Jobs and Dollars* (New York: Simon and Schuster, 1979); David Robertson and Dennis Judd, *The Development of American Public Policy: The Structure of Policy Restraint* (Glenview, Ill.: Scott, Foresman, 1989). On the EU side, see, for example, the divide between Liberals and Socialists on state aid in the European Parliament reported in "MEPs Split Over State Aid and Liberalization," Reuter European Community Report, 14 February 1996, BC Cycle. The only exception in the EU is in the United Kingdom, where the Labour government under Tony Blair continues the low-subsidy practices of its Conservative predecessors and strongly criticizes other EU members on their state aid policies.
15. "The Aid Plague," *Economist,* Survey of Business in Europe, 8 June 1991, 17.
16. This point was suggested to me by Barbara Jenkins.
17. For an extensive literature survey, see David Buchholz, "Competition and Corporate Incentives: Dilemmas in Economic Development" (Ph.D. diss., Duke University, 1998), Chapter 3.
18. Dan A. Black and William H. Hoyt, "Bidding for Firms," *American Economic Review* (December 1989), 1249–56.

19. Timothy J. Bartik, *Who Benefits from State and Local Economic Development Policies?* (Kalamazoo, Mich.: Upjohn Institute, 1991), 194–95.
20. Andrea Boltho, "European and United States Regional Differentials: A Note," *Oxford Review of Economic Policy* 5, no. 2 (summer 1989): 105–15, especially 106–07.
21. See CEC, *The Regions in the 1990s—Fourth Periodic Report on the Social and Economic Situation and Development of the Regions of the Community*, COM(90) 609 final, 9 January 1991, 8-2; and CEC, *Industrial Policy in an Open and Competitive Environment: Guidelines for a Community Approach*, COM(90) 556 final, 16 November 1990, 8; Douglas Yuill et al., *European Regional Incentives 1994–95* (London: Bowker-Saur, 1994), 100–102.
22. Peter S. Fisher and Alan H. Peters, *Industrial Incentives: Competition Among American States and Cities* (Kalamazoo, Mich.: Upjohn Institute, 1998), 26.
23. Of course, it would also be necessary to do a better job increasing the aid differentials between regions than the EU has so far been able to do; I take up this topic further in Chapter 6.
24. Bartik, *Who Benefits*, 192.
25. David Vogel, *Trading Up: Consumer and Environmental Regulation in a Global Economy* (Cambridge: Harvard University Press, 1995), 5–8.
26. See Russell Hardin's more rigorous discussion of group size and the prisoners' dilemma in *Collective Action* (Baltimore: Johns Hopkins University Press for Resources for the Future, 1982), 38–49.
27. Vogel, *Trading Up*, 6, 257.
28. Dennis Quinn finds that capital account liberalization has led to increased corporate tax revenues, according to most measures he used (although not that of Table 1-1). This surprising finding deserves further investigation; unfortunately, however, Quinn offers no theoretical explanation for it. He also finds—as one would expect on the basis of the analysis presented here—that capital account liberalization is associated with increasing levels of income inequality. See Dennis Quinn, "The Correlates of Change in International Financial Regulation," *American Political Science Review* 91, no. 3 (September 1997): 531–51.
29. Reducing property taxes is an odd response, however, because property taxes fell as a percentage of taxation and as a percentage of GDP throughout the 1965–80 period. In comparative perspective, of course, the U.S. tax burden as a proportion of GDP is virtually the lowest among all industrialized countries. See OECD, *Revenue Statistics 1965–1997*, Table 1, p. 78.
30. Geoffrey Garrett has shown that social-democratic governments have had to pay an interest rate premium for their more expansionary/infla-

tionary policies. See Geoffrey Garrett, "Capital Mobility, Trade, and the Domestic Politics of Economic Policy," in *Internationalization and Domestic Politics*, ed. Robert O. Keohane and Helen V. Milner (Cambridge: Cambridge University Press, 1996), 95.

31. Vic George, "The Future of the Welfare State," in *European Welfare Policy: Squaring the Welfare Circle*, ed. Vic George and Peter Taylor-Gooby (New York: St. Martin's, 1996), 25.

32. "How Will National Tax Systems Fare As Globalization Proceeds?" *IMF Survey*, 26 May 1997, 166. See also "Disappearing Taxes: The Tap Runs Dry," *Economist*, 31 May 1997, 21–23.

33. Jay Hancock, "S.C. Pays Dearly for Added Jobs," *Baltimore Sun*, 12 October 1999.

34. Sven Steinmo, *Taxation and Democracy* (New Haven, Conn.: Yale University Press, 1993), 156–58.

35. A typical example is Laura Reese, "The Role of Counties in Local Economic Development," *Economic Development Quarterly* 8, no. 1 (February 1994): 30. In addition to Reese's literature review (pp. 29–31), see Buchholz, *Competition and Corporate Incentives*, Chapter 2, and Fisher and Peters, *Industrial Incentives*, 13–20.

36. Reese, "The Role of Counties in Local Economic Development," 29. See also Scott Loveridge, "On the Continuing Popularity of Industrial Recruitment," *Economic Development Quarterly* 10, no. 2 (May 1996): 151–58.

37. On the current position of U.S. states, see the National Governors' Association (NGA) Policy on Economic Growth and Development Incentives, in Jay Kayne and Molly Shonka, *Rethinking State Development Policies and Programs* (Washington, D.C.: National Governors' Association, 1994). That document recognizes the existence of a problem but sees the solution in voluntary and cooperative actions by the individual states. Regarding the Canadian situation, the Canadian First Ministers adopted a first-ever Code of Conduct on Incentives as part of the July 1994 Agreement on Internal Trade—which, unlike the NGA policy, is legally binding on the provinces.

38. For example, state officials in New Mexico did not calculate the present value of tax revenues for an Intel plant, leading them to overstate the revenue received relative to that foregone (see Chapter 5).

39. See also Fisher and Peters, *Industrial Incentives*, 217–18.

40. Between 1979 and 1991, in the United States and Canada combined, there were thirteen new foreign-owned auto assembly plants against one closure; in the same period, there were sixteen closures of U.S.-owned assembly plants versus four new facilities. In other words, twelve U.S.-

owned facilities were replaced by an equal number of foreign-owned plants during this period. James M. Rubenstein, *The Changing U.S. Automobile Industry: A Geographical Analysis* (London: Routledge, 1992), Table 1.1, p. 3. See also Kenneth P. Thomas, *Capital Beyond Borders: States and Firms in the Auto Industry, 1960–94* (London: Macmillan, 1997), 142–43.

41. For example, an investment tax credit of *x* dollars per job created.

42. John Bachtler, "Grants for Inward Investors: Giving Money Away?" *National Westminster Bank Quarterly Review* (May 1990), 18; Douglas Yuill et al., *European Regional Incentives 1995–96* (London: Bowker-Saur, 1995), 14.

43. Bachtler, "Grants for Inward Investors," 18.

44. Yuill et al., *European Regional Incentives 1995–96*, 14. Yuill et al. also suggest that discretionary programs can create windfall gains because the lack of certainty about the extent of support means that firms must select investment locations as if they were not going to receive any subsidies. This conclusion is implausible, however, because site selection consultants (such as Plant Location International and Ernst & Young) can make good predictions about the likely level of support for investors' projects and help them conduct bidding wars among various governments for the investment. Investors can therefore make well-grounded assumptions about the likely level of support and incorporate these assumptions into their planning.

45. Steve Jordan, "Groups Attack States' Special Incentives for Firms," *Omaha World Herald*, 20 September 1995, 16.

46. Blum with Ginsburg, *The Mercedes Benz Subsidy Package*, i–ii.

47. Allen R. Myerson, "O Governor, Won't You Buy Me a Mercedes Plant?" *New York Times*, 1 September 1996, Section 3, p. 1.

48. This point is also strongly made by Robert O'Brien, *Subsidy Regulation and State Transformation in North America, the GATT, and the EU* (London: Macmillan, 1997), 91, though without a basis in estimates of his own.

49. See O'Brien, *Subsidy Regulation and State Transformation*, especially chapters 3–5, for a number of bitter subsidy disputes between the two countries.

2

The Market for Investment

Stephen Guisinger argues that there is a "market" for investment in which governments compete for investment and firms supply investment.[1] Yet the competition is not equal on both sides. As Karl Marx noted long ago, in a market, not only do sellers compete with each other and buyers compete with each other, sellers compete with buyers. Whether prices are high or low depends in part on whether buyers or sellers are better able to restrain competition among themselves.[2] In the contemporary language of game theory, we would say that buyers and sellers face a prisoners' dilemma, and the relative ability of each to solve it affects price. This latter insight has long been forgotten, yet it is quite central here. In the market for investment, firms generally have the upper hand: Firms compete for investment sites far less than governments compete for investment. This asymmetry is based on the relative ease with which capital owners can organize, information advantages that business has over governments, and the greater (and increasing) mobility of capital relative to governments. Over time, this asymmetry has tended to result in a reduction in tax and other burdens placed on capital. In the market for investment, then, the collective action problem faced by governments is more severe than that faced by firms, so the analysis here focuses on governments' collective action problem.

This chapter begins with an examination of the supply and demand for investment; it examines location theory and economic development practice in turn. It then explains in greater detail why I focus on the competition *for* investment rather than the competition *among* investors.

Next, the analysis proceeds to what I call the rising-n-person prisoners' dilemma (RNPD) model of investment attraction through incentives. This analysis shows the wastefulness of location subsidies and the necessity for cooperatively controlling them. The model is then illustrated by a case study of the automobile industry in the United States and Canada, where there has been substantial cross-border competition for investment since the signing of the Auto Pact in 1965. The rising trend of incentives given to automakers will show that the increased mobility of investment strengthened the Big Three automakers in their bargaining with governments on both sides of the border. Appendix 1 elaborates on the game of investment competition, showing that at very high levels of incentives, the game ceases to be a prisoners' dilemma and states more easily can refrain from offering location incentives. The evidence suggests, however, that before that point is reached, capital ceases to employ labor; instead, it substitutes for labor (see also discussion of Bartik in Chapter 1).

The Market for Investment

This section examines the supply of, and demand for, investment. The supply of productive capital (as opposed to financial capital) is the sum of business location decisions. Although location theory has matured over time, its fundamental principles have not changed. The increasing mobility of capital has made bargaining between investors and governments a more prominent aspect of location decisions, and smaller differentials between potential sites imply that there is a greater possibility of affecting the final decision by offering location subsidies.

The demand for investment is rooted in governments' dependence on firms for investment, combined with capital mobility; this demand is reflected in the economic development strategies chosen by different localities. Some localities are highly desirable locations for certain types of investments (for example, California's Silicon Valley) and do not have to offer as much in terms of location incentives or other policy concessions to attract investment. Nonetheless, even such favored jurisdictions compete for investment. The extent to which a government must make special efforts to attract investors can be comprehended by using theories developed for understanding bargaining power between multinational corporations and their hosts.

Supply of Investment

Location theory began with models that focus on transport costs and their minimization.[3] Over time, these models were elaborated to include multiple inputs and, more important, to incorporate production costs (including labor, taxes, government policies, and quality-of-life considerations) into the location decision. In a spatial model, this modeling could be accomplished by calculating the minimization point for transport costs (as with older models), then determining how much unit transport costs increased as one moved from this point. The low-cost production site was then determined, and if the unit production cost savings were greater than the additional transport costs, the facility would locate at that point. As Blair and Premus point out, location theory has had to incorporate other factors as transportation costs have fallen substantially over time:

> Other things equal, the higher the value of the product being shipped relative to shipping costs, the less importance businesses will attach to shipping costs in their location decisions. Thus, as industry became more "footloose" in location choices, the range of possible locations expanded, as did the list of possible locational determinants.[4]

This analysis is consistent with my argument elsewhere that a decline in transport costs increases capital mobility[5]—a point that will be critical in the analysis in this chapter.

Unfortunately, as more factors have been incorporated into location theory, its ability to predict has deteriorated. As Blair and Premus suggest, "Many areas have very similar locational characteristics"; they add that "the increased importance of state and local incentives has increased the difficulty of prediction."[6] What Blair and Premus fail to do in their analysis is to relate the difficulty in prediction to their point about the decline in transport costs: This decline in itself made potential location sites more similar from an overall cost perspective. Indeed, for automobile production in North America, there is a wide variety of sites with fairly similar transport costs, extending roughly from St. Louis, Missouri, to Oshawa, Ontario (GM Canada's headquarters, just northeast of Toronto).[7]

A critical issue for this study is whether investment incentives in fact affect site selection. Although Fisher and Peters note that, in a theoretical sense, investment incentives almost necessarily will affect locational decisions, they also point out that "small differences in labor costs can outweigh quite large differences in tax costs"[8] because labor costs are a much greater proportion of total cost than is tax. For this reason, some analysts doubt that tax and other location incentives actually affect siting decisions. Moreover, surveys of business officials about the determinants of their location decisions rarely give investment subsidies a high priority. As a result, many critics of incentives suggest that they are ineffective.[9] If this assessment is accurate, policymakers are irrational on a grand scale (see Appendix 1 for a brief game-theoretic presentation). Most recent literature suggests—though sometimes cautiously—that incentives do affect location decisions. Buchholz's review of the literature argues that more recent empirical studies are better specified than early ones and that they tend to reach the conclusion that incentives do affect location decisions.[10] Moran agrees; he sums up his review of studies of incentives on international location decisions as follows: "Grants, tax holidays, and reduced tax rates do, in short, play a role in multinational corporate choice among locations for investment."[11] Caves' review of literature on multinational corporations (MNCs) identifies "numerous recent time-series studies [that] have confirmed the finding that taxes strongly affect the location of foreign investment."[12] Fisher and Peters, for their part, see even recent studies as inconclusive, in part because of methodological problems; the conclusion to their own research, however (based on a "hypothetical firm" model in sixteen different industries) is that taxes and incentives have some effect on location choice—primarily screening out areas with high taxes that do not offset them with high incentives.[13] The consensus, then, is that incentives do matter to the location of investment; therefore, individual governments are not simply irrational to use them. The problem is that the collective outcome of their use is suboptimal, as discussed below.

Demand for Investment

On the demand side of the market for investment, two questions must be considered: Why do governments compete for investment in the first place, and why do they choose the economic development strategies they do? This section analyzes these two issues in turn.

Structural Dependence across Borders

Why do governments compete for investment? The short answer is that governments need capital and must negotiate with capital owners to receive investment, and capital is mobile across jurisdictional boundaries, requiring governments to compete among themselves for it.

Governments rely on business for economic activity to tax, as well as for job creation. Without these factors, they have neither the funds to carry out their jobs nor an economic performance that is likely to get them reelected.[14] Thus, maintaining an adequate level of investment is a prerequisite for a government to meet any other goals it might have.[15] Because business performance is so crucial to governments, its status is far more central than that of a special interest group: "In the eyes of government officials, therefore, businessmen do not appear simply as the representatives of a special interest, as representatives of interest groups do. They appear as functionaries performing functions that government officials regard as indispensable."[16] Government therefore is solicitous of business interests and, as Lindblom emphasizes, does what it can to "induce" capital owners to invest. In other words, government negotiates with business over the conditions of investment.[17]

This theory originally was developed in one-country models. The addition of more states and hence of the mobility of capital[18] greatly augments the power resources that owners of capital command and turns the bargaining relationship into a bidding situation because when an investor withholds capital, he or she must still do something with it.[19] Much capital is specific: If it cannot be moved across borders, its next-best use might have a much lower rate of return than if it could be transferred abroad and used in the same industry. Capital mobility removes some of this discrepancy between best and second-best uses of capital, thereby making threats to withhold investment or to disinvest less costly and thus more credible.

For the purposes of this book, the mobility that matters is that of productive capital. I have defined this type of mobility elsewhere as the potential to coordinate production on a wide-ranging geographical scale.[20] The most important determinants of this ability to move capital are technology, nontechnological innovation, degree of commitment of capital, and government policy.[21] Transport and communications technologies are the most significant factors that allow production to locate at a distance from the final consumer; costs in these sectors have plummeted since World War II (see below). Nontechnological innovations such as letters of credit have increased capital mobility in the finance sector;[22] the organizational innovation of "just-in-time" production methods may in fact decrease mobility by constraining production to locate near the final consumer.[23] As Raymond Vernon has shown, the act of committing or sinking an investment changes the bargaining dynamics between a firm and state; the ultimate reason, however, is not the changes in uncertainty identified by Vernon but the decrease in the mobility of the sunk capital.[24] In terms of government policy, restrictions on capital movements and trade barriers are major determinants of the feasibility of locating production offshore.

The combination of structural dependence and capital mobility means that governments at all levels—local, state/provincial, national, even supranational in the case of the European Union—must compete with each other for investment. This competition can be firm-specific or general; it can take many forms, including tariff protection, cash grants, tax breaks, free land and infrastructure, training funds, low-cost financing, deregulation, even repression of labor organizations. This situation obviously obtains for larger government entities, and the proliferation of economic development agencies among even quite small municipalities shows that exceptions are few and far between.[25] Nevertheless, the type of development strategy selected varies among governments.

Strategies of Economic Development

Given that governments compete for investment, what determines the strategies they follow? Despite Eisinger's prediction that supply-side activities such as location subsidies would give way to more entrepreneurial strategies, according to Scott Loveridge, "Local practitioners appear to see these new strategies as supplements, rather than replacements, for the tradition of industrial recruitment."[26] The clear evidence on the rising use of incentives in the United States (see Chapter 5) supports this view. Dana Hullinger argues that for most governments, the *structure* of incentive competition determines a *strategy* of trying for any opportunities that present themselves—which really is no strategy at all.[27] In Herbert Rubin's phrase, the main strategy is to "shoot anything that flies; claim anything that falls."[28]

The most important distinction, then, is the intensity of the use of location incentives, which depends primarily on the innate attractiveness of the polity to investors.[29] Attractive locations for investment provide the fewest inducements to prospective investors and may even seek to keep out certain types of economic activity. For example, a high-income suburb may be a natural location for high-end services such as financial and legal services, without special incentives; the city may simply provide no industrial zoning whatsoever. It may even remain completely residential; the only "investment" may be the purchase of homes to knock down and replace with larger homes ("teardown" homes). The factors that determine the need for and intensity of incentives or policy concessions to attract investment are the same as those identified in determining the bargaining power of multinational corporations with host states: the economic situation of the community (income, unemployment, size, and so forth), the availability of alternative projects, and the collective action possibilities of governments and firms.[30] Governments without resource needs are least likely to engage in competition for investment at all, although these governments are few and far between. Even Santa Clara, California—in the heart of Silicon Valley—provides property tax reductions, as well as piggybacking on state tax reductions for new investment.[31] Governments with alternatives to a particular investor have a stronger bargaining position than those without alternatives. Cooperation among states or firms can strengthen them in their bargaining.

This analysis points us again to the critical question raised in the introduction: Why is competition among governments for investment greater than competition among investors for investment sites?

Asymmetries That Favor Investors

Three factors account for the unequal position of government and corporate actors in the market for investment. First, capital is not only mobile; its mobility has been increasing for most of this century, especially in the post-World War II era. Second, it is generally easier for capital than governments to organize, and capital often need not even organize to act collectively. This situation is true even though there are far more potential investors than governments. Finally, there is a major information asymmetry at work: Firms have much better information about governments than governments have about firms; in particular, governments considering whether to bid on a particular investment project do not know when the next one will come along. I consider each of these factors in turn, then sharpen the focus to examine the competition among governments, as well as theoretical ways to control it.

Rising Capital Mobility

The mobility of productive investment is a function of several different factors, making it difficult to produce a single index of capital mobility.

In terms of enabling the movement of productive capital, the falling of trade barriers since World War II under the auspices of GATT and the WTO, as well as regional trade agreements such as the EU and NAFTA, make more locations more interchangeable for each other. In addition, there have been dramatic reductions in transportation and communications costs, see Tables 2-1 and 2-2.

As Tables 2-1 and 2-2 show, the real cost of a New York-to-London phone call has fallen more than 95 percent since 1945, and the real cost of transatlantic air transport declined more than 80 percent in the same period. Similarly, the annual cost of an Intelsat satellite communication circuit has fallen from about $60,000 in the late 1960s to below $5,000 by 1994.[32]

Because of the increase in capital mobility that these component measures suggest, the bargaining position of states relative to firms has decreased–particularly because the number of potential sites for

Table 2-1 **Cost of International Telephone Service, New York to London (constant 1981 dollars)**

Date	Cost
1946	56.40
1965	34.80
1967	14.58[a]
1970	8.28
1974	6.48
1978	6.30
1981	3.00
1990	2.31
1995[b]	1.99

[a]Indicates first availability of station-to-station calling. Previous rates are for person-to-person calling. All rates are for three-minute calls.
[b]Nondiscounted AT&T rates.

Sources: Historical Statistics of the United States, Colonial Times to 1970, Series R 89-92, 791; *Statistical Abstract of the United States*, 1975, Table 852, footnote 4; and *Statistical Abstract of the United States*, 1984, Table 948; "Calling Abroad," table of AT&T long-distance rates, *Wall Street Journal*, 4 October 1991, R10; rate quote from AT&T operator 14 November 1995. Calculated in 1981 dollars using Consumer Price Index data from *Historical Statistics of the United States, Statistical Abstract of the United States 1990*, and press reports (for September 1995 CPI number).

Table 2-2 **International Airline Travel Costs (constant 1981 dollars)**

Date	Average Revenue per Passenger-Mile
1945	0.4427
1950	0.2766
1955	0.2264
1960	0.1969
1965	0.1534
1970	0.1150
1980	0.0825
1985	0.0823
1990[a]	0.0751

[a]Last year for which revenue per passenger-mile was broken down between domestic and international operations.

Sources: 1945–1970: *Historical Statistics of the United States*, Series Q 577-590, 769–70; 1980–1990: *Statistical Abstract of the United States*, 1990, Table 1065, and *Statistical Abstract of the United States*, 1992, Table 1038. Calculated in 1981 dollars using Consumer Price Index data from *Historical Statistics of the United States, Statistical Abstract of the United States 1990*, and *Economic Report of the President 1993*.

a given investment is thereby increased. Not only does this trend mean that investors have more options open to them (which in itself would strengthen their hand); it also means that attempts by states to cooperate in holding down investment subsidies (or, indeed, any other policies that might affect location) is becoming more difficult as a result of the increased mobility of capital. This analysis brings us to the issue of whether there are structural dissimilarities in the ability of states and firms to cooperate among themselves.

How Capital Can Organize—If It Needs To

Returning to Marx's point about the importance of the relative ability of buyers and sellers to achieve collective action in understanding market outcomes, we find that asymmetries that favor capital exist here as well. At one level, this asymmetry is surprising: As Mancur Olson argued, the larger the group, the more difficult it is to overcome free riding (all other things being equal).[33] This dynamic helps to explain why it easier for firms to organize than for workers to unionize—but there are fewer governments than there are firms. Nevertheless, there are some striking examples of firms cooperating more effectively than states (even, on occasion, with far more relevant firms than states), and an analysis of this phenomenon will illuminate one of these asymmetries. Moreover, in many instances firms can each do the same thing without having to explicitly coordinate their actions, in ways that affect government behavior despite—and perhaps even because of—their lack of overt cooperation.

Cooperation among firms can take place precisely in situations in which cooperation among states cannot. Charles Lipson has shown that literally hundreds of banks cooperated during the debt crisis of the 1980s to prevent loan defaults, whereas the handful of major debtor nations was unable to coordinate action to advance their interests.[34] In the banks' case, the role of syndicate lending and the coordinating position of the syndicate agent explains how banks cooperate during debt crises.[35] Indeed, Lipson contrasts the ability of private banks to secure their debts even from revolutionary regimes with "the obvious failure of state sanctions to secure Iran's compliance on other issues [e.g., the U.S. freeze on Iranian assets during the hostage crisis of 1979–1981]."[36]

A further striking example is in the oil industry. According to Theodore Moran, corporate control of the industry was far more successful at maintaining monopoly rents than the Organization of Petroleum Exporting Countries (OPEC) has been, despite the fact that oil reserves expanded more—both absolutely and relatively—during the period of corporate control (1912–1971) than during OPEC's dominance.[37] In this case, the nationalization of production assets reduced the monitoring ability inherent in the ingenious contracts among the major oil companies that gave them shares of each other's production; these agreements also gave the companies automatic sanctioning capability against firms that produced more oil than agreed.[38]

The factors identified here—the existence of a coordinating agent and strong monitoring capabilities—obviously are not exclusive to companies, but they do help explain the advantages firms have in the bargaining situation. For example, although Saudi Arabia's coordinating role in OPEC—owing to its large share of world oil reserves—is well-known, an analogous situation does not exist among U.S.

states: California's share of gross state product is only 12.6 percent of the total.[39] The fact that greater concentrations necessarily exist among EU members and among Canadian provinces (because there are far fewer in both cases) may help to explain their greater cooperative success—a point to which I return in Chapter 7.

Some forms of coordination exist for firms in the market for investment. Much as credit rating agencies help coordinate investment decisions in the area of corporate and government debt,[40] site location consultants coordinate direct investment by sending investment toward particular areas and promoting specific government policies (i.e., to provide incentives). Location consultants are often quoted in the press (for example, Wilfred Vossen of Plant Location International), giving them ample opportunity to emphasize to governments and the public at large the need to provide investment incentives. Moreover, Buchholz argues that consultants play "pernicious" roles in the bidding-up of incentives by adding their expertise to the pre-existing information asymmetry. Indeed, many location consultants receive a percentage of any subsidy they negotiate—giving them further incentive to drive up the cost.[41]

Claus Offe and Helmut Wiesenthal's analysis of the differential organizing ability of capital and labor also suggests a further explanation for why cooperation is easier for firms than for states. In their view, firms and business associations reduce their needs to a single yardstick of money, whereas "unions are confronted with the task of organizing the entire spectrum of needs" of workers.[42] The same is true, I argue, for states, which must cooperate with each other on a broad range of issues—not all of which are measurable in monetary terms. This phenomenon produces a further systemic difference in the ability of states and firms to cooperate.

Finally, in many cases firms do not have to cooperate to achieve joint action. Although the use of location consultants may help to coordinate the behavior of investors (around the now-common demand that a community offer incentives if it is to be even considered for an investment), firms' individual decisions not to invest without receiving incentives can add up to a significant collective sanction without any such coordination by location consultants. Jeffrey Winters goes even further: He argues that the fact that sanctioning by capital may not be coordinated can make it "potentially devastating" because capitalists may even withhold or relocate investment to such an extent that it hurts them, as well.[43]

Information Asymmetries

The third main reason that companies generally hold an upper hand in the market for investment is related to information. A company searching for a site will collect a large amount of information about the localities in which it is interested; it also will be able to gather intelligence on political decision makers, actions of the relevant government body, and so forth. On the other hand, there is a great deal that government officials do not know about the firms:

> Only the firm knows with certainty its own degree of mobility (and propensity to take advantage of that mobility), what its criteria are for investment, and what value of incentives it would need to move or stay. In many cases, in fact, even the *identity* of the firm is kept secret, as location consultants seek out incentives for nebulous firms identified only by descriptions like "a large manufacturing firm."[44]

One might also add that officials do not always know if competing locations exist, and what the cost factors and incentives available there are.[45] As Bryan Jones and Lynn Bachelor conclude, this information asymmetry "leads to the extraction of more benefits from the public sector than are absolutely necessary to influence the corporate decision in regard to location."[46]

Beyond not knowing the mobility and decision criteria of firms, government officials also do not know when the next project they would want will come along. The most desirable facilities are not a dime a dozen. Between 1979 and 1991, for example, there were only twenty new automobile or truck assembly plants and five replacement facilities in the United States and Canada combined—and the new facilities were offset by twenty closures.[47] In all industries combined, there are only 200 to 300 major projects in the United States, with 15,000 agencies competing for them.[48] This uncertainty helps fuel the "shoot at anything that flies" approach to economic development.

Taken together, rising capital mobility, the greater likelihood of convergent (though not necessarily coordinated) action among firms, and information asymmetries between firms and governments lead to a stronger position for capital in the market for investment. Because government "cannot command" but can only "induce" investment,[49] the policy task before us focuses on only one side of the market for investment: that of governments bidding for investment. The following section breaks down the prisoners' dilemma among the bidders and presents prospects for its control.

Attracting Investment under Conditions of Rising Capital Mobility

Examples of competition for investment are everywhere. The Mercedes case described in Chapter 1 was only the tip of the iceberg in the automobile industry, which has seen bidding wars for facilities within Europe, the United States, and Canada, as well as between the United States and Canada. Piper Aircraft generated interest from nine of Canada's ten provinces when it considered moving there from the United States, and Trans World Airlines received offers from St. Louis, Kansas City, and New York City to be its new headquarters—despite the fact that the airline was in Chapter 11 bankruptcy proceedings at the time.

In one sense, this frantic scramble for investment is irrational. With regard to employment, the same number of jobs would have come to the state of Missouri regardless of whether St. Louis or Kansas City became the new headquarters of TWA. Yet the two cities offered local incentives to go with the state's incentive package. From the standpoint of the United States as a whole, the situation is even more irrational. Not only would the same number of jobs have been generated in New York City, Kansas City, or St. Louis, there were offsetting job losses at the company's former headquarters at Mt. Kisco, New York. Thus, subnational governments prepared three sets of investment incentives to reward TWA for creating *no* new jobs in the United States. The same irrationality exists from the Canadian national standpoint vis-a-vis the provinces and for the EU as a whole in relation to individual member states.

From the standpoint of *individual* governments, however, there is nothing irrational about their behavior. As Stephen Guisinger's "market for investment" model implies,[50] controlling government competition for investment is well modeled as a prisoners' dilemma.[51] All governments would be better off if they did not offer investment incentives, but an individual government would lose a significant amount of investment if it unilaterally ceased to offer location subsidies. As a result, governments continue to offer such incentives, though occasionally there have been attempts to control them.

Another way to think about the problem is to recognize that it involves delegation of regulation or enforcement. Konstantine Gatsios and Paul Seabright argue that subsidy control in the EU involves the delegation of regulatory authority from the member states to the European Commission. Indeed, they also analyze this issue in terms of the prisoners' dilemma and see the use of delegation as a way of strengthening the credibility of enforcement of cooperative agreements:

> But tacit co-operation can often break down, and in these circumstances the delegation of powers to the EC could be an alternative means of making co-operative outcomes credible. For this to work the EC's regulatory activity must itself be credible; but countries can and often do resist its application to themselves.[52]

Mitchell Smith makes a similar argument, claiming that delegation of enforcement power to the Commission in state aid cases "has lowered the net expected benefits of defecting from the state aid regime by increasing the likelihood of detection and punishment."[53]

Let us examine Guisinger's claim more closely.[54] In essence, Guisinger argues that if governments were *all* to refrain from offering investment aids to help persuade firms to locate within their jurisdictions, the resulting distribution of investment probably would be little different from the distribution that would result when all states provide such incentives.[55] Thus, if states did succeed in avoiding location subsidies, they would receive their "fair share" of investment while spending nothing on incentives—an improvement over the current situation, in which they must spend substantial amounts of money on location inducements to receive their fair share of investment. Nevertheless, the current situation is better for governments than not spending money for incentives *while other governments continue to do so* because they would thus receive less than their fair share of investment, and other states would receive more than their fair share.[56] The four possible outcomes can be ranked as follows and placed in the standard prisoners' dilemma 2×2 game matrix (using only two governments here for ease of exposition):

Best outcome (B): Your government provides incentives while the other one does not, increasing your investment share at the expense of the other government.

Second-best outcome (S): Your government does not provide incentives, nor does the other one; you receive your "fair share" of investment (as does the other government).

Third-best outcome (T): Your government provides incentives, and so does the other government—thereby giving you your "fair share" of investment, but at the cost of the incentives (this is also true for the other government).

Worst outcome (W): Your government does not provide incentives while the other one does, and you receive less than your "fair share" of investment.

Using these letters to designate payoffs produces a familiar prisoners' dilemma matrix (Government 1's payoff appears first in each cell):

	Government 2	
	Doesn't subsidize	Subsidizes
Government 1		
Doesn't subsidize	S, S	W, B
Subsidizes	B, W	T, T

This matrix clearly illustrates the basis for Guisinger's claim. If Government 2 doesn't subsidize, Government 1 gets a higher payoff by subsidizing (B) than by not subsidizing (S). If Government 2 does subsidize, Government 1 is still better off subsidizing (T) than not subsidizing (W). In other words, Government 1 is better off subsidizing no matter what Government 2 does. The same is true for Government 2,[57] so if each pursues its own interests without cooperating, both will subsidize—and both will receive lower payoffs (T, T) than if neither subsidized (S, S). This matrix also illustrates another important point: Neither government can move from the current situation (i.e., both subsidize) *by itself* without making itself worse off because its payoff for doing so would decline from T to W. This characteristic defines the situation as equilibrium. Because neither government has an incentive to change strategy by itself, they remain in the noncooperative equilibrium rather than the pareto-optimal situation in which neither subsidizes. If this prisoners' dilemma were played just once, the rational approach for both governments would be to subsidize.

This analysis does not imply that cooperation is impossible. As Russell Hardin and Robert Axelrod have emphasized, even without third-party enforcement of cooperation agreements, such cooperation can occur in situations in which the possibility of future benefits is high enough. In that case, non-cooperators can be punished by the loss of future benefits; their anticipation of this outcome may be sufficient to prevent their defection from cooperative agreements.[58]

With more than two actors, the problem of cooperation is more difficult still. As the number of players increases, cooperation is less likely because organizing the group becomes more complicated, because each actor still has a greater disincentive to cooperate, and because monitoring and enforcement of punishment for non-compliance is harder to achieve.[59] Although getting all parties to cooperate may not be necessary for the group to enjoy benefits from cooperation, there will be some minimum number that must cooperate to be net beneficiaries. Hardin refers to this situation as a *k*-group.

An example should make this concept clearer. If Ontario refrained from offering investment incentives but no other province did, Ontario would lose investment to other provinces. If both Québec and Ontario refrained, they might still lose out overall. If all the provinces except Prince Edward Island refrained from using subsidies, however, the nine cooperating provinces would surely benefit because Prince Edward Island can only absorb a small amount of Canadian investment. Determining exactly what the minimum would be is difficult,[60] but in this example it is between three and nine. By contrast, if provinces agreed not to use location inducements in the automobile industry (which is heavily concentrated in Ontario and secondarily in Québec), an agreement that included just Ontario and Québec would probably be sufficient for them to benefit regardless of what other provinces did because of the difficulty of establishing facilities far from presently existing ones. In this case, $k = 2$. As Hardin argues convincingly, the difficulty of achieving cooperation in an n-person prisoners' dilemma depends not on n but on k.[61]

Even this analysis is static, however. The prisoners' dilemma alerts us to the difficulty in achieving cooperation to obtain restraint of state aid; the failure of U.S. states in the Midwest and Northeast to maintain "no-raiding zones" only confirms this view.[62] In fact, under conditions of increasing capital mobility, the cooperation problem faced by governments grows increasingly difficult. The reason is precisely that the increasing mobility of capital implies that the number of feasible potential locations increases; in other words, it increases k.

As a result, governments seeking to attract investment do not simply face an n-person prisoners' dilemma. As a result of rising capital mobility, they face a situation in which n (and more important, k) is rising. That is, capital mobility makes more locations potentially substitutable for one another. Therefore, reaching and enforcing a cooperative solution is increasingly difficult.

In addition, not only is the number of actors sometimes quite large (fifty at the state level alone in the U.S. case, for example), the small number of really large projects (automobile assembly plants, aircraft maintenance facilities, and the like)[63] makes following the "tit-for-tat" (TFT) strategy advocated by Robert Axelrod and widely endorsed for national governments in the international arena impossible.[64] The small number of large projects prevents states from retaliating in a way that is distinguishable from business-as-usual competition for investment. Moreover, even with smaller projects, it is unclear that there are enough projects for TFT. Thus, the prospects that decentralized cooperation will emerge on this issue are negligible.

Because the moral of the prisoners' dilemma is precisely the difficulty of obtaining cooperation, the reason we have seen so little cooperation on this issue is immediately clear. The following section considers the rising-n-player prisoners' dilemma model as it has played out in a specific industry—namely, automobile manufacturing.

The Case of the Automobile Industry

The RNPD model predicts that under conditions of increasing capital mobility, governments will have increasing difficulty avoiding the use of location subsidies to attract investment. Moreover, the increasing mobility of capital also suggests that the bargaining power of mobile investors will rise vis-a-vis that of states—which will tend to increase the size of investment incentives, along with mobility.[65]

The case of the North American automobile industry provides a striking confirmation of these predictions. Not only has the industry benefited from the overall reduction in transportation and communication costs that have characterized the postwar economy, the mobility of automobile production in North America was increased by the Canada-U.S. Auto Pact in 1965 and the introduction of tri-level rail cars in 1960.[66] These developments made potential locations in the United States and Canada more nearly substitutes for one another and therefore increased the competition for automotive investments. In fact, there have been several cross-border bidding wars for auto plants, including the Lima, Ohio, Ford engine plant (decided in 1971); the Ford Essex Engine Plant in Windsor, Ontario (decided in 1978); a GM parts plant that had been slated in 1979 for Valleyfield, Québec, but ultimately was never built; the Marysville, Ohio, Honda assembly plant (decided in 1980); and Chrysler's St. Louis Assembly Plant #2 (decided in 1983).[67]

The combination of cross-border, interprovincial, and interstate competition since the signing of the Auto Pact has led to increasing levels of incentives being provided for auto plants in both countries. In Canada, the Duty Rebate/Auto Pact-era plants at Oakville (Ford Truck), St. Thomas (Ford Assembly), and Ste.-Thérèse (GM Assembly) all were built without receiving investment incentives, according to Simon Reisman.[68] The Ford Essex Engine Plant, announced in 1978, received $68 million (Canadian) in incentives for a $533 million facility—12.8 percent of the value of the investment. The GM/Suzuki joint venture, Canadian-American Motors Inc. (CAMI)—announced for Ingersoll, Ontario, in 1986—received $85 million (Canadian) in grants and forgivable loans for a $500 million plant, or 17 percent of the investment's value. The re-equipping of Ste.-Thérèse in 1987 received an interest-free 30-year loan of $220 million (Canadian) for the $450 million project—the equivalent of a grant of $197.1 million, or 43.8 percent of the investment.[69] Thus, for the Ford-Canada and GM-Canada negotiating dyads, the firms experienced improved outcomes during this period of increasing capital mobility.

In the United States, the situation has been similar. Chrysler (in Illinois and Missouri) and General Motors (in New York) received higher levels of incentives for projects in the 1980s than they received in the 1960s or 1970s.[70] Milward and Newman have shown that for major automobile projects announced in the 1980s, the level of state incentives provided per job has steadily increased: It was $11,000 per job for Nissan in 1980; $13,857 for Mazda in late 1984; $26,667 for Saturn in July 1985; $33,320 for Diamond-Star in October 1985; $49,900 for Toyota in December 1985; and $50,588 per job at the Subaru/Isuzu joint venture in December 1986.[71] This trend has continued with more recent plants (BMW and Mercedes). In 1992, South Carolina committed at least $130 million in incentives for the 2,000-

job BMW plant, or $65,000 per job.[72] Mercedes received an even larger package of at least $173 million for a $300 million plant that created just 1,500 jobs—a mammoth $115,467 per job.[73]

By contrast, there was a markedly different trend in the United Kingdom (UK) for investment incentives to Ford between 1960 and 1988. Subsidies rose from 10.7 percent of the investment in 1960 for Ford UK Expansion Plan #3 to 82.2 percent for the Bridgend Engine Plant in 1977—but fell sharply to 4.6 percent for Bridgend Engine Plant #2 in 1988. Other firms investing since that time have gotten quite low incentives, including Honda and Toyota.[74]

Conclusion: Cooperation—With and Without Anarchy

Theoretical work on cooperation suggests that for many prisoners' dilemmas, the only reliable way to achieve cooperation is for an outside party to enforce agreements.[75] In domestic politics, this third party normally would be government. In international politics, there is no such ultimate power to appeal to—hence the frequent description of international politics as an anarchic realm.[76] To obtain cooperation under anarchy, states must fall back on more fragile methods of obtaining cooperation, such as using long-term strategies to reward cooperators and punish non-cooperators. In some cases (the EU is arguably one of them), delegation of enforcement power may strengthen decentralized sanctioning.

The United States and the EU have low levels of internal trade barriers and are effectively "common markets"; combined with their other economic similarities, this situation makes them likely to see substantial competition for investment and thus good cases for comparison.[77] The main political difference is that EU member states are sovereign, whereas U.S. states are not. Cooperation among U.S. states could be enforced by the federal government; EU member states have had to cooperate without external enforcement of their agreements. To the extent that the European Commission and the European Court of Justice (ECJ) can be said to have achieved centralized enforcement power (which is widely debated), there is "third-party" enforcement, as could exist in the United States.

The ECJ has much more difficulty in enforcing its rulings against member states, however, than U.S. federal courts have in enforcing rulings against U.S. states.[78] In the past, some EU member states have simply refused to comply with state aid decisions even after action by the ECJ—and the ECJ or the Commission could do little. As Gatsios and Seabright argue, credible sanctions are necessary for regulation to be effective; the sanctions "must be large relative to the payoffs of [the regulated] but small relative to the payoffs of the regulators (since sanctions are typically costly for regulators too)."[79]

Until the Maastricht Treaty, the ECJ could give member states bad publicity for "being in violation of their Treaty obligations," but there was no bigger sanction short of expelling a country from the European Community—which clearly was too large a sanction to be credible. The Maastricht Treaty, however, amended Article 171 of the Treaty of Rome to provide for fines against member states that disobey ECJ orders—exactly the kind of midrange sanction that Gatsios and Seabright show is necessary. Given our theoretical understandings about when cooperation is most likely, it is striking that the independent members of the EU have been able to cooperate to reduce investment incentives, whereas U.S. states have not.

This contrast between the EU and North America animates much of the discussion in the remainder of this book. U.S. states are not independent and for much of the twentieth century have been subject to increasing direction from the federal government. In Canada, the provinces are relatively more autonomous from the federal government than are U.S. states, but they still are not independent. EU member states are indeed independent; to facilitate their many cooperative agreements, however, they have created quasi-federal institutions at the supranational level. Given the far greater efforts at subsidy control in the EU than in North America, the next two chapters focus on rules and institutions in the EU; the discussion then turns to the short history and (to date) fairly minimal accomplishments of North American control of investment competition.

Notes

1. Stephen E. Guisinger, "A Comparative Study of Country Policies," in *Investment Incentives and Performance Requirements*, ed. Stephen E. Guisinger (New York: Praeger, 1985), 11–14. Although Guisinger uses the term "competition for investment" as a section heading, he also refers to governments as *selling* investment sites to firms. For the purposes

of this book, what matters is not whether hosts or firms are the buyers or sellers but what factors strengthen the one or the other.

2. See, for example, Karl Marx, "Wage-Labor and Capital," in *Karl Marx: Selected Writings*, ed. David McLellan (Oxford: Oxford University Press, 1977).
3. This section draws strongly on John P. Blair and Robert Premus, "Location Theory," in *Theories of Local Economic Development: Perspectives from Across the Disciplines*, ed. Richard D. Bingham and Robert Mier (Newbury Park: Sage, 1993).
4. Blair and Premus, "Location Theory," 9–10.
5. Kenneth P. Thomas, *Capital Beyond Borders: State and Firms in the Auto Industry, 1960–94* (London: Macmillan, 1997).
6. Blair and Premus, "Location Theory," 23.
7. James Rubenstein, "The Changing Distribution of Automobile Assembly Plants," *Focus* (fall 1988), 14–15. Rubenstein states that a General Motors computation found that "distribution costs are comparable at other locations [than the cost-minimizing location] within a few hundred miles of the North American population center," which is near Vandalia, Illinois.
8. Peter S. Fisher and Alan H. Peters, *Industrial Incentives: Competition Among American States and Cities* (Kalamazoo, Mich.: W. E. Upjohn Institute, 1998), 13.
9. For numerous examples of this claim, see Stephen Guisinger, "Rhetoric and Reality in International Business: A Note on the Effectiveness of Incentives," *Transnational Corporations* 1, no. 2 (August 1992): 113–17. On business surveys, see pages 119–21.
10. David Buchholz, "Competition and Corporate Incentives" (Ph.D. diss., Duke University, 1998), chapter 2.
11. Theodore H. Moran, *Foreign Direct Investment and Development* (Washington, D.C.: Institute for International Economics, 1999), 100.
12. Richard E. Caves, *Multinational Enterprise and Economic Analysis*, 2nd ed. (Cambridge: Cambridge University Press, 1996), 205. Caves notes (p. 206) that one study identified the broad changes from U.S. tax reform in 1986 as a cause of higher foreign investment by U.S. firms. This analysis implies that such broad changes in taxation within a single country can have implications for world efficiency (by affecting global investment location) even if they do not necessarily reduce efficiency within the country.
13. Fisher and Peters, *Industrial Incentives*, 13–20 (literature review), 206–08 (authors' own conclusions). Fisher and Peters also find that, in general, the addition of incentives to the calculation increased the differences between cities rather than decreasing them.

14. Jeffrey Winters points out that the theory is equally applicable to nondemocratic societies; he discusses the case of Indonesia in *Power in Motion: Capital Mobility and the Indonesian State* (Ithaca, N.Y.: Cornell University Press, 1996), 15–16.
15. Winters also relates Lindblom's original theory to more general theories of resource dependence. See Winters, *Power in Motion*, 21–22.
16. Charles E. Lindblom, *Politics and Markets: The World's Political-Economic Systems* (New York: Basic Books, 1977), 175. For Lindblom's analysis of this "privileged position of business," see Chapter 13 more generally. Adam Przeworski and Michael Wallerstein call this the "Structural Dependence of the State on Capital," in an article by the same name in *American Political Science Review* 82 (March 1988): 11–29.
17. Lindblom, *Politics and Markets*, 173. Przeworski and Wallerstein formalize this bargaining situation in "Structural Dependence of the State on Capital."
18. According to Christopher Chase-Dunn, the existence of competing states rather than a world government "provides the political underpinning of the mobility of capital." See "Interstate System and Capitalist World-Economy: One Logic or Two?" *International Studies Quarterly* 25, no. 1 (March 1981): 31.
19. Thomas, *Capital Beyond Borders,* 44–45. See also Winters, *Power in Motion*, 16–22.
20. Thomas, *Capital Beyond Borders*, 55–57; for an analysis of the mobility of financial capital, see 53–55.

    Asset specificity is a related concept, but capital mobility cannot be reduced to it. Although nonspecific capital generally is more mobile than specific capital, specific capital's mobility is determined by the extent to which it can benefit from lower transportation and communication costs. This mobility can be viewed as the value/weight ratio of the goods the capital produces: Semiconductor production is more mobile than mass market automobile production, for example. Moreover, capital's bargaining strength derives not from its specificity but from its mobility. Threatening to remove capital outside a jurisdiction is far more potent than threatening to move it from the stock market to the bond market. See Kenneth P. Thomas, "Expanding the Debate on Capital Mobility," in *Structure and Agency in International Capital Mobility*, ed. Timothy J. Sinclair and Kenneth P. Thomas (London: Macmillan, 2000). In the present book, I am interested in specific, mobile capital.
21. David Andrews makes a similar argument but does not include degree of commitment of capital as a factor in mobility. See "Capital Mobility and State Autonomy: Toward a Structural Theory of International Monetary Relations," *International Studies Quarterly* 38, no. 2 (June 1994):

193–218. The difference between technological change and innovation is a very fine line, but at least some innovations apparently are not based in technological changes. In the auto industry, automakers in North America switched from production of all models for sale in a single region to national specialization by plants beginning in the 1960s. This change is an example of a technology-driven innovation because it was made possible by the reduction in transport costs for completed cars as a result of the introduction of tri-level railroad cars and intermodal freight. By contrast, "just-in-time" (JIT) production methods do not seem to be based on a technological improvement. JIT may reduce capital mobility, however, by constraining production to be closer to the final consumer. See James M. Rubenstein, *The Changing U.S. Auto Industry: A Geographical Analysis* (London: Routledge, 1992), 153–68, 197. Finally, war and war preparations tend to reduce capital mobility, often sharply. For a fuller discussion of these issues, see Thomas, *Capital Beyond Borders*, 32, 51–57.

22. Douglass North discusses this and several other nontechnological innovations affecting capital mobility in *Institutions, Institutional Change and Economic Performance* (Cambridge: Cambridge University Press, 1990), 125–26.

23. Thomas, *Capital Beyond Borders*, 144.

24. Raymond Vernon, *Sovereignty at Bay* (New York: Basic Books, 1971), 46–59. See also Thomas, *Capital Beyond Borders*, 56.

25. For example, in the St. Louis metropolitan area, several municipalities with a population of less than 50,000 have at least one full-time economic development official. Even cities without an economic development agency will carry out such an agency's functions through the office of a city manager or other city official.

26. Scott Loveridge, "On the Continuing Popularity of Industrial Recruitment," *Economic Development Quarterly* 10, no. 2 (May 1996): 152.

27. Dana Hullinger, "Risk Management in Local Economic Development Projects: Beginning the Transformation from Structure to Strategy to Process," unpublished paper, University of Missouri–St. Louis, December 1998.

28. Herbert J. Rubin, "Shoot Anything That Flies; Claim Anything That Falls: Conversations With Economic Development Practitioners," *Economic Development Quarterly* 2, no. 3 (August 1998): 236–51.

29. Although some governments target specific industrial sectors (such as pharmaceuticals and financial services in Ireland, for example), they compete for investment in those sectors and are subject to the prisoners' dilemma dynamic.

An interesting side issue is that size may change some of the aspects of structural dependence, at least with regard to the motivations of government officials. National and other large governments are held responsible politically for overall macroeconomic performance and must pursue strategies to obtain jobs and tax revenue. Smaller governments are often more concerned with tax revenue than jobs because voters do not expect a city of 20,000 residents to be responsible for overall macroeconomic outcomes.

30. Thomas, *Capital Beyond Borders*, 9–18; see especially Table 1.1.
31. See "Intel Given Tax Break," *Phoenix Gazette*, 21 September 1994, C1 (regarding tax incentives to Intel from Santa Clara County), and Vlae Kershner, "Legislators Warned to Allow Business Tax Breaks; Association Says State Should Attract Manufacture," *San Francisco Chronicle*, 17 March 1993, A11 (on state efforts to satisfy Intel).
32. United Nations Conference on Trade and Development, Division of Transnational Corporations and Investment, *World Investment Report 1994: Transnational Corporations, Employment and the Workplace* (New York: United Nations, 1994), 125.
33. Mancur Olson, *The Logic of Collective Action: Public Goods and the Theory of Groups* (Cambridge: Harvard University Press, 1971), 35.
34. Charles Lipson, "The International Organization of Third World Debt," *International Organization* 34 (October 1981), 603–31; "Bankers' Dilemmas," in *Cooperation Under Anarchy,* ed. Kenneth Oye (Princeton, N.J.: Princeton University Press, 1986), 200–225.
35. Lipson, "The International Organization of Third World Debt," 615–16.
36. Ibid., 607.
37. Theodore H. Moran, "Managing an Oligopoly of Would-Be Sovereigns: The Dynamics of Joint Control and Self-Control in the Oil Industry Past, Present, and Future," *International Organization* 41, no. 4 (autumn 1987): 575–607.
38. Ibid., 602.
39. U.S. Department of Commerce, *Statistical Abstract of the United States: 1998*, Table 719.
40. Timothy J. Sinclair, "Passing Judgement: Credit Rating Processes as Regulatory Mechanisms of Governance in the Emerging World Order," *Review of International Political Economy* 1, no. 1 (spring 1994): 144–45.
41. Buchholz, "Competition and Corporate Incentives," chapter 5.
42. Claus Offe and Helmut Wiesenthal, "Two Logics of Collective Action: Theoretical Notes on Social Class and Organizational Form," *Political Power and Social Theory* 1 (1980): 75.

43. Winters, *Power in Motion*, 14–15.
44. Buchholz, "Competition and Corporate Incentives," chapter 5.
45. Thus, government officials may be induced to mistakenly believe that there are more competitors for that investment than in fact are feasible. One European plant location consultant freely told me that he recommended to clients that they say they were considering other sites, even if they were not (telephone interview, 14 October 1993).
46. Bryan D. Jones and Lynn W. Bachelor, *The Sustaining Hand: Community Leadership and Corporate Power*, 2nd ed. (Lawrence: University Press of Kansas, 1993), 14.
47. James M. Rubenstein, *The Changing U.S. Auto Industry: A Geographical Analysis* (London: Routledge, 1992), Table 1.1.
48. Loveridge, "On the Continuing Popularity of Industrial Recruitment," 152.
49. Lindblom, *Politics and Markets*, 173.
50. Stephen E. Guisinger, "An Overview of Country Studies," in *Investment Incentives and Performance Requirements*, ed. Stephen E. Guisinger (New York: Praeger, 1985), 38–39.
51. Here I am using game theory in the sense of a "model" described by Duncan Snidal in "The Game *Theory* of International Politics," *World Politics* (October 1985), 32–34. In particular, I am extending Guisinger's use by asking if changing one of the main parameters (number of players) changes the outcome in ways suggested by previous analysis of the prisoners' dilemma (i.e., a greater number of players will have a more difficult time achieving cooperation, all other things equal).
52. Konstantine Gatsios and Paul Seabright, "Regulation in the European Community," *Oxford Review of Economic Policy* 5, no. 2 (1989): 45.
53. Mitchell Smith, "Autonomy by the Rules: The European Commission and the Development of State Aid Policy," *Journal of Common Market Studies* (March 1998), 62.
54. An important early statement of the problem—though without use of the term "prisoners' dilemma"—appears in Richard N. Cooper, "Economic Interdependence in the 1970s," *World Politics* 24, no. 2 (January 1972): 159–81, especially 168–71. Cooper long ago foresaw the possibility of tax base degradation and the difficulties involved in organizing a "constructive" (in my terms, cooperative) response; he also noted some other responses that are potentially useful for some of the other regulatory problems of capital mobility, such as extraterritoriality. Peter K. Eisinger, *The Rise of the Entrepreneurial State* (Madison: University of Wisconsin Press, 1988), 129, analyzes the situation of U.S. states in similar terms.

The best examination of the n-person prisoners' dilemma—one version of which is described as "the collective action problem"—is Russell Hardin, *Collective Action* (Baltimore: Johns Hopkins University Press for Resources for the Future, 1982).

William H. Riker and Peter C. Ordeshook also argue that some regulatory problems take the form of prisoners' dilemmas. In their view, the problem takes this form when regulations will benefit the regulated. As they conclude, "It may well be that all regulation to break Prisoners' Dilemmas is profitable both to the regulated and to society generally." See *An Introduction to Positive Political Theory* (Englewood Cliffs, N.J.: Prentice-Hall, 1973), 296–300 (quote from p. 300).

55. Partly for this reason, observers often argue that investment incentives are "ineffective." (The other reason is that these subsidies are rarely cited by firms among the top location determinants.) As Guisinger nicely demonstrates, the claim that incentives are ineffective is rhetorical sleight-of-hand. That is, many analysts who are critical of investment subsidies imply that they do not even affect investment location, which would necessarily make them bad policy. That is not my approach. I consider them bad policy precisely because they do affect investment location (as Guisinger makes quite clear); the prisoners' dilemma model of this chapter makes sense only with this precondition. See Guisinger, "Rhetoric and Reality in International Business," 111–23, for an excellent discussion of this issue.

56. The Guisinger study examined the importance of investment incentives by formulating questions of investors posed specifically with the prisoners' dilemma in mind. Thus, instead of asking firms how important incentives were to the decision, scholars taking part in the study asked whether investments would have been made in the absence of the incentives received, if all other countries continued to offer their incentives. Two-thirds of the projects surveyed in four industries (automobiles, computers, petrochemicals, and food processing) would have been located in other countries, according to their respondents (N = 74). See Guisinger, "A Comparative Study of Country Policies," 48–49. Given the contrast with the other way of posing the question, this result strongly confirms the prisoners' dilemma conceptualization of the problem.

57. We would then describe subsidizing as the dominant strategy for both governments because it provides a higher payoff than any other strategy. See Henry Hamburger, *Games as Models of Social Phenomena* (San Francisco: W. H. Freeman and Co., 1979), 45.

58. Hardin, *Collective Action*, 13; Robert Axelrod, *The Evolution of Cooperation* (New York: Basic Books, 1984), 12.

59. Hardin, *Collective Action*, 43–44, 173–87.
60. This determination is difficult because of the difficulty of determining in the abstract how many more provinces beyond Ontario and Québec would have to cooperate for all to benefit, even in the face of defection by the remaining provinces.
61. Hardin, *Collective Action*, 42–49.
62. On the Midwest, see Michael Gauf, "In the Midwest, It's Every State for Itself," *St. Louis Post-Dispatch*, 2 December 1992. On the Connecticut–New York–New Jersey case, see Steven Prokesch, "Despite Pact, New York and Region Spar for Jobs," *New York Times*, 30 November 1992, section C; Steven Lee Myers, "Giuliani Says Connecticut Broke Truce," *New York Times*, 14 October 1994, B1.
63. Loveridge, "On the Continuing Popularity of Industrial Recruitment," 152, reports that there are only 200 to 300 annually in the United States.
64. Axelrod, *The Evolution of Cooperation*, 109–23. For examples of the application of tit-for-tat to international prisoners' dilemmas, see Charles Lipson, "International Cooperation in Economic and Security Affairs," *World Politics* 37, no. 1 (October 1984): 1–23; see also many of the essays in Kenneth A. Oye, ed., *Cooperation Under Anarchy* (Princeton, N.J.: Princeton University Press, 1986). Moreover, for U.S. states many of the alternative means of sanctioning, such as tariffs and countervailing duties, are obviously unavailable.
65. This is the overall argument of *Capital Beyond Borders*.
66. For a discussion of both of these factors, see Kenneth P. Thomas, "Auto Bargaining in Canada, 1965–87," in *Foreign Direct Investment in a Changing Global Political Economy*, ed. Steve Chan (London: Macmillan, 1995).
67. On all of these cases except Honda, see Thomas, "Auto Bargaining in Canada, 1965–87." For Honda, see Edward M. Graham and Paul R. Krugman, *Foreign Direct Investment in the United States*, 2nd ed. (Washington, D.C.: Institute for International Economics, 1991), 134.
68. Telephone interview, 10 September 1991.
69. See Thomas, "Auto Bargaining in Canada, 1965–87."
70. Thomas, *Capital Beyond Borders*, 99–108.
71. H. Brinton Milward and Heidi Hosbach Newman, "State Incentive Packages and the Industrial Location Decision," in *The Politics of Industrial Recruitment: Japanese Automobile Investment and Economic Development in the American States*, ed. Ernest J. Yanarella and William C. Green (New York: Greenwood Press, 1990), Table 2.4. The absolute levels of the incentives were $33 million for Nissan, $48.5 million for

Mazda, $80 million for Saturn, $83.3 million for Diamond-Star, $149.7 million for Toyota, and $86 million for Subaru/Isuzu. Milward and Newman's analysis does not include Honda, which was announced in 1981. Honda benefited from $35.1 million in road widening and $1.7 million in other infrastructure, or $18,400 for each of 2,000 jobs (not including a local property tax abatement, for which no estimate is given). See Judy P. Blair, Carole Endres, and Rudy Fichtenbaum, "Japanese Automobile Investment in West Central Ohio: Economic Development and Labor-Management Issues," in the same volume (p. 123). Note that Milward and Newman's figures cover only *state* incentives; in some cases, local and/or federal benefits could be considerable. This was the case for Diamond-Star, which also received local incentives of almost $65 million and import duty savings of almost $30 million; see Nancy S. Lind, "Economic Development and Diamond-Star Motors: Intergovernmental Competition and Cooperation," in the volume edited by Yanarella and Green (p. 110).

72. See Leo Glade, "South Carolina: What Does BMW Know that You Don't?" *Expansion Management* (September-October 1993), 76; Robert Ebisch, "BMW's Site Selection in South Carolina," *Expansion Management* (January-February 1993), 24–25.

73. Ken Blum with Robert Ginsburg, *The Mercedes Benz Subsidy Package: Whose Benefits? Whose Losses?* (Chicago: Midwest Center for Labor Research, 1995), 1. These figures are lower than the $250–300 million range that is widely cited because, according to Ginsburg, those numbers represent the maximum that Mercedes could have gotten, whereas the Midwest Center's data reflect what the company will actually receive. For example, the firm decided not to try to exercise its option—which in any case was in dubious compliance with the state constitution—to use its employees' withheld state income taxes to pay off debt service on plant construction (telephone interview with Robert Ginsburg, 6 January 1997).

74. Thomas, *Capital Beyond Borders*, 94–99, 130. An epilogue (pp. 133–34) notes that the UK was able to give Ford lower subsidies in the 1990s for a Welsh engine plant to serve the European market than for a Jaguar plant that Ford threatened to relocate to the United States—beyond the EU's state aid regulatory reach.

75. See, for example, Dennis Mueller, *Public Choice* (Cambridge: Cambridge University Press, 1979), chapter 2.

76. One important analysis of this distinction between domestic and international politics is Kenneth N. Waltz, *Theory of International Politics* (Reading, Mass.: Addison-Wesley, 1979), 102–16.

77. See Guisinger, "A Comparative Study of Country Policies," 14–19. The United States and the EU are also good subjects for comparison with each other because their level of external trade (averaging exports and imports, excluding intra-EU trade) is comparable: about 8 percent of GDP for the United States and 9–10 percent of GDP for the EU. See Andrea Boltho, "European and United States Regional Differentials: A Note," *Oxford Review of Economic Policy* 5, no. 2 (summer 1989): 105.
78. Indeed, on several occasions in the 1950s and 1960s, federal troops were used against state governments that refused to carry out school desegregation orders. This situation would be inconceivable in the EU.
79. Gatsios and Seabright, "Regulation in the European Community," 45–46.

3

European Union Control of State Aid

This chapter begins the analysis of the state aid regime within the EU. It first describes the legal basis for the European Commission's regulation of various subsidies to business and the institutional arrangements used. It discusses the role of state aid policy within competition policy, the increased emphasis state aid policy received in the context of the Single European Act, and the relationship of state aid policy to regional development policy. It emphasizes the dual nature (legal and political) of policies on state aid and considers how important political divisions within the EU over state ownership and intervention affect policies on state aid.

Policymakers in the member states of the EU have long understood that a subsidy in one country can export unemployment to others. This dynamic is thought to be especially true in a situation such as that in the EU in which tariff and other trade barriers between countries have been removed. As Karel Van Miert, Competition Commissioner from 1993 to 1999, has argued:

> [I]f aid which is prejudicial to competitors in other Member States is not monitored by an independent body to see whether it is in the Community's interest, the *political* essence of the Treaty is in jeopardy. This is because the waiving of conventional protectionist measures such as trade restrictions and customs duties that was necessarily associated with the establishment of the common market can be demanded of the Member States only if they can be sure that their firms do not have to compete against rival firms in other member countries that operate with the backing of massive financial support from state resources.[1]

Moreover, as David Deacon has argued, supranational control is necessary because states "obviously . . . can only take account of national priorities."[2] For this reason, provisions to control subsidies to industry were written into the 1951 European Coal and Steel Community (Treaty of Paris) and the 1957 European Economic Community (Treaty of Rome) agreements. Indeed, regulation of state aid in Europe goes beyond attempts to control location incentives to footloose industries; it extends to any type of financial assistance to firms.

The legal basis for controlling state aid is formalized primarily in Articles 92 through 94[3] of the Treaty of Rome.[4] These provisions give the Commission wide-ranging powers to oversee and veto proposed state aids. In general, aid is considered to be incompatible with the common market unless it qualifies for a specific exemption, according to Article 92(1). Article 92(2) specifies three types of aids that are considered automatically compatible: aid "of a social character" provided to individuals, natural disaster aid, and aid for areas of Germany that had been affected by its postwar division (Berlin and areas bordering on the former East Germany). The issue of whether this last exception should now be applied to eastern Germany was raised before the ECJ in cases concerning disapproved aid to Volkswagen in Saxony.[5]

Article 92(3) specifies the sorts of subsidies that the Commission can, at its discretion, approve as compatible with the common market.[6] These categories are by far the most important of the derogations. Article 92(3)(a) provides for aid to the poorest areas of the Community; Article 92(3)(b) allows subsidies in the common European interest or to meet a serious disturbance in a member's economy. Finally, sectoral subsidies or regional subsidies (for areas lagging by national but not EU-wide standards) can be approved under Article 92(3)(c).

Article 93 includes the general requirement that states must notify the Commission before introducing state aids and prohibits their implementation until they receive Commission approval (the "standstill" requirement). It also empowers the Commission to keep state aid programs "under constant review" and provides that the Council of Ministers by unanimous vote can approve an aid scheme.[7] Article 94 enables the Council to make appropriate regulations for enforcing Articles 92 and 93; these regulations can be substantive or procedural. In 1998 the Council finally approved two Article 94 regulations for state aid, including a long-contentious procedural regulation.

These very general principles have been fleshed out by decades of Commission practice and jurisprudence by European courts (i.e., the Court of First Instance [CFI] or the ECJ—the latter being the equivalent of the U.S. Supreme Court).[8] The following two sections explain the main concepts used in EU practice, then summarize and organize the legal status of state aid law. (For a portrait of current state aid spending, see Appendix 3.)

State Aid Concepts

State Aid

The concept of state aid itself is very broad. Notably, it is not defined in the Treaty of Paris or the Treaty of Rome. Despina Schina suggests that "this omission may well have been intentional," giving the Commission wide-ranging powers of interpretation and keeping states from simply evading a fixed definition.[9] Three principles govern whether an advantage bestowed on a firm constitutes "state aid": Has there been an action by a state body (at any level of government) or a reduction of state resources?[10] Does the action favor *particular* firms or industries? An action that favors all firms—such as a reduction in interest rates—is considered to be general macroeconomic policy, not state aid. Does the action affect trade within the EU or competition between EU firms in third countries? If the first two tests are met, state aid exists; if the third one is also met, the Commission will consider whether the aid is incompatible with the Common Market or, conversely, eligible for one of the Article 92(3) exemptions. If the first two tests are not both met, the state aid rules are not applicable.

An example will make these considerations clearer. As noted above, activity by any level of government can lead to a state aid. In fact, the aid need not be administered by a governmental body at all; the only requirement is that some governmental action is involved. In 1972, France introduced a tax on clocks and watches to finance technical centers to provide research and development (R&D) and technical assistance to firms in the industry, especially small- and medium-sized companies. Although this action constituted no drain on the French treasury and was not administered by the government, the Commission did consider it an aid to the industry.[11] In terms of the foregoing criteria, it clearly included government action (the tax), and it was specific to a particular industry. Because timepieces were an item of Community trade, the Commission had to determine if the tax's impact on that trade was excessive. Ultimately, after the French government agreed not to tax imported clocks and watches to help finance the technical centers, the Commission ruled that the tax was compatible with the Common Market. With the change, the Commission deemed its effects on trade within the Community to be acceptably small.

A case in which extra-EU competition by EU firms was central was *Istituto Poligrafico e Zecca della Stato*; in that case, an Italian state-owned mint was ruled to have received aid through above-market compensation levels for coinage services. Although EU countries all mint their own coins—so there is no intra-EU trade in this service—the subsidization was deemed to have helped the company gain contracts in third countries at the expense of unsubsidized EU producers.[12]

Types of Aid

The EU classifies state aid into three main categories, according to their objective: regional aid, sectoral aid, and horizontal aid.

Regional aid is granted to areas that are lagging behind the development standards of the EU as a whole (often referred to as "92(3)(a)" regions after the relevant Treaty text) or the development standards of their own country ("92(3)(c)" regions). Regions are divided geographically by the Nomenclature of Territorial Statistical Units (NUTS). Table 3-1 shows the approximate size of the three levels of NUTS regions.

For state aid purposes, NUTS Level II regions are the largest that matter. As the examples above show, a Level II region can embrace an entire small country (before 2000, Ireland and Luxembourg each

Table 3-1 **Size of NUTS Regions**

Level	**Approximate Size**	**Example(s)**
Level I	German *Land*	Saxony
Level II	Italian *Regione*	Greater London Luxembourg Abruzzi
Level III	English County	Corse du Sud Oxfordshire

Sources: Fiona Wishlade, "Competition Policy, Cohesion and Co-ordination of Regional Aids in the European Community," *European Competition Law Review* 14, no. 4 (1993): 144 n. 12; Commission of the European Communities (CEC), *Competitiveness and Cohesion* (Luxembourg: CEC, 1994), Statistical Annex, Table A.1.

was a single NUTS II region). In determining eligibility for regional aid, NUTS Level II regions are the basis for classifying a region for Article 92(3)(a) status; regional aid requires a GDP per capita that is less than 75 percent of the EU average. Level III regions can be awarded Article 92(3)(c) designation on the basis of divergence from national averages for GDP per capita and unemployment. The richer the country, however, the more a region must differ from those averages.[13]

Regional development is now the most important focus of state aid programs in the manufacturing sector of the EU; it accounted for 57 percent of all state aid to manufacturing in 1995–97.[14] Every region of the EU has a maximum aid intensity (see definition below) that can be awarded in that region. There are substantial interactions between regional development and state aid (which are taken up in more detail below). Relative to other types of aid, the Commission is favorably disposed to regional aid.

Sectoral aid, as its name implies, is aid channeled to particular industries—usually those that are experiencing economic difficulties. Because of the pressure to support declining sectors, the Commission has taken an active role in coordinating such aid to prevent it from having an undue effect on intra-Community trade. To achieve this goal, the Commission has established several sectoral frameworks that outline its policies in industries such as textiles, shipbuilding, and automobiles. There also are special state aid rules for specific sectors: transport in the European Economic Community (EEC) treaty and coal and steel in the European Coal and Steel Community (ECSC) treaty.[15] Finally, of course, agriculture and fisheries are subject to common policies at the Community level. Sectoral aid totaled only 12 percent of manufacturing aid given by the member states in 1995–97.[16] Sectoral aid is considered most likely to distort competition.[17]

The Commission also classifies rescue aid under sectoral aid. This type of aid is financial support to individual firms that are in danger of bankruptcy. The relative frequency of rescue aid in western Europe compared to the United States represents a major difference in state aid practices between the two areas. Large firms are much more likely to be allowed to fail in the United States—as the airline industry shows in striking fashion. Whereas Air France, Olympic, TAP Air Portugal, Sabena, Iberia, and Aer Lingus have all received aid since 1991,[18] large U.S. carriers such as Pan American and People Express have been allowed to cease operations. Indeed, the most recent major bailout of a nonfinancial firm in the United States was the 1980 rescue of Chrysler.

Horizontal aid is not sectorally oriented; instead, it pursues specific goals across industries. The main horizontal goals are R&D,[19] small and medium enterprises (SMEs),[20] and trade/export. These three types of aid accounted for 19 percent of aid to manufacturing in 1995–97; all horizontal aid totaled 31 percent.[21] The Commission treats aid for SMEs, environmental aid, and R&D relatively favorably;[22] it treats aid to exports unfavorably (and absolutely bans aid for intra-Community exports).[23]

With the recent EU emphasis on reducing unemployment, aid for increasing employment and training has been added to the list of relatively favored horizontal aid. In 1995, the Commission adopted guidelines for employment aid that specify that it will treat such aid favorably as long as the aid is for job creation rather than job maintenance and is not in an overcapacity sector.[24] In 1998, a framework on training aid was established that gives priority to aid to SMEs and to general rather than firm-specific training.[25]

One final type of horizontal aid deserves mention because of its former importance, especially in terms of attracting inward investment. General investment aid (or simply "general aid") includes government support programs with no specific sectoral or regional focus. Such programs are available to any firm that satisfies their criteria, but these programs are different from general macroeconomic policy in that they provide advantages to specific enterprises. The Commission's policy has been to discourage general aid.

According to Reinhard Walther, state aid statistics chief in DG IV, the most important types of aid given to inward investors are regional aid, R&D aid, and general investment aid.[26]

Forms of Aid

State aid can take many forms, including direct grants, tax breaks, tax deferrals, soft loans, loan guarantees, above-cost procurement, below-cost provision of goods or services to firms, and government capital injections. Because direct grants and tax reductions are the easiest to assess (i.e., the most transparent), the Commission has attempted to persuade member states to use them in preference to other forms of aid, to improve its monitoring capacity. Recent cases have emphasized several forms of aid that are routinely provided to developers in the United States, such as free infrastructure in business parks.[27]

Aid Intensity

Intensity refers to the level of aid provided in relation to a benchmark—usually investment (although aid is sometime measured in relation to jobs). The Commission measures intensity primarily in terms of net grant equivalent (NGE). The NGE equals the after-tax value of the aid divided by the investment. Thus, if a company is investing $500 million in a project, a $100 million grant will have different NGEs depending on the tax treatment of the grant. If the grant is completely untaxed, the NGE would be 20 percent. If it is treated as ordinary income, and the tax rate is 25 percent, NGE is 15 percent ($75 million/$500 million). For some countries, however, aid limits are given in gross grant equivalent (GGE)—an inconsistent procedure that is based on differing national practices.[28] Further muddying the waters, the Commission's *Surveys on State Aid* calculate the total amount of aid given in each country on the basis of GGE, on the grounds that tax exemptions and corporate losses so reduce effective tax rates that ignoring tax treatment is less distorting than assuming maximum tax rates.[29]

Principles Governing State Aid Law and Policy

The legal status of state aid in the EU is constantly evolving, but a small number of concepts can help to organize the wide variety of legal decisions. Three general principles—compensatory justification, proportionality, and transparency—apply to state aid in general; two specific concepts—viable restructuring and the "market investor" rule—are important for understanding large subsets of state aid law.

"Compensatory justification" is an inexact translation of the French term *contrepartie*. This doctrine holds that aid can be granted to a firm only if it contributes to Community (not merely national) objectives and only if its objectives could not be achieved without the aid. According to the Commission, there must be "a contribution by the beneficiary of aid over and above the effects of normal play of market forces to the achievement of Community objectives as contained in derogations of Article 92(3) EEC" if the aid is to be approved under

Article 92(3).[30] This view was upheld by the ECJ in the landmark *Philip Morris* decision (see Chapter 4).[31]

"Proportionality" means that aid should not be excessive in relation to the goals it is designed to accomplish. This principle follows from the stricture in Article 93(3)c that aid should "not adversely affect trading conditions *to an extent contrary to the common interest*" (emphasis added). Among the general applications of the proportionality principle are differentiated aid maxima for various regions of the Community, whereby the amount of aid permitted depends on levels of unemployment, per capita income, and so forth in relation to EU averages.[32] Proportionality has been applied as well in specific cases—such as that involving Rover, in which the Commission rejected the British government's plan to completely write off the company's debt before selling it to British Aerospace, on the grounds that this action exceeded what was necessary to achieve the Community interest.[33]

Transparency is an important goal for the Commission that also is central to this study because of its importance for the Commission's monitoring ability. Briefly, "transparency" refers to the ability to detect and assess an aid in terms that are comparable with other aid. In other words, how easy is it to measure aid intensity for a particular type of assistance?[34] The various forms of aid can be ranked with regard to their transparency as follows: grants, tax reductions, soft loans or tax deferrals (such as accelerated depreciation),[35] guarantees, and equity injections.[36] Commission policy has been to encourage states to use more transparent forms of intervention and to move away from less transparent methods. The Commission has also begun to apply this principle to itself: It is providing greater access to information (for instance, to competitors of aid recipients) and making its operations more open to outside view in general—including an excellent Web site (http://europa.eu.int/comm/dg04/index_en.htm).

"Viable restructuring" is a crucial concept for a wide variety of rescue and sectoral aid programs. Absent extraordinary circumstances, the Commission is very unlikely to authorize aids to firms or industries that are in difficulty unless the government submits a plan detailing how the firm or industry will be restructured to regain long-run competitiveness. In particular, aid will not be authorized to increase productive capacity in industries that already suffer from overcapacity. Indeed, the Commission most likely will require capacity cuts to approve a sectoral aid program.[37] In one form or another, this requirement is longstanding. In 1971, the Commission wrote that it could authorize aid programs to help financially struggling enterprises "insofar as it is sufficiently exceptional and insofar as:

a. aid granted *is within the framework of a sufficiently well-defined reorganization programme* as to represent an effective contribution to the reorganization of the enterprises or regions concerned;
b. the field of sectoral or regional application where it is granted is defined with sufficient precision to enable its effect on competition and intra-Community trade to be assessed."[38]

In other words, the Commission would authorize aid as long as it was connected to viable restructuring and was transparent.

The viable restructuring requirement was emphasized further in the various sectoral frameworks mentioned above—as well as in the Commission's 1978 Communication on Sectoral Aid,[39] its 24 January 1979 letter on rescue aid,[40] and the 1994 Guidelines on Rescue and Restructuring Aid.[41]

A corollary of the viable restructuring requirement is that the Commission will very rarely authorize operating aid (sometimes called production aid) for companies that are losing money. If operating aid is not connected with a restructuring plan, it is unacceptable—as the Commission pointed out in rejecting a Belgian aid plan for the textile and clothing industry in 1978.[42] In 1988, however, the Commission decided that it would allow operating aid under certain circumstances in the worst-off (Article 92[3]a) regions of the Community.[43] As Fiona Wishlade points out, however, the Commission did so because it recognized that some peripheral areas have *permanent* cost disadvantages; a policy of allowing operating aid in those areas only on a *temporary* basis is inconsistent with that reality.[44] Only with the December 1997 regional aid guidelines did the Commission authorize permanent operating aid for transport costs in the "outermost regions" (French overseas departments, the Azores, Madeira, and the Canary Islands) or in areas with population density below 12.5 persons per square kilometer, in Article 92(3)(a) and (c) regions.[45]

The "market investor" principle applies to dealings between governments and state-owned or state-controlled enterprises.[46] To test whether a transfer (capital injection, loan, etc.) to a public enterprise (or a loan guarantee made on its behalf) constitutes state aid, the Commission will ask whether "a private investor operating under normal market circumstances" would have acted in the same way. If not, the action will be deemed to constitute state aid.[47] This approach was first enunciated by the Commission in 1984[48] (although it was foreshadowed at least as early as 1972, in the Commission's analysis of "Temporary official acquisitions of corporate capital by the State")[49]; it was upheld by the ECJ in the *Meura* decision.[50] Note that a "market investor" does not mean *any* investor: ECJ rulings[51] and Commission-sponsored studies emphasize that Commission decisions must ask what a *large* private investor would do. For example, Massimo Belcredi and colleagues suggest that a large firm would not simply allow a subsidiary to go bankrupt and let its unsecured creditors take a loss. It would have to pay them off, even though it was not legally required to, to protect its reputation.[52] Nonetheless, even large investors taking a long-term outlook will not support loss-making operations indefinitely.[53]

Taken together, these five principles cover the vast majority of state aid law and substantive Commission policy. To be approved, aid must achieve Community objectives that cannot be met without it, be proportional to the problem it addresses, and be transparent. If support is targeted to a company or industry in difficulty, it must be tied to a viable restructuring plan. If support provided to a state-owned firm would have been made by a private investor, it does not constitute state aid. If a private investor would not have made such a transfer, state aid is present, and its eligibility for exemption from the presumptive ban must be assessed.

The following section discusses how state aid law is carried out in practice, through a brief examination of Commission and court procedure.

State Aid Procedure

State aid policy is carried out by a relatively small bureaucracy in Brussels. Primary responsibility falls to the competition policy Directorate General (DG IV). Two of the eight directorates in DG IV are concerned with state aid; between them they have seven units and a special task force. Directorate G includes general state aid policy, horizontal aid, regional aid, and analysis/inventory. Directorate H includes sectoral aid I (shipbuilding, steel, non-ferrous metals, coal, cars, and synthetic fibers), sectoral aid II (textiles, paper, wood and wood products, mechanical and electrical equipment, chemical and pharmaceutical products, computers, electronics, other manufacturing), public enterprises and public services, and the task force on aid to the new *Länder* of Germany.[54] The directorate has a staff of about 100, 50 of whom are professional-level staff.[55] The small staff size means that there is a need to focus effort; it also constrains the amount of monitoring that can be done for non-notified aid. In fact, non-notifications usually come to DG IV's notice through news reports or complaints by competitors. Although DG IV has primary staff responsibility for state aid, actual decisions are made by majority vote of the entire twenty-person Commission.[56]

Not all aid is first considered by DG IV. Although DG IV recently took over much of the responsibility for aid in the transport sector,[57] aid for agriculture, fisheries, and energy is referred to their individual directorate generals (DG VI, DG XIV, and DG XVII, respectively).[58]

Finally, not all monitoring power is given to the Commission. The ECJ has ruled[59] that the final sentence of Article 93(3), which prohibits non-notified aids and implementation prior to approval by the Commission, has "direct effect." Thus, this provision can be enforced directly by national courts on application by an aggrieved party.[60]

In recent years, there has been increasing resort to Article 93(3) actions in national courts. Indeed, in 1995 the Commission sought to enlist national courts in the fight against aid that had not been notified in accord with Article 93(3) requirements.[61]

The Commission's Role in Theory and Practice

The notification and "stand-still" provisions of Article 93 are key to the Commission's monitoring power. In law—if not always in fact—governments submit to Commission oversight through the notification requirement. For the most part, this requirement is observed. At times, however, states have taken action in the gray areas of state aid policy, apparently unaware that what they were doing required notification. At other times, governments deliberately failed to notify the Commission because they felt they were unlikely to receive approval.[62] There has been substantial litigation over notification, post-notification Commission procedure, and non-notified aids (see Chapter 4). This latter category is of special interest in this study because it reflects directly on the extent to which the cooperative agreement about state aid control is actually succeeding.

A state aid case begins either with notification by a member state or through Commission discovery of a non-notified aid (either through the press or through complaints by competitors or other governments). A notification can be for a single project or for an aid program (for example, regional aid to firms meeting criteria specified in the notification). Certain aids must be individually reported even if they are reported under previously approved aid programs—notably in overcapacity sectors (specified under the sectoral frameworks mentioned above) or under the new Multisectoral Framework that is aimed at controlling bidding wars for large mobile investments using approved regional aid programs.[63] Once notified, the Commission has two months to approve the aid or open an investigation under Article 93(2)—sometimes called the "contentious procedure."[64] During the two-month preliminary stage, third parties (such as competitors of the aid recipient) have no right to be heard, even if their complaint started the investigation.[65] If the Commission opens the Article 93(2) procedure, third parties are then invited to submit comments. There is a time limit of eighteen months for this investigative procedure, which can result in approval (most likely of a modified version of the proposed aid), conditional approval, or a decision that the aid may not be implemented.[66] The Commission's decision (to not open the contentious procedure, or any outcome of that procedure) may be appealed to the European courts. In 1998, the Commission opened Article 93(2) proceedings or their ECSC analogue in 17.6 percent of new cases (excluding agriculture, fisheries, transport, and coal)—a significant jump over the long-term trend of about 10 percent.[67]

Although the process sounds neat and tidy in theory, in practice there are numerous ways it can be dragged out or circumvented.[68] Foot-dragging by member states can weaken the credibility and enforcement effect of the Commission's policy; on the other hand, Commission delays can infuriate states that wish to introduce an aid program promptly. Moreover, the wide discretion that the ECJ has allowed the Commission gives it ample room to pursue what some observers (for example, Michelle Cini) have characterized as an ideological agenda.

The first potential glitch in the process is that a government might not notify the Commission about an aid as required. As several authors have pointed out, the Commission's frequent statements reminding states of their requirement to notify is a sign of continuing problems.[69] To get some idea of the extent of the problem, consider that in 1998 the Commission received 317 aid notifications and 86 cases of non-notified aid; in 1997 there were 515 aid notifications and 140 cases of non-notified aid.[70] In 1995, the Commission made new efforts to improve compliance, including expanded efforts to force aid repayment in case of non-notification and issuing a notice on cooperation between the Commission and national courts to enforce compliance.[71] The November 1998 Procedural Regulation under Article 94 holds the most promise for getting control over non-notification. The ECJ has steadfastly refused to let the Commission declare a non-notified aid automatically illegal. Instead, although interim measures can be taken to stop the aid, the Commission must still open an Article 93(2) procedure and examine the aid scheme on its merits to declare it illegal.[72] Non-notification usually comes to light through monitoring of press reports or complaints from competitor firms or other member states.[73]

The Commission is not without leverage against non-notified aid or aid that is implemented without its approval. States that fail to comply with the rules can be ordered to secure repayment of illegal state aid, with interest, from the recipient firms. Though this sanction was established in principle in a 1973 ECJ ruling,[74] it was not used by the Commission until 1983.[75] This area of state aid law and practice is evolving rapidly.[76] With final adoption of the Procedural Regulation, national courts will no longer be able to prevent the "immediate and effective execution" of a Commission repayment order.[77] Previously, recipients of illegal aid could delay repayment by securing domestic court orders during appeal.[78] That route should now be closed.

As noted above, staff levels in Directorates G and H are not high, so there is a constant battle with backlogged notifications.[79] As Cini points out, the broad definition of a state aid means that states must report as much as possible[80]—thereby increasing workload problems. Over the years, the Commission had adopted three sets of responses to enable it to focus on top-priority cases; it did not achieve a breakthrough until May 1998, however, when a Council regulation under Article 94 enabled the Commission to sharply reduce the number of small notifications.

First, in line with longstanding member state desires but in contrast to its own past practice as well as court decisions,[81] the Commission introduced in its 1992 SME guidelines a *de minimis* rule providing that aid of less than 50,000 European Currency Units (ECU) (in each of two categories of expenditure—investment and non-investment—

for a possible total of 100,000 ECU) over a three-year period did not need to be reported. In January 1996, the Commission clarified that this exemption was available to firms of any size and replaced the two-category 50,000 ECU limit with a single 100,000 ECU limit.[82] With the adoption of the Enabling Regulation in May 1998, the *de minimis* rule's legal status was regularized.[83]

Second, the Commission frequently has been accused of extending its two-month deadline with requests for more information. Long-standing Commission practice holds that the clock does not start running until a notification is complete, with all necessary information for a decision at hand. By asking for more information, the clock is restarted—a practice that, not surprisingly, is poorly received by member states.[84]

Third, the workload is reduced through the use of informal notifications of aids that are considered to be very straightforward, wherein the member state will request a "comfort letter" that gives informal approval. No official statistics on such cases exist, and third parties are entirely uninformed. Naturally, if DG IV staff does not agree that the case is clear-cut, it must then be notified according to official procedures.[85]

Despite these efforts, focusing on the most important cases was difficult because, as one DG IV official noted, "We were flooded with small cases"; moreover, "With the introduction of the Court of First Instance, we were being brought into the courts much more often"—especially with competitors' challenges to Commission aid approvals.[86] On 7 May 1998, the Council adopted the Enabling Regulation, which should allow the Commission to rid itself of the workload associated with the many notifications of small amounts of aid. In addition to providing for a *de minimis* rule, the Enabling Regulation allows the Commission to exempt SME aid, aid for R&D, aid for environmental protection, aid for employment and training, and some regional aid from the notification requirement under conditions specified by the Commission. Member states are required to make annual reports on aid that utilizes these notification exemptions. The Commission issued draft block exemptions in July 1999 for SME aid and training aid, along with a *de minimis* regulation.[87]

Once a case enters the DG IV orbit through notification, complaint/discovery, or request for a comfort letter, a round of negotiation often ensues. That is, if the staff is not persuaded that the aid is eligible for exemption, it will enter into discussions with the member state on possible modifications to or, in more extreme cases, withdrawal of the aid program. As Cini writes:

> It should nevertheless be borne in mind that the move to the second detailed stage of the procedure is the exception rather than the rule. Problem aid is more likely to be dealt with informally early in the procedure. Member states will be informed that the aid is not likely to be authorised and this will put pressure on them to come to some arrangement with the directorate to alter it.[88]

Mitchell Smith also highlights the importance of negotiations between member states and DG IV, arguing (rightly, I believe) that these negotiations show far more about Commission effectiveness on state aid than the raw number of rejections.[89]

If agreement is not reached during the preliminary phase, discussions continue after the opening of an Article 93(2) investigation; the wrangling can last for years in cases in which a state is determined to introduce a new aid program. Negative decisions by the Commission are not final because they can then be appealed to the European courts; losses by the Commission in court are not final, either, if it loses on procedural grounds: The Commission can reopen the Article 93(2) procedure and fix its procedural errors, as it has in a number of cases. In the Air France case, the CFI ruled in 1998 on a lawsuit filed by competitors that the Commission's reasoning for its approval of FF20 billion in aid was inadequate. In response, the Commission issued a new decision that changed nothing except the reasoning that had been criticized.[90] In the "Rover sweeteners" case, British Aerospace successfully appealed to the ECJ against a Commission ruling that the company had to repay £44 million in illegal aid, but the Commission opened a new Article 93(2) procedure and successfully forced repayment.[91]

Even in highly contentious cases, a point of decision eventually will be reached. Because the ECJ has shown little inclination to question the Commission's substantive judgment,[92] Commission decisions are usually upheld in the absence of procedural error. At that point, if not sooner, the state must decide whether it will comply with the Commission decision. Non-compliance does occur, meaning that the state grants the aid without Commission approval; if such non-compliance is discovered, however, the Commission will sue to have the state declared in violation of its Treaty obligations and to force aid repayment. Until recently there was no ultimate sanction—aside from bad publicity—for states that still refused to comply. With the approval of the Procedural Regulation, the opportunities for aid recipients to delay repayment (often with state connivance, a Commission official told the *Financial Times*)[93] will be decreased substantially. Moreover, the Maastricht Treaty's revision of Article 171 now allows the Commission to propose fines of states that are in breach of their Treaty obligations, which could theoretically come into play if a state completely ignored ECJ rulings. This sanction, however, has not been threatened in a state aid case—not even the eighteen-month refusal by the German state of Saxony to reclaim disapproved aid it had paid to Volkswagen.[94]

Figure 3-1 shows the route of a state aid case from introduction to resolution.

Finally, an important difference in the treatment of new state aid programs and existing aids should be noted. The latter are harder to dislodge than the former, and the possibility of forcing aid repayment probably does not exist.[95] The Commission is empowered under Article 93(1), however, to monitor existing aid and propose "appropriate measures" when its examination suggests that the aid may no longer be compatible with the common market. This incompatibility can occur when economic circumstances have changed since the original aid approval—as in the "Offshore Supplies" cases. These cases concerned aid provided by the UK for purchases of oil rigs and supplies to be used in the North Sea. When the aid was first approved in 1976, the competitors were mainly the United States and Canada, so the aid program did not affect intra-Community trade. By 1979, however, French, Dutch, and German competitors had emerged; Article 93(1) proceedings were opened in light of the changed circumstances, and the British were forced to abolish the aid.[96] In the late 1980s, the Commission began to increase the use of its powers under Article 93(1) to examine such existing aid (see Chapter 4).

State Aid Policy and Competition Policy

State aid policy exists within a broader context that EU officials call "competition policy." This term encompasses antitrust policy as practiced in the United States and controls on state support of businesses that are the focus of this book. As Karel Van Miert has suggested,

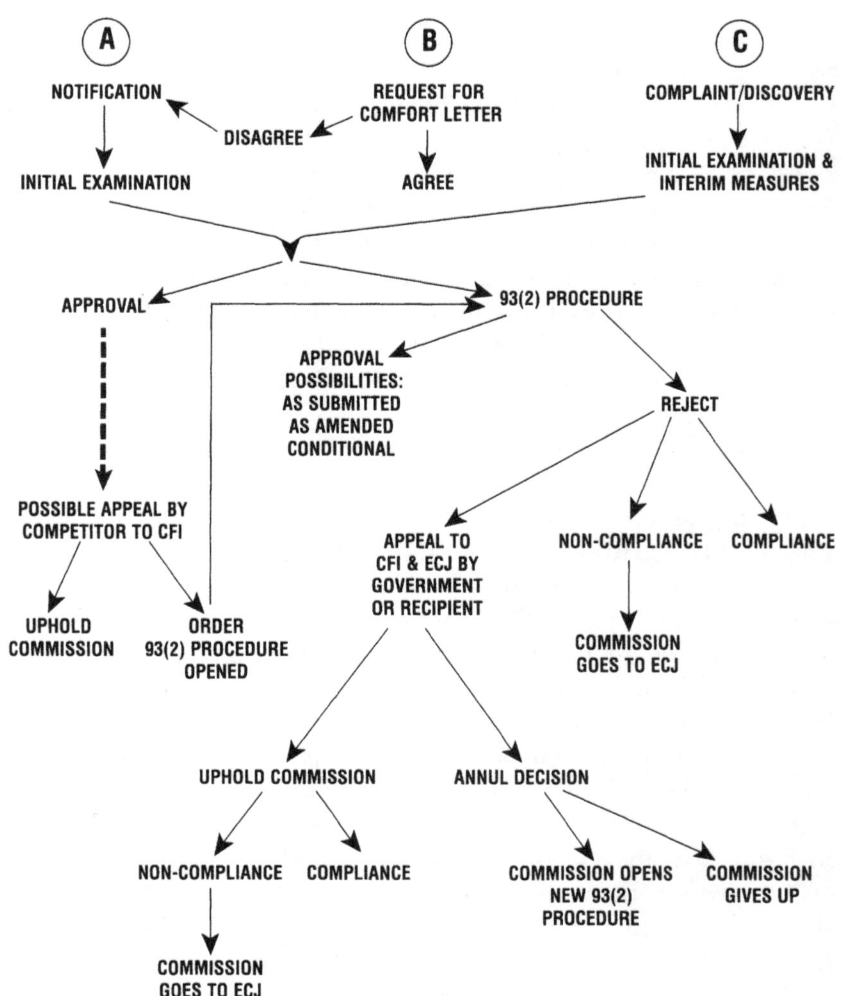

Figure 3-1 **Route of a State Aid Case**

state aid policy is very much about the distortion of competition, even when there may be good reasons for providing support to firms: "[A]ll aid, whether or not it is useful, has one thing in common: It distorts competition between businesses, since some of them receive grants or tax reliefs, while others do not. It is this damaging effect on competition which prompts the Commission to take action for the Community."[97] From the EU point of view, then, state aid control is a necessary part of competition policy.

There are important differences between competition policy in the United States and in the EU. What is known as antitrust policy in the United States translates into the EU taxonomy as three items: restrictive practices, abuse of dominant position, and merger control. All of these items, along with state aid control, fall within the purview of DG IV.[98] Within the United States, of course, there is no control over domestic subsidies (with minor exceptions); the only consideration of subsidies by the federal government relates to the Department of Commerce and the U.S. Trade Representative's interests in *foreign* subsidies and their trade impacts. In the EU, foreign subsidies are considered to be part of foreign commercial relations and are handled by DG I (External Affairs). Table 3-2 shows these differences:

Table 3-2 **U.S. and EU Competition Policy**

Policy Area	**U.S. Name/ Treatment**	**EU Name/ Treatment**
Mergers	Antitrust/DOJ	Merger Control/DG IV
Monopolistic Practices	Antitrust/DOJ	Abuse of Dominant Position/DG IV
Restrictive Practices	Antitrust/DOJ	Restrictive Practices/DG IV
Domestic Subsidies	None	State Aid/DG IV[a]
Foreign Subsidies	Subsidies/USTR	Subsidies/DG I

Note: DOJ = Department of Justice; DG = Directorate General; USTR = U.S. Trade Representative

[a]Plus other DGs as relevant.

Political Aspects of State Aid Control

State aid control presents two aspects: legal and political. Although there is a major legal component in ECJ rulings, as well as in the procedures of the Commission, Commission decisions themselves ultimately can be quite political. This political aspect is inevitable, given the fact that Commissioners are appointed by their home governments. Thus, intra-Commission negotiations form one of the most important ways in which cooperation over the control of state aid takes place in practice. For example, the Commission appears to have had an "unwritten rule" that state-owned airlines would not be allowed to simply fail,[99] although it has required layoffs, sale of routes or foreign subsidiaries, and other actions as conditions of approving aid.[100] At times, the Commission has appeared to pursue linkage strategies in its negotiations with governments over proposed state aids. For example, a proposed aid package for Ford Motors' Jaguar unit in the UK was the subject of very difficult negotiations—which became more difficult when the British government tried to block state aid to Irish Steel.[101]

Another political aspect of state decision making is the national identity of the Competition Commissioner and President of the Commission. For instance, it has been argued that aid for Renault received relatively lenient treatment during the mid-1980s (e.g., a 441 million ECU capital injection in 1986) because Jacques Delors was Commission President.[102] On the other hand, former Competition Commissioner Leon Brittan may have felt constrained to take a tough line on the "Rover sweeteners" case after his strong criticism of the Renault bailout.[103]

Finally, basic ideological differences mark the relationships of member states, and DG IV is not a neutral party; it is strongly in the economic liberal camp. Cini argues that DG IV staff thinks in terms of "good guys" and "bad guys"—with the UK, The Netherlands, and Denmark in the former group (Germany also is considered a DG IV ally) and Italy, Greece, Ireland, Belgium, and France ("to a slightly lesser extent") in the latter group.[104] The news media across the political spectrum also hold this view.[105] Although—as Smith argues—DG IV uses "the principle of neutrality of rules . . . as a defense against the threatening impact of politics,"[106] it does so in a way that advances a particular view of how the European economy should function.

These political divisions are long standing and have persisted to this day. In the preparation of the very first general system of control of regional aid (adopted in 1971), for example, the French and Italians opposed a Commission proposal for pre-notification of significant regional aids, whereas Germany and the Benelux countries supported it.[107]

In more recent battles, the battle lines have remained similar. For example, when Brittan announced in 1989 that he would focus on "aid for export, general investment and aid to nationalized industries and state holding companies,"[108] his statement was particularly galling to Italy and France. They charged that Brittan's goal was to challenge the mixed economy as such, not merely state aid. The issue is whether forcing all firms to operate on market criteria does that. According to the *Economist*, it does:

> This means that governments can no longer run state industries for social and political rather than economic ends. Therein lies the rub. What is the point of state ownership if the state must run its firms as if they were private ones? Rather than face this question, governments have turned aid cases into political footballs.[109]

Brittan's efforts were therefore very objectionable to member states with traditions of high levels of state ownership and intervention into the economy. For example, "Many French, Italian, and Spanish politicians argue that state planning and subsidies must continue if European industry is to survive the coming global competition," *Business Week* reported.[110] As Cini notes, although the Commission in the 1980s had a robust consensus on antitrust issues, "On the state aids side, however, this consensus was always more fragile."[111]

A final example of this dynamic was the FF20 billion aid provided to Air France in July 1994, which was opposed only by Brittan and Danish Commissioner Henning Christopherson (with an abstention by British Commissioner Bruce Millan). According to an editorial in *The Daily Telegraph*, "This decision went through the Council of Ministers and the Commission because other airlines in Greece, Portugal, Spain, Ireland and Belgium also want state aid, while the Germans were reluctant to upset their French friends."[112] The level of state interventionism, then, is an important aspect of state aid policy.

Finally, there has been activity by business associations and unions in the state aid field. In addition to the increasing number of complaints by businesses that lead to state aid investigations, there has also been policy activity by organizations such as the Union of Industrial and Employers Confederation of Europe (UNICE) and the Confederation of British Industry (CBI), an example of which is detailed in Chapter 4. Union activity has not been directed toward policy intervention but primarily toward individual cases in which state aid has contributed to job loss—such as the closing of Renault's Vilvoorde, Belgium, plant to move to Spain,[113] or the *Sloman Neptun* case, in which the company's works council argued that Germany's international shipping register was a state aid because it allowed the company to use cheaper foreign labor on German-flagged ships.[114]

State Aid and Regional Policy

Within many individual European countries as well as within the EU as a whole, there is a long tradition of regional policies designed to promote the development of areas that are suffering from some combination of below-average income, inadequate infrastructure, or high unemployment. Centralized regional policy is unknown in the United States, for the most part,[115] but an imperfect analogue does exist in the economic development efforts of the poorest U.S. states. For example, Mississippi was the first state to introduce a system of investment incentives to attract firms to its jurisdiction—in 1936.[116] Now, of course, all U.S. states engage in such activities.

As Tim Frazer argues, there is an inherent tension between regional policy and competition policy (including state aid control) because the former mandates intervention in the market and the latter tries to reduce interventions.[117] The Commission's job is to navigate these conflicting objectives, just as Stephen Wilks and Lee McGowan argue the Commission must reconcile the objectives of competition policy with the needs of international competitiveness and the environment.[118]

More specifically, regional policy is intimately related to state aid policy in three ways. First, one obvious method of improving incomes and reducing unemployment in lagging regions is to attract investment by offering location subsidies. In the EU, subsidies for regional development are subject to state aid rules just as any other subsidy would be (though, as elucidated above, their treatment under the Treaty of Rome is relatively favorable). It should be noted that regional aid awards are one of the most common types of state aid that can be used to attract mobile investment.[119]

Second, the effectiveness of locational subsidies for regional development depends on whether they make location in peripheral areas as attractive or more attractive than location in centrally located, high-income areas. This factor is a function of the difference between location incentives in peripheral and central regions. If company X will receive a grant equal to 20 percent of its investment whether it locates in rural Ireland or the suburbs of Paris, for example, the latter site is likely to be more attractive. If Ireland can offer 40 percent and France only 20 percent, however, the difference may offset problems associated with the Irish location. From the point of view of competition policy, an even better solution would be 20 percent in rural Ireland and zero in Ile-de-France. This approach reduces the distortions that are inherent in subsidies, yet it maintains the differential between the two locations.[120] Precisely for this reason, the Commission's current Guidelines on Regional Aid reduce the maximum levels of aid permitted throughout the EU, as well as the population coverage of areas eligible for regional aid.[121]

Third, regional policy is important for state aid policy because the EU itself funds certain investment incentives through the Community's Structural Funds, which now comprise the European Regional Development Fund (ERDF), the European Social Fund (ESF), the Guidance Section of the European Agricultural Guidance and Guarantee Fund (EAGGF), and the Funding Instrument for Fisheries Guidance (FIFG). Although the ERDF has the primary regional responsibility, all of these funds have developed regional dimensions.[122]

The rationale for regional policy is that although neoclassical economic theory tends to imply the leveling of regional differences if barriers to trade and capital movements are removed, in fact persistent differences in the levels of development of regions within the EU have remained.[123] Iain Begg argues that agglomeration advantages have been more important than high factor costs and congestion; economic integration, therefore, has benefited the central regions of Europe more than its peripheral areas.

Moreover, regional disparities are much greater within the EU than within the United States. Andrea Boltho[124] has pointed out that despite major similarities in the world's two largest markets (such as very low levels of extra-regional trade—under 10 percent in both cases), the United States has much smaller regional disparities than the EU as a whole, the EC-9, and (interestingly enough) even than the five largest EC economies. Boltho believes that labor mobility is the most likely reason for this phenomenon: Americans make two to three times as many interregional moves in their lifetime as Europeans. This movement is hardly surprising, given the much smaller variations of language and culture within the United States. Table 3-3, which uses updated data, shows how much wider income disparities are in Europe than in the United States—which helps explain the greater prominence of regional policy in Europe.

Within the EU, the poorest areas fall broadly in the Mediterranean and (since reunification) eastern Germany. Until the past few years, Ireland also was in this category, but recent economic growth has brought it above the EU average in GDP per capita.[125] The entire territory of Greece and almost all of Portugal are considered to be lagging in development by EU standards, as are much of Ireland, Spain, and the Mezzogiorno in Italy. These areas form the core of "Article 92(3)(a)" regions for state aid control purposes and thus benefit

Table 3-3 **U.S. vs. EU Regional Inequality**

	Ratio
U.S.: 50 States excluding D.C. (1997 personal income per capita), Top 5 : Bottom 5	1.66
EU: Top 8 Regions : Bottom 8 (GDP per capita at Purchasing Power Parity)	3.27
EU: Top 5 Countries : Bottom 5 (GDP per capita at market prices)	1.93

Sources: U.S. data were calculated from *Statistical Abstract of the United States 1998*, Table 727; data for EU regions were calculated from "46 Regions Below 75% of the EU Average," Commission press release no. 2198, 18 March 1998; data for EU countries calculated from Eurostat on-line statistical indicators (http://europa.eu.int/en/comm/eurostat/indic/indic16.htm, accessed 1 February 1999).

from a more favorable disposition for subsidy approval.[126] Ireland, Portugal, Spain, and Greece are also often referred to as "cohesion" countries; this term describes the EU goal of bringing these economies up to the standards of the rest of the members. As part of the political negotiations for the Single European Act and the Maastricht Treaty, these countries have bargained for and received higher levels of subsidies from the Structural Funds—including a special Cohesion Fund, of which they are the sole beneficiaries.

As suggested above, the concern for cohesion is also a goal to be promoted by DG IV. According to Karel Van Miert, the Commission's goal is to concentrate state aid in the poorer areas of the EU, precisely to promote cohesion.[127] Thus, the Commission has a policy of allowing higher levels of state aid per project in poorer areas of the Community, to maximize the differential between what richer and poorer regions can provide to firms.

Cohesion runs into the political difficulty that richer areas of the Community would prefer to run their national regional policies without consideration of their effects on poorer regions of the Community. DG IV's efforts to reduce state aid in general and maximize the differential that poor regions can provide in excess of rich regions have led to constant battles with national governments—in particular, France and Germany—over regional policy. In addition, R&D aid is disproportionately spent in central areas of the EU, with negative consequences for cohesion.[128] The Commission has not been completely successful in its efforts to control regional policy in the central regions. Part of the reason is that despite the theoretical differential provided by higher permitted aid levels in the periphery, experience has shown that richer areas can afford to provide up to the maximum allowed (and can fund a greater number of projects), whereas poor regions are generally unable to do so—thus reducing the differential and the relative attractiveness of poor regions to investment.[129] For example, when the entire country of Portugal was listed as having an aid maximum of up to 75 percent NGE, Ford and Volkswagen received only 33 percent for locating a minivan plant at Setubal. At about the same time, when Saab-Scania sought the 17 percent maximum grant allowed in Angers, France, the Commission only allowed half that amount.[130] Thus, instead of a 58 percentage point differential, there was only about a 25 percentage point difference in the grants actually awarded in the two regions. As Fiona Wishlade pointed out before the December 1997 regional aid guidelines reduced aid maxima, in neither Ireland, Greece, or Portugal is the aid maximum authorized by DG IV reached on a regular basis or even at all.[131]

Regional policy has been an important political issue within the EC/EU as a whole since the negotiations for the Treaty of Rome.[132] At that time, only the Mezzogiorno severely lagged EC social and economic indicators. According to Beverly Springer, "Italian negotiators bargained for provisions in the Treaty of Rome by which the EEC would assume some responsibility for Italian regional problems. Their success assured Italian support for the treaty."[133]

As the EC expanded to include poorer countries (Ireland in 1973, Greece in 1981, Spain and Portugal in 1986), disparities among member states widened and the stakes at issue became higher. In December 1974, Italy and Ireland threatened to boycott the Council meeting if the other members did not promise to support the ERDF.[134] With the introduction of the Single European Act and fears that it might further exacerbate regional disparities, the amount of money provided through the Structural Funds was doubled in real terms between 1987 and 1993.[135] In an attempt to concentrate the effects of these funds, five objectives for the Funds were specified (see Chapter 4).[136] Given the EC's intention to concentrate 80 percent of these funds in the most backward (Objective 1) regions, the richer states scrambled to make sure that their regions that previously were eligible for ERDF monies would still be eligible, and protracted negotiations took place over the designation of eligible regions.[137] The negotiations leading to the Maastricht Treaty prompted the introduction of a new "Cohesion Fund" for Ireland, Spain, Portugal, and Greece; the level of this fund was the subject of difficult debates as well. With the addition of Cohesion Funds, these four countries were assured of a doubling in real support between 1992 and 1999; the overall level of the Structural Funds plus the Cohesion Funds increased from 21.3 billion ECU in 1993 to 30 billion in 1999.[138] At the March 1999 Berlin Summit, funding for the 2000–2006 round of Structural Funds was essentially frozen at the 1999 level in a broader Agenda 2000 package that includes Common Agricultural Policy (CAP) reform and decisions on national contributions to the EU budget (see Chapter 4).[139]

Conclusion

This chapter examines the basic structure and policies of the EU toward state aid. It places state aid policy within its broader context of competition policy and shows that the increased prominence of competition policy under the Single European Act meant greater vigor in state aid enforcement. It also sets the groundwork for several themes that will recur in subsequent discussion—namely, the relationship between regional development and state aid and the interplay between issues of state intervention in the economy and subsidies to firms, especially government-owned enterprise. Chapter 4 puts these elements into play, analyzing how state aid policy and the Commission's powers have evolved since the establishment of the ECSC in 1951.

Notes

1. "Karel Van Miert's Guidelines and Intentions Over State Aid," *Europe Documents*, English edition, no. 1848, 9 July 1993, 3.
2. David Deacon, "Current State Aid Policy in the EC and the Implications of 1992," in *Producer Subsidies*, ed. Ronald Gerritse (London: Pinter, 1990), 65.
3. The Treaty of Amsterdam, which entered into force on 1 May 1999, changed the numbering of Treaty Articles; what had been Articles 92–94 became Articles 87–89. All referenced material uses the old numbers, however, and that practice is followed in this book. For all

renumbering relating to competition policy, see the DG IV Web site (<http://europa.eu.int/comm/dg04/amsterdam_treaty_art12.htm>).

4. An excellent summary appears in Despina Schina, *State Aids Under the EEC Treaty, Articles 92 to 94* (Oxford: ESC Publishing Ltd., 1987). Except where noted, my review here draws on her discussion (pages 42–61). For the full text of these Articles, see Appendix 2.
5. Ben Perry, "State Aids to the Former East Germany: A Note on the VW/Saxony Case," *European Law Review* 22 (February 1997): 85–91.
6. These exemptions are not automatic; they are at the discretion of the Commission. The ECJ definitively rejected the view that they are automatic in the *Philip Morris* case. See Schina, *State Aids Under the EEC Treaty*, 47, citing *Philip Morris v. Commission*, Case 730/79, [1980] ECR 2671 at 2690; [1981] 2 CMLR 321 at 341.
7. This latter provision is used relatively rarely (primarily in the agricultural sector). In 1996 and 1997, only one such case was approved. See CEC, *Twenty-seventh Report on Competition Policy* (Brussels-Luxembourg: CEC, 1998), 298.
8. Beginning on 1 August 1993, the CFI took over jurisdiction for appeals by firms against Commission decisions on state aid. Appeals of CFI decisions could be made only on legal issues. The ECJ remains the venue for appeals by member states. See CEC, *Twenty-third Report on Competition Policy* (Brussels-Luxembourg: CEC, 1994), point 381.
9. Schina, *State Aids Under the EEC Treaty*, 13.
10. Leigh Hancher et al., *EC State Aids* (London: Chancery Law Publishing, 1993), 22. These two tests are alternatives; only one must be met. Because state resources can be reduced by direct expenditure (subsidy) or by tax expenditure, the concept of state aid is necessarily wider than that of subsidy.
11. See CEC, *Second Report on Competition Policy* (Brussels-Luxembourg: CEC, 1973), section 109, and *Third Report on Competition Policy* (Brussels-Luxembourg: CEC, 1974), section 103.
12. CEC, *Twenty-eighth Report on Competition Policy* (Brussels-Luxembourg: CEC, 1999), point 196.
13. Fiona Wishlade, "Competition Policy, Cohesion and Co-ordination of Regional Aids in the European Community," *European Competition Law Review* 14, no. 4 (1993): 144–45.
14. CEC, *Seventh Survey on State Aid* (Brussels-Luxembourg: CEC, 1999), 20, Table 9.
15. See Hancher et al., *EC State Aids*, chapters 10 and 4, respectively.
16. CEC, *Seventh Survey on State Aid,* 20, Table 9. The sectors included in manufacturing are shipbuilding and "other," which normally means rescues of individual firms.

17. See, for example, CEC, *Fourth Survey on State Aid* (Brussels-Luxembourg: CEC, 1996), 27.
18. David Field, "Healthy airlines are livid over billions in subsidies for weak European rivals," *Washington Times*, 9 August 1994, B8.
19. Within the category of R&D, the Commission distinguishes among fundamental research, which is not directed toward particular products and is rarely subject to state aid rules; basic industrial research, which is concerned with general, but commercially usable, knowledge; and development (or applied R&D), which is devoted to the commercialization of innovative products or processes. See 1985 "Community framework for State aids for research and development," in CEC, *Competition Law in the European Communities, Volume II*, 134–39.
20. The Commission's definition of an SME has changed over time. Firms with up to 250 employees and up to 25 million euro in sales annually are considered "medium"; firms with 50 or fewer employees and sales up to 5 million euro are "small." In both cases, no more than 25 percent of the company can be owned by another firm not itself an SME. See Kostas A. Lavdas and Maria M. Mendrinou, *Politics, Subsidies and Competition: The New Politics of State Intervention in the European Union* (Cheltenham: Edward Elgar, 1999), 79, 117, n. 3–4.
21. *Seventh Survey on State Aid*, Table 9.
22. Andrew Evans and Stephen Martin, "Socially Acceptable Distortion of Competition: Community Policy on State Aid," *European Law Review* 16, no. 2 (1991), 107–08. Moreover, in connection with environmental and renewable energy aid, the Commission recently has been willing to allow operating aid for limited periods of time, in sharp contrast to its strong presumption against operating aid in most circumstances (see below). See *Twenty-eighth Report on Competition Policy*, points 221–22.
23. On intra-Community exports, see *First Report on Competition Policy*, point 187. More recently, the Commission has begun to investigate export to third countries more closely. See Cini, 261.
24. Henrik Mørch, "Summary of the most important recent developments (state aid)," *Competition Policy Newsletter*, summer 1995, 43–44.
25. *Twenty-eighth Report on Competition Policy*, points 218–20. The Commission considers much government support for training to be a general measure rather than state aid at all.
26. Personal communication, Brussels, 23 September 1993. As I note in Chapter 6, however, general investment aid has now been essentially ended in the EU.
27. For the Austrian case *Lenzing Lyocell*, see *Twenty-eighth Report on Competition Policy*, point 198.

28. See 1988 Communication on regional aid policy, in CEC, *Competition Law in the European Communities, Volume II*, 118–22; and Fiona Wishlade, "The Policy Relevance of the EU State Aid Rules," paper presented at the European Community Studies Association, Seattle, Washington, 29 May 1997, 29.
29. *Fourth Survey on State Aid*, 58.
30. *Tenth Report on Competition Policy*, point 213.
31. Case 730/79, 1980 ECR 2671.
32. The first regional aid coordination policy with full differentiation was introduced in 1975 (a 1971 program only had maxima for the central areas of the Community). See *Fifth Report on Competition Policy*, point 87.
33. See Hancher et al., *EC State Aids*, 167.
34. Fiona Wishlade has criticized this view of transparency as too formalistic. She argues that operating aid can be transparent even though it is by definition impossible to assess in terms of aid intensity. See "The Policy Relevance of the EU State Aid Rules," 24. In December 1997, the new guidelines on regional aid in fact added criteria of aid-per-kilometer and aid-per-unit-weight for areas with low population density. See CEC, "Guidelines on National Regional Aid," Annex II.
35. This combination may seem odd, but the intuition is that a tax deferral is essentially an interest-free loan from the government to the beneficiary.
36. *Second Survey*, 26–27.
37. For example, in 1978 the Commission raised no objection to a Dutch rescue scheme for ship repair yards because it reduced employment by 35 percent and cut capacity, whereas it challenged an Italian program for the same industry because of the probability that it would increase capacity. *Eighth Report on Competition Policy*, points 193–194.
38. *First Report on Competition Policy*, point 184.
39. See Hancher et al., *EC State Aids*, 90–91.
40. Hancher et al., *EC State Aids*, 68.
41. Henrik Mørch, "Summary of the Most Important Recent Developments (state aid)," *Competition Policy Newsletter*, autumn/winter 1994, 61.
42. *Eighth Report on Competition Policy*, points 201–03.
43. *Eighteenth Report on Competition Policy*, point 167.
44. Wishlade, "The Policy Relevance of the EU State Aid Rules," 23–24.
45. Guidelines on National Regional Aid, points 4.16, 4.17, and Annex II.
46. Article 222 (after Amsterdam, Art. 295) of the Treaty of Rome guarantees that states are free to have government-owned enterprises and in principle bans differential treatment of public and private ownership.

Michelle Cini suggests that in practice DG IV's culture has been relatively hostile to state intervention in the economy. See Michelle Cini, "Policing the Internal Market: The Regulation of Competition in the European Commission," Ph.D. diss., University of Exeter, 1994, 266: "As such, it appears that one of the state aid directorate's main functions is to work for an ideological victory over those states where direct interventionism is rampant."

An example of this is the treatment of privatization in state aid cases. As the *Twenty-fourth Report on Competition Policy*, point 360, notes:

> The Commission cannot impose a condition of privatization on an undertaking that has received aid for restructuring purposes. It can however take note of the commitment of a Member State to privatize the enterprise to be restructured. Through the viability condition, such a commitment can even become a binding element of the Commission's decision.

It goes on to argue that a commitment to privatization is evidence of eventual viability, which is hard to reconcile with non-discriminatory treatment of public and private enterprise.

47. Hancher et al., *EC State Aids*, 162.
48. See *Fourteenth Report on Competition Policy*, point 198.
49. *Second Report on Competition Policy*, points 122–25.
50. Case 234/84, Belgium v. Commission [1986] ECR 2263. Cited by Hancher et al., *EC State Aids*, 162.
51. See Hancher et al., *EC State Aids*, 162–63.
52. Massimo Belcredi et al., *The Aid Element in State Participation to Equity Capital* (Brussels: Commission of the European Communities, 1988), 7–8.
53. Hancher et al., *EC State Aids*, 163, discuss the *ENI-Lanerossi* case, in which this Italian clothing maker had lost money for more 10 years. The Court ruled that government capital injections under these circumstances clearly constituted state aid.
54. CEC, *Competition Policy Newsletter*, October 1998, 66.
55. "Community State Aid Policy: An Overview," RAPID Memo 94-67, 10 November 1994; personal communication with Panagiotis Alevantis, DG IV information officer, 21 August 1996.
56. For aid to coal and steel, which is governed by the ECSC Treaty, aid must be given under frameworks requiring unanimous Council of Ministers agreement. The actual monitoring procedure is essentially the same as for other state aid. See Hancher et al., *EC State Aids*, 77–78.

57. In part a result of Karel Van Miert's move from the Transport to Competition Directorate-General. See Lavdas and Mendrinou, *Politics, Subsidies and Competition*, 90, 93, 97–98, 107–08.

58. Hancher et al., *EC State Aids*, 240.

59. *Capolongo v. Maya*, Case 77/72, [1973] ECR 611; *Lorenz v. Germany*, Case 120/73, [1973] ECR 1471. See Schina, *State Aids Under the EEC Treaty*, 142–43.

60. Note, however, that it does not mean that the national court can rule on whether the aid is compatible with the common market. It can only rule on the issue of implementation without Commission approval.

61. *Twenty-fifth Report on Competition Policy*, points 152, 155.

62. James Flynn, "State Aid and Self-Help," *European Law Review* 8 (1983): 307–08.

63. "Multisectoral Framework on Regional Aid for Large Investment Projects," published in *Official Journal* (OJ C 107, 7 April 1998), available at DG IV's Web site: <http://www.europa.eu.int/dg04/lawaid/en/98c107.htm>, accessed 27 January 1999.

64. Schina, *State Aids Under the EEC Treaty*, 145. It also can take no action, but that is relatively rare.

65. Hancher et al., *EC State Aids*, 240. The Commission reaffirmed its view that this was proper in *Twenty-fifth Report on Competition Policy*, point 218.

66. Fiona Cownie, "State Aids in the Eighties," *European Law Review* 11, no. 4 (1986): 262, writes: "Very few grants of aid were approved by the Commission, once it had decided to initiate the procedure provided in Article 93."

67. Sixty-six investigations out of 274 new cases, according to the *Twenty-eighth Report on Competition Policy*, Table 5. This figure applies only to the initial decision to open the Article 93(2) procedure, not decisions resulting from that procedure. In 1995 and 1996, the figure was just over 10 percent, but 1997 saw an increase to 15 percent (*Twenty-fifth Report on Competition Policy*, point 219; *Twenty-sixth Report on Competition Policy*, point 228; *Twenty-seventh Report on Competition Policy*, point 320). For 1990–94, detailed investigations under Article 93(2) were launched 190 times, or in 7.9 percent of 2,410 new cases (CEC, *European Community Competition Policy 1994*, Table 1). J. A. Winter, "Supervision of State Aid: Article 93 in the Court of Justice," *Common Market Law Review* 30 (1993), 325, reports that about 10 percent of the cases decided from October 1986 and September 1990 went to the Article 93(2) procedure.

68. Cini, "Policing the Internal Market," Chapter 5, gives the most in-depth account of actual Commission practice in state aid cases.
69. See J. Knox, *Towards 1992: State Aids to Industry* (Trade and Tariffs Research, London, November 1989), 26; and Cini, "Policing the Internal Market," 280 n. 25.
70. *Twenty-eight Report on Competition Policy*, Table 3.1; *Twenty-seventh Report on Competition Policy*, point 320 and figure 7. These figures exclude agriculture, fisheries, transport, and coal.
71. *Twenty-fifth Report on Competition Policy*, points 153–55.
72. See Winter, "Supervision of State Aid," 313; Piet Jan Slot, "Facts, procedure and comments in Case C-301/87," *European Law Review* 16 (1991): 44–46; Hancher et al., *EC State Aids*, 237–38 (who note that there is no requirement to open an Article 93(2) investigation just because an aid is unnotified). The critical case here is Case C301/87 France v. Commission (Boussac) [1990] ECR I-307; see discussion in Chapter 4.
73. Fredrik Dahl, "European Firms Get Tough on EU State Aid Policy," *Reuter European Union Business Report*, 6 June 1996. As the *Twenty-fifth Report on Competition Policy*, point 152, notes, "Because firms are increasingly sensitive to aid granted to their competitors and are better informed about the opportunities for fair competition afforded them by the Community competition rules has [*sic*] resulted in their submitting more and more complaints to the Commission and more appeals to the Court of First Instance against Commission decisions to approve aid to their competitors." This was not always the case, however. Schina, writing in 1987, relates, "An English barrister, when it was suggested that the Commission be informed of an illegal aid granted against the interests of his client, replied, 'We don't do things that way in this country.' " *State Aids Under the EEC Treaty*, 175.
74. *Commission v. Germany*, case 70/72 [1973] ECR 813.
75. Schina, *State Aids Under the EEC Treaty*, 164.
76. See Hancher et al., *EC State Aids*, Chapter 18; and *Twenty-seventh Report on Competition Policy*, points 205, 311–16.
77. The quote is from Council Press Release no. 127 43/98, 16 November 1998. See also Emma Tucker, "Boost for Brussels Over Illegal State Aid," *Financial Times*, 16 November 1998, 4.
78. Lavdas and Mendrinou, *Politics, Subsidies and Competition*, 62, inexplicably ignore the substantial problems carrying out repayment orders, pronouncing the sanction "highly effective, both in substance and in procedural terms, in compelling state compliance." Yet to take one example, by the Commission's first publication of complete data on

repayments in 1993, Italy had not complied with any of six repayment orders totaling ECU 566.5 million, dating back as far as 1988. See *Twenty-third Report on Competition Policy*, Annex II, 450–52.

79. Cini, "Policing the Internal Market," Chapter 5, provides a highly detailed analysis of state aid policy administration that highlights staff time constraints. Others who have noted the work overload include Douglas Yuill et al., "European Regional Incentives (1992-93)," *Journal of Regional Policy* 12, nos. 3/4 (July/December 1992): 599; Joseph Gilchrist and David Deacon, "Curbing Subsidies," in *European Competition Policy*, ed. Peter Montagnon (New York: Council on Foreign Relations Press, 1990), 44; William Pitt, *More Equal Than Others . . . A Director's Guide to EU Competition Policy* (Hemel Hempstead: Director Books, 1995), 3.
80. Cini, "Policing the Internal Market," 280.
81. See Hancher et al., *EC State Aids*, 31.
82. Henrik Mørch, "Summary of the most important recent developments (State Aid)," *Competition Policy Newsletter*, spring 1996, p. 33. According to Lavdas and Mendrinou, "SMEs continue to be the main beneficiaries of the rule." *Politics, Subsidies, and Competition*, 85.
83. European Information Service, "State Aid: Commission and Council at Loggerheads Over Tighter Rules," *European Report* No. 2314, 9 May 1998.
84. Yuill et al., "European Regional Incentives 1992/93," 598; Cini, "Policing the Internal Market," 274, 292.
85. Cini, "Policing the Internal Market," 295–97; *Twenty-fourth Report on Competition Policy*, point 352.
86. Personal communication with DG IV official, Brussels, 18 May 1998. See also Mitchell Smith, "Autonomy by the Rules: The European Commission and the Development of State Aid Policy," *Journal of Common Market Studies* 36, no. 1 (March 1998): 73–75.
87. Council of Ministers Press Release, PRES 98/129, 14 May 1998; European Information Service, "State Aid: Council and Commission at Loggerheads over Tighter Rules," *European Report* No. 2314, 9 May 1998. For the announced block exemptions, see *Twenty-eighth Report on Competition Policy*, point 346; and European Information Service, "Commission Tables Draft Regulations for State Aid Exemptions," *European Report* No. 2249, 30 July 1999.
88. Cini, "Policing the Internal Market," 300.
89. Mitchell Smith, "Integration in Small Steps: The European Commission and Member-State Aid to Industry," *West European Politics* 19, No. 3 (July 1996): 564–65, 568–69, 576–77. His speculation that a "legitimization" of

the Commission's role had led to a decline in negative decisions (from 14 in 1990 to 3 in 1994) proved premature, however: Negative decisions rose to 23 in 1996, 9 in 1997, and 31 in 1998. *Twenty-eighth Report on Competition Policy*, Table 4.

90. Samer Iskandar and Michael Skapinker, "BA Angered at Outcome of Air France Subsidy Ruling," *Financial Times*, 23 July 1998, 26; Agence France Presse, "EU Commission Strengthens Arguments to Justify Rescue of Air France," 22 July 1998. For the Commission's view, see *Twenty-eighth Report on Competition Policy*, point 256.

91. Robert McDonald, "State Aids & the Effort to Ensure Fair Competition," *EIU European Trends*, No. 2 1992, 61–62; Cini, "Policing the Internal Market," 371. Cini provides an extended treatment of this affair on pages 360–73.

92. Evans and Martin, "Socially Acceptable Distortion of Competition," 80. Note, however, that this has begun to change recently, particularly in the CFI. See Smith's discussion of the *Sytraval* decision in "Autonomy by the Rules," 74.

93. Emma Tucker, "Boost for Brussels Over Illegal State Aid," *Financial Times*, 16 November 1998, 4.

94. Neil Buckley and Judy Dempsey, "Brussels fury over cash for VW," *Financial Times*, 31 July 1996, 2; Emma Tucker, "Commission Resolves VW Row," *Financial Times*, 19 November 1997, 2.

95. Schina, *State Aids Under the EEC Treaty*, p. 167.

96. Personal communication with Joseph Gilchrist, DG IV, Brussels, 14 September 1993; *Ninth Report on Competition Policy*, points 162–64.

97. "Karel Van Miert's Guidelines," 2.

98. Recall, however, that aid in the agriculture, fisheries, energy, and transport (except airlines) sectors are handled by their respective directorates general, not by DG IV.

99. "Spanish subsidies," *Financial Times*, 2 February 1996, 15.

100. In January 1996, for example, the Commission approved a capital injection of 87 billion pesetas ($694 million) into Spain's Iberia Airlines, but it required the company to divest itself of its controlling stake in Aerolineas Argentinas (and the latter's domestic subsidiary Austral) and scale back from 38 percent to 25 percent ownership of the Chilean airline Ladeco, as well as cutting 3,500 jobs. See "Spanish subsidies"; "Airlines: The Sky's the Limit for Iberia following Political Accord," *Transport Europe*, 19 January 1996; "Iberia Cash Infusion Shows European State Aid Still Flowing," *Airline Financial News*, 5 February 1996.

101. Emma Tucker and John Griffiths, "Aid deal for Jaguar could embarrass London," *Financial Times*, 2 February 1996, 2.

102. Motor Industry Research Unit, *State Aid to the European Motor Industry: Disaster Aversion or Strategic Investment?* (Norwich, England: University of East Anglia, 1987), 29.
103. Michelle Cini pointed this out to me.
104. Cini, "Policing the Internal Market," 246, 265.
105. Cini, "Policing the Internal Market," 260.
106. Smith, "Autonomy by the Rules," 62.
107. See CEC, *Competition Law in the European Communities*, Volume II: Rules applicable to state aids (situation at 31 December 1989), 97.
108. "EC Commissioner Outlines Areas of Aid Review," Reuters, 31 March 1989. He launched investigations of 6 billion FF of aid to Group Bull, 12 billion FF to Renault, $230 million to Italian trucking firms, and $1 billion to Sabena Airlines. See "The Aid Plague," *Economist* Survey of Business in Europe, 8 June 1991, 12–18.
109. "The Aid Plague," 17.
110. Jonathan Kapstein with John Rossant, " 'Subsidy' Becomes a Dirty Word," *Business Week*, 19 June 1989, 48.
111. Cini, "Policing the Internal Market," 216.
112. "City Comment: The Euro control tower believes a dodo can fly," *The Daily Telegraph*, 28 July 1994, 21; Mary Brasier and Christopher Lockwood, "Commission attacked over Air France aid," *The Daily Telegraph*, 28 July 1994, 20.
113. The Commission canceled ERDF subsidies that had been earmarked for the Spanish plant receiving the Vilvoorde work. Nathan Lillie, "Transnational Labor Mobilization in Europe: The Case of Renault-Vilvoorde," paper presented to European Community Studies Association annual meeting, Pittsburgh, 2 June 1999, 8–9. Mieke Damme, ed., *Perte Totale: La Fermeture de Renault-Vilvorde* (Antwerp: Hadewijch, 1997), 61, 115, relates that a delegation of Renault workers went to the home of Competition Commissioner Karel Van Miert on 24 March 1997 and later met with him and other officials after a demonstration on 4 April 1997. I thank Nathan Lillie for bringing this source to my attention.
114. Fiona Wishlade, *When Are Tax Advantages State Aids and When Are They General Measures?* Regional and Industrial Policy Research Paper Number 20, European Policies Research Centre, University of Strathclyde, June 1997, 8–9.
115. Peter K. Eisinger, *The Rise of the Entrepreneurial State* (Madison: University of Wisconsin Press, 1988), 66.
116. The program was known as Balance Agriculture With Industry. See William Schweke et al., *Bidding for Business: Are Cities and States Selling*

Themselves Short? (Washington, D.C.: Corporation for Enterprise Development, 1994), 14.

117. Tim Frazer, "The New Structural Funds, State Aids and Interventions on the Single Market," *European Law Review*, February 1995, 4.
118. Stephen Wilks with Lee McGowan, "Competition Policy in the European Union: Creating a Federal Agency?" in *Comparative Competition Policy: National Institutions in a Global Market,* ed. G. Bruce Doern and Stephen Wilks (Oxford: Clarendon Press, 1996), 258.
119. Personal interview, Reinhard Walther, Unit Chief for State Aid Inventory and Analysis, DG IV, 23 September 1993.
120. CEC, *Industrial Policy in an Open and Competitive Environment: Guidelines for a Community Approach*, COM(90) 556 final, 16 November 1990, 8.
121. Emma Tucker, "EU to Reconsider Regional Aid: Commission Plans to Focus Help on Areas Most in Need of Help," *Financial Times*, 19 December 1997, 2. The population limits for each country were announced in Commission Press Release IP/98/1133, "Commission Sets National Ceilings for Coverage of Regional Aid," 16 December 1998.
122. Douglas Yuill et al., *European Regional Incentives*, 10th edition (Strathclyde: European Policies Research Centre: 1990), 67. The FIFG dates from 1994. The European Investment Bank (EIB) formerly provided some funding for structural objectives. Ian Bache, *The Politics of European Union Regional Policy* (Sheffield: Sheffield Academic Press, 1998), 32, notes that even as early as 1979, "85 per cent of ESF funding went to regions eligible for ERDF assistance."
123. Iain Begg, "European Integration and Regional Policy," *Oxford Review of Economic Policy* 5, no. 2 (summer 1989): 90–104.
124. Andrea Boltho, "European and United States Regional Differentials: A Note," *Oxford Review of Economic Policy* 5, no. 2 (summer 1989): 105–15.
125. Patrick Smythe, "Corporation Tax Deal Could Lose Us EU Goodwill," *Irish Times*, 30 November 1998, 16.
126. Northern Ireland, despite exceeding the 75 percent threshold, was also classified as an Article 92(3)(a) area because of its exceptional political circumstances. With the 1997 regional aid guidelines, it was reclassified to Article 92(3)(c) status but was allowed to retain aid maxima otherwise only available in the poorer Article 92(3)(a) regions. See Fiona Wishlade, *RAGS and LIPS: New Weapons in the Commission's Regional Aid Control Armoury*, Regional and Industrial Research Paper Series, No. 31, European Policies Research Centre, February 1999, 13–14.
127. Van Miert, "Karel Van Miert's Guidelines," 5–6.
128. Jürgen R. Grote, "Diseconomies in Space: Traditional Sectoral Policies of the EC, the European Technology Community and their Effects on

Regional Disparities," in *The Regions and the European Community: The Regional Response to the Single Market in the Underdeveloped Areas*, ed. Robert Leonardi (London: Frank Cass, 1993), 27. This is confirmed by the data of the *Seventh Survey on State Aid*, Table 9, which show that all four cohesion countries spent less than the EU average proportion of manufacturing aid going to R&D (10 percent): Spain was the highest (7 percent), followed by Ireland (5 percent), Portugal (3 percent), and Greece (zero).

129. Yuill et al., *European Regional Incentives 1994–95*, 100–102; CEC, "Fair Competition in the Internal Market: Community State Aid Policy," *European Economy* no. 48 (September 1991): 72.
130. Robert McDonald, "State Aids & the Effort to Ensure Fair Competition," *EIU European Trends* no. 2 (1992): 61–62.
131. Fiona Wishlade, *EC Competition Policy and Regional Aid: An Agenda for the Year 2000?* Regional and Industrial Research Paper Series, No. 25, European Policies Research Centre, December 1997, 14.
132. The following discussion draws on Beverly Springer, *The European Union and its Citizens: The Social Agenda* (Westport, Conn.: Greenwood Press, 1994), chapter 7.
133. Springer, *The European Union and its Citizens*, 109.
134. Springer, *The European Union and its Citizens*, 110. For a more detailed account of the inauguration of the ERDF, see Bache, *The Politics of European Union Regional Policy*, 35–50.
135. R. Hall and D. van der Wee, "Community Regional Policies for the 1990s," *Regional Studies* 26, no. 4 (1992): 399–404.
136. Yuill et al., *European Regional Incentives*, 10th edition, 68. A sixth objective was added for thinly populated areas of Sweden and Finland, but there will be only three objectives in the 2000–2006 round of funding. On Objective 6, see Yuill et al., *European Regional Incentives 1995-96*, 84. On the new proposals for 2000–2006, see CEC, *Reform of the Structural Funds*, explanatory memorandum, COM (1998) 131 final, 18 March 1998, 11.
137. Fiona G. Wishlade, "Competition Policy, Cohesion and the Co-ordination of Regional Aids in the European Community," *European Competition Law Review* 14, no. 4 (1993): 145–47.
138. See Yuill et al., *European Regional Incentives 1995-96*, 74; CEC, *Competitiveness and Cohesion*, Table 17.
139. Brian Groom and Michael Smith, "Spain and UK the Biggest Winners: Regional Aid," *Financial Times*, 27 March 1999, 2.

4

The Development of the State Aid Regime

Chapter 3 considers the basic rules governing the EU's system of state aid control. This chapter provides a historical accounting of the development of European Commission procedures and powers and the changing background conditions in which state aid controls have existed. The goal of this chapter is not to provide the entire history of state aid control (which would require several volumes). Instead, it focuses on developments that bear most strongly on the Commission's ability to exercise effective control. The exposition in this chapter is partly chronological and partly thematic. That is, although this chapter deals with specific issues in their entirety, it treats them in the approximate chronological order in which they arose.

My analysis proceeds in seven stages. I begin with an examination of the first major application of state aid rules: export aid for intra-Community trade. Second, I turn to early Commission efforts in the area of regional aid, in which the system of differentiated aid maxima for different regions of the Community was created and expanded. Third, I consider the effect that the addition of new, poorer member states has had on state aid policy. Fourth, I consider Commission efforts in two important sectors: textiles and automobiles. Fifth, I analyze the introduction and development of the most important horizontal framework—that for R&D. Sixth, I shift the focus to the issue of efforts to evade the state aid rules and their application. In particular, I focus on Commission initiatives such as the rules on cumulation of aids and the inauguration of the *Surveys on State Aid* and especially the use of repayment orders beginning in the mid-1980s. I also consider crucial cases that have defined the powers of the Commission. Finally, I analyze the delicate relationship between rules on state aid and state-owned enterprises.

Introduction

When the Treaty of Paris that established the ECSC was adopted in 1951, the Community took the first step toward state aid control. As Article 4 of the ECSC Treaty states:

> The following are recognized as incompatible with the common market for coal and steel and shall accordingly be abolished and prohibited within the Community, as provided for in this Treaty:
>
> . . .
>
> (c) subsidies or aids granted by States, or special charges imposed by States, in any form whatsoever. . .

Article 54, furthermore, provides that the "High Authority" can impose fines on firms that receive state aid.[1] Similarly, the European Commission was given monitoring and enforcement powers in Article 93 of the European Economic Community Treaty (see Chapter 3).

Although the Commission had these powers from the dawn of the EEC, state aid control was a low priority until after the completion of the customs union in 1968.[2] Indeed, from 1958 to 1968 the Commission issued only three final decisions under Article 93(2) proceedings.[3] Kostas Lavdas and Maria Mendrinou suggest that state aid did not rise higher on the political agenda because of strong economic performance during the 1950s, whereas economic crises in the mid- to late- 1960s "had among their effects the strengthening of economic nationalism."[4] In the late 1960s and early 1970s, however, the situation began to change.

Aid for Intra-Community Exports

The first important application of state aid rules came in the area of intra-Community trade; specifically, the Community sought to ban the use of export subsidies for such commerce. In the joined cases *E.C. Commission vs. France: Re Export Credits* (cases 6/69 and 11/69),[5] the European Court of Justice ruled definitively that such subsidies on trade between member states were incompatible with the common market. This case involved the use by France of preferential interest rates for steel exporters in intra-European trade. The Commission had first tried to end this program in 1964, and the French finally agreed in May 1968. That same month, however, the country was hit with a massive political crisis, and the government reversed the decision to end the aid. In the ECJ's decision, the justices accepted the Commission's contention that a preferential lending rate was a specific act, not a general macroeconomic policy; therefore, it constituted state aid. The ECJ rejected several French arguments and concluded that France was in violation of its Treaty obligations.[6] As Despina Schina comments, "The use of export aids in the trade between Member States could threaten the unity and the functioning of the Community itself. It is, therefore, not difficult to understand why such aids were clearly blacklisted."[7] In other words, the fact that the *raison d'etre* for the EEC Treaty was to expand intra-Community trade explains why state aid that distorts such trade emerged as an issue early in the life of the Common Market.

A related issue arose in terms of aids for a sector that are financed through taxes on that sector ("parafiscal" levies). For example, France supported "occupational technical centers" in several industries, such as clockmaking. These centers provided R&D and technical assistance for French firms and were financed by taxes on all clocks sold in the country, domestic or imported.[8] Similar systems existed in other industries and in several other countries. The Commission explained its objections as follows:[9]

> From a purely national point of view, the levying of a tax and the granting of aid represent in fact a redistribution of revenue within one and the same sector. As regards intra-Community trade and competition, such systems raise important problems. Since the tax is also levied on products imported from other states, the direct competitors of those benefiting from aid contribute to this financing.

The ECJ upheld the Commission's position in a 1970 decision.[10] In 1971, therefore, the Commission requested that member states end all such systems in existence.[11] Although this goal was not accomplished immediately,[12] the general point was won, and the Commission was able to challenge similar aid programs that arose later.

Aid for intra-Community exports is a problem that has been largely solved.[13] More recently, the focus has become regulation of aid for outward investment (for instance, in Eastern Europe). The Commission has argued that such aid could well affect intra-Community trade, with especially negative effects on poorer member states. As a result, it opened an Article 93(2) procedure against several programs that promote outward investment. The Commission first published data on this type of aid in the *Seventh Survey on State Aid* (1999).[14] In addition, the Commission was seeking agreement among member states to end aid for export credit insurers[15]—again highlighting the Commission's relative success against more serious aids to intra-Community exports.

Systems of Regional Aid

In an important sense, the rules governing regional aid are the centerpiece of EU state aid control. These rules are central because the regional aid system specifies the maximum amount of support that can be given to a company in each and every location within the EU. This system has been elaborated over the course of three decades.

Discussions about a control system for regional aid began with a Commission proposal in 1968 for prior notification of major individual aid awards.[16] One of the major motivations for this policy was precisely the problem of bidding wars for investment:

> The various regions of the Community are therefore increasingly competing with each other to attract investments. . . . Part of the aid granted at present only achieves reciprocal neutralization with unjustified profits for the benefitting enterprises as the only counterpart. In fact, this process of outbidding cannot affect the aggregate flow of investments, which, at Community level, can be mobilized for the purpose of regional development.[17]

The Commission's proposed solution was unacceptable to Italy and France,[18] which preferred a more comprehensive approach. The Italian-French approach was adopted by the Council of Ministers in October 1971 and became effective in 1972.[19] First, the entire Community was divided into "central" and "peripheral" areas; an aid limit was established for the central areas only, leaving the periphery for later.[20] Second, an aid ceiling of 20 percent net grant equivalent (NGE) was established for the central region. Third, states were required to make aid transparent. Fourth, states were required to designate areas eligible for regional aid according to non-arbitrary criteria and relate aid intensity to the severity of a region's problems—illustrating, as Chapter 3 emphasizes, the importance the Commission attaches to the principle of proportionality. Fifth, states were required to track the sectoral distribution of regional aid awarded and provide the data to the Commission. Finally, member states were mandated to provide *ex post* notification of major individual awards.

The next stage of regional aid control, which was completed in 1975, required designation of aid maxima for the entire Community. Another problem to be addressed was that many regional aids in the periphery were not transparent, unlike those in the center. Many peripheral programs were based on job creation rather than investment, particularly in Britain and Italy. Those countries requested the creation of alternate maxima expressed in terms of cost per job.[21]

The 1975 coordination principles created four categories of region to replace the concepts of "center" and "periphery." In decreasing aid intensity allowed, these categories were as follows:[22]

- Ireland, Northern Ireland, West Berlin, Mezzogiorno—maintain existing maximum as of 1 January 1975.[23]
- French industrial premium areas, British assisted areas, and Italian center-north assisted areas—30 percent NGE.
- German Zonal Border Area, Danish assisted areas—25 percent NGE.
- All other regions—20 percent NGE.

The operating principles of the coordination system (transparency, regional specificity and proportionality, monitoring of sectoral consequences and large individual awards) remained the same.

The third stage of regional aid control came in 1978, when the Commission issued a communication on the subject that established cost-per-job limits in addition to the NGE limits set in 1975, as follows:[24]

- Worst-off areas: 75 percent NGE or 13,000 ECU per job created. For labor-intensive projects, the latter limit would be governing, even if aid exceeded 75 percent NGE. France's overseas territories (departments) were added to this category.
- For the aforementioned French, British, and Italian assisted areas, the 30 percent NGE limit was supplemented with a limit of 5,500 ECU per job, up to 40 percent NGE.
- For the Zonal Border Area and Danish assisted areas, the 25 percent NGE limit was matched by a 4,500 ECU per job cap, up to 30 percent NGE.

- For the rest of the Community, the limits were 20 percent NGE or up to 3,500 ECU per job, with a maximum of 25 percent NGE.

In theory, these formulations lent some bias to labor-intensive projects because higher NGE amounts were permitted if the ECU per job limits carried a project above the standard NGE limit. In practice, however, the Commission never used the ECU per job measure to evaluate regional aid.[25]

In 1988, new changes were made to the regional aid coordination principles.[26] Most important, the Commission for the first time issued detailed criteria for how regions should be designated for regional aid eligibility under either Article 92(3)(a) or Article 92(3)(c). The former category, which comprised the least developed areas of the Community, retained the 75 percent NGE limit. The Commission also stated that under certain circumstances it would authorize operating aid in such areas.

With this communication, the Commission codified to some extent its politically sensitive involvement in the issue of how member states draw their regional policy aid maps. According to Fiona Wishlade,

> As a result of Commission intervention, almost all of the northern, wealthier Member States of the European Community have seen a reduction in the spatial coverage of their regional aid policies in the last five years. Moreover, some of these countries are engaged in seemingly ongoing, often acrimonious, disputes with DG IV.[27]

These disputes have primarily involved Article 92(3)(c) areas, which are not as disadvantaged as Article 92(3)(a) areas. The Italian region of Abruzzi had been an Article 92(3)(a) region; because of diminishing economic backwardness, however, the Commission wanted to change its designation. At the same time, Abruzzi had been eligible for Community Structural Funds as an Objective 1 region (see below), further complicating the picture.[28]

Moreover, the Commission's intervention in map drawing was more deeply "counter-productive," in Wishlade's words. Some member states simply refused to discuss the issue and went so far as to introduce regional aid without notification rather than negotiate with the Commission.[29]

The 1988 communication also involved further differentiation among aid maxima, with some regions eligible for as little as 7.5 percent NGE as their maximum.[30]

Two major developments in regional aid policy occurred on 16 December 1997. On that day, the Commission adopted the Multisectoral Framework for inward investment as well as new guidelines for regional aid.

The Multisectoral Framework was designed specifically to address problems of competition for investment. Of the main types of aid used to affect investment location, regional aid is by far the largest. In negotiations with firms, many countries were able to evade Commission scrutiny of their investment attraction packages by giving aid under previously approved regional aid *programs*. If the investment was not in a sensitive sector with an existing framework (e.g., automobile or textiles), the member state did not need pre-approval of the individual aid award as long as it remained within the approved guidelines. The Multisectoral Framework closes this loophole and introduces new criteria for the maximum aid intensity for large projects. Specifically, it requires individual notification and Commission pre-approval of any investment in an industry that is not already covered by a framework (it also includes textiles and clothing, which did have their own framework) that either exceeds 50 million ECU in aid or includes an investment of at least 50 million ECU, with aid at least half of the region's aid maximum and a cost per job of at least ECU 40,000 (with lower limits for the textiles/clothing industry).

This framework is expected to apply to about twenty large projects annually, as a result of member state pressure to exclude projects by raising the limits and (at least initially) excluding most sectors that had their own sectoral framework. It imposes substantial monitoring requirements on member states, including a requirement that all aid contracts under the framework have a clawback clause.[31]

The framework also sets out a formula for adjusting the maximum allowable aid for a project that reduces aid in declining industries, penalizes capital-intensive projects, and rewards projects that are likely to have high indirect job creation. To assuage the fears of member states that such individual reviews could drive investment outside the EU altogether, the framework requires the Commission to reach a decision within two months; this deadline can be waived only with the member state's consent. The framework came into effect on 1 September 1998 for a trial period of three years; it will be assessed by September 2001. If this framework is successful, it will likely be used to replace all of the existing sectoral frameworks.[32]

The Multisectoral Framework was accepted by all member states except Germany. (Spain had also opposed early Commission proposals, whereas the UK strongly supported them.)[33] Thus, in May 1998, the Commission opened Article 92(3) proceedings against Germany and concluded that it was also bound by the framework. Germany had objected to the rules on capital intensivity and had been one of the countries that worried that the framework might reduce investment, but the Commission rejected all of its arguments in July 1998.[34]

The new regional aid guidelines replaced several previous Commission policies[35] and introduced new policies that reduced aid maxima and population coverage, allowed permanent operating aid in the "outermost regions" and low-population-density areas (see Chapter 3), reduced aid for capital-intensive projects, more closely aligned maps for regional aid and Structural Funds (giving member states more discretion over area designation, within the population limits determined), and required aided investment to remain in place for five years.[36]

The new guidelines also reduced aid maxima. Whereas all Article 92(3)(a) regions formerly had a 75 percent NGE limit, the new guidelines divided these regions into those below 60 percent of EU per capita GDP and those with 60–75 percent of the average. The poorest regions were given a new maximum of 50 percent NGE; those with 60–75 percent of EU per capita income now have a 40 percent NGE aid limit. In both cases, somewhat higher limits are possible in the outermost regions and in low population-density areas. For Article 92(3)(c) regions, the 25 percent maximum was reduced to 20 percent—and the maximum is only 10 percent if the region is poor by national standards alone but unemployment and per capita GDP are better than the EU average. According to Wishlade, this reduction was "relatively uncontroversial" by itself; combined with the Multisectoral Framework, however, it could cause constraints for policymakers in providing aid to large projects.[37]

Concurrently, the proportion of the EU population living in regions that are eligible for regional aid was reduced from 46.7 percent to 42.7 percent. This figure apparently was selected to keep the population in EU assisted areas under 50 percent after expected enlargements between 2000 and 2006.[38] Over the course of 1998, the Commission and member states negotiated over the national limits; initial Commission proposals called for drastic cuts for some states. For example, Ireland's strong economic growth and its status as a single Level II NUTS statistical entity would have led to a significant shift in its status: where it had been a 100 percent Article 92(3)(a) area, under the Commission's proposal only half of the country would have been designated as an Article 92(3)(c) area; Ireland also would have lost Objective 1 status for the Structural Funds. Only the statistical division of the country averted this shift (see below). In the end, the national population coverage limits ranged from a low of 15.0 percent in The Netherlands to 100 percent in Greece, Ireland, and Portugal.[39]

Regional aid policy has been politically controversial and technically complicated. Beginning with the first regional framework, however, the Commission has steadily extended the system's coverage and inserted itself directly into national regional development programs through its oversight of area eligibility and its scrutiny of aid programs and individual awards. This approach has brought the Commission into conflict with national governments and, at times, the Regional Policy Directorate General (DG XVI).[40] Yet DG IV has moved steadily forward in this area, most recently with the Multisectoral Framework and the new regional aid guidelines. Taken together, these trends could well mark a direct assault on competition for investment.[41]

At the same time, the accession of poorer countries and regions from 1973 to 1990 has increased the importance of regional policy on a Community scale. Vastly increased EU-provided Structural Funding for regions since the Single European Act, on top of nationally provided regional aid, also contributed to challenges for the system of state aid control.

Enlargement and Regional Problems

The enlargements of the EC that began with the 1973 accession of Ireland, Denmark, and the UK vastly widened economic disparities among member states. For instance, Irish gross national product (GNP) per capita at accession was 59.2 percent of the EC average in 1973.[42] The addition of the new countries meant that some of the state aid rules that seemed definitively in place—such as the ban on intra-Community exports—had to be relearned. In the Irish case particularly, this norm conflicted with the essential setup of the national industrialization strategy.

Ireland: From Export Aid to Tax Competition

Since the late 1950s, Ireland has pursued an economic development strategy centered on the attraction of foreign multinational corporations.[43] A key investment incentive was export sales relief (ESR), which exempted 100 percent of profits on export sales for manufacturing firms from corporate income tax. Because ESR clearly violated the ban on intra-Community export aid, the Commission took the position that it would have to be changed eventually. In the accession negotiations, Ireland pressed for, and obtained, "guarantees that any revised incentive scheme required by EEC codes would be equally effective."[44]

In 1978, Ireland announced a system to replace ESR that involved a reduction in corporate income tax for manufacturing industry to 10 percent.[45] Although this policy shift did achieve DG IV goals on banning export aids, it was an expensive victory. On one hand, Ireland's Industrial Development Authority (IDA) has used the low tax rate as one of its main selling points.[46] At the same time, the government has contended that the tax arrangement is not state aid at all but a general macroeconomic measure. The Commission accepted this view until July 1998, when it ruled that the 10 percent manufacturing tax rate did indeed constitute an aid; indeed, the Commission charged that the arrangement constituted an operating aid that could no longer be justified on the basis of Ireland's former Article 92(3)(a) status (which ended 31 December 1999).[47]

The value of this tax expenditure (for 1997) was not included in the estimates of Irish state aid contained in the EU's *Surveys* of state aid spending until the seventh survey (1999). Throughout this period, Ireland's tax arrangement has been a clear and *unregulated* element in the country's competition for investment.[48] Although the Commission has reached a compromise with Ireland in which the country agreed to raise the tax rate to 12.5 percent (which includes lowering non-manufacturing taxes from 32 percent to 12.5 percent), other countries, particularly France, clearly will keep pressure on this issue in the future.[49]

Teaching New Countries Old Tricks

The problem of export aid also came up at various times with regard to other new member states. For instance, in 1988 the Commission made an Article 93(1) proposal[50] to Spain that it change its program for aid to the press because of two elements. First, only Spaniards were eligible. Second—and more important here—the aid was based on consumption of Spanish newsprint only, thereby discriminating against foreign newsprint producers. This clear impact on intra-Community trade was disallowed by the Commission.[51]

The reunification of Germany also had a substantial impact on state aid policy. Besides the high level of subsidies provided to promote the transition to a market economy (an average of 19.2 billion ECU per year in 1993–95 and 13.5 billion ECU per year in 1995–97)[52] and the large increase in DG IV's caseload,[53] there have been major violations of the state aid rules in eastern Germany. Much of the DM 850 million in state aid provided to Bremer Vulkan AG—Germany's largest shipbuilder—to modernize shipyards in eastern Germany was diverted to the company's West German subsidiaries. When the fraud was uncovered, the company went bankrupt and its former chairman was arrested; the Commission had to approve more aid for the East German yards, and repayment of DM 788.7 million is being pursued through the bankruptcy proceedings as well as from Bremer Vulkan's offspring companies.[54] In the *Land* of Saxony, the government refused to follow a Commission order not to pay Volkswagen DM 241 million in state aid, paying an initial DM 91 million in July 1996. After more than a year of negotiations and legal skirmishing, the Commission finally secured a repayment agreement in November 1997.[55] Both of these affairs were deeply embarrassing to the German federal government.

Enlargement to Poorer Areas and the Structural Funds

In addition to requiring that new members learn old rules (such as the ban on export aid), enlargement has also affected state aid because (as noted above) several of the new members had standards of living that were much below average. Besides Ireland, Greece (admitted in 1981), Portugal (1986), and much of Spain (1986) had lower standards of living than the rest of the Community. After the reunification of Germany in 1990, the EC added a new region, the former East Germany, that was even poorer than those four. Table 4-1 shows the dimensions of the disparity.

Cohesion is the term used to describe the goal of bringing the least economically developed regions of the EU up to the standards of the richer nations. After the accession of Spain and Portugal in 1986, the disparities within the Community required an increase in funding for the four poorest countries (often called the "cohesion countries"): Ireland, Greece, Portugal, and Spain. As a result, the EC undertook

Table 4-1 **GDP per Capita of Cohesion Countries and New *Länder* (1991) at Purchasing Power Parity**

Spain	78%
Ireland	70%
Portugal	59%
Greece	47%
Former East Germany	38% (1991–92)

Source: CEC, *Competitiveness and Cohesion*, Tables A.20 and A.23.

what is now commonly referred to as the "first reform" of the Structural Funds. This reform consisted of a doubling, in real terms, of the money going into these Funds between 1987 and 1993[56] and the specification of five objectives for the Structural Funds:

- Objective 1: Structurally backward regions (GDP per capita less than 75 percent of EC average)
- Objective 2: Regions of industrial decline
- Objective 3: Long-term unemployment
- Objective 4: Youth employment
- Objective 5a: Adjustment of agriculture
- Objective 5b: Development of rural areas.[57]

Overall, a total of 60 billion ECU (at 1989 prices) was allocated for 1989–93. Of this amount, 80 percent was earmarked for Objective 1 regions.[58] Although the Commission's goal was to concentrate these funds in the four poorest countries, each member state also wanted to make sure that it received some of the funding.[59] Wishlade writes, "The highly political nature of these early negotiations is reflected in the criteria for designating eligible areas, especially for Objectives 2 and 5b." This battle coincided with the battle over aid maps and yielded striking anomalies. The designations for Structural Funds did not fully coincide with those for national regional aids. Overall, 46.8 percent of the Community's population was in non-assisted areas, 40.0 percent was in regions eligible for national and EC regional aid, 7.4 percent was in areas eligible for national aid only, and 5.7 percent was in areas eligible for EC aid only.

The Directorate General for Regional Policy (DG XVI) and most member states argued that there should be more coherence between the two sets of aid maps—in particular, that areas designated as

Objective 1 should be eligible for Article 92(3)(a) treatment for state aid, and that Objective 2 and 5b areas should receive Article 92(3)(c) status. DG IV, however, was not persuaded that the two sets of designations had to be coordinated in such a fashion, claiming that because regional policy and competition policy had different aims, there was no reason the two should have exactly the same maps. In the negotiations for the 1993–99 Structural Funds, however, member states generally reasserted their authority on issues such as area designation and additionality (i.e., not simply using Structural Funds to replace national spending), which strengthened the states in bargaining with DG IV on maps for national state aid as well.[60] This factor was further reflected in the December 1997 regional aid guidelines: The Commission came around to the view that there should be close coordination between the maps for the Structural Funds and state aid. Interestingly, the UK took the position that map alignment was not necessary.[61]

In addition to the intensely political nature of the designation exercise, one other aspect of the expansion of the Structural Funds had important consequences for state aid control and for competition for investment in general. Historically, much of the structural funding had gone toward improving infrastructure in the worst-off member states. The doubling of the Structural Funds in the 1989–93 round was accompanied, however, by an increased emphasis on aiding investment. Hall and van der Wee write:

> Whereas support for investment in transportation, telecommunications, energy and water infrastructure accounted for 80 percent of total Regional Fund expenditure in the pre-reform years of 1987 and 1988, this figure has been reduced to 55 percent in Objective 1 regions and to a mere 16 percent in Objective 2 areas. Meanwhile, a far greater proportion of resources—40 percent in Objective 1 and 80 percent in Objective 2—will be used to support investment in industry and services, to improve the business environment and to develop human resources.[62]

This trend means, of course, that the Commission has moved increasingly into the area of itself funding aid granted to firms for investment, as Yuill and colleagues note:

> In absolute terms, Community spending on encouraging productive investment in Objective 2 areas is clearly much smaller than in Objective

> 1 regions. Nevertheless, it is somewhat perverse that the Commission should contribute to the "bidding-up" process that characterises many international location decisions by supplementing, directly or indirectly, the funds available for encouraging productive investment in the wealthier Member States.[63]

For the 1994–99 round of Structural Funds, there was a further increase in allocations. Expenditures on the Structural Funds and the Cohesion Fund (established by the Maastricht Treaty)[64] were to rise from 21.3 billion ECU (1992 prices throughout this paragraph) in 1993 to 30 billion ECU in 1999, of which 74 percent would go to Objective 1 regions. This figure compares with a budget for the Common Agricultural Policy of 38.4 billion ECU in 1999. Over the 1993–99 period, Structural Action would rise from 30.8 percent of the EU budget to 35.7 percent, whereas the CAP would fall from 50.9 percent to 45.7 percent.[65] In addition, as a result of the accession of Sweden and Finland, a new Objective 6 was added for regions with extremely low population density, such as Lapland.[66]

Again, the more prosperous states lobbied furiously to receive as much of the Structural Funds as possible. This lobbying paid off. Six member states successfully obtained Objective 1 status for regions that had not been so designated in 1988. In three cases—eastern Germany, Cantabria (Spain), and Flevoland (Dutch lands reclaimed from the Ijselmeer)—the primary criterion of GDP per capita below 75 percent of the EU average was met. One other area that was designated Objective 1 although it was just above the threshold—the Highlands and Islands area of Scotland—was not surprising because it had already been eligible for 75 percent NGE aid for very small enterprises despite only being an Article 92(3)(c) region.[67] Also receiving Objective 1 designation, however, were part of Hainaut in Belgium along with part of Nord-Pas de Calais just across the border from Hainaut in France, as well as the Liverpool area in England. Only one area—Abruzzi in Italy—was removed, but even that removal involved a three-year transition period.[68] Moreover, as an example of how regional policy and the Structural Funds interact, the Commission wanted to see Abruzzi (in the Mezzogiorno) become an Article 92(3)(c) region and have offsetting de-designations in the center-north of Italy. Because of the problems caused by northern secessionism, however, Italy was loath to de-designate any areas and finally persuaded the Commission to relent (in an unpublished decision).[69]

The negotiations over the 2000–2006 round of Structural Funds were equally furious. These negotiations did not conclude until the March 1999 Berlin summit. Caught up in the overall battle over the EU's budget, the Structural Funds issue was linked to the issues of richer countries' contributions (of particular interest to Germany and the UK), CAP reform, and shifting of the Structural Funds to the much poorer candidate states of Central and Eastern Europe. Germany had proposed a ceiling of E 210 billion for the Structural Funds and Cohesion Fund. Spain and Greece called for E 240–250 billion, and Greece threatened to veto the entire Agenda 2000 deal if the German proposal were adopted.[70] France and the UK, by contrast, called for spending on the order of under E 200 billion. Regional Affairs Commissioner Monika Wulf-Mathies had proposed 239 billion ECU. The final figure of E 213 billion came about after a 5:30 am compromise between the Germans and the Spanish that was one of the keys to the budget deal.[71]

Area designations again were heavily lobbied. A year before the deal, only South Yorkshire was slated for new Objective 1 designation, whereas several areas appeared set to lose it.[72] For example, Ireland's strong economic growth in the 1990s had put it above the 75 percent of GDP threshold for Objective 1 status, so the government decided that it needed to divide the country into regions so that part of it would still be eligible for Objective 1 designation. The IDA had predicted that if the country were to lose Objective 1 status entirely, it would suffer a substantial decline in inward investment, especially because some competitor regions in the UK would retain Objective 1 status. Therefore, the Irish government proposed a fifteen-county area to Eurostat for continued Objective 1 designation; this area contained thirteen counties from recognizable regions (Border, Midlands, and West), plus two others (Kerry and Clare) rumored to have been added for political reasons. Eurostat rejected the two additional counties, however, and Ireland accepted this decision.[73] Overall, Ireland still lost more than half of its Structural Funding, and it is expected to lose Cohesion Funds after a 2003 review.[74]

In addition to South Yorkshire, Cornwall and West Wales also received Objective 1 designation, as did the areas of northern Finland and Sweden that previously had been designated as Objective 6 (low population density). The UK government fought strongly to retain Objective 1 designation for the Highlands and Islands area of Scotland because the area's per capita GDP was only 1.4 percentage points above the cutoff and its population density was only slightly higher than the standard under which the Finnish and Swedish areas were included (9.5 vs. 8 persons per square kilometer). Moreover, GDP per capita in the Highlands and Islands area was lower than that of most of the Swedish and Finnish communities that were added to Objective 1.[75] In the final agreement, however, Highlands and Islands was de-designated, though it did receive a substantial transitional package—as did the other de-designated areas around the EU: Northern Ireland, Flevoland, Cantabria, Corsica, East Berlin, Lisbon, Hainaut, Nord-Pas de Calais, and Molise (Italy). Britain also benefited from an agreement that no country could have its Objective 2 funding cut by more than one-third; overall, however, the UK still saw its Structural Funds decline because of falling unemployment.[76]

The European Economic Area and Europe Agreements

Another aspect of enlargement and state aid policy has been the European Economic Area (EEA) agreements. Although the EEA as a whole is outside the scope of this book, in the state aid field, the members of the European Free Trade Association agreed to bind themselves by EU rules. With the accession of Austria, Finland, and Sweden, this Agreement has become a footnote, although Norway, Iceland, and Liechtenstein still remain bound by it.[77] Austria's 1972 free trade agreement with the EC had already bound that country to the subsidy rules—a factor that came into play when Austria provided incentives for Chrysler to locate a minivan plant there.[78]

Similarly, the "Europe Agreements" that established rules for EU commerce with the central and east European (CEE) countries, with a view to eventual accession, also include provisions on state aid. These provisions "boil down to a transposition of Article 92 and the guidelines, frameworks and decisions that follow from it" into the various agreements.[79] The ten CEE candidate countries (Hungary, the Czech Republic, Slovakia, Latvia, Lithuania, Estonia, Slovenia, Poland, Bulgaria, and Romania) were all expected to establish independent competition bodies and begin state aid reporting similar to that in the EU's *Surveys*.[80] By 1998, all 10 CEE countries had established competition authorities, and in May 1998 the fourth Competition Conference was held in Bratislava. The first formal agreement on state aid was adopted in June 1998 for the Czech Republic.[81]

Generally speaking, however, the Commission was critical of the candidate countries' efforts in the state aid field (whereas they had done much better in antitrust), arguing that they still needed inventories of existing aid programs and better aid monitoring capacity.[82] In addition, the EU's Berlin summit budgeted pre-accession structural funding of E 1.04 billion annually, plus E 2.08 billion for technical assistance and agriculture.[83]

This brief survey shows how the expansion of the EU has created new challenges for the enforcement of state aid rules. The Irish case was particularly difficult because an export aid was central to the country's economic development strategy. The solution created problems of its own that linger to this day. Ireland's planned harmonization of corporate income tax at 12.5 percent will definitively remove it from potential consideration as a state aid but would still leave it as a key investment attraction strategy. Beyond Ireland, enlargement has meant that new officials had to be socialized to the state aid rules. The greatest difficulty in achieving strict control, however, may be continuing political pressures to designate regions in richer countries for Community regional funds and expanded use of those monies to fund the competition for investment.

Controls over Sectoral Aid

As Chapter 3 notes, an important difference between industrial support in the United States and the EU is the latter's far greater emphasis on aiding firms and industries in difficulties. Whereas the United States occasionally has massive bailouts (such as with Lockheed or Chrysler), support for entire industries in Europe is at least as common. At the same time, European officials recognize that subsidy wars for declining industries are just as counterproductive as bidding wars for new investments. As the Commission stated regarding the textile framework in 1977:

> The Commission considers that the present situation requires that certain aspects of the framework be given greater precision with a view to ensuring that the proposed solutions for overcoming the problems regarding structures, surplus capacity and imports from non-member countries *are not rendered ineffective by ruinous outbidding*.[84]

If one state provides subsidies to an uncompetitive firm, it effectively exports unemployment to other member states. If all states subsidize, jobs may be preserved in all of the firms, but at the high cost of diverting needed funds to less-efficient uses. Thus, sectoral aid may well be more problematic than supporting new firms, insofar as the latter are likely to be more efficient.

The Commission has tried to balance several competing objectives. When whole industries become uncompetitive on a global scale, massive layoffs and dislocation for the workers in those sectors can ensue. The Commission has looked relatively favorably on aid to firms that will directly benefit their laid-off workers as the firms move to a smaller but more competitive size. At the same time, as a fundamentally market-oriented organization, the Commission also stresses the need for efficient production and minimization of subsidies. Finally, when an industry's problems are thought to be the result of unfair actions by foreign competitors, the Commission also takes trade initiatives to supplement its aid policies.[85] To control the potential for aid wars, the Commission's preferred approach has been to introduce sectoral frameworks, two of which are discussed here: textiles and autos. In general, these sectoral frameworks can be regarded as a controlled shrinking of industries in difficulties.[86]

Textiles

Like its American counterpart, the European textile industry has been in a long-term decline as a result of the rise of low-wage manufacturers in less-developed countries (LDCs). Along with the United States, the European Commission pushed for trade restrictions to control the market share of LDC producers; these efforts led to the Multi-Fiber Agreement (MFA).[87] At the national level, governments responded to the problem by subsidizing their domestic industries: "Aids, which up to a few years ago were still limited, have tended to increase," the Commission reported in 1972.[88]

The textile framework was introduced in July 1971; in many ways it was the prototype for later sectoral frameworks. In particular, the Commission laid down the principles that aid must not increase capacity in the sector; that it must take into account the Community state of the industry, not just the national situation; and that operating aid was prohibited. Furthermore, the Commission strongly emphasized that the aid that was most likely to win approval was aid that was designed to bring about genuine restructuring leading to long-term viability.[89] The following year, the Commission followed up by creating an inventory of all aid given to textile firms, regardless of the category under which the aid was given (e.g., sector-specific, general investment, regional). The Commission notified member states that even aids that were not specific to the textile industry had to be reported in advance for consideration from the point of view of the situation in that sector.[90]

An early example of the framework's application that illustrates an extremely common pattern in the use of the Commission's state aid regulatory functions is provided by an aid program for the British clothing industry proposed in 1975. This scheme had three elements: a Productivity Center for the industry, 50 percent grants for hiring consultants for firm modernizations, and 20 percent grants for plant and equipment. DG IV staff solicited comments from other member states in the course of its preliminary investigation; DG IV concluded that the first two elements were acceptable but that the third was not because of its potential to increase capacity in the industry. Faced with Commission objections on this point, the UK government modified its proposal to make clear that investment aid could be given only if there were no capacity increases. In particular, funds allocated to the program would be used in part to finance the closing of unprofitable operations.[91] Knox points out that the Commission interprets the framework as applying to types of aid that are disproportionately provided to the textile industry, citing the example of the UK's Temporary Employment Subsidy, which was introduced by the Labour government in 1975.[92]

Needless to say, the introduction and elaboration of this framework did not mean the end of the industry's problems. Indeed, difficulties spread to related sectors, such as synthetic fibers, for which the Commission adopted a similar framework in 1977.[93] The elaboration of frameworks has meant that the member states have a clear set of criteria around which to design aid programs, however, and that all parties involved (including recipient firms and their competitors) can expect consistent treatment of aids. Nonetheless, as with other aspects of state aid control, excessive delays and attempts at circumventing the rules sometimes weaken the Commission's position. As Schina concludes:[94]

> A close examination of instances where the Commission had to deal with notified aids to the textile industry demonstrates that the Commission has adhered strictly to its principles. Nevertheless, the effectiveness of the

Commission's control is weakened by the long delay which often occurs between the notification of a plan of aid and its removal or modification by the notifying Member State, not to mention the occasional failure to obey the Commission's decisions.

Automobile Industry

Again as in the United States, the European auto industry has suffered from the rise of Japanese exports; more recently, the EU has been a location for substantial Japanese automotive investment, particularly in the UK. From 1970 to 1980, Japanese imports increased from less than 1 percent of the British and West German markets to more than 10 percent of both; the Japanese market share in small European countries such as Belgium, Ireland, and Greece ranged from 20 percent to 40 percent in 1980.[95] This market penetration represented a substantial problem for European policy because the auto industry is one of the world's most important in terms of production and employment.[96] According to one estimate, auto firms and their suppliers are responsible for 15 percent of total EU employment.[97]

After the onset of serious problems for the industry in 1980, the Commission signaled its willingness to approve "strictly necessary and temporary aid schemes" to allow European producers to restructure. The following year the Commission announced that it would require annual accounting of all aid given to the industry, whether from sector-specific or other sources.[98] In this relatively permissive environment, subsidies to the automobile industry reached high levels, as the Commission reported in the *Eighteenth Report on Competition Policy*:[99]

> A compilation of the Commission's experience concerning aids in this sector revealed that most major car producers had benefitted from substantial aid flows. Rough estimates based on incomplete information show that this sector has received at least ECU 11 billion in national aid between 1981 and 1986. Over half of this amount was paid to restructure loss-making State-owned companies. Regional aids have also been an important feature in this sector.

Among the more important of these cases were Renault (2.82 billion ECU approved in 1988, and 35 million ECU ordered repaid; a further 846 million ECU was ordered repaid in 1991, however),[100] Rover (a £469 million capital injection was allowed; the Commission later discovered that the UK government had given the company's buyer, British Aerospace, an additional £44.4 million in aid that the Commission forced British Aerospace to repay),[101] and 615 billion lire in aid associated with Alfa Romeo's 1987 sale to Fiat.[102]

Based on its experience in these and other cases, the Commission in December 1988 adopted a framework for the automobile industry that became effective at the beginning of 1989. This framework provided that all individual automotive projects receiving aid must be reported in advance if the investment totalled more than 12 million ECU.[103] In at least one case, the Commission challenged aid that appeared to have been chopped up into smaller pieces to evade the 12 million ECU threshold.[104]

This framework has been politically controversial. At the time of its original adoption, Germany stated that it would not accept it, apparently "concerned that the Commission [would] use the new arrangement to ensure that southern European car industries [would be] allowed to receive more state aid than West Germany's larger and more profitable auto manufacturers."[105] Spain, by contrast, opposed the framework because it feared that there would be *less* opportunity for state intervention. The Commission opened Article 93(2) procedures against both countries to force their compliance with the framework.[106] Although Germany has come around to the Commission's view on subsequent renewals, Spain remains the only member state that opposes the framework, challenging it (sometimes successfully) before the ECJ at every opportunity.[107]

Overall, the automotive framework appears to have improved the Commission's monitoring capacity in this sector, as well as signaling to member states and potential aid recipients what is likely to be approved. According to Hancher and colleagues, "The impression one gets from reading the Commission's Decisions and Notices is that the Commission is gradually getting a grip on these extensive aid operations." They go on to note that the Commission's rulings "did achieve extensive restructuring of the industry."[108] This conclusion is supported by the early 1997 battle with Renault, in which the company simultaneously closed plants in Belgium and France while seeking aid to expand in Spain. Negative publicity forced Spain to withdraw its aid offer while the Commission sought to draft rules to prevent cases like this in the future.[109] In terms of hard numbers, there has been a clear decline in the amount of state aid approved under the framework: from the 11 billion ECU in 1981–86 to 5.9 billion

ECU from the framework's inception in 1989 through the end of 1996.[110]

Effects of Sectoral Frameworks

Sectoral aid frameworks have had some success in controlling aid awarded in crisis sectors, though that evaluation does not necessarily mean they would receive a positive evaluation when viewed through a broader lens (for example, that of LDCs vis-a-vis the MFA and the textile aid code). Although space limitations preclude full treatment here, the steel industry has had two aid frameworks, with substantially different outcomes. The crisis of the 1980s saw steel-producing member states cut capacity and eventually phase out aid entirely (recall that aid is specifically prohibited by the ECSC Treaty); the December 1993 steel agreement collapsed, however, because member states failed to deliver on their promised capacity cuts.[111] In December 1996, however, the Council unanimously agreed on a new steel aid code, effective until the expiration of the ECSC Treaty in July 2002.[112] The shipbuilding industry has had a framework since 1969 in the form of successive Council Directives with varying levels of maximum aid allowed; the longevity of these directives, the paucity of negative decisions, and weak compliance, however, mark the shipbuilding framework as anything but a success.[113]

Nonetheless, we should not conclude on the basis of these cases that frameworks are wholly unsuccessful in controlling aid in sectors in which there is strong pressure to subsidize industry. As Hancher and colleagues suggest (see above), there has been substantial progress in the automotive sector in reducing planned aids and in forcing restructuring on the industry. Richard Jacques also held this opinion, pointing out, "When you have a sectoral regime, you get lots of lobbying and pressure groups—AND the Commission gets a lot of information as a result."[114]

Indeed, some outside observers have regarded the EU's use of aid frameworks as one of the stronger points of its control mechanism. Mark Ronayne strongly suggests that Canada can learn directly from the EU in this regard, arguing that the frameworks for specific activities (both sectoral and horizontal) have been helpful in reducing the Commission's enforcement costs.[115] Similarly, Edward M. Graham and Mark A. A. Warner's call for a North American Competition Commission would be based on "a set of standards with respect to what are, and what are not, acceptable types and magnitudes of subsidy, . . ."[116]—exactly the sort of thing aid frameworks do. Although their suggestion is broader than sectoral policy and, indeed, envisions a sort of DG IV for NAFTA, there is no reason that some of the standards could not be sectorally based (for example, in the automobile industry).

In terms of overall outcomes, sectoral aid has declined substantially as a percentage of total aid to manufacturing: 33.1 percent in 1981–86; 26.8 percent in 1986–88; 21 percent in 1988–90, 15 percent in 1990–92, 11 percent in 1992–94, 13 percent in 1994–96, and 12 percent in 1995–97.[117] These declines come in the context of falling overall aid to manufacturing, as Chapter 6 shows. These figures suggest that the sectoral frameworks have reduced aid, particularly in steel and shipbuilding.

Horizontal Frameworks

Horizontal frameworks are similar to sectoral frameworks in their ability to provide a set of policies around which expectations can converge. They represent announcements by the Commission about the approach it plans to adopt when it analyzes similar aids. Horizontal frameworks differ from sectoral frameworks, however, in their effort to promote broader goals that can apply in a variety of industries. The most important single "horizontal" goal—taking up 10 percent of all manufacturing aid in 1995–97—is support for research and development.[118] (This term refers only to aid given by member states; the EU itself also provides substantial support for R&D, averaging about 3.3 billion ECU annually for the "research and technological development framework programme" in 1996–97).[119]

Commission guidelines on R&D originally grew out of sectoral concerns, particularly in the aircraft and computer industries. With regard to aircraft, the Commission deplored the widely varying subsidy practices of several member states and argued that a transnational program was absolutely necessary to meet the dominant position of U.S. producers.[120] The Commission proposed a major program of allowable support, including "advance credits of up to the total amount of R and D costs . . . reimbursable from the yield on sales when the aircraft are marketed," loan guarantees for production costs, and marketing aid including "long-term credit. . . , insurance against the commercial risk; [and] guarantees against exchange fluctuations or . . . abnormal and unforeseeable upward cost movements. . . .[121] This program, of course, was the basis of the Airbus program. What is notable for our purposes is the extraordinarily lenient treatment it announced for R&D aid.

Over subsequent years, this lenient treatment was confirmed in several Commission decisions: allowing the German government to absorb 75 percent of the losses of a venture capital firm for R&D by SMEs;[122] grants to cover losses as the French firm Compagnie International pour l'Information (CII) was merged with Honeywell-Bull, as well as 50 percent grants for R&D in the German data processing industry;[123] 50 percent grants for research and 25 percent grants for development (with 50 percent grants for development when more than one company was involved) in the UK;[124] and a German program of 40 percent grants for R&D staff, available in any industry, without a requirement that firms hire any new R&D staff.[125]

By 1985, however, some member states clearly were taking advantage of this permissive attitude to skirt the rules, particularly with regard to notification. States were also packaging their aid to appear as if it were R&D oriented, even if that was not the case. As a result, "state aids for R&D have become one of the largest if not in many Member States the largest form of government intervention in support of industry."[126] For example, in 1981–86 state R&D aid represented 22 percent of German aid to manufacturing, 41 percent of Danish aid, 11 percent of Dutch aid, and 16 percent of British aid.[127] This situation set the stage for the December 1985 adoption of the R&D framework. The Commission insisted that prior notification of all programs was an absolute necessity and further required the notification of individual projects of more than 20 million ECU in size. The Commission stated that fundamental scientific research was generally not subject to the state aid rules and that such research carried on in universities or research institutes was definitely not affected unless it was carried out with or for a for-profit enterprise. Finally, it promulgated new aid intensity limits that were lower than many it had approved in the cases listed above: 50 percent for basic industrial research and lower levels (generally 25 percent) for development.[128]

As Hancher and colleagues point out, the introduction of this framework by no means suggested that the Commission had become less favorable toward R&D aid—merely that it wanted to improve transparency in this area. The Commission made 520 decisions on

R&D aid between 1986 and 1994, opening the Article 93(2) procedure only fifteen times and issuing no final negative decisions. When the contentious procedure was opened, it led to negotiated changes in the proposed programs, as is commonly the case (see Chapter 3).[129]

On 20 December 1995, the Commission issued a new R&D framework that took into account the higher levels of aid permitted by the GATT Agreement on Subsidies and Countervailing Measures (SCM); it also incorporated the Commission's standard practices since the adoption of the first framework. As a result of the changed U.S. position on R&D subsidies in the Uruguay Round after the election of President Clinton, the EU's problem in those negotiations changed from one of keeping the limits from falling far below those of its 1986 framework to one of reacting to higher limits than it provided.[130] The 1995 R&D framework made it possible to reach the new SCM limits of 75 percent (basic industrial research) and 50 percent (precompetitive development) in cases in which non-EU competitors had received or were about to receive such high levels of aid. In addition, the new framework elaborated the existing system of bonuses to the 50/25 system for categories such as SMEs, backward regions, and transnational cooperation. Finally, it raised the notification thresholds to 5 million ECU of aid or a project of greater than 25 million ECU.[131]

Like the sectoral frameworks, the horizontal frameworks on R&D have codified an important area of state aid regulation, giving all parties concerned a consistent set of expectations on how proposed aid would be treated. In contrast to the case of sectoral aid, there is no general presumption against R&D aid in DG IV; this attitude is reflected in the fact that R&D aid has received about the same proportion of manufacturing aid throughout the 1981–97 period: 9 percent in 1981–86, 11 percent in 1986–88, 10 percent in 1988–90, 10 percent in 1990–92, 7 percent in 1992–94, 9 percent in 1994–96, and 10 percent in 1995–97.[132]

The framework appears to have been useful in reducing nonnotification problems in R&D cases. For example, in 1995 only two research aid programs were introduced without notification—one each in Germany and the UK. In addition, ten French cases of non-notified aid under the EU's Eureka program for R&D from previous years were settled in 1995. In 1996, one Dutch R&D program was introduced without notification and four French Eureka cases were settled. There appear to have been no non-notified research and development aid cases in 1997.[133] These figures suggest that the Commission has made progress in its goal of transparency in R&D aid. At the same time, there is evidence that some "packaging" of aid as allegedly R&D still occurs, most recently in the cases of semiconductor manufacturer SGS-Thomson and pharmaceutical maker Hoffman-LaRoche—which was the first-ever rejection of an R&D aid. Then-Commissioner Karel Van Miert announced DG IV's intention to look more carefully at problems with R&D aid, so new action is likely in the future.[134]

Policing the Rules, Evading the Rules, and Expanding the Commission's Powers

This section describes the strengthening of the Commission's powers in the area of state aid. Although the foregoing discussion has suggested a gradual development of policy and expertise, the 1980s saw an acceleration in policy initiatives, largely as a result of the Single European Act's general revitalization of the European idea. Under Commissioners for Competition Policy Peter Sutherland (Ireland, 1985–88) and Sir Leon Brittan (United Kingdom, 1989–92), DG IV's role increased enormously because of the very centrality of its mission to successfully removing the remaining economic barriers between member states. As Sutherland said in an interview, "Competition policy was brought to the fore by the 1992 initiative. It required an activist policy on antitrust and state aid affairs, and, in both cases, state intervention was the most intractable and, at the same time, the most important issue."[135] Sutherland and Brittan both believe that failure to control state aid could lead to new distortions of competition that would undermine the 1992 program's removal of trade barriers.[136]

This section also contains a heavy dose of legal history. The reason is that although Commission initiatives are ultimately political as well as legal actions, they are invariably challenged before the ECJ. The ECJ's decisions were critical in determining whether the Commission could make a policy initiative stick. Therefore, I examine several central decisions: *Philip Morris* (1980), which confirmed the Commission's general powers and many of its preferred modes of analysis; *Leeuwarder* (1983), in which the ECJ set standards for the economic analysis the Commission was required to perform to justify its decisions; a whole series of cases on aid repayment from the 1970s through the 1990s; and *Boussac* (1990), which concerned procedures to follow for non-notified aid.

After considering ECJ cases, this section turns to specific Commission initiatives, including the cumulation rules to combat attempts to circumvent aid limits, the inauguration of the *Surveys* on state aid, the campaign against general aid, and increased use of Article 93(1) procedures against "existing" aid.

Introduction

As anyone who has studied regulation is well aware, regulation isn't forever: The regulated will seek ways to evade regulation when it is in their interest to do so. EU member states have often sought ways to evade state aid rules without actually violating them. One way is simply in the way particular subsidies are packaged for presentation to the Commission. For example, some states have packaged aid as R&D to take advantage of the Commission's favorable attitude toward such aid.[137] Similarly, member states have sought to evade the rules by combining different types of aid that are eligible under different approved aid programs (for example, giving a firm regional aid and R&D aid for a single investment). This strategy has provoked responses by the Commission to address evasion techniques, notably rules on cumulation of aids of different types.

One very vulnerable point in the state aid regime is the necessity for states themselves to notify the Commission of their intent to award aid to firms; non-notification can greatly undermine the effectiveness of the system. Naturally, non-notification is most likely to occur when the state fears that the Commission would not approve the aid in question.[138] Even if the aid is eventually discovered, non-notified subsidies can have pernicious effects if they manage to get a firm through a difficult period when it would have gone bankrupt but for the aid. The problem for the Commission, then, is how to deal with the discovery of non-notified aid in a way that sufficiently penalizes the recipient without violating its rights under EU law. The Commission's preferred approach would have been to declare all procedurally illegal aid to be automatically incompatible with the common market. The ECJ blocked this route in the *Boussac* case, however, requiring that the decision on incompatibility be made on substantive rather than procedural grounds.

Instead, the Commission has focused on *ex post facto* sanctioning of non-notified, incompatible aid. The method chosen has been to order repayment (with interest) of illegal subsidies to the granting state, which at least until the signing of the Maastricht Treaty was the *ultima ratio* of state aid control.[139] Although member states strongly resisted repayment orders at the ECJ, advancing a variety of legal theories against this sanction, the Court swept them all aside, leaving the Commission the clear victor.

In late 1996, however, the Commission moved to augment this sanction, announcing its intention (after having rejected the idea in 1990) to propose to the Council of Ministers a set of implementing regulations for state aid as provided for under Article 94. This proposal led to the Procedural Regulation adopted by the Council of Ministers in November 1998. If this regulation works as designed, it will sharply reduce delays in compliance that ensued when governments appealed to national courts against repayment orders.

Philip Morris

Philip Morris was a landmark case: the first ever to consider the Commission's powers and discretion in state aid cases.[140] Yet it was a surprising case to become the landmark it became. As Cini points out, there was virtually no mention of it in the *Reports on Competition Policy* until after the Court's decision.[141] What started as a routine denial of investment aid to Philip Morris Holland BV became a *cause célèbre* when the company, unsupported by the Dutch government,[142] challenged virtually the entire legal basis of state aid control. Although the case also was noteworthy for the procedural fact that it established the standing of the proposed aid beneficiary to sue the Commission,[143] it was far more important because the company challenged the Commission's discretion in determining exemptions under the statutory derogations of Article 92(3) and because it attacked the entire concept of compensatory justification. In ruling for the Commission, the ECJ in essence endorsed both of these principles: that the Commission could decide whether an aid was justified by one of the conditions set forth in Article 92(3)[144] and that the Commission's requirement for a compensatory justification for awarding an aid was correct. As Evans and Martin conclude, "State aid that distorts competition will be permitted only to accomplish Community goals and only in the presence of market failure. If market forces would accomplish the goal without state aid, and state aid will distort competition, then state aid will not be permitted."[145] Beyond being a legal landmark, however, *Philip Morris* was also—as Cini emphasizes—a "political landmark . . . [that made] a public statement about DG IV's right to restrict the freedom of national and subnational aid-donors in choosing where and when to grant subsidies."[146]

Leeuwarder and Requirements for Economic Analysis

One goal the Commission did not achieve in *Philip Morris* was that the ECJ did not say that state aid *automatically* distorts competition.[147] Had it done so, it would have relieved the Commission of much of its burden of proof. Nevertheless, the Commission's economic analysis in state aid cases continued to remain superficial in the view of many observers—to say nothing of the member states. The ECJ put an end to this trend in *Kingdom of the Netherlands and Leeuwarder Papierwarenfabriek BV v. Commission*, one of the earliest cases in which the Commission ordered aid repayment. Whereas in *Philip Morris* the Commission had specified the company's market share in the Netherlands and established that 80 percent of the plant's output would be exported within the Community, in *Leeuwarder* the Commission had not specified either of these central economic datums. Furthermore, the Commission had not raised the important issue of possible overcapacity in the market. Given these shortcomings in the Commission's economic analysis, the ECJ annulled the decision against the aid and, as Schina says, "forced on the Commission a change in attitude."[148] The ECJ ruled that if the Commission did make a clear statement of its economic analysis, however, it created a strong (though rebuttable) presumption that the aid threatened to distort competition (or did so, if already introduced).[149] Between *Philip Morris*, in which the ECJ ruled that there was no need for the extensive economic analysis required in anti-trust cases under Articles 85 and 86, and *Leeuwarder*, the ECJ created a standard of analysis that was subsequently followed by the Commission.

Some member states saw *Leeuwarder* and similar decisions of the period (such as *Intermills*) as providing a new way around the state aid rules: Prevent the Commission from conducting an adequate economic analysis by not giving it the information to do so.[150] In one example, *France v. Commission,* Case 102/87 (judgment of 13 July 1988), the French government objected to the Commission's estimate of the prevailing interest rate in France[151] but had offered no information itself. Relying on the requirement of EEC Article 5 that member states must cooperate in the achievement of Community purposes, the Court ruled against France.

More recently, a 1994 ECJ decision has muddied this area somewhat. In *Federal Republic of Germany and Pleuger Worthington GmbH v. Commission*, Cases C-324/90 and C-342/90, the ECJ ruled that its *Boussac* decision (see below) had essentially given the Commission subpoena powers to order member states to provide necessary information—and that if the Commission did not use these powers, it could not claim that the state in question had failed to provide adequate information for a decisions. It therefore overturned a Commission negative decision and repayment order in the case.[152]

Repayment of Illegal Aid

As noted above, aid repayment has been the *ultima ratio* for controlling non-notified, incompatible aid since the mid-1980s. The Commission's right to order repayment was established in the ECJ's ruling in *Commission v. Germany*, Case 70/72 [1973] ECR 813. Although ruling against the Commission on other grounds in this case involving aid to the coal mining industry, the ECJ said of the Commission's request for repayment:[153]

> Such a request is admissible since the Commission is competent, when it has found that aid is incompatible with the Common Market, to decide that the State concerned must abolish or alter it. To be of practical effect, this abolition or modification may include an obligation to require repayment of aid granted in breach of the Treaty, so that in the absence of measures for recovery, the Commission may bring the matter before the Court.

Despite this aspect of the ruling, the Commission did not announce that it would begin using this sanction until ten years later.[154] On 24 November 1983, the Commission sent a Communication to member states notifying them that it would take all possible measures to ensure that notification requirements were adhered to and informing potential aid recipients that they may be subject to having to repay illegally received state aid.[155] To facilitate a "gradual implementation of this principle," the Commission decided to focus on cases in which the aids were incompatible with the common market and had been introduced illegally.[156]

Not surprisingly, given the potential power of repayment orders to undo government decisions, these orders were strongly contested by many member states. In several ECJ cases, the appellant states argued that repaying aid would be in violation of domestic law. For example, Belgium argued in *Commission v. Belgium*, Case 5/86 ([1988] 2 CMLR 258), that refunding a state injection of equity capital violated Belgian company laws. The ECJ rejected these arguments, as it rejected similar arguments in *Re Tubemeuse,* Case 142/87 ([1988] 2 CMLR 601), that undoing that equity participation "would conflict with national company law on the relative status of shareholders and creditors."[157]

Another argument raised in some repayment cases was that repaying the aid would force the recipient into bankruptcy. In *Belgium v. Commission*, Case 52/84, the ECJ ruled that repayment should still be enforced even if bankruptcy were required. This case also established that the only acceptable reason not to obey a repayment order was the factual impossibility of doing so.[158]

A third argument, which was raised in several appeals by different member states, appealed to the legal principle of legitimate expectations—that is, that the aid recipient should have been able to rely on the national actions to be binding. As Germany argued in *Deufil*, Case 310/85, the company had a legitimate "expectation that a national decision granting the aid would be definitive."[159] The ECJ ruled that this argument was not correct: The notification requirement of Article 93(3) is definitive—all the more so because Community law is binding on all member states.

Ross suggests that the ECJ upheld a consistent line that only factual impossibility, not legal impossibility, was a permissible reason to not obey an aid repayment order from the Commission. He concludes, "The Court seems determined to resist the development of any easily-satisfied escape-route for Member States faced with demands to repay aids."[160]

Table 4-2 shows the increasing use by the Commission of repayment orders through January 1998.

The Commission was able to expand this power in the 1990s. First, it began requiring interest to be paid on illegal aid in the case of the Spanish firm Intelhorce SA, which it determined to have received an illegal capital injection.[161] When the German firm Siemens challenged an interest charge before the CFI (Intelhorce had appealed on other grounds), the Court upheld the Commission on 8 July 1995.[162]

Table 4-2 **Commission Use of Aid Recovery Orders**

Year	No. of Cases	Countries Involved[a]	Amount (MM ECU)
1982	3	B, NL	67.59
1983	2	B	25.17
1984	6	B, F, NL, UK	177.51
1985	2	D	5.71
1986	3	B, D	6.90
1987	6	B, D, F	829.34
1988	5	F, I	214.18
1989	5	E, F, GR, I	403.90
1990	5	D, F, GR, I	15.399
1991	4	F, I, UK	42.79
1992	5	B, D, E	130.00
1993	3	D, F, UK	125.09
1994	1	D	8.3
1995	6	F, E, B, NL, D	34.87
1996	15	B, D, E, F, I	525.72
1997	10	DK, D, F, I, E	389.567
1998	24	D, NL, I, L, A, F, E	530.13

[a]D = Germany, E = Spain, B = Belgium, NL = Netherlands, F = France, UK = United Kingdom, I = Italy, GR = Greece, L = Luxembourg, A = Austria

Source: Twenty-Seventh Report on Competition Policy, Part II, state aid Table F, 306–15; *Twenty-Eighth Report on Competition Policy,* Part II, state aid Table 2, 309–11.

Second, in the case of the German firm Textilwerke Deggendorf, the Commission established that it could withhold approval of *legal* aid until illegal aid had been repaid. This decision was upheld by the ECJ on 15 May 1997.[163]

Nevertheless, member states have continued to create new ways of circumventing repayment orders. In 1993, Italy adopted a law amending its bankruptcy provisions for large firms that allowed a company made bankrupt by having to repay illegal state aid to be taken over by the state and have its debts guaranteed—in essence receiving new aid. The Commission opened the Article 93(a) procedure against this law in December 1994 and ruled against it in March 1996, demanding the repeal of the new law and an aid repayment it was blocking.[164] In another case from Italy, the ECJ ruled on 29 January 1998 that a member state could not merely claim that repayment was absolutely impossible in the absence of positive action on its part to secure repayment or to offer alternatives to the Commission that would cure the distortion to competition.[165]

The foregoing review shows that once the Commission began using repayment orders as a sanction for rules violations, the European courts backed it up. As Ross points out, the ECJ has allowed no excuses from member states seeking to avoid repayment, and more recent history has shown ECJ support for expanding use of the repayment sanction. In Chapter 6, I consider the outcome of repayment orders from the substantive rather than legal angle and assess their impact on improving rule compliance by member states.

Trying to Sanction Non-Notification: The Legacy of *Boussac*

In *France v. Commission* [*Boussac*], Case C-301/87, 14 February 1990, the French government attempted to overturn a negative decision and a partial repayment order for non-notified aid it gave to textile producer Boussac Saint-Frérès in 1983. This case highlights the many problems the Commission has encountered in trying to control non-notified aid. According to Piet Jan Slot's account, the Commission discovered the aid in July 1983, but France did not provide all necessary information to the Commission concerning the aid until May 1987; the aid was declared incompatible with the Common Market in July 1987.[166] As Slot remarks elsewhere, "Long and tedious negotiations such as took place in the Boussac Case and the Peugeot aid plans weaken the credibility of the Commission and, for that matter, the Community."[167]

Needless to say, a state is unlikely to be deterred by a sanction the outcome of which is uncertain (the Commission only required that about one-third of the aid be repaid) and the effective date of which may be years away (seven years in this case; some German cases have taken more than eight). Given this obvious problem, the Commission tried to persuade the ECJ that non-notified aids are *per se* illegal, which would greatly strengthen its hand in bargaining with non-notifiers. The ECJ did not accept this argument,[168] but it did say that the Commission could issue interim orders and demand an immediate suspension of aid payments.[169] On the substantive side of the case, the ECJ rejected a wide variety of French claims (inadequate reasoning,

Commission delays, disproportionate punishment [i.e., repayment], and an argument that the capital injections and soft loans did not constitute an aid because a market investor would have done the same) and upheld the repayment order.[170]

The mixed decision on the procedural side drew varying reactions from observers. Slot regarded it as giving no sanction against non-notification, except for using national courts to enforce the directly effective notification requirement,[171] whereas K. P. E. Lasok regarded it as only delaying the inevitable, at worst.[172]

The Commission's view has moved ever closer to Slot's in recent years. Although the Commission initially focussed on making interim orders,[173] by 1995 it decided to recruit national courts more directly into enforcing the notification requirement.[174] In addition, it stepped up its use of injunctions to demand information from member states—as for instance in its 1996 decision in the Italian road haulage case.[175] In 1996, however—in a sharp turnabout from its position at the beginning of the decade—the Commission proposed implementing regulations under Article 94, which the Industry Council encouraged in its November 1996 meeting.[176] Before that, DG IV officials had shied away from Article 94 because the Commission already had almost exclusive control of state aid policy, and a regulation could give more power in this area to the Council. The need to establish better control over non-notified aid pushed the Commission to finally propose a Procedural Regulation, however.[177] Moreover, as one member state representative suggested, the decision in the *Sytraval* case worried the Commission that the courts would take a bigger hand in defining state aid procedures, so it sought a Council regulation to codify its practices. In particular, this representative believed the Commission was seeking to minimize third-party intervention, which threatens to "clog up the process"—much as it is felt to do in anti-trust cases.[178]

The Procedural Regulation was approved by the Industry Council in November 1998, and final approval by the Council of Ministers came in March 1999.[179] One of its main goals is to strengthen the Commission's powers regarding non-notified aid. The problem, from the Commission's point of view, is that appeals in national courts against repayment orders have delayed their implementation for years, compounding the damage to competition caused by illegally awarded aid.[180] Thus, the proposed regulation calls for member states to recover aid in immediate and effective fashion; it also requires member states to "take all necessary steps which are available in their legal systems" to enforce recovery orders. The original Commission proposal had specified, however, that appeals to national courts "shall not have suspensive effect," meaning that national courts could not permit the firm to keep the aid until it had been disapproved by the Commission and all appeals exhausted. Initially, Germany, France, Austria, and Italy all had misgivings on this point—with Germany (by far the worst offender on notification, as Table 6-19b shows) arguing that this provision would constitute a harmonization of member states' laws that is not provided for by Article 94. In the May 1998 Council meeting, there were "a number of stormy exchanges" between Van Miert and members of the Council, according to one report, and Van Miert apparently threatened to withdraw the proposal entirely rather than allow the Commission's powers to be weakened.[181] At the November 1998 Council Meeting, a compromise was unanimously agreed to: The "suspensive effect" language was dropped in favor of the weaker language given above, and rules limiting appeal to national courts were accepted by objectors in return for strict time limits on Commission investigations (two months for preliminary investigation, eighteen months for the Article 93(2) procedure) that could be waived only with member state agreement. The regulation also provides for a ten-year "statute of limitations" on aid recovery, beginning from the date the aid was awarded (in contrast to the often years-earlier approval of the program under which the aid was disbursed), on-site inspections when there are apparent compliance problems, reductions in translations, and new rules on the rights of competitors of the aid recipient.[182] Business organizations were not happy with the provisions on third-party rights, arguing that they did not do enough to make "a clear recognition that the complainant was an important part of the process. In the final document, third-party rights were treated rather cursorily," according to Cyrus Mehta, head of the Confederation of British Industry's State Aid Working Group.[183] Similarly, the Union of Industrial and Employers Confederations of Europe (UNICE) registered concerns about protections for third parties, but it was also concerned that the Council had weakened the regulation too much by removing the "no suspensive effect" statement. Eric Berggren of UNICE's Company Affairs Department argued that there should be a harmonization of national law regarding state aid procedure, which the removed statement would have provided. He proposed the adoption of a "remedies directive"—such as exists in the area of public procurement—to eliminate the wide disparities in national legal treatment of aid repayment orders, which he termed "distortive."[184]

Nevertheless, the Procedural Regulation is a landmark because it strengthens the Commission's monitoring capacity (through on-site inspections) and its sanctioning capacity (through the repayment rules). Its adoption should improve the Commission's hand greatly in cases of non-notification. Moreover, as Berggren noted, in practice the ECJ may interpret the regulation to prohibit suspensive effect—although there is no way to be certain of that until an appropriate case is heard.

Evasion Techniques: The Case of Cumulation

Given the incentive that states have to avoid the rules when it is in their interest to do so, it is important to consider some of the evasion techniques available. Non-notification and packaging (primarily under the R&D rubric) have been discussed above; one other option has been used frequently: "cumulation" of aids—that is, awarding more than one aid of different types to the same project.

For example, a state with a regional aid maximum of 30 percent might provide a 25 percent NGE regional aid for an investment as well as a 10 percent NGE R&D grant for the same investment. Although both would be within the normally permitted maxima for that type of aid and likely would not even have to be reported (assuming that the programs under which they were given had already been notified and approved), the total aid would be in violation of the overall maximum for the region in question. Because neither aid would be individually illegal, however, the Commission would be unlikely to hear about the violation unless there were a complaint from another state or from a competitor of the recipient. To prevent situations such as this from occurring, particularly in the context of bidding for inward investment,[185] the Commission introduced, in a 1985 Communication, "Rules applicable to cases of cumulation of aids for different purposes."[186] These rules required the notification of individual cases when two or more types of aid were cumulated and either the aid came to 25 percent NGE or greater or the investment was greater than 12 million ECU.

These rules were not immediately accepted by all member states. France, Germany, and Greece all either rejected them or refused to apply them. The Commission instituted infringement proceedings against France before the ECJ for failing to notify aid cumulation procedures; France agreed in 1988. With Germany, the Commission instead opened Article 93(2) proceedings against the Fourteenth and Fifteenth Framework plans for federal/*Länder* regional aid to pressure Bonn on the cumulation question. Germany reached agreement with the Commission in 1987, and Greece did so in 1988—also after a 93(2) procedure.[187]

The evidence is mixed on whether the cumulation rules have fully addressed the problem. Certainly in its first few years, the Commission's calls for transparency in this area suggested that problems remained.[188] Similarly, in 1994, Cini suggested that the problem of cumulation "remains a major problem for the DG IV."[189] Yet neither the twenty-sixth, twenty-seventh, nor twenty-eighth *Report on Competition Policy* mentions cumulation as an issue, so perhaps a case can be made that the situation is now better than in the 1980s.

Other Commission Initiatives

As Cini has argued, Sutherland's inauguration of the *Surveys* on state aid was crucial in providing a quantitative snapshot of the entire state aid field that subsequently was used to inform new policy initiatives.[190] She notes how the negative example of Italy as a high aid giver was constantly held up in the first two *Surveys*, as was the apparent treatment of aid as *in itself* bad.With the information gained from the *Surveys*, the Commission was able for the first time to say that state aid comprised *x* percent of country Y's GDP, or the government's budget, or its budget deficit. This information added to the Commission's ability to argue that the total amount of state aid was too high. Moreover, DG IV also produced a comprehensive listing of all aid programs in effect; although this listing was never published (because of member state pressure), it helped focus attention on the far greater amounts of subsidies given under existing aid as opposed to new aid programs.[191]

In 1989, as part of his policy review, Commissioner Brittan announced that general investment aid would be an important target and that previously approved ("existing") general aid programs would come under scrutiny as well.[192] DG IV moved swiftly to challenge several of these programs; the Dutch and Belgians agreed to end general investment programs, and the British undertook to individually notify every general aid offered under Article 8 of the Industrial

Development Act.[193] As a result of this pressure, general aid has fallen as a proportion of total aid to manufacturing from 5 percent in 1981–86 to just 1.6 percent in 1992–94 and essentially zero in 1995–97 (see Table 6-15).[194]

Beyond general aid, existing aid programs were a high priority because an estimated 80 percent of all aid was granted under existing schemes, as opposed to new aids. Already under Sutherland, the use of Article 93(1) reviews to examine existing aid was on the upswing.[195] Under Brittan and Van Miert, however, it became a more regular feature of DG IV practice. For example, the Commission completed reviews of existing aid under Article 93(1) in seven cases in 1996, six in 1997, and five in 1998.[196]

Evolution of Law and Policy

This section has demonstrated the increasingly rapid pace of state aid law and policy since 1980. Beginning with the *Philip Morris* decision, which created a firm case law base for DG IV's work, the Commission has become more confident in its handling of state aid policy. Although this trend by no means changes the incentives states face to try to evade the rules, the Commission's efforts, upheld by the ECJ, have increased the sanctions for transgressions. This change has intensified the ways in which EU powers have clearly reduced the sovereignty of member states. The following section highlights one of the most sensitive aspects of this development: the interaction between state aid law and the use of public ownership of enterprise.

State Aid to State-Owned Firms

State-owned firms and state aid control are mutually problematic. Transactions between the state and state-owned enterprises tend to be less transparent than "arms' length" transactions. Moreover, as Gatsios and Seabright have argued, there may be inherently less credibility for a state to pledge not to reimburse losses of a state-owned firm than for the state to make the same commitment vis-a-vis privately owned companies.[197] Both of these factors make regulating aid to public enterprises more difficult than controlling subsidies to private firms.

At the same time, the inherent threat to sovereignty that state aid control represents is especially sharp in relation to state-owned firms. The legitimacy of state ownership is guaranteed by Article 222[198] of the Treaty of Rome, and many countries have used public ownership as a key ingredient of their industrial strategy. State aid regulation necessarily impinges on decisions of industrial policy, but the special targeting of aid to public enterprises—as occurred particularly under Sir Leon Brittan's tenure as Competition Commissioner—seems to undermine the Treaty's neutrality between public and private ownership. As the *Economist* has asked, "What is the point of state ownership if the state must run its firms as if they were private ones?"[199]

The Commission's approach to the state-owned sector has changed over the years. This section focuses on the Commission's early analysis of state ownership before turning to the first landmark in this area of state aid control, the Transparency Directive of 1980. Next, I consider the Brittan initiative against aid to the public sector and the conflicts it generated. Finally, I focus on recent developments, where the most important justification for allowing subsidies to state-owned enterprises has been for the performance of public service requirements (such as providing postal service throughout a country's territory, regardless of the differential cost of serving different locations).

Karel Van Miert was replaced by former Internal Market Commissioner Mario Monti shortly before this book went to press. It is still too early to determine what effect this change will have on aid to publicly owned firms.

Temporary Acquisition of Shareholdings by the State

In the *Second Report on Competition Policy*, the Commission addressed the question of state ownership at length.[200] Commenting on several Italian, French, and Belgian programs for temporarily acquiring shares of firms in difficulties, it turned Article 222 on its head:

> . . . the Commission took the view that the principle of neutrality set out by the EEC Treaty (Article 222) with regard to ownership arrangements in the Member States prevents the latter from using their power to intervene in the ownership of production facilities to take measures which, if other intervention techniques were used, would be incompatible with Article 92 *et seq.*, since these distort intra-Community competition and trade. Any other interpretation would entail unacceptable discrimi-

> nation between Member States or between differing measures adopted by the same Member State, but in fact having the same objectives.[201]

In other words, not only does Article 222 imply that state ownership cannot be burdened by EU decisions, it cannot be *privileged*, either.

The Commission acknowledged that it could not decide in the abstract whether the agencies set up to obtain such temporary shareholdings (such as the Instituto Mobiliare Italiano—IMI) were in fact dispensing state aid; it could make such determinations only through examination of their actual practices. The Commission decided that the French, Italian, and Belgian agencies would have to provide reports on each firm assisted under by them, with regional and sectoral data included. In particular, it noted that aid would be considered to be present when any of the following could be demonstrated:

- that the acquisition of holdings are used as an alternative to or a factor strengthening traditional forms [of state aid];
- that these holdings are provided for firms in liquidation that would disappear from the market without such assistance;
- that the purchases of holdings do not ensure normal remuneration of the capital committed or that they are eventually sold to the partners falling short of the acquisition price.[202]

This last point strongly foreshadowed the Commission's later "market investor" rule (see Chapter 3).

The Transparency Directive

In June 1980, the Commission adopted Directive 80/723/EEC on "the transparency of financial relations between Member States and public undertakings."[203] This decision requires governments to maintain, for five years, records covering all financial transactions between governments authorities and state-owned or state-controlled firms, including the specific uses of funds provided to them, to be provided to the Commission upon request.[204] A pitched legal battle ensued, as two of the most interventionist states (France and Italy) challenged the Directive before the ECJ, as did the UK. Intervening on behalf of the Commission were the Netherlands and Germany—states with far lower levels of state ownership. Britain's position was somewhat anomalous: It did not oppose the goal of the directive; it joined the appeal on the basis that the Commission was usurping the Council's legislative powers.[205] In ruling in the Commission's favor, the ECJ stated that the directive did not place an unfair burden on public firms because the financial relations between states and state-owned firms were of a different nature than those involving privately owned firms. When the Commission in 1991 issued a Communication requiring annual reporting of information on state-owned firms, however, the ECJ annulled its decision.[206] In response, the Commission issued a new directive incorporating the annual reporting requirement.[207] Through these directives, the Commission has increased the quantity and quality of information available to it for controlling aid to the state-owned sector.

Commissioner Brittan's Initiative Against Aid to State-Owned Firms

In 1989, Sir Leon Brittan took over the Competition portfolio from Peter Sutherland. Following Sutherland's activism, Brittan announced his priorities for state aid control in several speeches given that March. In particular, he identified a reduction in the overall volume of aid, a review of "existing" (i.e., previously approved) aid, subsidies for exports to non-EC countries, general investment aid, aid for "national champions," and—most important for the present analysis—aid to state-owned firms. As Brittan said in one speech, "The feather-bedding of nationalized industries must be stopped"—hardly a surprising statement from a one-time Industry Secretary under Margaret Thatcher.[208] Although Brittan's comments certainly reflected his own political views, his attack on aid to public firms also underlines the difficulties in regulating such aid. For example, Commission estimates suggest that the ECU value of non-notified aid is ten times greater for state-owned firms than for private companies.[209]

As Cini has pointed out, Brittan's approach to his portfolio was to "concentrat[e] on the most controversial cases."[210] Among the more important cases of aid to state-owned firms on which he focused were Groupe Bull (FF 6 billion in aid) and Sabena ($1 billion).[211] Yet in these cases, the Commission eventually approved the aid in question. In the case of Bull, the Commission was persuaded to approve the aid (despite the company's longstanding losses) by promises of capacity cuts and the fact that IBM and NEC had bought minority stakes in the company.[212] Regarding the Sabena aid, Trevor Soames and Alan

Ryan comment that it—along with aid for state-owned Air France and Iberia—was approved "with barely a murmur from the European Commission."[213]

One high-profile case that Brittan inherited was that of Renault, in which the French government wrote off FF 12 billion of the company's debt in early 1988.[214] This action followed capital injections of FF 8 billion (1.13 billion ECU) over the previous three years that had been paid without Commission approval.[215] The case was complicated by the fact that the write-off was originally intended by a Conservative French government as a precursor to privatization, but when the Socialists returned to power later that year they balked at privatizing the company. Indeed, the new government refused to take the first step envisioned—changing Renault's status from a "Régie" (the equivalent of a government department) to a normal firm (Société Anonyme). The Commission had originally agreed to the write-off when it was to be followed by the ending of its Régie status, but with the new government's change of plans, the March 1988 aid approval was voided and the Commission threatened that Renault would have to repay the FF 12 billion debt write-off.[216] The Commission split on this issue along a Brittan-Delors axis, but eventually a compromise was reached. In view of a partial change in the company's legal status (remaining a Régie, but subject to normal commercial law) and the completion of about half of the capacity cuts envisioned in the March 1988 decision, the Commission agreed that Renault would only have to repay FF 6 billion, with the other 6 billion approved subject to the conditions of the original decision.[217]

Recent Developments

Since Flemish Socialist Karel Van Miert replaced Brittan as Competition Commissioner in 1993, the level of rhetoric surrounding aid to state-owned firms seems to have declined somewhat.[218] Nevertheless, important work on public sector aid has continued, and new ground is being broken. The largely state-owned airlines have felt new pressure on the subsidies they once received with little notice in the past, and state-owned firms in several sectors have had to justify the subsidies they receive to carry out "public service" requirements.

After a spate of aid awards to airlines in the early 1990s, the industry's difficulties led to even larger awards—topped by FF 20 billion to Air France in 1994. By this time, according to Soames and

Ryan, the Commission began to impose more stringent restructuring requirements on the airlines in return for the aid—largely as a result of lobbying campaigns by privately owned airlines—beginning with aid for Aer Lingus that was authorized in December 1993.[219] The aid to Air France was challenged by British Airways and six other airlines in the CFI, which held in June 1998 that the Commission had not provided sufficient justification for two aspects of the aid package (the purchase of seventeen new planes and its analysis of the competitive situation outside the European Economic Area). Four weeks later, the Commission submitted a response to the CFI on these issues and pronounced the aid approved by a 13–3 vote.[220] A capital injection to Iberia was approved in January 1996 with a decision that it did not constitute state aid; yet restructuring requirements were still imposed, including a cut of 3,500 jobs and the sell-off of some of Iberia's South American subsidiaries.[221]

Public service requirements have become increasingly prominent in discussions of aid to the public sector. Although there are few such requirements in the airline industry, Ireland's have been criticized by Aer Lingus' competitors as being set up so that only Aer Lingus can practically serve them (Community rules require an open bidding process for serving poorly traveled routes a country wants to keep open)—and thus a further subsidy.[222] Another important public service case involved the French Postal Service; the Commission decided that no aid existed because:

> the value of the tax relief is less than the costs of the public service obligations imposed on the post office, namely to provide post offices throughout the country and deliver mail throughout the territory of France irrespective of the fact that the prices for this service may not always correspond to the costs.[223]

Similarly, in November 1996 the Commission decided that payments received by the Portuguese state-owned broadcasting firm RTP did not constitute aid because the payments were less than the cost of the channel's public service requirements (covering the entire territory, including the Azores and Madeira, religious broadcasting, etc.), which the commercial complainant did not share.[224]

Conflict over aid to state-owned firms appears certain to continue for the foreseeable future. Privately owned companies in industries such as steel and airlines have become increasingly vocal about the aid given to state-owned competitors; such complaints have now begun in areas formerly occupied by government monopolies, such as television broadcasting (targeted by new Competition Commissioner Mario Monti in his confirmation hearings)[225] and postal and telecommunications services. In particular, the issue of whether subsidies to cover public service requirements give government enterprises advantages in competitive markets is bound to stay at or near the top of DG IV's agenda as complaints come in from private competitors.[226] As the "no aid present" decisions in cases such as those involving the French Postal Service and RTP Broadcasting show, however, state-owned firms are by no means simply going to be swept from the scene by aggressive use of the state aid rules.

Conclusion

This chapter reviews the gradual expansion of the Commission's powers in the state aid field and how important environmental events such as enlargement have affected state aid policy. Several themes clearly stand out.

First, the legal aspects of state aid policy have proved crucial at several junctures. Because the really controversial issues are appealed to the EU courts, the attitude of the courts has played a major role in the development of state aid policy. In particular, the fact that the ECJ (and more recently, the CFI) has generally supported the Commission's actions has lent the Commission a strong hand in prosecuting its policy.[227] This factor stood out in the *Philip Morris* case and in the long series of cases on the Commission's power to order aid repayment that have defended this authority and allowed the Commission to extend it via interest charges and through withholding legal aid until illegal aid is repaid. In terms of constraints on the Commission, *Boussac* is the most important case insofar as it kept from the Commission what would clearly have been a powerful lever against non-notification; *Sytraval* provided one of the proximate motivations for the Commission to seek a Council Regulation under Article 94.

Second, an ever-widening area of policy has been codified. Until the mid-1980s, this codification occurred largely in reaction to crises, both sectoral (shipbuilding, textiles, steel, etc.) and horizontal (i.e., environmental and technological). The Commission's enumeration of these two types of frameworks has made for speedier handling of aid in the affected areas, as well as guiding member states toward proposing programs that were likely to be approved.

Third, compliance with the Commission's authority has been uneven among the member etates, but efforts at non-compliance have been met with increased enforcement efforts by the Commission. This trend has been especially evident in the introduction of the R&D framework and cumulation rules, and most importantly in the use of aid repayment orders. The Procedural Regulation should strengthen the Commission's hand on enforcement even further.

Fourth, there has been a sharp expansion in the volume of activity by the Commission. From only twenty-one cases and one negative decision in 1970, the Commission's activity expanded fivefold by 1980. During the 1980s the number of negative decisions generally was in double digits; the Commission reviewed more than 400 cases for the first time in 1988. In 1998 the Commission issued 784 decisions, including a record 40 negative decisions in all sectors.[228]

Fifth, the Commission moved from a reactive to a proactive approach to state aid under Peter Sutherland and Sir Leon Brittan. The period of policy activism during the 1980s has left its mark on DG IV.

Sixth, the enlargement of the EU beginning in 1973 has posed challenges to state aid policy. Most obviously, enlargement has meant the socialization of new groups of officials to the rules, such as those banning export aid for intra-Community trade. More fundamentally, the increasing number of members has meant a larger group of actors trying to cooperate on this policy—which cooperation theory warns us is an increasingly difficult task. This trend has been exacerbated because many of the newer areas are substantially poorer than the original six member states, creating the dilemma of how to increase growth in the cohesion countries while simultaneously avoiding pressures for races to the bottom in environmental policy, labor, and social policy and increasing levels of investment location subsidies. Some of the choices made along the way (such as allowing Ireland to levy only a 10 percent corporate income tax on manufacturing without considering it at the time to be a state aid) have intensified rather than ameliorated competition for investment.

Finally, the overall thrust of the Commission's efforts has been to require increasing transparency in state aid policy on several dimensions. This effort includes enforcing the notification requirement more diligently, encouraging member states to use more transparent forms of aid (discussed further in Chapter 6), publishing more details of Commission rules and decisions, and compiling and publishing the *Surveys* on state aid. The amount of information available on state aid in the EU is now quite substantial.

By contrast, as Chapter 5 shows, the same cannot be said for either the United States or Canada. Not only are there few central rules on subsidies and tax expenditures that favor firms, there are no comprehensive data in either country that show the total support given to companies at the federal and subnational levels. In Chapter 5, I turn to the task of generating ballpark estimates and analyzing what regulation does exist.

Notes

1. CEC, *Competition Law in the European Communities*, Volume II: Rules applicable to state aids (situation at 31 December 1989) (Brussels-Luxembourg: CEC 1990), 14–15.
2. Cini, "Policing the Internal Market," 151.
3. *Sixth Report on Competition Policy*, Annex, p. 195. Compare this with the 32 final decisions taken in 1997 under Article 93(2) or the similar steel aid code procedures. See *Twenty-seventh Report on Competition Policy*, point 320.
4. Lavdas and Mendrinou, *Politics, Subsidies and Competition: The New Politics of State Intervention in the European Union* (Cheltenham: Edward Elgar, 1999), 29.
5. *Common Market Law Reports* [1970] Part 41, 43–76.
6. EC Commission vs. France, 1970 CMLR 41, pp. 64–69.
7. Schina, *State Aids Under the EEC Treaty*, 46.
8. *Second Report on Competition Policy*, point 109.
9. *First Report on Competition Policy*, point 181.
10. Case 47-69, *France v. Commission* [1970] ECR 487.
11. *First Report on Competition Policy*, point 183.
12. For some of the cases brought by the Commission to enforce this position, see *Second Report on Competition Policy*, points 108–11; *Third Report on Competition Policy*, points 102–04; *Fourth Report on Competition Policy*, points 159–62; *Seventh Report on Competition Policy*, points 220–21. Indeed, it came to light in 1980 that France had not complied with the ECJ decision in Case 47/69, and the Commission instituted infringement proceedings with the ECJ. See *10th Report on Competition Policy*, point 211.

13. In 1980, *The Ninth Report on Competition Policy*, point 139, declared, "The Community discipline eliminating aid in intra-Community trade has become fully effective." Three cases of aid for intra-Community exports over the 1985–89 period (all Italian) are identified by Elaine Ballantyne and John Bachtler, *Regional Policy Under Scrutiny: The European Commission and Regional Aid* (Glasgow: European Policies Research Centre, 1990), 43. Following Greece's accession to the EC, its export aid program was allowed to continue as a transition measure. In 1986, however, the Commission ordered its phase-out by 1 January 1990. *Sixteenth Report on Competition Policy*, point 258.
14. *Twenty-fifth Report on Competition Policy*, point 209; *Seventh Survey on State Aid*, 15 and Table 7.
15. *Twenty-fourth Report on Competition Policy*, point 390; *Twenty-fifth Report on Competition Policy*, point 210.
16. *First Report on Competition Policy*, point 143.
17. *First Report on Competition Policy*, points 141–42.
18. CEC, *Competition Law in the European Communities*, Volume II: Rules applicable to state aids (situation at 31 December 1989), 97; Cini, "Policing the Internal Market," 227.
19. *First Report on Competition Policy*, points 147–53.
20. The "center" at that time consisted of the entire EC except for Berlin, Germany's Zonal Border Area (the area bordering East Germany), the Italian Mezzogiorno, and west and southwest France.
21. *Fifth Report on Competition Policy*, point 86.
22. *Fifth Report on Competition Policy*, point 87.
23. This evolved into a 75 percent net grant equivalent limit, because that was the existing maximum in the Mezzogiorno at that time. See Douglas Yuill et al., *European Regional Incentives 1994/95* (London: Bowker-Saur, 1994), 100.
24. Published as the Commission Communication of 3 February 1979, included in *Competition Law in the European Communities*, Volume II: Rules applicable to state aids (situation at 31 December 1989) (Brussels-Luxembourg: CEC, 1990), 99–108. In addition to the Communication itself, see the discussion of it in *Eighth Report on Competition Policy*, points 152–53.
25. Personal communication with Reinhard Walther, DG IV, Unit Head for Inventory and Analysis, Brussels, 23 September 1993.
26. Commission communication on the method for the application of Article 92(3)(a) and (c) to regional aid, in *Competition Law in the European Communities,* Volume II, 109–22.

27. "Competition Policy, Cohesion and the Co-ordination of Regional Aids in the European Community," *European Competition Law Review* 14, no. 4 (July/August 1993): 145.
28. Yuill et al., *European Regional Incentives 1994/95*, 96. Its Objective 1 status ended 31 December 1996.
29. Wishlade, *EC Competition Policy and Regional Aid*, 23.
30. CEC, *Competition Law in the European Communities,* Volume II, 118–22. In some cases, the limits were specified in terms of gross grant equivalent.
31. Wishlade, *RAGS and LIPS: New Weapons in the Commission's Regional Aid Control Armoury*, Regional and Industrial Research Paper Series, Number 31, European Policies Research Centre, February 1999, 31.
32. See "Multisectoral Framework on regional aid for large investment projects," available at <http://www.europa.int/comm/dg04/lawaid/en/98c107.htm>, and "Large Investment Projects. New State aid framework approved for large investment projects," *Competition Policy Newsletter* (February 1998), 70–71.
33. Wishlade, *RAGS and LIPS*, 28.
34. Madeleine Tilmans, "The Commission decided that Germany must apply the multisectoral framework on regional aid to large investment projects," *Competition Policy Newsletter*, October 1998, 50; "EU Commission says German objections to regional aid rules are unacceptable," *AFX News*, 14 July 1998.
35. For the list, see "Guidelines on Regional Aid," n. 2.
36. Emma Tucker, "EU to Reconsider Regional Aid: Commission Plans to Focus Help on Areas Most in Need of Help," *Financial Times*, 19 December 1997, 2; Wishlade, *EC Competition Policy and Regional Aid*, p. 21.
37. "Guidelines on National Regional Aid," point 4.8, which includes further detail on exceptions to the rules. See also Tucker, "EU to Reconsider Regional Aid"; and Wishlade, *RAGS and LIPS*, 23, 32.
38. Wishlade, *RAGS and LIPS*, 12, n. 33.
39. "Commission Sets National Ceilings for Coverage of Regional Aid," Commission Press Release IP/98/1133, 16 December 1998; Tucker, "EU to Reconsider Regional Aid;" Wishlade, *EC Competition Policy and Regional Aid*, 34–37.
40. Cini, "Policing the Internal Market," 230, suggests that DG XVI has been relatively weaker than DG IV. Ballantyne and Bachtler, *Regional Policy Under Scrutiny*, 50, note the "protracted, complex and often acrimonious argument between Brussels and national government departments."

41. Wishlade also argues that the combination of the Multi Sectoral Framework and new regional aid maxima will put more constraints on investment incentives than they have in the past. *EC Competition Policy and Regional Aid*, 39–40.
42. John Kurt Jacobsen, *Chasing Progress in the Irish Republic: Ideology, Democracy and Dependent Development* (Cambridge: Cambridge University Press, 1994), 197.
43. Jacobsen, *Chasing Progress in the Irish Republic*, Chapter 4.
44. Jacobsen, *Chasing Progress in the Irish Republic*, 99.
45. Industrial Development Authority, *Annual Report 1979* (Dublin: IDA Ireland, 1980), 93. See also *Tenth Report on Competition Policy*, point 173. The Commission also objected to ESR on the grounds that it was an operating aid.
46. See, for example, the following promotional material: IDA Ireland, *Ireland: Put Yourself in Our Hands in the 1990s* (Dublin: IDA Ireland, 1991), 1; IDA Ireland, *Guide to Taxes and Tax Reliefs in Ireland* (Dublin: IDA Ireland 1991), 3—which describes the tax rate as "A Unique Tax Incentive into the 21st Century" and trumpets the tax rate on the cover.
47. For the old view, see *Second Survey on State Aid*, Annex 1, 1–2. This caused a downward revision of the estimated value of ESR for the 1981–86 period covered by the *First Survey* (because the benchmark against which it was measured was thereby lowered). That the Commission accepted it as a general measure rather than state aid is even more puzzling in light of its treatment of certain extensions of the 10 percent rate to non-manufacturing operations as state aid. See Wishlade's sharp criticism on this point in *When Are Tax Advantages State Aids and When Are They General Measures?* Regional and Industrial Policy Research Paper, Number 20, European Policies Research Centre, June 1997, 19–21. On the new view that several Irish tax programs (besides the 10 percent manufacturing tax rate, the same rate in the Dublin International Financial Services Centre, and the Shannon Customs-Free Airport Zone) constitute operating aid, see Commission Press Release IP:98/691, "Commission Addresses Recommendations to Ireland Regarding Corporate Tax," 23 July 1998; and *Twenty-eighth Report on Competition Policy*, point 210. See also *Seventh Survey on State Aid*, 4.
48. It should be noted that the Irish had already considered ending the 10 percent tax rate at its scheduled expiration in 2010. This was the argument of 1992's Culliton Report from the Industrial Policy Review Group. See Douglas Yuill et al., *European Regional Incentives 1993-94*, 13th edition (London: Bowker-Saur, 1993), 5.
49. With the single tax rate, manufacturing would no longer be singled out for special treatment; despite the low rate, it would no longer be

considered a state aid. Subsequently, however, an investigation by the Internal Market Directorate (which is responsible for tax policy) threatened to undermine the agreement. The dispute was finally resolved in June 1999. John Murray Brown, "Dublin Ends Tax Dispute with EU," *Financial Times*, 23 July 1998, 2; John McManus and Fiona McHugh, "Irish Tax Strategy Blocked by EU," *Sunday Times*, 4 October 1998; and Sean Mac Carthaigh and Eibhir Mulqueen, "EU Tax Policy Aimed at Reducing Overall Rates," *Irish Times*, 19 June 1999, 19. For further discussion of tax competition, see Chapter 7.

50. Again, this procedure is used with existing aids; see Chapter 3.
51. *Eighteenth Report on Competition Policy*, point 234.
52. *Seventh Survey on State Aid*, 7, Table 3. The figures are expressed in 1996 prices.
53. Mitchell Smith, "Integration in Small Steps: The European Commission and Member-State Aid to Industry," *West European Politics*, July 1996, 570. Fully one-third of all aid decisions in 1998 pertained to Germany; see *Twenty-eighth Report on Competition Policy*, 87, figure 8.
54. Imre Karacs, "Bremer head detained in search for missing money," *The Independent*, 21 June 1996, 21; "State Aid: Commission Extends Bremer Vulkan Investigation," *European Report* no. 2173, 13 November 1996; European Information Service, "State Aid: Commission to Bail Out East German Shipyards," *European Intelligence* no. 113, 7 March 1996; Madeleine Tilmans, "State Aid: Principaux développements du 1er mai au juillet 1998," *Competition Policy Newsletter*, October 1998, 57–58.
55. "EU Gives Germany Till Aug 10 to Fix VW Subsidies," Reuter European Community Report, 2 August 1996, BC Cycle; European Information Service, "Volkswagen Row Escalates as Bonn Takes Commission to Court," *European Report* no. 2157, 14 September 1996; "Deal Near on Illegal Aid to VW," *Financial Times*, 25 October 1997, 2; Emma Tucker, "Commission Resolves VW Row," *Financial Times*, 19 November 1997, 2.
56. R. Hall and D. van der Wee, "Community Regional Policies for the 1990s," *Regional Studies* 26, no. 4 (1992): 400.
57. Yuill et al., *European Regional Incentives*, 10th edition, 68.
58. Hall and van der Wee, "Community Regional Policies for the 1990s," 400. For information on the negotiations over the expansion of the Structural Funds (as well as other aspects of the EC budget), see Simon Alterman, "Spanish Drive for Better EC Deal Poses Summit Threat," Reuter Library Report, 9 February 1988; and David Buchan and Tim Dickson, "An End to the Nay-Saying," *Financial Times*, 15 February 1988, 21.

59. Fiona G. Wishlade, "Competition Policy, Cohesion and the Co-ordination of Regional Aids in the European Community," 146–47. The quote that follows is from page 146.
60. See Bache, *The Politics of European Union Regional Aid Policy*, Chapter 4; and Wishlade, *EC Competition Policy and Regional Aid*, 26.
61. Brian Groom, "Minister Attacks Proposed Changes to EU Aid," *Financial Times*, 6 February 1998, 10.
62. "Community Regional Policies for the 1990s," 400.
63. *European Regional Incentives 1994-95*, 101–02.
64. This fund specifically benefits only Ireland, Greece, Portugal, and Spain—which normally are referred to as the "cohesion countries." The addition of the Cohesion Fund guaranteed that these four countries would see their assistance double in real terms between 1992 and 1999. See Yuill et al., *European Regional Incentives 1995-96*, 74.
65. CEC, *Competitiveness and Cohesion*, 26, Tables 17 and 18.
66. CEC, *Competitiveness and Cohesion*, 133.
67. CEC, *Competition Law in the European Communities,* Volume II, 120.
68. CEC, *Competitiveness and Cohesion: Trends in the Regions* (Brussels-Luxembourg: CEC, 1994), 129. For a taste of the intense bargaining over this package, see Chris Porter, "Commission Loses Out in Bruising Regional Aid Battle," Reuter European Community Report, 20 July 1993; and "European Community: Poorer than Thou," *Economist*, 10 July 1993, 41.
69. Fiona Wishlade, *EC Competition Policy and Regional Aid: An Agenda for the Year 2000?* Regional and Industrial Research Paper Series, Number 25, European Policies Research Centre, December 1997, 15–16.
70. "EU Summit Roundup: Talks Suspended but Agenda 2000 Deal Expected Tonight," *AFX News*, 25 March 1999.
71. Brian Groom and Michael Smith, "Spain and UK the Biggest Winners: Regional Aid," *Financial Times*, 27 March 1999, 2; Peter Norman, "Twenty-Hour Talk Marathon Ends in Compromise," *Financial Times*, 27 March 1999, 2.
72. Charles Bremner, "Regions Will Lose in EU Spending Reform," *The Times* (London), 19 March 1998, 23.
73. Mark Brennock, "Axe Will Not Fall Suddenly on All EU Funding," *Irish Times*, 22 March 1999, 13.
74. Patrick Smyth, "Ireland Suffers Cut of More Than Half in Total Receipts from EU Funds," *Irish Times*, 27 March 1999, 14.
75. David Ross and Benedict Brogan, "Sea Lochs the Key to Subsidy," *The Herald* (Glasgow), 24 March 1999, 7.

76. Groom and Smith, "Spain and UK the Biggest Winners." See also "Berlin European Council—Presidency Conclusions," press release, 25 March 1999; and for background, Kitty Holland, "Regionalisation Has Shallow Roots in Our Traditions," *Irish Times*, 21 November 1998, 10; and Ian Bache, *The Politics of European Union Regional Policy*, 130–32. Final list of eligible regions kindly provided by Ciaran Dearle, DG XVI, personal communication, 13 April 1999. Some parts of Sweden's former Objective 6 area do not qualify for Objective 1 but will receive a special package with similar levels of funding.
77. *Twenty-fifth Report on Competition Policy*, point 220.
78. Kevin Done, "Chrysler to go to law against EC," *Financial Times*, 11 November 1992, 4; Edward M. Graham, *Global Corporations and National Governments* (Washington, D.C.: Institute for International Economics, 1996), 82.
79. Claude Rakovsky et al., "Summary of the most important recent developments (International Dimension of Competition Policy)," *Competition Policy Newsletter*, autumn/winter 1995, 55.
80. *Twenty-sixth Report on Competition Policy*, point 231.
81. Joos Straiger, "Competition Conference in Bratislava," and Maria Blässer, "Implementing Rules for State Aid—Czech Republic," both in *Competition Policy Newsletter*, October 1998, 59–60.
82. *Twenty-eighth Report on Competition Policy*, points 300–02.
83. "Berlin European Council—Presidency Conclusions," Press release, 25 March 1999.
84. Commission letter and annex on textile and clothing industries, 4 February 1977, in CEC, *Competition Law in the European Communities*, Volume II: Rules applicable to state aids (situation at 31 December 1989), 50. Emphasis added.
85. Needless to say, EU trading partners may regard these initiatives not as benign but as themselves protectionist. These disputes are beyond the scope of this volume.
86. Cini, "Policing the Internal Market," 236; Schina, *State Aids Under the EEC Treaty*, 81.
87. The MFA, which many LDCs bitterly resented as proof that the industrialized nations only favored free trade when it was beneficial to them, was slated for phase-out only as a result of the Uruguay Round GATT agreement.
88. *First Report on Competition Policy*, point 171.
89. *First Report on Competition Policy*, point 172.

90. *Second Report on Competition Policy*, point 97.
91. *Fifth Report on Competition Policy*, points 107–09.
92. F. Knox, *Towards 1992: State Aids to Industry,* Trade and Tariffs Research, London, November 1989, 17–18. See also *Seventh Report on Competition Policy*, points 237–41.
93. See Schina, *State Aids Under the EEC Treaty*, 85. The synthetic fibers industry includes products with industrial uses as well as textile/clothing uses.
94. Schina, *State Aids Under the EEC Treaty*, 84–85.
95. For a good discussion of the early penetration of U.S. and EU markets by Japanese firms, see Dennis Patrick Quinn, *Restructuring the Automobile Industry: A Study of Firms and States in Modern Capitalism* (New York: Columbia University Press, 1988), 104–18. For Japanese market share in EU countries over the course of the 1970s, see figures 4.14 and 4.15, 152–53.
96. See, for example, Kenneth P. Thomas, *Capital Beyond Borders: States and Firms in the Auto Industry, 1960-1994* (London: Macmillan, 1997), 75.
97. See Lavdas and Mendrinou, *Politics, Subsidies and Competition*, 108.
98. The quote is from *Tenth Report on Competition Policy*, point 206. On the reporting system, see *Eleventh Report on Competition Policy*, point 215. See also Hancher et al., *EC State Aids*, 112–13.
99. Point 164.
100. *Eighteenth Report on Competition Policy*, point 227; Hancher et al., *EC State Aids*, 113–14; Robert McDonald, "State Aids & the Effort to Ensure Fair Competition," *EIU European Trends*, No. 2, 1992, 61; and "The Aid Plague," *Economist* Survey of Business in Europe, 8 June 1991, 17. Useful background on this case appears in Krish Bhaskar and the Motor Industry Research Unit, *The Effect of Different Aid Measures on Intra-Community Competition, Exemplified by the Case of the Automotive Industry*, Commission of the European Communities Document, March 1990, 2, 16–18.
101. The most extensive treatment of this case is Cini, "Policing the Internal Market," 347–73. Cini also notes (page 356) that £78 million in regional aid was authorized.
102. Hancher et al., *EC State Aids*, 117; McDonald, "State Aids," 61; Krish Bhaskar and Motor Industry Research Unit, *The Effect of Different Aid Measures on Intra-Community Competition*, 18–19. Italy was ordered to reclaim the entire amount of this aid.
103. *Eighteenth Report on Competition Policy*, point 164; Hancher et al., *EC State Aids*, 119–21.

104. Max Pemberton, *Europe's Motor Industry After 1992*, EIU Special Report no. 2090, January 1991, 122. This was an investigation of six small Volkswagen investments in Belgium.

105. Reuters, "European Commission and Germany Head for Clash Over Subsidies," 7 April 1989, AM cycle.

106. Krish Bhaskar and the Motor Industry Research Unit, *The Effect of Different Aid Measures on Intra-Community Competition*, 12.

107. For example, see "European Commission reestablishes right to monitor state automobile aid," *AFX News*, 5 July 1995; Reuter Textline, "EU: Spain Attacks Commission Decision to Extend State Aid Framework to Car Sector," 21 September 1995; "EU probes Spanish state aid for motor industry," *AFX News*, 21 September 1995; "EU orders Spain to notify car sector state aid projects over 17 mln Ecu," *AFX News*, 20 December 1995; European Information Service, "State Aid: Commission's Extension of Motor Industry Aid Code Not Justified," *European Report* No. 2216, 16 April 1997.

108. Hancher et al., *EC State Aids*, 121–22.

109. "EU's Wolf-Mathies to look at ways of preventing plant transfers for subsidies," *AFX News*, 10 March 1997; David Gow, "Euro Eye: First Shots in a Long and Bloody Battle Over Jobs," *The Guardian*, 15 March 1997, 22.

110. Data on "State aid cases under the EC Framework to the motor vehicle industry" kindly provided by Terence Whaley, DG IV Information Officer, electronic transfer, 27 May 1997.

111. For a general discussion of the early 1980s aid code—often called the "Davignon Plan"—see *Fifteenth Report on Competition Policy*, points 177–81. On the 1993 plan and its collapse, see *Twenty-fourth Report on Competition Policy*, point 365. Both are covered in Lionel Barber, Andrew Baxter, and Michael Lindemann, "Steel Back in the Melting Pot: The Collapse of the EU Rescue Plan for the Industry," *Financial Times*, 26 October 1994, 22.

112. On the new steel aid code, see Wolfgang Mederer, "State Aid: Summary of the most important recent developments," *Competition Policy Newsletter*, autumn/winter 1996, 46.

113. Hancher et al., *EC State Aids*, 125–27, 134; Mederer, "State Aid," 46–47. Shipbuilding is further complicated by the fact that there is an OECD agreement on aid to the industry. The most recent version of this agreement, designed as a binding treaty to take effect in July 1996, is in limbo because the United States has yet to ratify it. See OECD-DSTI-Shipbuilding, "The Agreement Respecting Normal Competitive Conditions in the Commercial Shipbuilding and Repair Industry—

Overview," available at: <http://www.oecd.org/dsti/sid/sp7.html>, and Mederer, "State Aid," 46.

114. Personal communication with Richard Jacques, office of the Permanent Representative of the United Kingdom to the European Union, Brussels, 20 May 1998.

115. Ronayne, *Disciplining Industrial Incentives*, 86–87, 106.

116. Edward M. Graham and Mark A. A. Warner, "Multinationals and Competition Policy in North America," in *Multinationals in North America,* ed. Lorraine Eden (Calgary: University of Calgary Press, 1994), 479.

117. Data for 1981–86 calculated from *Second Survey on State Aid*, Annex I, Table X B (a revision of data from the *First Survey*); 1986–88 data calculated from *Second Survey on State Aid*, Annex IV, 2–13; 1988–90 data drawn from *Fourth Survey on State Aid*, Table 7; 1990–92 data from *Fifth Survey on State Aid*, Table 7; 1992–96 data from *Sixth Survey on State Aid*, Table 9; 1995–97 data from *Seventh Survey on State Aid*, Table 9. Note that these figures include steel and shipbuilding, which were extremely high in the early 1980s and have been the focus of other sectoral frameworks. Without steel and shipbuilding, the figure for 1981–86 falls to 16 percent and the figure for 1986–88 falls to 20 percent (*Second Survey on State Aid*, Table IX).

118. *Seventh Survey on State Aid*, Table 9.

119. *Seventh Survey on State Aid*, Annex Table A.

120. *Second Report on Competition Policy*, points 100–03.

121. *Second Report on Competition Policy*, points 102–03.

122. *Fourth Report on Competition Policy*, points 171–74.

123. *Sixth Report on Competition Policy*, points 237–38.

124. *Eighth Report on Competition Policy*, point 210.

125. *Ninth Report on Competition Policy*, point 195. The Commission did say that it would confirm that the amount of aid going for existing employees was not disproportionate and that the aid was not being concentrated in particular industries to an extent liable to affect intra-Community trade.

126. *Fifteenth Report on Competition Policy*, point 218. See also the Gatsios and Seabright quote below.

127. *Second Survey on State Aid*, Table IX. These figures exclude aid to steel and shipbuilding.

128. CEC, *Competition Law in the European Communities,* Volume II, 134–37; *Fifteenth Report on Competition Policy*, point 218; Hancher et al., *EC State Aids*, 222.

129. Hancher et al., *EC State Aids*, 219. Data on number of cases, Article 93(2) procedures, and the lack of negative decisions are from *Twenty-Fourth Report on Competition Policy*, point 383.
130. For more information on these negotiations and the U.S. flip-flop, see Robert O'Brien, *Subsidy Regulation and State Transformation* (London: Macmillan, 1997), 119–21.
131. *Twenty-fifth Report on Competition Policy*, point 201.
132. *Second Survey on State Aid*, Table IX; *Third Survey on State Aid*, Table 6; *Fourth Survey on State Aid*, Table 6; *Fifth Survey on State Aid*, Table 6; *Sixth Survey on State Aid*, Table 8; *Seventh Survey on State Aid*, Table 9. Note that the 1981–88 data of the *Second Survey* exclude aid to steel and shipbuilding.
133. Information on total nonnotified cases was tabulated from the *Twenty-Fifth* through the *Twenty-Seventh Report on Competition Policy*, "List of state aid cases in sectors other than agriculture, fisheries, transport and the coal industry." Discussion of some of these cases comes from case summaries in *Twenty-fifth Report on Competition Policy*, 235–37. Except for the Dutch case in 1996, all of these proposed aids were approved by the Commission without opening the Article 93(2) procedure.
134. For Van Miert's comments on R&D aid, see Emma Tucker, "Cresson Halts EU Block on State Aid to Chips Venture," *Financial Times*, 20 June 1997, 2. Italy later withdrew the proposed aid after it became apparent the Commission would not approve it. On Hoffman-LaRoche, see "European Commission Rejects Austrian Aid Proposal," *Pharmaceutical Manufacturing Review*, June 1997, 38.
135. Bureau of National Affairs, "Sutherland Reflects on Success and Setbacks in EC Competition Policy," *Antitrust and Trade Regulation Report* 56, no. 1403 (16 February 1989): 253.
136. Buraff Publications, "State Aids: Brussels Faces Tough Task in Controlling State Subsidies," *1992—The External Impact of European Unification*, Vol. 1, no. 6, p. 5. On the extent to which subsidies might substitute for the reduction of trade barriers more generally, see André Blais, *A Political Sociology of Public Aid to Industry* (Toronto: University of Toronto Press, 1986).
137. Compare Konstantine Gatsios and Paul Seabright, "Regulation in the European Community," *Oxford Review of Economic Policy* 5, no. 2 (1989): 56.
138. James Flynn, "State Aid and Self-Help," *European Law Review* 8 (1983): 307–08.
139. The Maastricht Treaty empowered the Commission to propose fines to the ECJ for member states that violated their treaty obligations

(which includes following the state aid rules and complying with ECJ decisions upholding Commission decisions).

140. *Thirteenth Report on Competition Policy*, point 226.

141. Cini, "Policing the Internal Market," 328, 343 n. 50.

142. The law under which the aid was given specifically stated that aids that were not approved by the Commission would not be granted. See Andrew Evans and Stephen Martin, "Socially Acceptable Distortion of Competition: Community Policy on State Aid," *European Law Review* 16, no. 2 (1991): 79–111. Except as noted, the following account draws on their treatment of this case on pages 86–91.

143. Schina, *State Aids Under the EEC Treaty*, 156.

144. Schina, *State Aids Under the EEC Treaty*, 45.

145. Evans and Martin, "Socially Acceptable Distortion of Competition," 90.

146. Cini, "Policing the Internal Market," 347. Note, however, that she is incorrect to suggest that the case is ironic because the aid to Philip Morris would now be considered exempt under the Commission's *de minimis* rules. Although the aid intensity of under 4 percent would meet one test of these rules, the several million dollars in absolute level of aid was far above the 100,000 ECU maximum allowed under the rule.

147. Schina, *State Aids Under the EEC Treaty*, 25. Except as otherwise noted, this paragraph relies on her analysis (pages 25–26).

148. Schina, *State Aids Under the EEC Treaty*, 25.

149. Evans and Martin, "Socially Acceptable Distortion of Competition," 89.

150. Malcolm Ross, "A Review of Developments in State Aids 1987-88," *Common Market Law Review* 26 (1989), 179.

151. This case involved a below-market rate loan given to a brewery. Nowadays, the Commission even posts the disputed interest rate, known as the "reference rate," on its Web site.

152. *Twenty-fourth Report on Competition Policy*, point 491.

153. Quoted in Schina, *State Aids Under the EEC Treaty*, 163.

154. Schina gives some very vague reasons why this was the case: ". . . either because of practical or social problems or for reasons of public policy. . . ." Strangely, her citations on this point all come from European Parliamentary questions that precede this court decision (Schina, *State Aids Under the EEC Treaty*, 164, including notes 78–80). More likely, I suggest, is that the onset of the recession after 1973's oil price hikes led the Commission to be more willing to approve state aid and consequently less concerned with strict enforcement of the rules. Regarding the increases in aid given in the late 1970s—though no good quantification exists—see Cini, "Policing the Internal Market," 246.

155. CEC, *Competition Law in the European Communities*, Volume II: Rules applicable to state aids (situation at 31 December 1989), 36.

156. The quote is from *Twelfth Report on Competition Policy*, Introduction, 11; the discussion of the focus is from *Fifteenth Report on Competition Policy*, point 171.

157. Ross, "A Review of Developments in State Aids 1987-88," 187–88.

158. See Schina, *State Aids Under the EEC Treaty*, 166; Hancher et al., *EC State Aids*, 511–12.

159. Ross, "A Review of Developments in State Aids 1987-88," 181.

160. Ross, "A Review of Developments in State Aids 1987-88," 188.

161. Hancher et al., *EC State Aids*, 252, 487–92. This position was upheld by the ECJ in September 1994; see Wolfgang Mederer, "Summary of the most important recent developments (state aid)," *Competition Policy Newsletter*, autumn/winter 1996, 50.

162. *Twenty-Fifth Report on Competition Policy*, point 154, n. 87.

163. *Twenty-Fifth Report on Competition Policy*, point 154, covers the case through the ruling of the CFI. On the ECJ's upholding of the decision, see "Court Dismisses Textilwerke Challenge to State Aid Decision," Reuter European Community Report, 15 May 1997.

164. *Twenty-Fourth Report on Competition Policy*, 519; European Information Service, "Commission Outlaws Italian Law on State Aid for Bankrupt Firms," *European Report*, 16 March 1996. On Italy's bad record of compliance with Commission decisions in general, see Maria Mendrinou, "Non-Compliance and the European Commission's Role in Integration," *Journal of European Public Policy*, March 1996, figure 2.

165. *Twenty-Eighth Report on Competition Policy*, point 288.

166. Piet Jan Slot, "Facts, procedure and comments in Case C-301/87," *European Law Review* 16 (1991): 38–40, 42–43.

167. Piet Jan Slot, "Procedural Aspects of State Aids: The Guardian of Competition Versus the Subsidy Villains?" *Common Market Law Review* 27 (1990): 759–60.

168. Slot, "Facts, procedure and comments in Case C-301/87," 45–56.

169. Slot, "Facts, procedure and comments in Case C-301/87," 41–42.

170. Slot, "Facts, procedure and comments in Case C-301/87," 42–44.

171. Slot, "Facts, procedure and comments in Case C-301/87," 45–46.

172. K. P. E. Lasok, "The Commission's Powers Over Illegal State Aids," *European Competition Law Review* 11, no. 3 (1990): 127.

173. See the discussion of *Boussac* in *Twentieth Report on Competition Policy*, point 172, and of the Commission's use of those powers in the *Pari*

Mutuel Urbain case in *Twenty-First Report on Competition Policy*, point 274.

174. *Twenty-Fifth Report on Competition Policy*, point 155.

175. See "Commission Asks Italy to Suspend Aid to Restructuring of the Road Haulage Sector and Requests Further Information," RAPID press release IP/96-364, 30 April 1996.

176. Wolfgang Mederer, "The Future of State Aid Control," *Competition Policy Newsletter*, autumn/winter 1996, 12.

177. Personal communication with Commission official, Brussels, 18 May 1998.

178. Personal communication with Richard Jaques, office of the Permanent Representative of the United Kingdom to the European Union, Brussels, 20 May 1998. According to Wolfgang Mederer, in late 1996, "80 state aid cases [were] pending before the courts, the majority of them brought to court by competitors"; "The Future of State Aid Control," 13. For information on *Sytraval*, see "Business and the Law: Decision on French Aid Annulled—European Court," *Financial Times*, 3 October 1995, 13; and "Commission's Duties on State Aid Clarified," *Financial Times*, 21 April 1998, 24.

179. The entire (draft) regulation can be obtained at the DG IV Web site, <http://europa.eu.int/comm/dg04/lawaid/en/98com73.htm>. See also European Information Service, "EU Approves Changes to Procedural Regulations," *European Report* No. 2393, 24 March 1999.

180. As one official told the *Financial Times*, "The Commission has never been able to recover aid in Germany more quickly than eight years." Emma Tucker, "Boost for Brussels Over Illegal State Aid," *Financial Times*, 16 November 1998, 4.

181. European Information Service, "State Aid: Commission and Council at Loggerheads over Tighter State Aid Rules," *European Report* No. 2314, 9 May 1998; personal communication with Commission official, Brussels, 18 May 1998.

182. Tucker, "Boost for Brussels Over Illegal State Aid"; Council of Ministers Press Release, PRES 98/381, 22 January 1999, "2133rd Council meeting INDUSTRY Brussels, 16 November 1998."

183. Telephone interview, 22 March 1999.

184. "UNICE Disappointed with Proposed State Aid Rules," *European Report* No. 2293, 21 February 1998; personal communication with Eric Berggren, UNICE, 23 March 1999.

185. *Fourteenth Report on Competition Policy*, point 199.

186. CEC, *Competition Law in the European Communities,* Vol. II, 146–48.

187. Ballantyne and Bachtler, *Regional Policy Under Scrutiny*, 40 and Appendix pp. 5–7. On Greece, see *Eighteenth Report on Competition Policy*, point 168.
188. This point is emphasized by Ballantyne and Bachtler, *Regional Policy Under Scrutiny*, 40; Knox, *Towards 1992*, 76.
189. Cini, "Policing the Internal Market," 229.
190. Cini, "Policing the Internal Market," 246–54.
191. Fiona Wishlade, *When Are Tax Advantages State Aids and When Are They General Measures?* Regional and Industrial Policy Research Paper, Number 20, European Policies Research Centre, June 1997, 5 n. 1.
192. "New Resolve to Control State Aids," *Financial Times Business Law Brief*, April 1989; Cini, "Policing the Internal Market," 260–61; *Nineteenth Report on Competition Policy*, point 121.
193. CEC, "Fair Competition in the Internal Market: Community State Aid Policy," *European Economy* 48 (September 1991): 71. See also Cini, "Policing the Internal Market," 260–61.
194. *Second Survey on State Aid*, Table IX; *Fifth Survey on State Aid*, 17; *Sixth Survey on State Aid*, Table 8.
195. The 80 percent figure is given in *Eighteenth Report on Competition Policy*, point 169. The same volume makes reference to Article 93(1) reviews in 1988 for Belgium, The Netherlands, and Portugal at points 175, 182, and 184, respectively.
196. *Twenty-sixth Report on Competition Policy*, 345; *Twenty-seventh Report on Competition Policy*, 356; *Twenty-eighth Report on Competition Policy*, 343.
197. Gatsios and Seabright, "Regulation in the European Community," 56.
198. After the Treaty of Amsterdam, this became Article 295. See note 3 in Chapter 3.
199. "The Aid Plague," *Economist* Survey of Business in Europe, 8 June 1991, 17.
200. This account is drawn from points 122–25.
201. Point 124.
202. Point 124.
203. CEC, *Competition Law in the European Communities,* Vol. II, 23. This Directive appears on pages 23–26.
204. Several sectors of the economy were excluded from the original Directive but were later included in a 1985 amendment. See Hancher et al., *EC State Aids*, 159.
205. A. H. Hermann, "The EEC power struggle," *Financial Times*, 13 July 1982, 2.

206. Hancher et al., *EC State Aids*, 160–161. A Communication is a weaker legal instrument than a Directive.

207. *Twenty-third Report on Competition Policy*, point 399.

208. This account comes from David Buchan, "Brussels Threatens to Cut State Subsidies to European Industry," *Financial Times*, 10 March 1989, 18; Reuters, "EC Commissioner Outlines Areas of Aid Review," BC Cycle, 31 March 1989; "New Resolve to Control State Aids," *Business Law Brief*, April 1989; and Jonathan Kapstein, " 'Subsidy' Becomes a Dirty Word," *Business Week*, 19 June 1989, 48. For more detail on aspects of this policy review beyond its effects on state-owned firms, see Cini, "Policing the Internal Market," 254–62.

209. David Gardner, "EC loses state aid case: Court rules against closer public sector scrutiny," *Financial Times*, 17 June 1993. This estimate appears to count 1 ECU of capital injection as equal to 1 ECU of grant, however, when in fact the (net or gross) grant equivalent of capital injections often is far below that of grants. On the other hand, determining just how much below is a tedious process, underscoring the fact that capital injections are a very non-transparent form of aid.

210. Cini, "Policing the Internal Market," 218.

211. "The Aid Plague," *Economist* Survey of Business in Europe, 8 June 1991, 16.

212. *Twenty-Second Report on Competition Policy*, point 425.

213. Trevor Soames and Alan Ryan, "State Aid and Air Transport," *European Competition Law Review* 5 (1995): 290.

214. "The Aid Plague," 16.

215. *Eighteenth Report on Competition Policy*, point 227.

216. Peter Cope, "1992: The Anxieties of the Motor Sector," *European Trends* no. 4 (1988), 53; *Nineteenth Report on Competition Policy*, point 187. See also Krish Bhaskar and the Motor Industry Research Unit, *The Effect of Different Aid Measures on Intra-Community Competition, Exemplified by the Case of the Automotive Industry*, Commission of the European Communities Document, March 1990, 16–18.

217. On the Brittan-Delors split, see Cini, "Policing the Internal Market," 217. For the final decision, see *Twentieth Report on Competition Policy*, point 259.

218. Stephen Wilks and Lee McGowan offer a similar assessment in "Competition Policy in the European Union: Creating a Federal Agency?" in *Comparative Competition Policy: National Institutions in a Global Market,* ed. G. Bruce Doern and Stephen Wilks (Oxford: Clarendon Press, 1996), 257–58. Wilks and McGowan regard Van Miert as "more

conciliatory" than Brittan, at least as strict in most areas of competition policy, but "pragmatic" in state aid control.

219. Soames and Ryan, "State Aid and Air Transport," 290.

220. Samer Iskandar and Michael Skapinker, "BA Angered at Outcome of Air France Subsidy Ruling," *Financial Times*, 23 July 1998, 26; Agence France Presse, "EU Commission Strengthens Arguments to Justify Rescue of Air France," 22 July 1998.

221. "Spanish subsidies"; "Airlines: The Sky's the Limit for Iberia following Political Accord," *Transport Europe*, 19 January 1996; "Iberia Cash Infusion Shows European State Aid Still Flowing," *Airline Financial News*, 5 February 1996.

222. Soames and Ryan, "State Aid and Air Transport," 308.

223. *Twenty-Fifth Report on Competition Policy*, 226. The CFI effectively upheld this decision in February 1997, holding—contrary to the Commission—that the tax benefits the Postal Service enjoyed did constitute state aid but that it was legitimate insofar as it was less than the cost of its public service obligations. See "French State Aid Lawful," *Financial Times*, 4 March 1997, 14.

224. "Financing of Public TV in Portugal: No aid involved," *Competition Policy Newsletter*, autumn/winter 1996, 48.

225. Alasdair Murray, "Monti Signals Intent to Attack All State Subsidies," *The Times* (London), 2 September 1999.

226. As Cini, "Policing the Internal Market," 283, n. 33, notes, "Complaints are the lifeblood of the directorate." This is equally true whether the aid recipient is public or private.

227. As noted, for example, by James Flynn, "State Aid and Self Help," 312.

228. *Twenty-eighth Report on Competition Policy*, Table 4.

5

The North American Nonregimes

Whereas the EU has developed a well-institutionalized policy for dealing with state aid (see Chapter 4), in North America there has been virtually no policy to address the competition for investment. The lack of a policy does not mean that there is no recognition of the problems that result from bidding wars for investment. Indeed, these problems are widely recognized by state and provincial officials, quasi-governmental organizations such as the National Governors' Association, and nongovernmental organizations (NGOs) across the political spectrum. For the most part, however, this recognition has not translated into an institutionalized response.

This situation highlights the features of the rising-n-person prisoners' dilemma model (see Chapter 2). In the United States, the actors include fifty states and countless county and municipal governments that are involved in investment attraction. For any particular project, rising levels of capital mobility have increased the number of feasible sites seeking it—the "rising-n" of RNPD. In Canada, there are only ten provinces, and subprovincial governments are for the most part forbidden from offering location subsidies. These differences may help explain why Canada has a Code of Conduct on Incentives whereas the United States does not. Nevertheless, because of falling transport and communications costs and the signing of several trade agreements with the United States, Canadian provinces are subject to the same dynamic: They need to cooperate with a growing number of potential competitor sites for investment.

The institutional vacuum is most pronounced in the United States. Despite substantial funds devoted to subsidizing business activity at the federal, state, and local levels, there is almost no federal legislation that controls it. One major reform came in the 1986 Tax Reform Act, which capped the use of Industrial Revenue Bonds (which provide subsidized finance) at the state level.[1] Several battles have been fought to ban the use of federal funds to lure firms from one state to another. Such anti-piracy bans exist for Small Business Association (SBA) and

Economic Development Administration (EDA) programs, Community Development Block Grant (CDBG) funds, Puerto Rico Industrial Tax Exemption Act subsidies (which provide indirect control over Section 936 tax breaks), and Workforce Investment Act (formerly Job Training Partnership Act, JTPA) funds—though the latter appears to be widely violated. Many of these reforms owe their existence to battles over subsidized relocations. As Greg LeRoy, a participant in many of these campaigns, states, "Behind every reform, there lies a horror story—a company that failed to deliver or a company that got subsidies but then did something to offend the public."[2]

At the regional level, there have been two voluntary attempts by groups of states to reduce competition for investment among themselves—one in the Midwest and one among Connecticut, New York, and New Jersey. The failure of these efforts underlines the argument that competition for investment is a prisoners' dilemma in need of a third-party solution. Some states, however, have reduced competition for investment among their municipalities by banning local tax abatements.

The real story of the politics of controlling investment competition in the United States is at the NGO level. There probably are scores of groups, in Washington and in most states, that actively organize against "corporate welfare."[3] As we will see, not all of these groups are motivated by the same critique of state aid to corporations: Many—perhaps most—are motivated by equity concerns, but more conservative groups focus on efficiency problems associated with subsidies, and environmental groups focus on subsidies that encourage environmentally unsound practices. Yet these groups often have worked together to eliminate subsidy programs they agree should be cut—proving beyond any doubt the old adage, "Politics makes strange bedfellows." At the state level, a wide range of organizations has been active in a variety of campaigns to improve disclosure, accountability, the environmental performance of firms receiving subsidies, and the wages paid by such companies.

In Canada, the most important exception to the general dearth of policies for controlling bidding for investment is contained in the 1994 Agreement on Internal Trade: a first-ever Code of Conduct on Incentives. Most significantly, the code bans the offering of subsidies to firms relocating from one province to another. It also urges provinces not to engage in bidding wars, though this latter provision does not have force of law. In addition, most provinces have banned local governments from awarding any location subsidies to firms (Ontario may be strictest)—a practice they call "bonusing."

Nongovernmental organizing against "corporate welfare" in Canada appears to be growing as well. Originally it was a preserve of the Left, but there has been growing involvement by business interests (especially small business) in recent years. The New Democratic Party (NDP) made corporate welfare the theme of its 1972 parliamentary campaign and remains active on issues of tax equity. The NDP's status as a minority party nationally has reduced its impact on these issues at the federal level, however, although it has had some provincial successes. Other Canadian critics of subsidies to business come from the labor movement and social justice organizations, small business, and taxpayers' groups.

Canada also has a history of failed voluntary cooperation among provinces. According to Mark Ronayne, such efforts in Atlantic Canada and the western provinces "have been largely ineffective."[4]

This chapter begins by making an estimate of subsidies provided in the United States and Canada, highlighting the fact that there are no data comparable to those generated by the EU (see Chapter 6). It then discusses federal controls on state and local subsidies, as well as two failed attempts at voluntary state cooperation. Next, the discussion turns to the rich history of popular response to corporate welfare, reviewing federal and state campaigns on these issues. The focus then turns to Canada, considering governmental action (especially the 1994 Agreement on Internal Trade) and NGO efforts to rein in subsidies to business.

Dimensions of (Quasi) State Aid in North America

In international trade negotiations, the United States has always portrayed itself as a low-subsidy country, and trade analysts often accept this view uncritically.[5] The U.S. position would appear to be true on the basis of national accounts definitions of subsidy, as Table 5-1 shows.

National accounts statistics do not include tax expenditures, however, and the United States uses tax expenditures for industrial support far more than other industrialized countries do.[6] Thus, the figures in Table 5-1 are very misleading. The amount of subsidization in the United States is open to some dispute (see below) as a result of different

Table 5-1 **Subsidies by National Accounts Definitions, Percentage of GDP**

	U.S.	Canada	Japan	EU-15	EC-12[a]
1960	0.24	0.80	0.53	1.40	1.42
1965	0.44	0.86	0.71	1.67[b]	1.75
1970	0.49	0.94	1.10	2.07	2.18
1975	0.32	2.47	1.49	2.69	2.74
1980	0.39	2.68	1.50	2.85	2.87
1985	0.56	2.44	1.14	2.98	2.98
1990	0.52	1.66	1.09	2.50	2.45
1994	0.50	1.47	0.88	2.45	2.39[c]
1996	0.45	1.11	0.75	2.22	—

[a]Without Austria, Finland, and Sweden.

[b]1966.

[c]1993 (the last year for which the OECD calculated EC-12 rather than EU-15; EU-15 for 1993 was 2.55 percent).

Note: This table uses OECD data based on current prices and 1990 exchange rates to the U.S. dollar.

Sources: Except for EC-12 and 1996: 1960, 1966–94, data are calculated from OECD, *National Accounts, Vol. 1 (1960–94)* (Paris: OECD, 1996); data for 1965 and EC-12 are calculated from OECD, *National Accounts, Vol. 1 (1960–93)* (Paris: OECD, 1995). Data for 1996 are calculated from OECD, *National Accounts, Vol. 1 (1960–96)* (Paris: OECD, 1998).

definitions of what should count as a subsidy or tax expenditure and what treatment to give to broad-gauged programs such as accelerated depreciation. This section therefore attempts to clarify the amount of business support provided in the United States and Canada.

United States

There is nothing in the United States comparable to the EU's *Surveys* on state aid, which aggregate data at the national and subnational levels in Europe. We must therefore sift through several estimates of support to business to consider their plausibility and determine how comparable they are to EU data. At the federal level, a small number of studies by the Congressional Budget Office (CBO) and the Joint Committee on Taxation (JCT) form the basis for most estimates on corporate subsidization, thereby reducing many of the differences in estimates of "corporate welfare" to ideology. At the state level and below, there are no consistent estimates for all fifty states; indeed, there are none covering as many as fifteen states.[7] Only about a dozen states produce highly detailed tax expenditure budgets. As a result, analysts have had to rely far too much on press reports of individual large investment packages,[8] and the estimates that can be derived for total subsidization at the state and substate level are not nearly as accurate as those for the federal level.

Calculating Federal Subsidization

The U.S. federal government often seems little interested in knowing the full extent of business subsidies. Not only has there never been an effort such as that represented by the EU's *Surveys* on state aid, the only times that relatively comprehensive data on business support have been produced are those in which there was a popular perception of unfairness to individual taxpayers. The early 1980s was one such period because the 1981 tax reforms sharply reduced the business tax burden and caused a proliferation of business tax avoidance schemes. In response, the CBO published *Federal Support of U.S. Business* in 1984. The CBO did not revisit the issue until 11½ years later, when a wide variety of NGOs across the political spectrum were calling for an end to "corporate welfare." The publication of *Federal Financial Support of Business* in 1995 offers the best recent benchmark for measuring business support and, along with two other federal reports,[9] forms the ultimate basis for current estimates of "corporate welfare."

One other federal source is noteworthy—though unhelpful. Under the 1994 General Agreement on Tariffs and Trade, GATT members were required to report their subsidies to the newly formed WTO (see Chapter 7). After two rounds of notifications, however, substantial shortcomings remain for the purposes of this book. Many federal programs reported in the CBO exercise are omitted because the United States contends that these programs do not constitute "subsidies" as defined by the Agreement on Subsidies and Countervailing Measures. Furthermore, although the United States reports state-level subsidies in the most recent notification, very few of the programs that are included have associated expenditures provided.[10] Therefore, the U.S. WTO notification is not considered here, although Chapter 7 discusses it further in the context of the development of the GATT/WTO subsidies regime. Instead, the focus here is on estimates made by NGOs on the basis of the main federal studies mentioned above.

NGOs whose work on "corporate welfare" is most useful include the Center for the Study of Responsive Law/Essential Information (EI—organized by Ralph Nader), the Cato Institute (a libertarian think tank), the Progressive Policy Institute (PPI—a think tank affiliated with the centrist Democratic Leadership Council and once chaired by then-Governor of Arkansas Bill Clinton), Citizens for Tax Justice (CTJ), and the Center on Budget and Policy Priorities (CBPP). The estimates range from $46.6 billion a year (PPI) to $167 billion annually (EI). By making adjustments to the estimates to bring them closer to EU and OECD concepts of subsidization, however, we can narrow the gap considerably; we find that estimates of federal corporate welfare fall into a fairly narrow range. This section analyzes the estimates of EI, the Cato Institute, PPI, Citizens for Tax Justice, and CBPP.[11] The discussion begins with the raw estimates of each group, as shown in Table 5-2.[12]

To put these figures in context, we can compute them as a percentage of U.S. GDP ($7,253.8 billion in 1995) and compare them with similar data for EU state aid. The foregoing figures correspond to a range from 0.64 percent of GDP for the PPI estimate to 2.30 percent of GDP for the EI estimate. By comparison, in the EU, total "state aid" (which includes direct subsidies, tax expenditures, soft loans, etc.) in 1995–97 was 1.2 percent of GDP.[13]

The spread among the estimates is smaller than the raw numbers in Table 5-2 show, however, in large part because the numbers are "derivative" inasmuch as they are all based on a small set of mostly federal reports, as noted above.[14] The various estimates agree on a

Table 5-2 **Raw Estimates of Federal Corporate Welfare (billions of dollars per year)**

Group	Estimate
Essential Information	167.2
Center on Budget and Policy Priorities	100.0
Cato Institute	87.3[a]
Citizens for Tax Justice	69.2[b]
Progressive Policy Institute	47.7

[a]Direct subsidies only; no tax expenditures.
[b]Tax expenditures only; no direct subsidies.

Sources: See note 11.

Table 5-3 **Largest Federal Programs Identified by CBO (excluding accelerated depreciation and agriculture)**

Program	**1995 Amount ($)**
Tax expenditures	
Reduced rates on first $10 million of corporate taxable income	3.9 billion
Tax credit for corporations with income from U.S. possessions	3.7 billion
Exception to source rule for sale of inventory property	3.5 billion
Tax credit for low-income housing	2.2 billion
Special treatment of life insurance companies' reserves	2.1 billion
Spending programs	
National Institutes of Health—applied biomedical research	3.7 billion
Department of Energy—technology development for new energy sources	3.4 billion
Community Development Block Grants	0.5 billion
Technology Reinvestment Project	0.5 billion

Source: Federal Financial Support of Business, Tables 2 and 3.

large proportion of the items they label "corporate welfare," so it is possible to focus on the main deviations of each.

First, however, it is useful to identify the largest federal programs, which are generally cited by most of the organizations whose individual estimates are discussed below. Table 5-3 shows the five largest federal tax expenditure programs and four largest spending programs listed by the CBO (excluding accelerated depreciation, which is discussed separately).

To begin with the highest estimate, several of the "corporate welfare" programs identified by EI—including by far the largest one—entail failures of the government to collect taxes that have never been collected before, including taxes on water and air pollutants and on ozone-depleting chemicals not currently taxed totaling $3.8 billion, $55.1 billion, and $0.2 billion, respectively. I deduct them from the EI estimate because they are not comparable to other existing state

Table 5-4 **Adjustments to Essential Information Estimate (billions of dollars)**

Category	Amount
Original estimate	167.2
Impose minimum tax on foreign-owned businesses	0.2
Raise marginal tax rates on corporations	3.9
Failure to collect taxes from large corporations	4.5
Failure to collect taxes from small corporations and sole proprietors	6.0
Impose excise taxes on water pollutants	3.8
Impose excise taxes on air pollutants	55.1
Tax additional ozone-depleting chemicals	0.2
Total adjustments	73.7
Revised estimate	93.5

aid/subsidy measures—though it is not beyond imagination that a failure to impose such taxes could someday be considered a subsidy. A Canadian trade expert once suggested that this approach might well be a natural evolution of international trade law on subsidies. Table 5-4 summarizes adjustments to the EI estimates.

The second-highest raw estimate, from CBPP, is closest to the main federal sources cited above. CBPP points out that the government estimates in *Federal Financial Support of Business* are conservative. "In comparing its list of business subsidy programs with the lists prepared by the Progressive Policy Institute, the Cato Institute, and the Heritage Foundation, CBO found that 'generally, CBO's tally is the most conservative, mainly because it includes only programs with a stated business focus whereas the other studies include programs that may help business but have no such stated focus.' "[15] CBPP thus accepts the CBO's estimate of $30 billion in spending programs[16] and $68 billion in tax expenditures, adding a further $2 billion identified by Rep. Bill Archer (R-Tex.), Chairman of the House Ways and Means Committee. Because of the close adherence of CBPP figures to CBO figures, I leave the former unadjusted.

The Cato Institute estimates differ the most from the others. As noted in Table 5-2, they do not include any tax expenditures. The reason is that Cato "reject(s) the notion that allowing a company to keep its earnings and pay less in taxes is somehow a 'subsidy.' " Moore and Stansel instead suggest that all of the tax expenditures identified

Table 5-5 **Adjustments to Cato Institute Estimate (millions of dollars)**

Program	Amount
Original estimate	87,300.0
Research and development to university researchers	11,641.0
Independent agencies[a]	4,211.0
Department of Transportation[b]	13,321.4
Department of Labor	5,622.1
U.S. Geological Survey	547.6
Public housing construction	413.0
U.S. Army Corps of Engineers	2,872.9
U.S. Department of Defense[c]	13,047.3
National Oceanic and Atmospheric Administration	1,126.1
Department of Agriculture foreign assistance	1,067.6
Total adjustments	53,870.0
Revised estimate	33,430.0

[a]Cato estimate minus $308 million listed in CBO study.
[b]Cato estimate minus two subsidies listed in CBO study.
[c]Cato estimate minus Advanced Research Project Agency (ARPA) subsidy listed in CBO study.

by PPI should be eliminated in conjunction with a tax cut, "on a revenue-neutral basis, or as a net tax cut."[17] According to Stansel, "The Left wants to close tax loopholes, but if that's all you do, it's a tax hike."[18] In addition, the Cato study targets for elimination numerous whole programs—many apparently on the grounds that they should be privatized (for example, $8.7 billion for the Federal Aviation Administration). The report also targets weapons procurement, training for employees, basic research performed at universities, and cleanup of Department of Energy facilities. Finally, according to the CBO report, "Moore and Stansel double-counted (and in some cases triple-counted) some federal technology programs."[19] Table 5-5 categorizes $50 billion in adjustments that remove items that are not considered state aid in the EU and would put Cato in the same ballpark with the other estimates, if tax expenditures are included. More detailed analysis would probably reduce the Cato estimate further.

This revised Cato estimate of $33.4 billion, if added to the $68 billion in tax expenditure the CBO found, would put Cato in the same range as the other estimates.

CTJ estimates business and investment tax expenditures provided to corporations of $69.2 billion in fiscal 1996. As noted in Table 5-2, this figure does not include an estimate of spending subsidies; this approach arises from the group's focus on tax policy rather than from an ideological choice (as in the case of Cato). If we add the CBO's $30 billion estimate of positive subsidies to the CTJ estimate, we arrive at a figure of $99.2 billion—virtually the same as the CBPP estimate (they rely on the same sources).

PPI lists $26.1 billion in spending subsidies and $21.6 billion in tax subsidies for fiscal year 1998.[20] Where PPI differs most dramatically from groups such as EI, CBPP, and CTJ is in its treatment of accelerated depreciation (listed by CBO as worth $32.2 billion to corporations in 1995).[21] Adding this item alone would transform the PPI estimate to $79.9 billion. Other major subsidies that are included by CBO but not by PPI are reduced tax rates on the first $10 million in corporate income ($3.9 billion in 1995) and expensing (as opposed to capitalizing and then depreciating) up to $17,500 of capital assets in the year of purchase ($1.5 billion).[22] In all likelihood, these items would be considered state aid in the EU because they primarily benefit small businesses (SMEs, in EU parlance). Adding these two programs would raise the PPI estimate to $85.3 billion.

The issue of accelerated depreciation is central to calculations of federal-level subsidization of business because by itself it represents about 0.4 percent of GDP. Because the OECD measure of subsidies is only 0.50 percent (see Table 5-1), accelerated depreciation by itself substantially increases the observed federal level of support to business, even before we consider other programs. There are arguments for and against its inclusion from the standpoint of the present exercise, however. The most important consideration that favors inclusion is that generally available accelerated depreciation increases after-tax income and functions as a way to attract investment. The most important argument against including accelerated depreciation is that although *targeted* accelerated depreciation is considered state aid in the EU, *generally available* accelerated depreciation would not be. This situation contrasts with most of the programs identified by the CBO, which would be considered specific (but because of their nature as tax breaks, they tend to be automatic rather than discretionary). In the EU, however, such non-aid accelerated depreciation is probably far below 0.1 percent of GDP.[23] This latter fact leads me to believe that we should consider accelerated depreciation in the United States to be functionally equivalent to state aid because it attracts some investment that might go to other countries.[24] My estimate includes it—but in a fashion that allows it to be clearly separated for analysis if the reader wishes to do so.

Calculating State and Local Subsidization

Calculating the amount of state aid provided at the subfederal level in the United States is impossible. As at the federal level, the majority of aid to firms is provided through tax expenditures, and few states keep tax expenditure budgets in enough detail to identify support to enterprises. Moreover, many states jealously guard their data on overall subsidization precisely to avoid giving away information to other states for future bidding wars. Finally, below the state level there are literally thousands of government entities that themselves subsidize firms (again, usually through tax expenditures), and—except for Minnesota (as a result of 1995's "Corporate Welfare Law") and Maine (which should soon have such data after the November 1998 adoption of a law patterned on Minnesota's)—there is no tracking of their aid whatsoever. We are left with partial figures and educated guesses—to which we now reluctantly turn.

One review of tax expenditure budgets provided data for eleven states in the year 1992.[25] Based on the methodology described below, this review implied an estimate for state and local subsidies of about $30 billion annually.[26] More recent data on state-level subsidies, some of which use the Corporation for Enterprise Development's "Unified Economic Development Budget" methodology,[27] are listed in Table 5-6.[28]

Except for the four states in Table 5-6 where there is a significant proportion of local incentives in the estimate, estimates of local subsidies can only be an educated guess. Iris Lav of CBPP suggests that the ubiquity of local property tax abatements places total local spending at approximately the same level as state tax expenditures.[29] If this claim seems surprising, consider that in 1996, Cincinnati and Columbus, Ohio, plus the Columbus suburbs, provided more than $600 million in property tax abatements. Similarly, in Syracuse, New York, government support for industry averages $400 million per year.[30] The use of tax abatements varies among cities, but a few examples such as this rapidly bring the figures to the level of state tax expenditures. Accepting Lav's hypothesis, then, we can (very cautiously) double the state estimates for the four states in Table 5-6 without local estimates to represent these local tax abatements.

Table 5-6 **Estimates of State (or state/local) Corporate Subsidies, ca. 1996 ($ million)**

State	State Amount	State/Local Amount
California	3,143	6,286
Iowa	885	1,770
Louisiana		919
Massachusetts	755	1,510
Michigan		459
Minnesota		1,127
North Carolina	507	1,014
Ohio		1,500
Total		14,584

Sources: Author's calculations from sources in note 28. State-only numbers are doubled to generate state/local numbers when a state/local estimate is not available.

The real challenge for calculating state level subsidies is determining how to extrapolate the eight-state figure to the United States as a whole. I use share of U.S. GDP as the basis for this extrapolation, although that calculation is not ideal.[31] These eight states accounted for 29.9 percent of U.S. GDP in 1996,[32] which suggests an estimate of $48.8 billion in state and local subsidies. Although this figure may seem surprisingly high, the estimate left out some states that are known to have high subsidies (such as Kentucky) because of lack of available data, and for the most part it does not include accelerated depreciation (California is an exception, but accelerated depreciation there came to only $230 million). Moreover, as Fisher and Peters point out, "standing incentive offers are not trivial in comparison with the much publicized one-time deals."[33] We should not assume, then, that states that are left out of this estimate (which does include 30 percent of U.S. GDP) will differ sharply in their subsidy practices, although the possibility exists that there is some bias in these estimates (see note 31).

Summing Up U.S. Business Subsidization

Given the fragility of the data, my estimate of "state aid equivalent" support to firms in the United States must be very tentative. Nevertheless, even excluding accelerated depreciation, U.S. levels of subsidization clearly are comparable to those of EU member states (see Table

Table 5-7 **Total U.S. Business Subsidization ($ billion), 1995–1996**

Type	Amount
Federal accelerated depreciation	32.2
All other federal tax expenditures	35.8
Federal positive expenditures	30.1
State/local (extrapolated from Table 5-6)	48.8
Subtotal	146.9
(Less agriculture)	(15.6)
Grand total	131.3
Total without accelerated depreciation	99.1

Sources: Federal Financial Support of Business; Table 5-6.

6-2). If accelerated depreciation is included—as I believe it should be—the United States would fall in the upper range of EU state aid givers. Table 5-7 summarizes my federal, state, and local estimates.

The grand total in Table 5-7 excludes agriculture because virtually all agricultural aid in the United States is farm income support[34] that is most comparable to the EU's Common Agricultural Policy. CAP spending is not included in DG IV data of national state aid (national aid to agriculture is included in the state aid *Surveys*, but it is excluded from the calculation of aid as a percentage of GDP [see Table 6-2]), so it is excluded here to provide better comparability with EU data.

Overall, the data suggest that state aid or quasi-state aid in the United States ranges from $99.1 billion to $131.3 billion annually, depending on how one treats accelerated depreciation. This sum is not trivial. It equals 13.7–18.2 percent of 1995 gross fixed nonresidential investment (the state/local figure alone comes to 6.7 percent) of $723.0 billion. As a percentage of GDP, it represents 1.37–1.81 percent of 1995's figure of $7,253.8 billion. By comparison, state aid as a percentage of non-agricultural GDP in the EU for 1995–97 ranged from 0.43 percent in Finland to 1.71 percent in Italy, with an EU average of 1.20 percent.[35] At 1.81 percent, the United States would rank first of the sixteen countries (EU-15 + United States); at 1.37 percent, it would rank third, behind only Italy and Germany (see Table 6-2).

Again, the fragility of these data cannot be overemphasized. In particular, the estimate for local level support is poorly grounded; at the same time, there is no doubting the fact that local property tax abatements are used by literally thousands of jurisdictions. Until systematic reports of local business support are produced that rival the EU state aid *Surveys*, we are limited to educated guesses. The state-level data, though better grounded, may be subject to sampling bias because the states with the best tax expenditure budgets might have adopted them *because* they were perceived to have high tax expenditures. Ultimately, even if we accepted a substantial reduction in the estimate (on the order, say, of $10 billion), the range would be 1.23 percent to 1.67 percent of U.S. GDP—still comparable with Italy and Germany at the top of the EU range (*not* far below it, as national-accounts subsidies data would suggest). The common claim that the United States subsidizes industry much less than Europe does is a fiction.[36]

Canada

As with the United States, there is no comprehensive report of state aid in Canada that is comparable to the EU's *Surveys*.[37] Indeed, a 1995/96 report on incentives, mandated by the Agreement on Internal Trade, is confidential. Nevertheless, business support in Canada appears to be considerably more transparent than aid in the United States because Canada exhibits greater reliance on grants than tax expenditures.[38] Thus, national accounts data on subsidies will be more reliable for Canada than for the United States. Table 5-8 includes subsidies, capital transfers,[39] and federal tax expenditures.[40]

Besides subsidy reductions at the federal level, Progressive Conservative governments in Ontario and Alberta have sharply cut back on business assistance. Ontario cut grants to businesses by 43 percent between 1995–96 and 1996–97. By 1999, Premier Mike Harris claimed to have saved Ontario C$300 million in subsidies and declared that there would be no giveaways to the Ottawa Senators hockey team.[41] Alberta passed a Business Financial Assistance Limitations Act in 1996 that restricted the provincial government's ability to provide subsidies by requiring legislative approval to provide funds to business.[42]

One other important trend (not shown in these data) is the increasing proportion of support that comes from the provincial level as opposed to the federal level. As Ronayne shows, this trend dates at least to the 1980s.[43] Provincial subsidies first exceeded federal subsidies in 1990, and they have remained higher since 1992. Capital transfers

Table 5-8 **Corporate Subsidies, Capital Transfers, and Federal Tax Expenditures in Canada (billions of Canadian dollars)**

Year	Subsidies	Capital Transfers[a]	Tax Expend[b]	Total	GDP	% of GDP
1990	10.1	2.4	5.4	17.9	678.1	2.64
1991	12.9	2.7	4.8	20.4	683.2	2.99
1992	12.3	2.0	3.3	17.6	698.5	2.52
1993	10.4	1.5	4.0	15.9	725.0	2.19
1994	9.6	1.4	5.2	16.2	767.5	2.11
1995	8.7	1.6	6.0	16.3	807.1	2.02
1996	8.1	1.2	5.8	15.1	833.9	1.81
1997	8.6	1.2	6.3	16.1	873.9	1.84
1998	9.8	1.3	6.1	17.2	895.7	1.92

[a]This category includes the former category of "capital assistance" (grants related to capital formation), plus loan forgiveness and loan write-offs.
[b]Sum of separately estimated federal tax expenditures. This figure cannot take account of interactions, which would likely reduce the total if all relevant tax expenditures were abolished simultaneously. Figures for 1997 and 1998 are projections. The sources do not include estimates for accelerated depreciation.
Note: Totals may not sum because of rounding. Revised figures are used when available. Except for tax expenditures, all figures include federal, provincial, and local data.

Sources: Subsidies/capital transfers—personal communication, Dan Finnerty, Statistics Canada, 13 September 1999. Revised GDP data—personal communication, Dan Finnerty, Statistics Canada, 16 September 1999. Tax expenditures—OECD, *Tax Expenditures: Recent Experiences* (Paris: OECD, 1996), 46; Department of Finance, *Tax Expenditures 1999*; Department of Finance, *Tax Expenditures 1997.*

have fallen dramatically at the federal level over the 1990s; a plurality is now provided at the local level.[44]

Summary: Canada

Canadian subsidy levels historically have been higher than those in the United States. Recent declines have brought Canada down to the top of the range given for the United States above (i.e., including accelerated depreciation for the United States). The lack of Canadian data on accelerated depreciation means this comparison is not complete, however, suggesting that Canadian subsidy levels are still higher than in the United States—but by nowhere near as large a margin as the national accounts statistics of Table 5-1 would suggest.

Federal Subsidy Control in the United States

Peter K. Eisinger has outlined the main federal programs with an effect on state and local economic development in *The Rise of the Entrepreneurial State*.[45] The focus here is narrower: to cast light on the ways in which the federal government constrains subnational competition for investment in the United States. As Chapter 1 suggests, the federal government has done little to constrain competition for investment by state and local governments. There have been two types of federal intervention in this competition: regulation of industrial revenue bonds (IRBs, also known as industrial development bonds) beginning in 1968 and culminating in changes included as part of the Tax Reform Act of 1986 and inclusion of "anti-piracy" provisions in major federal programs that help fund state and local economic development efforts, which ban their use to induce firm relocation.

Competition for investment in the United States is rooted not in sovereignty, as in the EU, but in the American federal system.[46] As David B. Robertson and Dennis R. Judd write:

> Since [American state and local officials] have virtually no power to limit the movement of business out of their jurisdictions, they are especially reluctant to intrude on business, more willing to accommodate its needs, and more cautious about initiating public programs to rectify the risks and inequalities that result from market capitalism.[47]

The states have engaged in a wide variety of ways to compete for investment, including non-financial means such as passage of union-weakening "right-to-work" laws (which ban "closed shops") and weakening of workers' compensation laws to make them less expensive to business.[48] In fact, according to Earl Fry, "Between 1988 and 1993 three of every four higher-paying manufacturing jobs in the United States were created in the 21 states that have right-to-work laws but that only represent 35 percent of the nation's total population."[49] The focus of this book, however, is the financial incentives that states provide for investment; this chapter focuses on the relatively few ways in which the federal government has regulated these incentives.

The first type of regulation of financial incentives concerns IRBs. These instruments are tax-exempt bonds issued by state or local governments to lower the cost of borrowing for private investors. As with any other municipal or state bond, the interest is not taxed by the federal government, making it possible for the state or locality to offer lower interest rates than for taxable bonds. The first use of such bonds was Mississippi's issuance of a similar bond in 1936, although they did not become common until the 1970s.[50] As an inducement to business location, IRBs had numerous advantages for state and local officials:

> From the state and local point of view IRB financing was a nearly ideal program until the 1980s. The entire cost of the program was borne by the federal treasury in the form of foregone tax revenues. Decisions about the volume of bond activity, however, lay entirely with state and local officials. Even the administrative costs incurred by the issuing authority could be recovered through fees levied against the beneficiary firms. IRBs, therefore, offered subnational officials an essentially cost-free inducement to hold out to industry. But Congress eventually became concerned over the mounting size of a federal subsidy over whose volume it had no control.[51]

This analysis shows the key reason for federal control in this area: Even though IRBs were a local program, the federal government was paying the entire tab. As Eisinger relates, the federal response began in 1968 with regulations specifying permissible uses of the bonds; this action was followed by further controls on purposes in 1982, state volume caps in 1984, and lowered state volume caps—along with beneficiary company maxima—in the Tax Reform Act of 1986. Although nonmanufacturing uses were disallowed in 1986, the use of IRBs to support manufacturing facilities is still authorized.[52]

The other significant type of legislation at the national level concerns the use of federal funds by the states in their investment attraction efforts. Several federal programs include an "anti-piracy" provision that bans the use of federal funds to induce relocation of a facility from one part of the country to another. Many of these provisions were adopted after major local battles over abuses—as with the provisions for the CDBG program discussed below. Indeed, many of the battles were fought by unions trying to prevent plant shutdowns caused by subsidized relocations that used federal funds for part of the subsidy.

The Urban Development Action Grant (UDAG) program prohibited the use of federal funds to " 'facilitate the relocation of . . . plants or facilities from one area to another' unless it is determined that there is no adverse effect on the area suffering the loss."[53] According to Greg LeRoy, this provision was enforced in practice by requiring approval from the mayor of the job-losing city. LeRoy cites a case in which a United Auto Workers local was able to block a UDAG grant to J. I. Case, preventing its relocation from Wisconsin.[54] The UDAG program was terminated in 1988,[55] but a number of other federal programs have similar provisions.

The EDA contains perhaps the strongest anti-piracy provision. Not only is there a four-year ban on moving jobs from one "commuting area" to another but transgressions are penalized through repayment with interest of the EDA funds received.[56] This arrangement, of course, is similar to EU policy on repayment of illegal state aid with interest.

The SBA restricts the use of SBA loan guarantees for relocations—in particular, disallowing them when it would "cause serious unemployment in the present location" or when it would "nullify a labor union contract or a commitment to negotiate a collective bargaining agreement."[57] This rule was upheld in the case of Athletic Helmet Inc., which moved fifty unionized jobs from Knoxville, Tennessee, to Salem, Illinois, in 1995. The SBA had granted a $750,000 loan guarantee for the Salem plant because it had not been informed that it would result in the Knoxville facility's closure. When the Amalgamated Clothing and Textile Workers Union (ACTWU) objected, the loan guarantee was rescinded—although the firm moved anyway, using state and local incentives and a CDBG loan guarantee (then legal).[58]

The Workforce Investment Act (WIA; formerly the JTPA) has anti-piracy provisions, but the evidence suggests that they are not enforced.[59] At the June 1995 White House Conference on Small Business, Mark DiSalvo—a business owner from Massachusetts—recounted how numerous states had approached him offering incentives to relocate his operations. DiSalvo said he received solicitations "every month" to move his software and woodworking businesses;

when he asked whether trained workers were available, he was told not to worry because JTPA funds were available for his training needs.[60]

Anti-piracy provisions apply indirectly to Internal Revenue Code Section 936 tax credits for businesses in Puerto Rico because Puerto Rico's Industrial Tax Exemption Act requires that firms benefitting from Puerto Rico's tax incentives (invariably combined with Section 936 credits) could not be given to firms relocating from the mainland United States. This requirement came about after Textron closed six factories and moved to Puerto Rico in 1947; it lay dormant from its 1948 enactment until 1991—when the Oil, Chemical, and Atomic Workers Union (OCAW) cited it in Racketeer-Influenced and Corrupt Organizations (RICO) lawsuits against American Home Products (which was closing an OCAW-organized plant in Elkhart, Indiana) and the Governor of Puerto Rico (who, the suits alleged, had not enforced the clause).[61] American Home Products settled this suit for $24 million in 1992.[62] Although the union was not successful in introducing an explicit anti-piracy clause into Section 936, the benefits available under Section 936 were sharply reduced in 1993.[63]

The biggest recent battle to control the use of federal funds for relocation subsidies revolved around CDBG funds. In May 1994, Briggs and Stratton announced that it would move 2,000 jobs from suburban Milwaukee to five locations, including two in Missouri and Kentucky for which it would receive $855,000 in subsidies (including CDBG funding). By July 1994, the Wisconsin Congressional delegation had successfully passed a CDBG piracy ban in the House, but it fell to a filibuster threat by Senator Kit Bond (R-Mo.) in the Senate. These provisions were not added to the CDBG law until November 1998.[64]

As the foregoing examples show, federal involvement in subnational investment competition has been growing. Aside from limiting industrial revenue bonds—for which the federal government was paying 100 percent of the cost of the subsidy—most of the changes in federal law have been outgrowths of specific local abuses.[65] Unions, in particular, have been involved with these developments because relocation subsidies were often used as a tool to run away from a unionized workforce. Union alliances with community groups have affected local subsidy policies as well (see below). Moreover, further organizing probably will take place over controls that are not currently well enforced, such as the WIA anti-piracy rules.

Nevertheless, this situation does not constitute a comprehensive federal solution, and the occasional proposals made in Congress (such as that of Minnesota Rep. David Minge) at present have little chance of passage.[66] Given the lack of what the model in Chapter 2 would describe as "third-party" control of cooperative forms of avoiding investment competition, the discussion now turns to attempts by groups of states to achieve the same purpose voluntarily. As the model predicts, the incentive to defect (increasing competition for investment) is strong, and in the cases examined here, states have been unable to resist it. The failure of such voluntary cooperation among states has led back to discussion of a greater federal role.

Voluntary Cooperation by U.S. States

State and local government officials understand that untrammeled investment competition has significant drawbacks. As the NGA declared in 1993:

> The accelerated use of direct development incentives by states to attract economic investment is symptomatic of the continuing slow growth of the nation's economy. State government finds itself pressured to take whatever steps are necessary to support job creation that otherwise might occur unaided under more healthy economic conditions. . . . Governors must be prepared to withstand the political pressure that may result when they announce that their state will not engage in a bidding war for a high-visibility, high-impact project.[67]

In the same document, however, the nation's governors declared their opposition to "the threat of punitive measures or federal intervention," arguing that restraint in awarding investment incentives should be followed because it is "good public policy."[68] Not surprisingly, then, there have been voluntary attempts by states to restrain their use of investment subsidies—most particularly in terms of agreements to refrain from luring existing firms in one state to relocate to another. There have been two attempts to create such "no-raiding" zones: one in the Midwest and one comprising New York, Connecticut, and New Jersey. In both cases, these efforts have been unsuccessful.

In the Midwest, a 1980s attempt by the Council of Great Lakes Governors to create a no-raiding zone failed just before it was signed when one state violated it before it even went into effect.[69] Similarly, the ink was barely dry on a 1991 agreement between New York, New Jersey, and Connecticut when the latter two states passed new incentives programs that they aimed at New York City employers. As Charles Mahtesian notes, "New Jersey's Governor James Florio broke [the truce] within months. Worse yet, he rubbed New York's face in it by creating a recruitment fund paid for out of revenues from the World Trade Center—jointly owned by both states."[70] As a result of Connecticut's and New Jersey's aggressive recruitment, some firms relocated—such as First Chicago Corporation, which received $50 million to move to New Jersey. Even when companies did not move, however, the offers enabled them to demand new incentive packages from the city to keep them from moving.[71] A long list of retention subsidies was topped in 1998 by a package estimated to be between $600 million and $900 million to keep the New York Stock Exchange in New York City.[72]

As these examples show, the prospect for voluntary cooperation between states is not good—notwithstanding the NGA's view. As the RNPD model predicts, achieving cooperation on control of investment incentives is extraordinarily difficult in the absence of third-party enforcement.[73] Instead, the real story of attempts to control subsidies to investment in the United States is about nongovernmental organizations and their organizing efforts.

Popular Response to "Corporate Welfare"

Given the lack of overall federal regulation and the difficulty that individual states have in refraining from competing for investment, the main initiative in coping with the problem of business subsidies comes, not surprisingly, from the NGO sector. This NGO involvement has occurred at the national level and the state level. This section examines the activities of these NGOs, assessing their successes and failures as well as the likely evolution of their efforts.

Among the NGOs working to end or regulate "corporate welfare" are national and local organizations; reflecting the multiple critiques of corporate subsidies, these NGOs span the political spectrum. Among the better-known national groups are the Center for the Study of Responsive Law; the Cato Institute; the PPI; Friends of the Earth (an environmental NGO); and the American Federation of State, County, and Municipal Employees (AFSCME). Other national groups include the Association of Community Organizations for Reform Now (ACORN), which has local chapters in most parts of the country; Good Jobs First; the Corporation for Enterprise Development; and the Grassroots Policy Project. Examples of local organizations include Alabama Arise, the Minnesota Alliance for Progressive Action, and the Southwest Organizing Project (New Mexico).

These groups differ in their implicit criticism of subsidies. General critiques of location incentives can be made on efficiency or equity grounds (see Chapter 1). A more restricted critique of some corporate subsidies can be made on environmental grounds, attacking precisely the subsidies that harm the environment.

In the United States, the efficiency argument is the central motivation behind the participation of conservative and libertarian organizations in the anti-"corporate welfare" movement. This description would apply to the Cato Institute and some of the member organizations of the Friends of the Earth's "Green Scissors" coalition, such as the Concord Coalition and Taxpayers for Common $ense. The environmental argument motivates Friends of the Earth itself, as well as the other ecology NGOs in the Green Scissors campaign. The equity argument motivates many of the more liberal citizen's groups (e.g., ACORN, CTJ, CBPP, and the Center for Responsive Law) as well as union participants.[74] PPI focuses equally on the efficiency and equity problems of subsidization.[75] In Canada, the breakdown is similar: Left-wing and right-wing criticism of subsidies are in evidence, and social-justice and taxpayer organizations are both represented. Again, North American experience is in sharp contrast with the politics of subsidies in the EU, where the efficiency critique is paramount, and the Left (outside the UK, where the Labour government remains critical of other member states' subsidies) is critical of EU state aid policies.

National-Level Activities

Given the large number of groups involved in campaigns against corporate welfare, this discussion is illustrative rather than exhaustive.[76] In particular, I examine two "strange bedfellows" campaigns and several other recent national developments.

Friends of the Earth (FoE), the U.S. Public Interest Research Group (U.S. PIRG), and Taxpayers for Common $ense (TC$) sponsor the Green Scissors campaign, targeting environmentally damaging subsidies. According to Gawain Kripke, about two dozen other organizations, mostly environmental, take part in Green Scissors.[77]

Beginning with the 1993 publication of "The Green Solution to Red Ink" (the name was changed to "Green Scissors" in 1995), these groups have claimed success in eliminating $25 billion in spending and subsidies—including the TPX fusion reactor and Advanced Neutron Source project, both of which created substantial waste disposal problems. Green Scissors' most recent report, *Green Scissors 99*, identifies seventy-two programs—focusing primarily on energy, public lands, water, agriculture, and highways—with an estimated savings of $50.8 billion over five years.[78]

The Stop Corporate Welfare Coalition brought together several Nader organizations, FoE, the Cato Institute, and conservative groups such as the Heritage Foundation. These groups announced a "Dirty Dozen" of corporate welfare programs that all of these organizations agreed should be terminated or sharply modified. This January 1997 effort—similar to a June 1995 "Dirty Dozen" released by EI, Cato, and PPI—identified the Overseas Private Investment Corporation, Market Access Program, highway demonstration projects, and U.S. contributions to the International Monetary Fund's General Agreements to Borrow as programs to terminate. The five-year savings of the coalition's Dirty Dozen were projected to be $11.5 billion.[79]

Although these groups agreed on the twelve programs to be cut and that total corporate welfare is substantially higher, they disagreed with regard to what should be done with the savings. As Shields points out:

> While conservatives and progressives agree on the need to cut corporate welfare, old differences re-emerge when the groups are faced with the question of the freed funds. The Competitive Enterprise Institute, for example, would use budgetary savings to reduce the deficit. Essential Information would ensure that needy people have access to safe shelter, nutritional food, affordable health care and quality education.[80]

Another set of national developments has been spearheaded by researchers at the Federal Reserve Bank of Minneapolis. In 1994, staffers Arthur Rolnick and Melvin Burstein wrote an influential article, "Congress Should End the Economic War Among the States," that was reprinted in many newspapers around the country. One lawmaker who responded to its call was Ohio State Senator Charles Horn, a Republican. He was instrumental in organizing the September 1995 declaration by more than 100 Midwest economists for an end to firm-specific investment incentives. Organized by conservative think-tanks in five states (Ohio, Indiana, Illinois, Nebraska, and Michigan), the mostly conservative signers argued instead for "broad-based tax relief for all businesses and citizens."[81]

Following this declaration, in May 1996 Horn led the Ohio Senate to unanimous passage of "a resolution requesting federal assistance in halting the interstate smokestack chase. Specifically, the first-of-its-kind measure urged Congress to explore initiatives to mitigate interstate economic warfare and to identify and eliminate the federally funded programs that are currently used to lure businesses from other states."[82] Also in May 1996, Minnesota Public Radio and the Ford Foundation sponsored a conference in Washington called "The Economic War Among the States." More than 70 people, primarily critics, attended the conference; many joined Rolnick and Burstein in calling for an end to competition for investment.[83]

In November 1996, a regional presidential commission—the Northern Great Plains Rural Development Commission—called for a Congressional ban on relocation subsidies.[84] Beginning in December 1996, Midwest governors resumed discussions on regional restrictions on investment competition under the aegis of the Council of Great Lakes Governors, but no agreement came out of them.[85]

Local Campaigns

At the local level, many organizations are working to reduce subsidies to corporations. Relatively speaking, conservative groups are less well-represented at this level than at the national level. Again, this disparity reflects the early campaigns against plant shutdowns that used subsidies as an organizing handle.

In Alabama, three groups (Greater Birmingham Ministries, Alabama New South Coalition, and the Alabama Coalition Against Hunger) came together to create Alabama Arise (AA) in 1988.[86] By 1996, the coalition had grown to nearly 100 members, including anti-poverty groups, unions, churches, and other organizations. AA's efforts on tax equity issues in the early 1990s led it into a campaign against the "Mercedes Law" that provided generous tax breaks and other benefits for investors in the state. Although this legislation initially was passed for the Mercedes project discussed in Chapter 1, within just one year the state had pledged tax breaks totalling $3 billion to eighty-six other corporations.

This law exempted companies that built or expanded facilities from the state's corporate income tax and provided them the right to use its employees' personal state income tax withholding to pay off debt related to the construction of facilities. The latter provision potentially conflicted with mandates of the state constitution that designate income tax revenue for the Education Trust Fund; this provision particularly incensed the state teachers' union, the Alabama Education Association, which threatened a lawsuit over the issue.

Alabama Arise contracted with the Midwest Center for Labor Research to conduct an analysis of the Mercedes package. Armed with the finding that Mercedes received at least $118 million in direct subsidies (such as paying the entire wage bill for the first year of the plant) and $55 million in tax subsidies,[87] AA was able to mobilize an even larger coalition to challenge the law and lobby for a new Industrial Tax Credit Act to replace it.

The showdown over the law came in the 1995 legislative session. AA and its allies made one major gain in the new law: removal of the constitutionally dubious pledge of personal income tax revenue to investing firms. A second, more mixed, gain was that the tax credits had to be tied to construction costs rather than promised job creation. This provision, however, raised the possibility that highly capital-intensive projects could receive large subsidies while creating few jobs.

The new law had many other drawbacks as well. Republican Governor Fob James and the legislature ignored major AA recommendations, such as improved monitoring of firm compliance with agreements, clawbacks, and cost-per-job limits. Moreover, the wage requirements of the Mercedes Law were deleted for rural employers in the new law.

Since then, Governor Don Siegelman has attempted to raid the state's tobacco settlement funds ($3.2 billion over twenty-six years) for industrial recruitment, in conjunction with a Honda plant announced in 1999. Alabama Arise fought this action, arguing that the money should go to children's health. In the end, the state legislature designated only $350 million for recruitment. "We took this to mean the legislature wouldn't give away the store," AA's Kimball Forrester said, "but it was still quite generous."[88]

The Minnesota Alliance for Progressive Action (MAPA), a coalition of about twenty-five organizations, was the driving force behind the most significant legislative victory in the country. In 1995, it helped pass the "Corporate Welfare Reform Law," which requires the granting authority to set job and wage goals for any business assistance (including grants, tax breaks, and tax increment financing) over $25,000 to a single firm; it also requires clawbacks if these goals are not met within two years of the award. It further requires the state Department of Trade and Economic Development to compile an annual report of all subsidies.[89] This legislation makes Minnesota a model in terms of subsidy transparency and accountability (as noted, Maine passed a similar law in November 1998); it also has created an unprecedented (for the United States) database for assessing the use, cost, and effects of subsidies.

These data were used in a comprehensive study of Minnesota's subsidies by Good Jobs First, which analyzed more than 550 projects in February 1999. This analysis showed that many projects awarded more than $35,000 in assistance per job, that two-thirds had wages that were more than 20 percent below the local average for the industry, and that tax increment financing projects were especially problematic in terms of high cost per job and frequent financing of intrastate relocations.[90]

Armed with this analysis and its own identification of problems in the original law, MAPA sought to strengthen the law in several ways. While its bill was blocked in committee, MAPA's allies in the legislature were able to attach the reforms to omnibus tax legislation that passed on the final day of the session. The new legislation contained three major changes from the 1995 law. First, all local subsidies greater than $100,000 and all state subsidies greater than $500,000 require public notification and hearings, and they can only be given by elected officials—not by administrative bodies. Second, previous accountability provisions were improved through the provision of fines for corporations that fail to fulfill their goals, and government bodies that do not make proper reports cannot provide further subsidies until they do so. Third, granting bodies must hold public hearings and establish transparent criteria for how they will grant subsidies, including job and wage requirements.[91]

In Rio Rancho, New Mexico (a suburb of Albuquerque), the Southwest Organizing Project (SWOP) fought local governments in 1993 over a huge incentive package given to Intel for a $2 billion wafer fabrication plant that promised 2,400 jobs. The company considered locations (all of which were adjacent to existing facilities) in New Mexico, Arizona, Texas, Utah, California, and Oregon and chose Rio Rancho after receiving a mammoth package that included industrial revenue bonds, property and sales tax abatements, job training funds, corporate income tax credits, and the right to keep its employees' withheld state income taxes; the incentives were worth $289 million in 1994 dollars, according to the *Albuquerque Tribune*.[92]

After landing the plant, Rio Rancho hit an immediate financial crisis. According to David Friedman:

> In 1994, when the town created a new school district, it could only raise $27 million in taxes, far less than it needed to pay for its current, let alone future, educational needs. Rueful officials publicly admitted that they could have obtained 10 times more funding had Intel's decades-long tax holiday not been on the tax rolls.[93]

The problem persisted until September 1995, when Intel agreed to pay $28.5 million for a new high school. In return, Rio Rancho agreed to issue *$8 billion* in revenue bonds for the company.[94]

According to SWOP director Jeanne Gauna, the group had already been tracking the industry because of the chemical poisoning of its workers, most of whom were women of color: "Two hundred women of color were poisoned by GTE in Albuquerque; then we found out we were paying for it!"[95] Among SWOP's demands in the aftermath of the Intel subsidies were impact studies on the environmental, economic, social, and cultural consequences of the huge project; a review of the state's economic development policies; and a commitment by Intel to cleaner (Intel has three Superfund sites in Silicon Valley) and safer operations.[96] After eight meetings with Intel, however, the only concession the company made was to set up a public participation plan, which Gauna calls "the same old shuck and jive."[97]

Some campaigns on subsidies have focused on making them more accountable, rather than banning them. One important issue that has been raised has been wages paid by recipients of tax abatements or other subsidies. ACORN—a national alliance of low- and moderate-income citizens' action groups—has organized "living wage" campaigns in Chicago, New York, Boston, St. Louis, Denver, and other cities, as well as participating in coalition efforts in Minneapolis/St. Paul and Los Angeles. These efforts are aimed at requiring firms that receive local subsidies (and sometimes firms that receive contracts from local governments) to pay wages that would lift a family of four above the federal poverty line. The law that passed in Los Angeles in April 1997, which is one of the strongest in the country, is fairly typical in its provisions: Firms that receive city subsidies of $100,000 per year or $1 million total, or contracts of more than $25,000, must pay workers at least $7.25 per hour plus benefits, or $8.50 per hour without benefits. Nevertheless, the law's coverage was so narrow that it was expected to affect only 5,000 workers. Similar laws that passed in early 1997 in Minneapolis and in St. Paul also had narrow coverage as a result of exemptions for small business and other provisions. Subsequent campaigns in the Twin Cities aimed at expanding coverage and negotiating with individual employers.[98] In New York—which also has passed a living wage ordinance—ACORN supplemented its efforts by negotiating directly with a major recipient of city subsidies (Viacom) for a training and job program.[99]

The Impact of NGOs

The foregoing histories represent only the tip of the iceberg in terms of nongovernmental organizing on issues of "corporate welfare." Although local organizing is not always victorious, it has achieved more concrete victories than national efforts and in many ways is the precursor of national efforts. The Minnesota legislation has the strongest provisions and is likely to be a model for groups in other states. The difficulties faced at the local level should not be underestimated, however. Economic development officials are accustomed to providing location incentives, and firms' ability to play hardball is increasing as capital mobility makes the number of feasible locations for any particular project grow. In the long run, accountability efforts are helping to put the issue of federal control on the agenda.

At the same time, except for the living wage movement—in which a single national organization (ACORN) has a high profile even when it is in coalition with other groups—describing the campaigns against corporate welfare as a unified movement would be a mistake. In the United States, the groups involved come from both ends of the political spectrum, with substantial participation by conservative and libertarian organizations (especially at the national level).[100] This deep fissure may undermine efforts to reduce "corporate welfare" because it means there are sharp differences over what is considered an inappropriate subsidy. At the same time, there seems to be little dissent among the various groups that location subsidies (and even more clearly, *relocation* subsidies) are bad policy on equity and efficiency grounds.

Canadian Action on Subnational Competition for Investment

According to Mark Ronayne, "The provision of industrial incentives in Canada is subject to few basic framework rules or guidelines. Rather the Canadian Constitution Act, outside of certain limitations, has not greatly restrained their use by either provincial or federal governments."[101] Provinces in the Canadian federal system are stronger, relative to the central government, than are U.S. states; for example, the sort of barriers to trade that would be banned under the Commerce Clause of the U.S. Constitution are commonplace in Canada. Thus, there is wide scope for interprovincial competition for investment.

Perhaps the most extreme recent example of such bidding wars occurred over Piper Aircraft. In July 1991, Piper filed to reorganize under Chapter 11 of the U.S. Bankruptcy Code. Cleveland financier Cyrus Eaton, Jr., conceived the idea of buying the company and relocating it from the United States to Canada to avoid U.S. product liability laws. Despite the fact that Eaton had not obtained control of the company (his bid was pending with the Bankruptcy Court), he began negotiating with officials from Investment Canada and provincial economic development agencies. Before the soap opera concluded, nine of Canada's ten provinces had attempted to land the investment. Saskatchewan put together a C$64 million package in which the province would provide C$25 million, the company would borrow C$29 million, and Eaton's group would put up C$10 million. A Danish-Canadian consortium made a $50 million purchase offer for the company with the intention of moving it to British Columbia. In the end, Piper emerged from bankruptcy and didn't leave Florida—and Eaton never gained control of the company.[102] Although the Piper affair was humorous in some ways, it demonstrates that Canada's experience has been no different from that of the United States: There have been bidding wars for new investments (some of which had U.S. participants as well) and attempts by the provinces to lure firms to relocate from one to another (called "poaching" in Canada, as opposed to the usual U.S. term, "piracy"). New Brunswick, in particular, has developed a reputation for aggressive efforts to induce relocations.[103]

Thus, the same prisoners' dilemma logic of investment attraction applies in Canada as in the United States and the EU. Moreover, voluntary attempts by Canadian provinces (like those between U.S. states) to refrain from incentive wars have been ineffective. As Ronayne notes, the Maritime Premiers' Council (covering Nova Scotia, Prince Edward Island, and New Brunswick) and the Western Premiers' Conference (British Columbia, Alberta, Saskatchewan, and Manitoba) have issued calls for the control of location incentives. Neither, however, can be regarded as successful—nor were earlier all-province attempts.[104]

The Code of Conduct and Other Governmental Actions

Against this background, the adoption in 1994 of a Code of Conduct on Incentives—Annex 607.3 of the Agreement on Internal Trade (AIT)—is a potential landmark. Under Article 3, Prohibited Incentives, the Code provides:

> No Party shall provide an incentive that is contingent, in law or in fact, and would directly result in an enterprise, located in the territory of any Party, relocating an existing operation into its territory.[105]

For the first time, Canada adopted a legally binding ban on poaching. In addition, the provinces agreed to a "best efforts" provision to avoid bidding wars for new investments in Article 4, Avoidance of Certain Incentives.[106]

One attractive aspect of the ban on poaching is that it breaks the cooperation problem into manageable pieces, which makes it a logical first step.[107] Despite the negative consequences of competition for investment, it is difficult to imagine governments simply agreeing to a ban on all location incentives, as the logic of prisoners' dilemma tells us. Of all location subsidies, however, the problems inherent in relocation incentives are most evident because no new jobs are created by such moves. By tackling a small but significant and clearly egregious part of the overall problem, U.S. states might be able to similarly launch themselves into greater cooperation in avoiding investment subsidies.

Unfortunately, the Canadian experience to date (summer 1999) shows that even this small first step can be difficult to take. In January

1995, New Brunswick offered United Parcel Service (UPS) C$11 million in incentives to relocate some of its operations from British Columbia, Manitoba, and Ontario; as a result, UPS moved 870 jobs to New Brunswick. The following year, British Columbia complained under the AIT. Informal negotiations between the two provinces were fruitless. In September 1996, British Columbia claimed that New Brunswick had refused to enter the formal stage of dispute resolution; New Brunswick argued that the UPS deal had been completed prior to the June 1995 signing of the standstill agreement and therefore was not covered by the agreement at all. New Brunswick further charged that British Columbia was simply using its complaint as a pretext to pull out of the AIT. Although the complaint was never formally withdrawn, it has effectively become inactive.

As this account shows, the dispute-settlement procedure is cumbersome—perhaps to the point of ineffectiveness.[108] Several other violations have been alleged, including the transfer of Air Canada's call center from Montréal to St. John, New Brunswick, and the relocation of 300 meat packing jobs from Vancouver to Saskatoon, Saskatchewan.[109] The Internal Trade Secretariat has established a working group to strengthen the anti-poaching provisions.[110]

Although the Code of Conduct on Incentives has not yet lived up to its promise in Canada, a federal law in the United States banning relocation incentives probably would be easier to enforce. Because U.S. states do not have the powers of Canadian provinces, the cumbersome dispute-resolution mechanism of the AIT would be unnecessary. Instead, such a law presumably could be enforced through the federal courts. Alternatively, the law could provide for financial penalties levied by the federal government, much as the threatened loss of federal highway monies forced some recalcitrant states to raise their drinking age to 21.

There is one further way in which Canadian governments have held down competition for investment. In most provinces, local governments are prohibited from providing incentives of any sort to firms.[111] As Laura Reese notes, Ontario's ban on local incentives may be the most strict:

> Cities in Ontario are prohibited from offering tax abatements, loans, loan guarantees, and lease-back arrangements. Any land owned, developed, or "banked" by the municipality must be sold to developers at current market cost. The only exception to these regulations is aid to small

business, in which case cities may sell and/or lease property below market value.[112]

This virtual blanket ban prevents the kind of situation in which two or more municipal governments within a single U.S. state offer incentives for an investment—in addition to whatever package the state has assembled.[113] Moreover, because of the absolute nature of Ontario's ban, it is much easier to police than the EU's rules, which allow state aid in a wide variety of circumstances (again, remember that the EU's rules are applied to national governments, whereas Ontario's are applied to local governments). The evidence also suggests that compliance with the rules is very high. As Katherine McGuire remarks, "I haven't heard of any case in which a municipality wished to get around" the rules on bonusing.[114] Her comments were echoed by a municipal economic development director: "Many of us strongly objected" when the Rae provincial government discussed ending the bonusing ban. Moreover, this official said that he was not aware of any attempts to evade the rules, and he thought about the only way to try to do so was to provide land or facilities at below market value because determining that value is sometimes difficult.[115]

Reese's findings are similar: Her comparison of local economic development agencies in Ontario and Michigan found very little evidence that Ontario cities used banned methods. Pre-survey interviews had turned up some instances of such practices, but her survey of forty-two cities in Ontario found only four cities using sale/lease-back arrangements and even fewer using other banned techniques. Reese's pre-survey work turned up no evidence of tax abatements, tax increment financing, bond issuance, or downtown development authorities, so she did not ask about these financing measures in her Ontario survey; in Michigan, however, these types of incentives were used by 83 percent, 68 percent, 39 percent, and 60 percent of cities, respectively.[116] Thus, Ontario's ban on local incentives has been highly successful and has had an impact compared to normal economic development practice in the United States.

"Corporate Welfare" Campaigns in Canada

Although the corporate welfare issue in Canada was long a preserve of the Left (dating in particular to the New Democratic Party's 1972 federal election campaign on that theme), in more recent years groups such as the Canadian Taxpayers Federation have also focused on the issue, providing more of the two-pronged critique of subsidies characteristic of U.S. debates.

On the Left, the NDP has focused most of its research and organizing on the many inequities of the Canadian tax system (no inheritance tax or corporate minimum tax, adoption of the regressive Goods and Services Tax), according to NDP Policy Coordinator Judy Randall. It has devoted far less attention to direct subsidies.[117] The same focus also characterizes unions and social justice groups that are active in campaigning on corporate welfare.[118] Because tax expenditures are more prevalent in the federal tax system than in provincial systems, Canadian corporate welfare campaigns have tended to have a federal focus.[119] However, the NDP's general lack of electoral success at the federal level (it did enter the government as a junior partner with the Liberals after the 1972 election; after the 1997 elections, it had 21 MPs among 301 in the House of Commons) has sharply limited its impact on federal tax policy. As Randall admits, successes at the federal level have been "few and far between." The NDP has been more effective when it has formed provincial governments. For example, in Ontario under Bob Rae, the party introduced a corporate minimum tax.[120]

Groups such as the Ontario Coalition for Social Justice and the Ontario Federation of Labour have also been active in campaigning for a more equitable tax system. Their joint publication, *Unfair $hares*, points out that businesses in Canada receive more in subsidies and tax expenditures than they pay in corporate income taxes[121]—a situation that has also characterized the EU. Their goals for the tax system are similar to those of the NDP: reductions in corporate tax expenditures, imposition of a wealth tax, and a corporate minimum tax.[122]

On the Right, the Canadian Taxpayers Federation (CTF) in April 1998 released a two-volume report that documented C$11 billion in Industry Canada programs from 1982 to 1997 that the group considered to have been wasted.[123] The report pointed out that seventy-five firms accounted for more than half of the funds received, including well-known firms such as Pratt & Whitney Canada, Bombardier, and GM Canada. CTF was especially critical of R&D programs that used "repayable contributions"—where little, if any, of the money given was repaid (in the only individual case that survived Access-to-Information censoring, Bombardier had repaid only 5 percent of the money it received for twenty-one individual projects)—and called for the "immediate cessation" of the major Canadian R&D program, Technology Partnerships Canada.[124]

Although Industry Canada defended the program as a significant improvement over its predecessor (which it characterized as a subsidy, whereas the new program was an "investment"), further materials were leaked to CTF director Walter Robinson suggesting that the use of repayable contributions was a smokescreen to try to hide them from GATT/WTO rules.[125] Despite Industry Canada's efforts, the WTO made a final ruling in August 1999 that Technology Partnerships Canada was an export subsidy.[126]

The CTF also was a major player in the battle for Alberta's Business Financial Assistance Limitations Act. According to Robinson, "The government came to us and asked us what they should do. We were then kept in the loop as they drafted a bill and provided advice"[127]—which Alberta Premier Ralph Klein confirmed in a published interview.[128]

The Future of Canadian Subsidy Control

Because Canada's provinces have greater autonomy from the central government than do U.S. states, it is no surprise that the dynamic of investment competition takes place there as well. Indeed, Canadian provinces often get into bidding wars for investments with U.S. states as well as with each other. The Code of Conduct on Incentives may provide a way to gain control over these battles, however (despite its lack of success in the UPS case). Moreover, as pressure heats up against "corporate welfare" from the Left and the Right, the issue is gaining prominence on the national and provincial levels. As in the United States, this issue will not go away.

Conclusion

Control of competition for investment in North America ranges from weak to non-existent. In the United States, a vast array of subsidies to business favor companies locating here rather than elsewhere. Because most of these subsidies are provided in the form of tax expenditures, subsidy data on a national accounts basis is highly misleading and would have us sharply underestimate business subsidization in the

United States. Approximately $84 billion a year goes to non-agricultural business in the form of federal programs and tax expenditures. At the state and local levels, there is as much as $50 billion in additional support, much of it designed to influence investment location *within* the United States and thus wholly irrational from a national perspective.

Federal control efforts in the United States are still relatively weak. States have used federal funds such as CDBG or JTPA monies in packages designed to induce the relocation of a firm from one state to another, even when such use is specifically prohibited. These abuses have led to campaigns to create and enforce anti-piracy provisions in such programs—most recently (November 1998) with the inclusion of such provisions in the CDBG program. Beyond that, the most successful efforts against subsidies in the United States have been the 1986 Tax Reform Act's limitations on tax-exempt industrial revenue bonds (although we have seen in the case of Intel that much higher levels of *taxable* IRBs can be issued) and the same law's curtailment of the investment tax credit and other subsidies to firms that were born in the tax changes of 1981.

At the state level, the situation is repeated for most states, since few place any restrictions on substate government efforts to recruit investment. As a result, two or more local governments will offer competing investment incentive packages to a firm in addition to incentives from the state government.[129]

At the regional level, two attempts by groups of states to reduce bidding for investment, particularly the piracy of existing investment, have been complete failures. This failure highlights the compelling prisoners' dilemma logic of competition for investment and suggests the need for federal regulation.

NGOs have stepped into the vacuum in the United States at the national and the state levels, fighting against individual investment subsidies and competition for investment more generally. This "corporate welfare" campaign has united groups across the political spectrum, with the Left motivated by the equity critique, the Right by the efficiency critique, and environmental organizations by the ecological critique of subsidies to business. Many of the federal changes have grown out of local activism, which so far can count more concrete successes than the strictly federal campaigns across ideological boundaries. Nevertheless, the movement as a whole has been gathering momentum and is likely to have more impact on policy in the future. Rarely does an issue prompt Republicans to call for greater federal government activism—as happened in the Republican-majority Ohio Senate.

The situation is only slightly better in Canada. In most provinces, local governments do not have the authority to offer any kind of subsidies to firms, a rule that is relatively easy to police because of its absolute nature. This approach also appears to be widely supported by local economic development officials, whose role is thus limited to marketing and red tape clearance rather than financial underwriting of investment. On this dimension, the Canadian experience is clearly better than that of the United States.

In other ways, however, the two countries are much more similar. Bidding wars for investment *between* Canadian provinces are common, and—as in the United States—voluntary efforts by groups of provinces to stem the tide have been unsuccessful. "Poaching" of existing investment is as much a problem in Canada as "piracy" is in the United States. In contrast to the U.S. experience, however, Canadian provincial and federal officials have attempted to formally deal with this problem in the 1994 Code of Conduct on Incentives. The Code's first big test, however, revealed the dispute-resolution mechanism to be a weak instrument for control of relocation subsidies. Whether the Code will mature into a valuable instrument is an open question. It is, however, attractive as a practical way of dividing up the prisoners' dilemma of investment competition into smaller, more manageable steps;[130] moreover, it would be easier to enforce in the U.S. context than in Canada, given the fact that provinces have relatively more power vis-a-vis the federal government than U.S. states do.

At the NGO level, there is relatively less activity in Canada than in the United States. Moreover, unlike the situation in the United States, ideologically diverse coalitions against corporate subsidies in Canada have yet to emerge. According to CTF's Walter Robinson, there has been only a small evolution toward Left-Right cooperation in Canada—and that only on issues such as access to information.[131] Although "corporate welfare" has been a part of the NDP lexicon at least since 1972, the party's lack of electoral success at the federal level has naturally limited its ability to influence federal subsidy policies. Provincial NDP governments have had some impact, however—such as the corporate minimum tax enacted by the Rae government in

Ontario. Judging from newspaper citations, the term "corporate welfare" is now primarily associated with the Canadian Right.

In a development that parallels those in the EU, some provincial governments—notably the Klein government in Alberta and the Harris government in Ontario—have turned away from business subsidies as part of their commitment to budget cutting. Again, this trend flows from the efficiency-based concerns of their Conservative governments.

One common thread that runs through the Canadian and U.S. cases is the lack of precise data on state aid to business. Neither country has anything like the detailed reports on state aid that the EU's DG IV now produces on an annual basis. In the United States, the lack of information is most pronounced at the local level, but it is also substantial at the state level—as my estimates make clear. In Canada, subsidy data are better captured by national accounts statistics, given the lesser use of tax incentives in Canada than the United States, but the data situation is by no means satisfactory. Both countries have taken part in OECD exercises to estimate industrial subsidies, but both worked to end the data gathering in 1998 (see Chapter 7). Both countries have reported their subsidies to the World Trade Organization, but their notifications fall far short of the level of detail provided by the EU. The definitive work on subsidy levels in North America remains to be done; my estimates are only a beginning.

We turn next to an evaluation of the EU's state aid control policies. As this chapter has shown, there is virtually no regulation of competition for investment in North America. Chapters 3 and 4 showed that there is a substantial body of regulation and case law on state aid in the EU. The logical question, then, is, Does it make a difference? Chapter 6 attempts to answer that question.

Notes

1. It also sharply restricted or abolished a wide variety of subsidies to business at the federal level, including accelerated depreciation and the investment tax credit. This reduced corporate tax expenditures from 201 percent of corporate income tax paid before the reform to 60 percent of tax paid in 1996. See Citizens for Tax Justice, *The Hidden Entitlements* (Washington, D.C.: Citizens for Tax Justice, 1996), 5–6.
2. Personal communication, 10 May 1999.
3. Some groups criticize this term; they argue that it implies that social welfare programs for individuals are themselves undesirable policies.

4. Mark Ronayne, "Disciplining Industrial Incentives to Promote Competitive and Efficient North American Markets," Industry and Science Canada discussion paper, August 1993, 53.
5. Gary Clyde Hufbauer and Joanna Shelton Erb, *Subsidies in International Trade* (Washington, D.C.: Institute for International Economics, 1984), 2–5, is a well-known and representative example.
6. OECD, *Industrial Support Policies in OECD Countries, 1986-1989* (Paris: OECD, 1992), 40, reports that during the period covered by the study, the share of reported subsidization using this method of finance in the United States was between 84 percent and 93 percent. Robert Ford and Wim Suyker, "Industrial Subsidies in the OECD Economies," *OECD Economic Studies* no. 15 (autumn 1990): 52, suggested that, at the federal level, "tax expenditures for the industrial sector are about three times as large as current grants." If tax concessions are even more important at the state and local level than grants (as seems plausible), these two OECD figures are entirely compatible. See also Ronayne, "Disciplining Industrial Incentives," 89–91.
7. OECD did survey 19 states for a 1996 study of industrial support, but most programs reported for this work did not have the associated expenditure listed.
8. As Peter S. Fisher and Alan H. Peters, *Industrial Incentives: Competition Among American States and Cities* (Kalamazoo, Mich.: W.E. Upjohn Institute for Employment Research, 1998), 3, point out, even economic development literature often "fail(s) to distinguish the nominal value of the awards and their actual value to the firm" and does not identify how this differs among different types of aid to a firm (such as infrastructure, loans, and grants). Indeed, many analysts fail to calculate the present value of an award, rather than its nominal value. Even economic development officials sometimes fail to take this elementary step—as the story of Intel in New Mexico shows.
9. Joint Committee on Taxation, *Estimates of Federal Tax Expenditures for Fiscal Years 1996-2000* (Washington, D.C.: Congress, 1995); Congressional Budget Office, *Reducing the Deficit: Spending and Revenue Options* (Washington, D.C.: CBO, 1994).
10. The U.S. notification, along with those of all other WTO members, is available at the Commerce Department's Electronic Subsidies Enforcement Library Web site, <www.ita.doc.gov/import_admin/records/esel>.
11. Janice Shields, *Aid for Dependent Corporation (AFDC) 1995* (Washington, D.C.: Essential Information, 1995); Stephen Moore and Dean Stansel, *Ending Corporate Welfare As We Know It* (1995), available at: <http://www.cato.org/main/pa225.html>; Robert J. Shapiro and Chris

Soares, *Cut-and-Invest to Grow: How to Expand Public Investment While Cutting the Deficit* (Washington, D.C.: Progressive Policy Institute, 1997); Citizens for Tax Justice, *The Hidden Entitlements* (Washington, D.C.: PPI, 1996); Pauline Abernathy, Bob Greenstein, and Richard Kogan, "Will Corporate Welfare Be Reined In? Congressional Action Related to Business Subsidies" (Washington, D.C.: Center on Budget and Policy Priorities, November 7, 1995).

12. The United States uses a different method to calculate tax expenditures than any other OECD country: an "outlay equivalent" approach that attempts to estimate the amount of federal spending that would be necessary to achieve the same benefit for the recipient. The rest of the OECD uses a "revenue foregone" calculation that merely estimates the revenue loss due to a particular tax provision. See OECD, *Tax Expenditures*, 14. Fortunately, the CBO study, *Federal Financial Support for Business*, appears to use the revenue foregone method, as a comparison between it and *Tax Expenditures* shows. (This OECD publication gives U.S. tax expenditures using both methods.) However, estimates of tax expenditures by groups that are based, for instance, on the Joint Committee on Taxation's work may rely on the other definition, which in practice usually results in higher values. See the comparison in OECD, *Tax Expenditures*, Table 19. My estimates are based on the CBO study, so their international comparability is not affected.

13. Commission of the European Communities, *Seventh Survey on State Aid* (Brussels-Luxembourg: CEC, 1999), 50, Table 19. These figures may not be entirely comparable. On one hand, the U.S. figures do not include subfederal amounts, whereas the EU data do. On the other hand, the U.S. numbers may fall relative to the EU statistics because Shields's and other estimates count accelerated tax depreciation, which is considered a "general measure" in the EU and therefore not counted. In addition, the EU data for national aid to agriculture (i.e., exclusive of the Common Agricultural Policy) may be understated because of reliance only on budgetary figures, without consideration of tax expenditures.

14. Personal communication, Robert Shapiro, Progressive Policy Institute, Washington, D.C., 7 June 1996.

15. Abernathy, Greenstein, and Kogan, "Will Corporate Welfare Be Reined In?" 3.

16. For loans and guarantees, CBPP states that they have used "the administrative cost and subsidy value of the loans and guarantees in terms of the discounted present value of the government's expected net losses" (Abernathy et al., 5 n. 6), which is far more comparable to EU and OECD practice than the all-too-often form in which such subsidies

are reported in the media (i.e., the total amount of the loan or guarantee).

17. Moore and Stansel, *Ending Corporate Welfare*, 8.
18. Personal communication, Washington, D.C., 11 June 1996.
19. The quote and the examples preceding it are taken from Congressional Budget Office, *Federal Financial Support of Business* (Washington, D.C.: CBO, 1995), 4.
20. Robert J. Shapiro and Chris Soares, *Cut-and-Invest to Grow: How to Expand Public Investment While Cutting the Deficit* (Washington, D.C.: Progressive Policy Institute, 1997), 28–36.
21. CBO, *Federal Financial Support of Business*, 19.
22. CBO, *Federal Financial Support of Business*, 18–21.
23. Personal communication with Reinhard Walther, Unit Chief for State Aid Inventory and Analysis, DG IV, 24 September 1996. Mr. Walther does not consider it to be the equivalent of state aid because it is generally available.
24. See Richard Caves's discussion of the effects of taxation on international location choices in *Multinational Enterprise and Economic Analysis*, 2nd edition, 205–06.
25. Robert G. Lynch, *Do State & Local Tax Incentives Work?* (Washington, D.C.: Economic Policy Institute, 1996), 26 n. 1. This survey included California, Florida, Louisiana, Maryland, Massachusetts, Michigan, Missouri, Ohio, Pennsylvania, Washington, and Wisconsin. In addition, the state of New York regularly had corporate tax expenditures on the order of $1 billion annually, but it did not report 1992 data. If New York is included, the total for 12 states comes to about $7.3 billion.
26. This includes an estimate of about $1 billion in state spending programs, based on my analysis of National Association of State Development Agencies, *State Economic Development Expenditure Survey/Summary: Analysis and Tables* (Washington, D.C.: NASDA, n.d.), viii.
27. William Schweke and Carl Rist, *Managing for Higher Returns: What Does North Carolina Actually Spend on Economic Development and How Can These Investments Be Better Managed?* (Washington, D.C.: Corporation for Enterprise Development, 1997).
28. Schweke and Rist, *Managing for Higher Returns*; Bruce Kimmel, Eric Rothman, and Alexis Thompson, *Increasing the Visibility and Accountability of Economic Development Spending: A Unified Development Budget for Massachusetts* (Cambridge, Mass.: Kennedy School of Government, 1997); California Budget Project, *California Unified Economic Development Budget*, May 1999 draft; Osterburg Consulting, *Corporate Welfare in Iowa* (January 1997); Nora Ranney and Alexa Bradley, *1996 Corporate*

Welfare Handbook: A Comprehensive Handbook on Corporate Welfare in Minnesota (St. Paul: Minnesota Alliance for Progressive Action, 1996); office of Senator Charles Horn (Ohio); Kristy Daugherty, *Gambit Magazine* (Louisiana); Michigan: data on tax abatements provided by Michael LaFaive, Mackinaw Institute, average property tax rate in state provided by Jeff Horner, Citizens Research Council of Michigan, plus press reports on the MEGA program. In several places I eliminated items from these estimates to improve their international comparability and to remove agricultural subsidies (see discussion below).

29. Personal communication, Washington, D.C., 7 June 1996. Furthermore, Jeff Goodman, vice president and chief financial officer of Mancon Tax Incentive LLC, notes that there are more tax abatement programs on the local level than on the state level. Although he was unable to say that tax expenditure *spending* also was higher, it must be substantial (personal communication, 7 January 1997).

30. Jim Woods, "City Doesn't Squander Abatements, Study Says," *Columbus Dispatch*, 13 March 1998, 1; William P. Barrett, "Willis Carrier's Ghost," *Forbes,* 29 May 2000, 152.

31. The reason it is not ideal is that these eight states do not constitute a random sample. It is quite conceivable that these states have tax expenditure budgets precisely because their citizens perceived that corporate tax expenditures were high, which would bias this estimate upward. Because neither the U.S. WTO notifications nor the OECD's stratified sample of state support to manufacturing include usable spending data, however, the procedure used here is the best available. (For its 1996 survey of industrial support in member countries, the OECD constructed a stratified sample of 20 U.S. states. See OECD, *Industrial Subsidies: A Reporting Manual* [Paris: OECD, 1995], 71–72.)

    Buchholz, *Competition and Corporate Incentives*, extrapolates from the relative size of a state's budgetary expenditure—and uses only one state (Massachusetts) as his base. This procedure is suspect because tax expenditures may vary inversely with on-budget expenditure, rather than directly. That is, states with low on-budget expenditure may use high levels of tax expenditure. I believe this is more likely to be the case than direct variation between the two, although it cannot be determined without complete data on tax expenditures.

32. *Statistical Abstract of the United States*, 1998, Table 719, 454.

33. *Industrial Incentives*, 210–11.

34. CBO, *Federal Financial Support of Business*, 30.

35. *Seventh Survey on State Aid*, 50, Table 19. Despite appearances, this table does not include aid to agriculture. Personal communication from

Reinhard Walther, DG IV Inventory and Analysis Unit, 25 August 1999.

36. Agriculture is another story, but that subject is beyond the scope of this book.

37. Mark Ronayne, "Disciplining Industrial Incentives," 31 n. 59.

38. Ronayne, "Disciplining Industrial Incentives," 89–90. He reports that one study found, for the pulp and paper industry, that direct grants constitute more than half of Canadian aid in the 1980s but an "insignificant" amount in the United States. He also suggests that Canadian support to industry is more transparent than that of the EU.

    Tax expenditures are about 70 percent of U.S. federal support for business and an even higher proportion at the state and local level. In Canada, Blais reported estimates on the order of 2 percent of GDP for grants and tax expenditures in the early 1980s. See André Blais, *A Political Sociology of Public Aid to Industry*, 29, 47.

    The data presented in Table 5-8 also support the interpretation that grants are a far greater proportion of total aid to business in Canada than in the United States, although the proportion of tax expenditures in Canada is increasing.

39. For a discussion of these subsidies and capital assistance (a subcategory of capital transfers), see Ronayne, "Disciplining Industrial Incentives," 30–31.

40. See also footnote b in Table 5–8. According to Jim Turk of the Ontario Coalition for Social Justice, tax expenditures are relatively minor at the provincial level (personal communication, 5 September 1996). The following were the main federal tax expenditures added: low tax rate for small businesses, low tax rate for manufacturing and processing, low tax rate for credit unions, scientific research and experimental development investment tax credit, Atlantic investment tax credit, special investment tax credit (a regional program), small business investment tax credit, investment tax credits claimed in current year but earned in prior years, Canadian film or video production tax credit, film or video production services tax credit, resource allowance (and the offsetting nondeductibility of Crown royalties and mining taxes), and earned depletion. See Department of Finance, *Tax Expenditures 1999*, available at: <http://www.fin.gc.ca/taxexp>.

41. "Ontario Creates Jobs and Attracts Investments Without Hand-outs to Business—Palladini," Canada NewsWire, 19 February 1998 (this report by Economic Development, Trade and Tourism Minister Al Palladini also showed that loans and loan guarantees had been cut by 69 percent as well); Kellie Hudson, "Premier Rules Out 'Handouts' for NHL," *Toronto Star*, 8 April 1999.

42. Ian Gray, "Alberta to Restrict Province's Investments," *Financial Post*, 4 April 1996, 8; personal communication with Walter Robinson, Canadian Taxpayers Federation, 23 July 1999.

43. Ronayne, "Disciplining Industrial Incentives," Table III-3.

44. Data kindly provided by Dan Finnerty, Statistics Canada, Income and Expenditure Accounts Division (personal communication, 13 September 1999).

45. Peter K. Eisinger, *The Rise of the Entrepreneurial State: State and Local Economic Development Policy in the United States* (Madison: University of Wisconsin Press, 1988), especially Chapter 6.

46. David B. Robertson and Dennis R. Judd, *The Development of American Public Policy: The Structure of Policy Restraint* (Glenview, Ill.: Scott, Foresman, 1989), 11–14.

47. Robertson and Judd, *The Development of American Public Policy*, 13.

48. Indeed, changing workers' compensation was one of the most popular incentives in the 1990s: From 1990 through 1996, 9 to 21 states did this every year (an average of 13 per year). See Keon S. Chi and Drew Leatherby, *State Business Incentives: Trends and Options for the Future* (Lexington, Ky.: Council of State Governments, 1997), 5.

49. Earl H. Fry, *The Expanding Role of State and Local Governments in U.S. Foreign Affairs* (New York: Council on Foreign Relations Press, 1998), 82.

50. Eisinger, *The Rise of Entrepreneurial State*, 158–59.

51. Eisinger, *The Rise of the Entrepreneurial State*, 161. The average annual revenue loss was $4.8 billion from 1984 to 1988, according to Eisinger, 162.

52. Eisinger, *The Rise of the Entrepreneurial State*, 161–63.

53. Eisinger, *The Rise of the Entrepreneurial State*, 121.

54. Greg LeRoy, *No More Candy Store: States and Cities Making Job Subsidies Accountable* (Chicago: Federation for Industrial Retention and Renewal and Washington: Grassroots Policy Project, 1994), 137–38. This work included the first comprehensive analysis of anti-piracy regulations at the federal and state levels and should be consulted for more detail on several such provisions.

55. Ann Mariano, "Senate Votes to Cut Off Development Grants; Decade-Old Program for Troubled Areas Succumbs to Deficit Pressures," *Washington Post*, 14 July 1988, A17.

56. LeRoy, *No More Candy Store*, 142–43.

57. SBA Standard Operating Procedures, section 50-10-3. I thank Greg LeRoy for providing me with this information.

58. Amy Geisel, "Federal Aid for Knox Plant's Illinois Move is Put on Hold," *Knoxville News-Sentinel*, 15 March 1995, A1; correspondence from SBA to National Bank of Mt. Olive, Illinois, 16 February 1995 (provided by Greg LeRoy, who consulted for ACTWU on this issue) (personal correspondence from Greg LeRoy, 31 August 1998).

59. Personal communication with Ken Poole, National Association of State Development Agencies, 31 May 1996.

60. Quote from Aaron Zitner, "Mass. Seeks Curb on States' Job 'Poaching,'" *Boston Globe*, 3 June 1995, 59; personal communication with Greg LeRoy, Good Jobs First, 31 August 1998; personal communication with Marcia Howard, economic policy analyst, Public Policy Department, AFSCME, Washington, D.C., 6 June 1996.

61. Julia Abedian, *Exposing Federal Sponsorship of Job Loss: The Whitehall Plant Closing Campaign and "Runaway Plant" Reform* (New York: Garland, 1995), 37–38, 54–55.

62. Abedian, *Exposing Federal Sponsorship*, 105.

63. Abedian, *Exposing Federal Sponsorship*, 124–26.

64. See Charles Mahtesian, "Saving the States from Each Other," *Governing*, November 1996, 15; Greg LeRoy, personal communication, 31 August 1998; Center for Community Change, "CDBG and Job Piracy," *Organizing*, December 1998, available at: <http://www.communitychange.org/organizing.cdbg11.htm> (last accessed 24 March 1999).

65. I owe this point to Greg LeRoy.

66. See Mike Meyers, "Relocation Subsidies Target of Minge Bill," *Minneapolis Star Tribune*, 3 December 1997, 1D.

67. National Governors' Association Policy on Economic Growth and Development Incentives, in Jay Kayne and Molly Shonka, *Rethinking State Development Policies and Programs* (Washington, D.C.: National Governors' Association, 1994), 25–26.

68. Kayne and Shonka, *Rethinking State Development Policies and Programs*, 25.

69. William Schweke, Carl Rist, and Brian Dabson, *Bidding for Business: Are Cities and States Selling Themselves Short?* (Washington, D.C.: Center for Enterprise Development, 1994), 70. See also Michael Gauf, "In the Midwest, It's Every State for Itself," *St. Louis Post-Dispatch*, 2 December 1992.

70. Charles Mahtesian, "Romancing the Smokestack," *Governing*, November 1994, 38.

71. Schweke et al., *Bidding for Business*, 28–29; Steven Prokesch, "Despite Pact, New York and Region Spar for Jobs," *New York Times*, 30

November 1992, section C; Steven Lee Myers, "Giuliani Says Connecticut Broke Truce," *New York Times*, 14 October 1994, B1.

72. Greg LeRoy, "The Terrible Ten Candy Store Deals of 1998," in *The Progressive* magazine, available at: <http://www.progressive.org/leroy9905.htm>. For details on some earlier examples, see Schweke, Rist, and Dabson, *Bidding for Business*, 28–29.

73. Note, however, that Schweke, Rist, and Dabson, *Bidding for Business*, 70–72, are slightly more optimistic about voluntary regional agreements than I am.

74. AFSCME is an especially good example of this; see Marcia Howard, *A Corporate Welfare Reform Agenda* (Washington, D.C.: AFSCME Public Policy Department, 1994).

75. Shapiro, *Cut-and-Invest*.

76. For further examples, see Kenneth P. Thomas, " 'Corporate Welfare' Campaigns in North America," *New Political Economy* 2, March 1997, 117–26. Appendix 4 provides a more complete listing of organizations involved in organizing on issues of corporate welfare.

77. Personal communication, 21 May 1996.

78. Friends of the Earth, *Green Scissors 99* (Washington, D.C.: Friends of the Earth, 1999).

79. Press release from Janice Shields, Corporate Welfare Project Coordinator, 29 January 1997.

80. Janice Shields, "Ending (Corporate) Welfare As We Know It" (1996), available at: <http://www.emf.net/~cr/govreform/corpwelf-012596>, 6–7.

81. The quote is cited in Steve Jordan, "Groups Attack States' Special Incentives for Firms," *Omaha World Herald*, 20 September 1995, 16. This section also draws on "Editorial: States Should Embrace Tax-Incentive Backlash," *Dayton Daily News*, 28 September 1995, 10A; Debra Jasper, "Horn Seeks End to Tax Breaks," *Dayton Daily News*, 21 September 1995, 7B; Kristin Matz, "Economists Call for End to Incentive Packages," *Lafayette Business Digest*, 30 October 1995, section C, 2.

82. Charles Mahtesian, "Saving the States from Each Other," *Governing*, November 1996, 15. Horn's own position goes beyond this; he is willing for Ohio to "unilaterally disarm" in the economic development wars. David Friedman, "The New Civil War," *Inc. Special Issue: The State of Small Business*, 21 May 1996, 104. By late 1997, ten legislatures had passed such resolutions. See Meyers, "Relocation Subsidies Target of Minge Bill."

83. Peter Behr, "Battle to Attract Firms, Teams Hurting Some States, Experts Agree," *Washington Post*, 24 May 1996, F01, and interviews with participants. The papers presented at this conference can be accessed at the Web site of the Minneapolis Fed: <http://woodrow.mpls.frb.fed.us/sylloge/econwar/index.html>
84. Mike Meyers, "Ban Urged on States' Financial Competing for Business; Regional Presidential Commission Urges Halt to Subsidies for Teams, Industries," *Minneapolis Star-Tribune*, 26 November 1996, 8D.
85. Paul Souhrada, "Fewer Battles Urged," *Dayton Daily News*, 24 December 1996, 5B; "Highest Bidder: Competition for New Firms Unfair," editorial, *The Cincinnati Enquirer*, 27 March 1997, A18; personal communication with Jeff Edstrom, Council of Great Lakes Governors, 6 April 1999.
86. Except as otherwise noted, this account comes from Hany Khalil and Theresa Gardella, "Reforming Alabama's 'Mercedes Law,' " in *Public Subsidies, Public Accountability: Holding Corporations to Labor and Community Standards,* ed. Sandra Hinson, Richard Healey, Jim Benn, and Kary L. Moss (Washington, D.C.: Grassroots Policy Project, 1998), 28–32.
87. Some published reports put the figure at as much as $300 million; according to Robert Ginsberg (the Midwest Center for Labor Research analyst on the Mercedes project), however, these figures reflected everything Mercedes could conceivably have been eligible for, not what the company actually received.
88. Personal communication, 5 August 1999; Jay Reeves, "Honda Deal with Ala. Less Sweet Than 1993 Package to Mercedes," *Chattanooga Times*, 8 May 1999, C1; Karl Ritzler, "Alabama Proposal Attracts Honda: State Probably Will Use Tobacco Money to Fund Incentive-Laden Plan for Manufacturing Plant," *Atlanta Journal and Constitution*, 6 May 1999, 1A. The value of this subsidy ($102.7 million in site preparation and training, $55.6 million in tax breaks) may not be that much less than the actual cost of the Mercedes deal, which is substantially less than the widely published figure of $253 million, as explained above.
89. Jessica Whalen, Jesse Bacon, and Alexa Bradley, *Minnesota Corporate Welfare Law . . . 2 Years Later* (St. Paul: MAPA, 1997), 1.
90. Greg LeRoy and Tyson Slocum, *Economic Development in Minnesota: High Subsidies, Low Wages, Absent Standards* (Washington, D.C.: Good Jobs First, 1999), 1–3.
91. "Legislature Reins In Corporate Welfare," *MAPA Bulletin*, 18 May 1999; Monte Hanson, "Legislature Puts Clamps on Corporate Welfare," *Finance and Commerce* (Minneapolis), 20 May 1999, 1, 7; text of revisions

of Minnesota Corporate Welfare Reform Law, provided by MAPA, 20 May 1999.

92. See SouthWest Organizing Project, *Intel Inside New Mexico*, revised edition (Albuquerque: SouthWest Organizing Project, 1995), 36, 40–45. The *Tribune* article—Tony Davis, "Good Business or Public Burden?" (28 July 1994)—is reprinted as Appendix VII. As an example of the unequal bargaining power between New Mexico and Intel, Davis found that the state's cost-benefit analysis did not assign present values because the state economic development official did not know how to do it. Davis quotes him: "I don't frankly understand present value calculations." *Intel Inside New Mexico*, 126.

93. Friedman, "The New Civil War," 100.

94. *Ibid*. Note that these IRBs were taxable, hence not subject to the limits established in the 1986 federal tax reform.

95. Personal communication, 27 November 1996.

96. *Intel Inside New Mexico*, 13, 73–78.

97. Personal communication, 18 February 1997.

98. Greg Krikorian, "Council Overrides Veto, OK's Wage Law," *Los Angeles Times*, 2 April 1997, Metro Part B section, 1; Kevin Diaz, "Minneapolis Aims for Compromise on Living-Wage Rule," *Minneapolis Star Tribune*, 5 March 1997, 1B; "Living Wage Movement Scores New Victories, Keeps Rolling," *The ACORN Report*, April 1999, 1–2.

99. Personal communication, Jen Kern, ACORN, 28 May 1996.

100. At the local level, conservative and libertarian think tanks have been important in the Midwest, rallying behind Ohio Republican state senator Charles Horn's call for unilateral disarmament in the subsidy wars. In North Carolina, the libertarian John Locke Institute supported the legal challenge by William Maready to the state's subsidy programs, which won at the lower court level but was overturned by the state supreme court in March 1996. See John Greenwald, "A No-Win War Between the States," *Time*, 8 April 1996, 44; Neil R. Peirce, "To Curb Tax Giveaways: Bring on the Feds," *Nation's Cities*, 25 December 1995, 14; David Friedman, "The New Civil War," 99–106.

101. Mark Ronayne, "Disciplining Industrial Incentives," 30.

102. "Canada: Piper Aircraft Corp to Investigate Location of all New Operations," *Financial Post*, 21 November 1991, 3; "Nine Provinces Trying to Woo Piper Aircraft," *Globe and Mail*, 10 December 1991, B6; "Canada: Piper May Locate to Canada if Funds Can Be Arranged," *Financial Post*, 18 December 1991, 7; "USA: Piper Aircraft Rescue Deal in Sight," *Financial Post*, 6 March 1992, 4; "USA: Piper Aircraft Ready for British Columbia Landing by Dancan Investments," *Financial Post*, 11 June

1992, 4; "Canada: Piper Bid Dead," *Financial Post*, 1 May 1993, p. 4; Paul Proctor, "Fear of New Taxes Dims Glow from Sales," *Aviation Week and Space Technology*, 25 September 1995, 45.

103. See, for example, John DeMont, "Fast Frank: How New Brunswick's Premier Turned His Province Into Canada's Social Laboratory," *Maclean's*, 11 April 1994, 26, on poaching and on a bidding war for Purolator Canada between New Brunswick and Manitoba. Some other bidding wars included the Toyota plant that went to Cambridge, Ontario (beating out six other provinces), in 1985 (Christopher Waddell, "Ontario to get $300 million Toyota plant," *Globe and Mail*, 19 October 1985, A1); the Suzuki-GM plant that chose Ingersoll, Ontario, over Québec (Gary Lamphier, "Suzuki set for auto plant: But it's Québec vs. Ontario for location," *Financial Times of Canada*, 21 April 1986, 3; James Daw, "GM-Suzuki plant includes $85 million aid packages," *Toronto Star*, 28 August 1986, A1); the Litton Systems Canada radar plant that chose Nova Scotia over Prince Edward Island in 1986 (Robert Martin, "Nova Scotia wins bidding war for $18 million Litton plant," *Globe and Mail*, 26 July 1986, A3). Some examples of relocations include Crown Life Insurance Co. (Ontario to Saskatchewan; "Crown jobs to relocate to Regina as promised," *Toronto Star*, 28 May 1992, D1) and DynaTek Automation Systems (Ontario to Alberta; "Growing firm lured away from Ontario," *Calgary Herald*, 28 December 1992, C2).

104. Ronayne, "Disciplining Industrial Incentives," 52–54.

105. Internal Trade Secretariat, *Agreement on Internal Trade: A Guide* (Ottawa: Internal Trade Secretariat, 1994), 14.

106. Personal communication with Emmy Verdun, Industry Canada, 19 July 1994. Verdun was a negotiator of the Agreement on Internal Trade.

107. See Robert Axelrod, *The Evolution of Cooperation* (New York: Basic Books, 1984), 131–32.

108. Keith Damsell, "B.C. Files Objection to Loss of UPS to N.B.," *Financial Post*, 27 April 1996, 14; Alan Toulin, "Canada: Provincial Trade Pact Starting to Crumble," *Financial Post*, 14 September 1996, 1; "Canada: Editorial—Provincial Trade Agreement Doesn't Pass Crucial Test," *Financial Post*, 19 September 1996, 10; personal communication with Norm Treneman, British Columbia Ministry of Employment and Investment, 26 March 1999.

109. On Air Canada, see Chris Morris, "Province Offers $5.3M 'Loan' to Lure Air Canada Call Centre," *Ottawa Citizen*, 30 August 1996, D10. On Intercontinental Packers Ltd., see Lindsay Kines, "Meat Plant Closure 'Job Poaching,' Union Says," *Vancouver Sun*, 2 December 1996, B4.

110. Personal communication with Norm Treneman, 26 March 1999.

111. Katherine McGuire, Director of Trade Policy for the Ontario Ministry of Economic Development and Trade, reported that she did not know of any provinces that allowed local governments to provide incentives—a situation she was certain of for all the provinces east of Ontario (personal communication, 29 January 1997).

112. Laura Reese, "Local Economic Development Practices Across the Northern Border," *Urban Affairs Quarterly* 28, no. 4 (June 1993): 576; personal communication with Katherine McGuire, Director of Trade Policy, Ontario Ministry of Economic Development and Trade, 29 January 1997. I thank Barbara Jenkins for bringing the "bonusing" ban to my attention.

113. For example, both St. Louis and Kansas City prepared incentive packages to move Trans World Airlines from Mt. Kisco, New York, to Missouri. See Kenneth P. Thomas, "EU Regulation of State Aid to Industry: Lessons for North America," in *Economic Integration in the Americas,* ed. Christos C. Paraskevopoulos, Ricardo Grinspun, and George E. Eaton (Cheltenham: Edward Elgar, 1996), 138.

114. Personal communication, 29 January 1997.

115. Personal communication with a municipal economic development director in Ontario, 26 November 1996.

116. Reese, "Local Economic Development Practices," Table 6.

117. Judy Randall, Canada's New Democrats, personal communications, 19 August 1996 and 11 September 1996.

118. See Ontario Coalition for Social Justice and Ontario Federation of Labor, *Unfair Shares: Corporations and Taxation in Canada* (Don Mills, Ontario: Ontario Coalition for Social Justice and Ontario Federation of Labor, 1996).

119. Personal communication, Jim Turk, Canadian Union of Public Employees, 5 September 1996.

120. Personal communication, Judy Randall, Canada's New Democrats, 11 September 1996.

121. Ontario Coalition for Social Justice and Ontario Federation of Labour, *Unfair $hares,* 2.

122. New Democrat press release, "McDonough Details Program to Reduce GST," 30 May 1996.

123. Canadian Taxpayers Federation, *Corporate Welfare: A Report on Sixteen Years of Industry Canada Financial Assistance* (Ottawa: Canadian Taxpayers Federation, 1998).

124. Lorne Gunter, "Canada's Corporate Trough-Dippers Unmasked," *Ottawa Citizen*, 22 June 1998, A9; Daniel Leblanc, "Big Business's Best

Friend: The Cash Cow on the Hill: 'Corporate Welfare' Recipients Evade Millions in Payments: Report," *Ottawa Citizen*, 5 June 1998, A1; Daniel Leblanc, "Corporate Welfare Costs Citizens Billions: Study," *Ottawa Citizen*, 17 April 1998, A12.

125. Gunter, "Canada's Corporate Trough-Dippers"; Leblanc, "Big Business's Best Friend."
126. "Canada, Brazil Both Claim Win in WTO Aircraft Ruling," *Vancouver Sun*, 3 August 1999, C8.
127. Personal communication, 23 July 1999.
128. "Alberta May Ban Business Investments by Government," Canadian Press Newswire, 17 August 1995.
129. A recent study of Minnesota data shows the widespread use of tax increment financing for corporate relocations within the state. Greg LeRoy and Tyson Slocum, *Economic Development in Minnesota: High Subsidies, Low Wages, Absent Standards* (Washington, D.C.: Good Jobs First, 1999), 29–33.
130. See Robert Axelrod's analysis of "decomposing" prisoners' dilemmas in *Evolution of Cooperation*, 132.
131. Personal communication, 23 July 1999.

6

How Much Bang for the Euro?

We have seen that the EU has well-institutionalized procedures and built-up case law for controlling subsidies and other state aid by member states. Whether this arrangement is any better than the unrestrained bidding for business in the United States depends on the extent to which EU procedures have succeeded, particularly with regard to controlling aid to mobile investment. Some observers are dubious: Edward Graham writes, "In practice, however, investment subsidies are rife, and little has been done at the level of the European Union to stem them."[1] We must ask, however: "rife" compared with what? Other writers have evaluated Commission control more positively: Damien Neven and Georges Siotis argue that a subsidy of 80,000 ECU per job may not be excessive, "at least in regions where employment prospects are particularly poor. Further intervention to reduce these subsidies might not, therefore, be a priority for European competition policy."[2] Here, too, the appropriate counterfactual for comparison is key. This methodological problem, in fact, is central for evaluating EU state aid control policy.

The approach adopted here is to compare outcomes in the EU with those in other industrialized countries. This approach encounters certain difficulties because the data for EU state aid are far better than anything available for other countries. For example, because the vast majority of U.S. support to firms is provided through tax expenditures, national accounts data on subsidies present a completely uninformative picture. Therefore, we must make two cuts at analyzing European performance. First, how have trends in state aid in the EU compared with developments in other industrialized nations? Much of this work is done in Chapter 5, which attempts to categorize U.S. and Canadian industrial support in terms of whether it would be considered "state aid" in the EU. In this chapter, I also present data on trends for the OECD as a whole. The second evaluative move requires us to compare outcomes with Commission goals, to get at what Michelle Cini has called policy "effectiveness."[3]

Accordingly, we must ask what the Commission's—or more precisely, DG IV's—goals have been. I take these goals to be as follows:

- Reduce the overall volume of state aid and the total aid that flows to the manufacturing sector. This reduction is easily discerned from the *Surveys* on state aid; it follows from Cini's comments about the anti-interventionist bias of DG IV.[4]
- Reduce bidding for investment projects.[5]
- Improve cohesion by reducing "central" aid compared to "peripheral" aid.[6]
- Improve transparency to ease the monitoring process by encouraging the use of transparent forms of aid and getting rid of non-transparent forms of aid or those that are easily abused. (See discussion of transparency in Chapter 3.)
- Ensure more generally that the Commission's rules are followed. This goal speaks in particular to the importance of notification and compliance.[7]
- Achieve certain specific goals that have changed through time, such as eliminating aid for intra-Community exports and reducing general investment aid that is not targeted to regional, sectoral, or horizontal purposes.

This chapter tries to show the extent to which the Commission has succeeded in its goals, as well as comparing the EU with other industrialized countries.[8] To preview the results, the total amounts of national state aid, aid to manufacturing, and aid in the categories that are most likely to go to mobile investment projects have fallen in real terms over the period covered by the seven *Surveys* on state aid (1981–97), once the impact of German reunification has been factored into the equation. Although these outcomes imply Commission effectiveness, several caveats are in order. First, aid given by the EU itself through its regional policies has offset the decline in national aid available for mobile investment, though not the decline in manufacturing aid or total state aid. Second, there are important ways of evading the rules for mobile investment, although they are not without their limits. Thus, although the overall evaluation of the Commission's efforts on aid amounts is positive, it is not uniformly so.

In terms of its effect on cohesion, state aid control has only recently had a positive impact. For some years, the overall reductions in aid were more substantial in the poorer countries than in the richer ones.

Since 1992–94, this trend has been reversed: Aid has actually increased in the cohesion countries, on top of increased allocations from the Structural Funds. All of the cohesion countries give below-average proportions of their aid to R&D efforts, however, which may slow their growth in the future.

Beyond the amount of aid, the data show that, except in reunifying Germany, the Commission has been successful in channeling aid into more transparent forms (grants and tax reductions) while significantly reducing the share of aid provided through capital injections and guarantees (the most opaque instruments). This trend should help improve the Commission's monitoring capacity in the long run.

Turning to the important issues of notification, compliance, and enforcement, clearly governments still often fail to abide by their Treaty obligation to report aid in advance. At the same time, the likelihood of being caught in non-notification is also substantial: 22.1 percent of all new aid cases in 1998 were non-notified but discovered. Obviously, this problem is by no means solved. In terms of compliance and enforcement, the number of negative decisions rose sharply beginning in 1981 and generally stayed in double digits through 1990. Negative decisions declined in the early 1990s but jumped to record highs of twenty-six in 1996 and thirty-one in 1998.[9] Commission vigilance in this area has been supplemented by the use of repayment orders since 1982. An analysis of these orders suggests that although some countries have been more likely than others to have broken the rules to such an extent that negative decisions have included repayment orders, Germany stands out: Several long-running cases have been subject to multiple court decisions and prolonged appeals.

Finally, this chapter analyzes two specific Commission initiatives: aid for intra-Community exports and general (investment) aid. The former has been virtually non-existent since 1979; the latter has died out in the past few years. Both of these results are in accord with Commission initiatives.

Total Volume of State Aid

The trend for total state aid is obviously central to evaluating the substantial effort put into its control. The EU is unique with regard to the amount of detailed information it publishes on state aid. Neither the United States nor Canada has collected anywhere near as much information on practices within their borders, and the two other multilateral organizations with subsidy information—the WTO and the OECD—have grave shortcomings. WTO subsidy notification only began with the implementation of the Uruguay Round's Subsidies and Countervailing Measures agreement in 1995 and is incomplete in many ways; the OECD project was terminated in May 1998 (see further discussion in Chapter 7). The detailed nature of the EU data provides a fairly exact picture of the trends in EU state aid. Table 6-1 gives the total volume of aid for the period 1981–1997. Note that, unless otherwise specified, this table and the tables that follow cover *national* aids—not those given by the EU itself.

Table 6-1 shows that there has been a generally downward trend of state aid in real terms (which would look even more consistent if agricultural aid data were available for 1992–94). Note that the EC-12 declines since 1988–90 are even more significant than the table shows because of the inclusion of aid to the former East Germany for the first time (at least 6.6 billion ECU)[10] and because of the

Table 6-1 **Total State Aid (annual averages) and Percent Change (billions of ECU, constant 1996 prices)**

	EC-10	EC-12	EU-15	Percent Change
1981–86	114.2			
1986–88	102.1			−10.6
1986–88		112.7		
1988–90		113.2		+0.4
1990–92		104.2[a]		−8.0[a]
1992–94		91.3[b]		−12.3[b]
1993–95		101.5[c]		+11.2[c]
1995–97		88.5	95.1	−12.8

[a]There is substantial missing data for agricultural aid (though most aid comes from the CAP);[11] see *Fifth Survey*, 25–26 and Table 9.
[b]Includes no data for agricultural aid; see *Sixth Survey*, 31, 41.
[c]Agricultural aid reincorporated at a value of 10.8 billion ECU; see *Seventh Survey*, 27–28.

Sources: EC-10 for 1981–1986 and 1986–88, *Second Survey*, 39, Table XI; EC-12 for 1986–88, *Third Survey*, 38; Table 13; 1988–90, *Fourth Survey*, 38, Table 13; 1990–92, *Fifth Survey*, 34, Table 14; 1992–94, *Sixth Survey*, 41, Table 17; 1993–95 and 1995–97, *Seventh Survey*, 49, Table 18. Amounts converted to 1996 prices using the EU-15 consumer price index (CPI), *Eurostat Yearbook '97*, 425.

economic difficulties of the early 1990s, which tend to increase demand for state support.[12]

Table 6-2 amplifies the findings of Table 6-1 by relating total state aid in EU member states to their GDP. Table 6-2 shows that total aid as a percentage of GDP has fallen for the EU as a whole, as well as for most of the individual members.

At the level of all national state aid, the Commission's efforts appear to be paying off. State aid has steadily reduced in real terms since the Commission began its *Surveys*, and aid has fallen as percentage of GDP as well. This trend is especially striking in the recessionary 1992–94 period, when the EU registered a decrease in state aid as a percentage of GDP even as it was absorbing eastern Germany—a region that was poorer than any of the cohesion countries.

State Aid to Manufacturing

Knox suggests that to understand the success (or lack thereof) of EU state aid control, it is necessary to focus on aid to manufacturing rather than all aid. He argues that support for agriculture, fisheries, transport, and coal is "probably allowable" in most cases, so manufacturing subsidies have the greatest likelihood of violating state aid rules.[13] Given the focus of the *Surveys* on the manufacturing sector as well, the Commission appears to share this view. This section analyzes data for manufacturing aid. To provide a comparative standard, the results of the most recent OECD study on industrial support also are considered.

EU State Aid to Manufacturing

Returning again to the *Surveys*, Table 6-3 shows state aid to manufacturing[14] for 1981–1997. The first comparison omits steel and shipbuilding, both of which saw very high aid in 1981–1986.

Table 6-3 shows that there was a consistent downward trend in state aid to manufacturing over the 1981–94 period, if the extraordinary effect of German reunification is excluded. Since then, as aid to the new *Länder* has fallen, there has been a greater increase in aid in other member states—although that increase is almost entirely accounted for by *ad hoc* aid in the financial services and air transport sectors. Table 6-4 shows manufacturing aid as a percentage of value

Table 6-2 **Total State Aid as a Percentage of GDP**

Country[a]	1981–86	86–88	88–90	90–92	92–94	94–96	95–97
Austria	—	—	—	—	—	0.6	0.65
Belgium	4.1	3.2	2.8	2.9	1.5	1.3	1.17
Denmark	1.3	1.0	1.1	1.0	0.9	0.9	0.89
Germany	2.5	2.5	2.5	2.4	2.3	1.9	1.64
Greece	2.5	4.5	3.1	1.9	1.3	1.1	0.98
Spain	—	2.7	1.8	1.3[b]	1.1	1.2	1.16
Finland	—	—	—	—	—	0.4	0.43
France	2.7	2.0	2.1	1.7	1.2	1.1	1.12
Ireland	4.0	2.7	1.9	1.2[b]	1.0	0.8	1.10
Italy	4.0	3.1	2.8	2.4[b]	2.2	2.0	1.71
Luxembourg	6.0	4.0	3.9	2.4[b]	2.1	1.0	0.50
The Netherlands	1.5	1.3	1.1	0.9	0.6	0.7	0.61
Portugal	—	1.5	2.0	1.5	0.8	0.9	0.98
Sweden	—	—	—	—	—	0.7	0.76
United Kingdom	1.8	1.1	1.2	0.5	0.3	0.5	0.52
EU-10/12/15[c]	2.8	2.2	2.1	1.8	1.5	1.4	1.20

Note: Beginning with the *Sixth Survey* (1992–94), aid is calculated as a percentage of non-agricultural GDP because of weakness of agricultural aid data (see Table 18). Although this factor is not stated in the *Seventh Survey*, it is also true there.

[a]This table follows alphabetization used in the *Surveys*, in which Germany, Greece, and Spain are ordered by their own-language names (Deutschland, Ellas, and España).

[b]No data for agricultural aid in this period; see *Fifth Survey*, 26, Table 9.

[c]EU-10 in 1981–86, EU-12 in 1986–94, EU-15 for 1994–96 and beyond.

Sources: Second Survey, 42, Table XII; *Third Survey*, 39, Table 14; *Fourth Survey*, 41, Table 14; *Fifth Survey*, 35, Table 15; *Sixth Survey*, 42, Table 18; *Seventh Survey*, 50, Table 19; personal communication from Reinhard Walther, DG IV Inventory and Analysis Unit, 25 August 1999. In all cases in which figures were revised, the most recent data have been used.

Table 6-3 **State Aid to Manufacturing (annual averages) and Percent Change (billions of 1996 ECU, constant prices)**

	EC-10	EC-12	Percent Change	EC-11[a]	Percent Change
1981–86[b]	47.4				
1986–88[b]	41.6		−12.2		
1986–88[b]		47.4			
1988–90		44.3	−6.6	35.6	
1990–92		44.9	+1.3	29.1	−18.1
1992–94[c]		44.0	−1.9	23.5	−19.4
1993–95[d]		44.2	+0.5	25.0	+6.6
1995–97[e]		40.3	−8.8	26.8	+7.2
1995–97[e]		41.6			

[a]Excluding Germany. The reunification of Germany led to high and rising aid in the new *Länder,* partially offset by substantial aid cuts in the old *Länder.*

[b]Excludes steel and shipbuilding, both of which saw very high aid in 1981–86. Including these sectors would make the decrease even larger.

[c]Includes ECU 41.4 billion manufacturing, 0.66 billion air transport, and 0.34 billion financial services.

[d]Includes ECU 41.8 billion manufacturing, 1.3 billion air transport, and 1.1 billion financial services.

[e]EU-15; includes ECU 36.4 billion manufacturing, 1.2 billion air transport, and 2.7 billion financial services.

Sources: Calculated from *Second Survey*, 31, Table X; *Third Survey*, 10, Table 3; *Fourth Survey*, 10, Table 3; *Fifth Survey*, 7, Table 3; *Sixth Survey*, 9, Table 3 (manufacturing), and 35 (air transport and financial services); *Seventh Survey*, 7, Table 3 (manufacturing), 40 (air transport), and 47 (financial services). Amounts converted to 1996 prices using EU-15 consumer price index, *Eurostat Yearbook* '97, 425. All periods except 1995–97 use data from the succeeding *Survey* to incorporate revisions.

added, underscoring the decrease in aid to manufacturing. This table has been divided into two tables, corresponding to the exclusion of airline and financial services from the definition of "manufacturing" beginning in 1992–94.

Tables 6-4a and 6-4b present a more mixed picture for manufacturing aid, with a large decrease by 1986–88 (i.e., after the end of the Davignon aid program for the steel industry and high aid allowed for the shipbuilding industry),[15] little change through the early 1990s, then renewed decline since 1994. Few countries have shown a consis-

Table 6-4a **Manufacturing Aid as a Percentage of Value Added (includes airlines and financial services)**

Country	1981–86	1986–88	1988–90	1990–92	1992–94
Belgium	6.4	4.3	5.0	7.9	4.8
Denmark	2.8	1.9	2.3	1.9	2.8
Germany	3.0	2.7	2.6	3.5[a]	4.8
Greece	12.9	24.3	16.9	12.5	10.5
Spain	—	6.8	3.7	2.1	1.7
France	4.9	3.8	3.7	2.7	3.3
Ireland	7.9	6.4	3.9	2.7	3.5
Italy	9.5	6.2	7.8	8.9	8.4
Luxembourg	7.3	2.3	3.4	3.5	2.9
The Netherlands	4.1	3.1	3.2	2.5	2.1
Portugal	—	2.2	7.3	4.6	4.4
UK	3.8	2.6	1.9	1.4	0.8
EU-12[b]	4.8	4.0	3.8	3.8	4.0

[a]Data for former East Germany first incorporated.
[b]EU-10 in 1981–86.

Sources: Second Survey, 10, Table I; *Third Survey*, 10, Table 3; *Fourth Survey*, 10, Table 3; *Fifth Survey*, 7, Table 3. In all cases in which figures were revised, the most recent data have been used.

tent decline; the UK has been the most prominent to do so. The high levels, and occasional increases, in rich countries such as Belgium, Denmark, and Luxembourg are difficult to square with the Commission's goal of promoting cohesion (an issue to which I return below).

WTO and OECD Data

What was the trend of manufacturing support spending in other industrialized countries during this time? Nothing even remotely comparable to the EU's data exists for the manufacturing sector yet. Although the Uruguay Round of the General Agreement on Tariffs and Trade produced an Agreement on Subsidies and Countervailing Measures that requires subsidy notification, some WTO members had not reported their subsidies even in the second round of "new and full" notifications (1998); others implausibly claimed to have no subsidy programs or made substantially incomplete notifications.[16] An examination of the U.S. and Canadian notifications, for example, shows

Table 6-4b **Manufacturing Aid as a Percentage of Value Added (not including airlines and financial services)**

Country	1992–94	1993–95	1994–96	1995–97
Austria	—	—	1.3	1.5
Belgium	2.5	2.5	3.0	2.4
Denmark	2.5	2.7	2.9	3.0
Germany	4.4	4.4	3.8	3.1
Greece	6.5	5.2	6.3	5.6
Spain	1.8	2.1	2.7	3.0
Finland	—	—	1.6	1.6
France	2.4	2.1	1.8	2.0
Ireland	1.7[a]	2.4	1.5[a]	2.2
Italy	6.4	6.1	5.8	5.3
Luxembourg	2.6	2.2	2.3	2.3
The Netherlands	1.5	1.1	1.4	1.2
Portugal	2.5	2.7	1.9	2.8
Sweden	—	—	0.8	1.0
United Kingdom	0.9	0.8	0.9	0.9
EU-12	3.5	3.5	[b]	2.9
EU-15	—	—	3.0	2.8

[a]The Commission deemed these figures inaccurate but did not provide revisions in the *Seventh Survey*.[17]
[b]No figure provided.

Sources: Sixth Survey, 9, Table 3; *Seventh Survey*, 7, Table 3.

that they are very different from the figures presented in Chapter 5. The WTO process will not produce adequate data for comparative purposes for some time.

A better comparative source is the OECD's 1996 study, *Public Support to Industry*, which covers the period from 1989 to 1993.[18] Though now somewhat dated, the stated focus of this study was similar to the focus on "manufacturing aid" in the EU *Surveys*. The real drawback to the OECD study, however, is that its spending data in essence are provided only in aggregated form for the entire database because there are no individual data available for the United States or Canada—though there are data (updated since 1993 in many cases) for most other OECD members. Moreover, the coverage between this study and its predecessor covering 1986–89 changed so radically that

Table 6-5 **"Industrial Support" versus "State Aid to Manufacturing" (billions of 1989 dollars or 1993 ECU)**

Year	**OECD Amount**	**EU Amount**
1988	no data	E 47.37
1989	39.0	36.18
1990	41.8	43.78
1991	48.4	39.83
1992	46.0	41.20
1993	42.2	43.89
1994	no data	42.83
Percent change 1988–94	N/A	–9.6
Percent change 1989–92	+17.9	+13.9
Percent change 1989–93	+8.2	+21.3
Percent change 1990–93	+1.0	+0.3
Percent change 1989/90–1991/92	+18.0	+1.4
Percent change 1989/90–1992/93	+9.2	+6.4
Percent change 1989/91–1991/93	+5.7	+4.3

Sources: EU 1988–89, *Fourth Survey*, 1990–94, *Fifth Survey*, 5, Table 1; OECD, *Public Support to Industry*.

Note: EU amounts for 1988 and 1989 converted to 1993 prices using the EC-12 CPI, *Eurostat Yearbook '95*, 238.

they are not really comparable.[19] In addition, the OECD data also suffer from problems of obtaining reliable subfederal subsidies, as well as gaps in support by way of tax expenditures. Bearing in mind these differences, Table 6-5 compares OECD data for industrial support from 1989 to 1993 with EU state aid for manufacturing from 1988 to 1994 (the third through fifth *Surveys*). The figures are in constant 1989 U.S. dollars (OECD) or constant 1993 ECU (EU).

These data are very difficult to compare, in particular because the results are very sensitive to the base year chosen and the choice between annual data and multi-year averages.[20] Given the extreme variability with annual data, multi-year averages would seem to be more reliable; several such comparisons above show that the EU increase in manufacturing aid is slightly less than that for the OECD as a whole. Moreover, the *Fifth Survey* made upward revisions to the 1990–92 data that should be replicated in the OECD data; because they have not been, the EU data are biased upward relative to the OECD data, especially when 1989 is taken as the base year (note, too, that 1989 is the EU's local minimum—magnifying the apparent increase when it is used as the base year).Thus, the EU's performance is slightly better than the raw data show. Though the lack of complete comparability could upset this comparison, in the recessionary 1989–93 period (for which both data sets have complete coverage), EU state aid to manufacturing grew somewhat more slowly than the average for all OECD members. This finding means that non-EU OECD members did even worse than the table shows because collectively they would have to have had grown more rapidly than the OECD average. (Again, this finding discounts the 1989–93 change because 1989 is the local minimum for the EU—a factor that is corrected with multi-year averages.) All of these considerations point to better performance by the EU in restricting state support of manufacturing industry.

The evidence on state aid to manufacturing, then, again points to Commission success in reducing this important category of aid. The volume of support to manufacturing fell substantially in real terms over the period 1981–97. Despite the addition of five new member states and the new *Länder* of Germany, the real value of manufacturing aid was lower in 1995–97 than in 1981–86. Moreover, if we exclude Germany entirely[21] to isolate the extraordinary effect of reunification, the decline of the early 1990s emerges in even more vivid relief, and the increases in the EU-11 since 1992–94 result almost entirely from bailouts of banks and airlines. Expressed as a share of value added in manufacturing, however, aid remained flat from 1986–88 (after the sharp reductions in aid for steel and shipbuilding) to 1992–94. Only since 1994 has aid fallen as a percentage of value added in manufacturing—and part of the lower levels results from changes in data keeping. The data show that some countries have reduced their aid to manufacturing less than others; indeed, some have increased it. Whereas France, The Netherlands, and the UK (as well as Germany until reunification) have all had generally decreased aid to manufacturing, Belgium and Denmark have generally increased manufacturing aid since 1986 (see Table 6-4).

How does EU aid to manufacturing compare with that of the rest of the industrialized world? The evidence here is weaker than for state aid or subsidies as a whole, but the overall conclusion must still be that aid is under more control in the EU than elsewhere. As Table 6-5 shows, different ways of expressing the same data for 1988–94 suggest that aid to manufacturing in the EU grew more slowly than in the OECD as a whole; this trend is clearest in a comparison of multi-year averages. This finding implies that control over aid was better in the EU than in the rest of the OECD.

Aid for Mobile Investment

Placing controls on bidding for investment projects has been an important rationale for state aid policy, especially in the field of regional aid.[22] Yet only in December 1995 did the Commission produce a draft framework for the control of regional aid for large inward investments, and this proposal was not accepted until two years later.[23] Determining whether state aid policy has been effective in this regard is relatively difficult. There are two major data problems involved here. First, the Commission does not categorize aid in a way that identifies mobile projects, so data must be extracted from the *Surveys*. That procedure is followed in the following section. A second problem, however, is that some critics of state aid policy are commercial enterprises (i.e., site selection consultants) that do not make their underlying data public. On the basis of several interviews with location consultants, this chapter pieces together potential problems in the Commission's control of bidding for investment.

Evidence from the State Aid *Surveys*

Because the Commission's reports on state aid do not total the amount going to mobile investment projects, the present analysis identifies the types of aid that are most likely to go to such projects, then follows its trends over the 1981–97 period covered by the *Surveys*. This analysis does not constitute an estimate of aid to mobile investment *per se*; instead, it identifies the total amount that is *potentially available* for such projects. According to Reinhard Walther, a statistical expert in the Directorate for State Aids of DG IV, the types of aid that are likely to go to mobile investments are regional aid, aid for R&D, and general aid.[24] Examination of spending in those categories confirms that overall spending potentially available for mobile projects has decreased from the period of 1981–86 (*First Survey*) to 1995–97 (*Seventh Survey*), as Table 6-6 shows.

Table 6-6 **State Aid: R&D, General, Regional (annual averages), and Percent Change (millions of 1996 ECU, constant prices)**

	EC-10	EC-12	% Change	EC-11[a]	% Change
1981–86	24,154.8				
1986–88	21,785.7		−9.8		
1986–88		22,612.5			
1988–90		22,089.9	−2.3	15,085.3	
1990–92		25,459.5	+15.3	14,819.0	−1.8
1992–94		28,602.7	+12.3	13,047.7	−12.0
1995–97		24,739.2	−13.5	13,889.2	+6.4
1995–97 (EU-15)		25,509.5			

[a]Excluding Germany. The reunification of Germany led to high and rising aid in the new *Länder*, which was partially offset by substantial aid cuts in the old *Länder*. Moreover, the vast majority of regional aid in the new *Länder* was privatization aid, meaning a lower proportion of regional aid there went to greenfield investment than in other countries.

Sources: 1981–86 and 1986–88, *Second Survey*, 31, Table X; 1988–90, calculated from *Third Survey*, Annex Tables A4/1-A4/12; 1990–92, calculated from *Fourth Survey*, Annex Tables A5/1-A5/12; 1992–94, calculated from *Fifth Survey*, Annex Tables A4/1-A4/12; 1995–97, calculated from *Seventh Survey*, Annex Tables A4/1-A4/15. Amounts converted to 1996 prices using the EU-15 CPI, *Eurostat Yearbook '97*, 425.

As Table 6-6 shows, spending on these three categories of aid fell in real terms by 9.8 percent from 1981–86 to 1986–88 and by 2.3 percent from 1986–88 to 1988–90. With the reunification of Germany, there was a sharp increase of 15.3 percent in these categories from 1988–90 to 1990–92, with a further 12.3 percent increase by 1992–94. After that, aid in these categories fell by 13.5 percent to 1995–97. Excluding Germany would be more appropriate for our purposes (excluding eastern Germany only would *overstate* Commission effectiveness) to evaluate how well the Commission has been able to control these categories of aid, given that eastern Germany is poorer than any cohesion country and the Federal Republic has substantial resources to provide aid there. There was a decrease of 1.8 percent between 1988–90 and 1990–92 for the eleven countries (excluding Germany) and a substantial drop of 12.0 percent between 1990–92 and 1992–94. This latter decrease is especially striking, given the economic difficulties facing the EU during this period.[25] Between 1992–94 and 1995–97, however, these eleven countries saw an increase of 6.4 percent.

Although the general downward trend in the value of the types of aid that are most likely to go to mobile investment (EC-11) provides some support for the hypothesis that the Commission's policies have had that effect, the data do not yet constitute proof that aid to mobile investment has declined. They do show, however, that the overall pool of money from which investment incentives are drawn has shrunk.[26] Given that not all aid in any of these categories is provided solely to attract mobile investment, an increase in awards to mobile projects is still consistent with the decreased size of this pool. Achieving a smaller pool and larger awards per project, however, requires that fewer projects receive funding or that governments spend less on other ways of achieving their R&D and regional objectives, or both. At a gross level, then, the Commission may still be entitled to claim some success in this area.

Nevertheless, some plant location consultants have stated publicly that aid for new investment projects has increased over the last few years.

Views of Plant Location Consultants

Site selection consultants occupy a role in the world economy that is analogous to the role that Sinclair has argued characterizes credit rating agencies (CRAs).[27] CRAs, in Sinclair's view, provide information to potential investors and in effect help coordinate their behavior.[28] In the process, their views of "proper" government policy receive wide dissemination and are strongly taken into account by governments. Sinclair identifies these views as consistent with a shrinking of the economic role of the state and a removal of certain economic decisions (i.e., monetary policy) from the arena of politics.[29]

Like CRAs, location consultants have developed specialized knowledge that helps coordinate the investment process, but their effect on government policy is narrower than that of CRAs (i.e., location consultants are restricted to attempting to influence policy for attracting direct investment) except in the longer run. By nature, site selection agencies encourage governments to compete for investments at the level of initial investments and in terms of developing policies for negotiating with investors that in the long run will increase subsidies to investment. That is, they encourage governments to use cost-benefit analyses to determine the amount of investment support the government will provide firms; the way such analysis is cast takes into account the costs and benefits only in the jurisdiction offering the investment aid. In other words, these consultants encourage governments to ignore the collective irrationality of the process of investment competition (see Chapter 2).

All three of the site selection consultants with whom I have spoken asserted that the Commission's efforts at constraining aid to mobile investment have been unsuccessful. That is, they agreed that aid intensity (at least for the most desirable investments) has increased over the past few years. None would provide underlying data on which they base their assessments, however, so analyzing closely their overall conclusions is impossible. Nonetheless, their comments do underline genuine problems for the Commission's control policy.

First, there is a problem in measuring aid intensity, whether intensity is measured in NGE or GGE. The reason for this difficulty is that the denominator—the investment itself—is open to interpretation and manipulation. Recall that aid intensity = aid ÷ investment. If the investment consists of land, plant, and equipment that costs $20 million and the government provides a $5 million investment grant, then aid intensity (GGE) is 25 percent. If the Commission in practice will not allow aid greater than 20 percent in that region, the aid would be disallowed, or the Commission would try to persuade the government to provide only $4 million. As one of the consultants pointed out, however,[30] if the investment is construed to include acquisition of know-how and technology from the parent company, the denominator grows—thereby increasing the allowable numerator for what is in fact the same investment. In the foregoing example, if these latter items are counted as an additional $5 million investment, the total investment grows to $25 million—and $5 million in aid would then be allowable.

Germany now allows "intangible" assets to be counted as part of the investment; Ireland includes licensing and royalty charges. Italy includes licenses, establishing offices, and distribution network creation. Luxembourg allows the purchase of "know-how" and technology acquisition via patents and licenses. These examples are part of a "movement in recent years to increase the 'softer' component of policy, including also measures to improve the general business environment."[31]

Although the Commission generally approves of this approach (most recently in the December 1997 regional aid guidelines), it is at variance with previous EC policy[32] and clearly increases the effective value of aid. In addition, inclusion of items such as "know-how" and technology means that transfer prices become relevant to determining the denominator. As Richard Caves documents, these items—precisely those for which no "arms-length" transactions exist (unlike, for example, automobile spark plugs)—have the widest scope for abusive manipulation of transfer prices.[33] If a subsidiary is overcharged for patents, for example, the "investment" appears larger than it really is, again making possible Commission approval of higher aid.

A second method identified by the consultants to legally evade state aid rules is the use of alternative forms of financing. In the United States, a common method is IRB financing, whereby a state issues tax-exempt bonds to help finance a private project (see Chapter 5). In Europe, tax-inspired leasing can provide negative-interest finance without the involvement of the state. For example, before Irish banks were subject to the same 10 percent corporate income tax paid by manufacturing firms, they could buy capital goods, take the 100 percent depreciation allowance against their 40 percent tax rate, and lease the equipment to manufacturing firms at negative interest rates.[34] This arrangement was completely immune to the state aid rules because the major contours of tax policy are considered to be general macroeconomic measures rather than state aid. In 1997, however, the Commission acted against a Dutch extension of the use of sale-leaseback arrangements to *intellectual* property, opening an Article 93(2) procedure against the "technolease" tax plan under which electronics giant Philips sold technology to Rabobank in 1993. The Commission suspected that this tax provision was not genuinely available to all companies and that it was designed as a means of propping up Philips, which was in financial difficulty at the time.[35]

Two of the plant location consultants I interviewed pointed to the use of training grants as a third way to evade the intent of Commission policies. This strategy is sometimes possible because such funds lie at the dividing line between state aid and general measures (fiscal, social security, or employment policy). The Commission's comments in the *Fourth Survey on State Aid* reflect this dilemma:

> Insofar as such [training or employment] schemes are not industry-specific and are available across the whole economy and in fact genuinely constitute part of a general system of employment measures, they are not to be considered state aids. Although a number of training and employment schemes have been treated by the Commission as state aids,

> not all Member State's measures in these fields have up to now been examined in detail. Therefore, in order to present figures that are comparable between Member States, no training and unemployment measures have been analyzed in the present report pending completion of this detailed examination.[36]

In fact, however, presenting *no* data on training or employment aid is itself distorting in a situation in which such measures are very unevenly used—which in fact is the case. The clearest example of this distortion is the fact that training grants were available in only six EU countries in 1995: France, Germany, Ireland, Portugal, Sweden, and the UK (Northern Ireland only).[37]

In the United States, too, training grants seem to be growing in importance. These grants also provide a way around the provisions in many U.S. state constitutions that ban direct state grants to private companies.[38] Because money is fungible, we might well wonder if such training grants (whether in North America or the EU) do anything but provide an extra means of funding for firms. One site consultant wondered just how much training actually gets done and how much of the funding is directed to other uses.[39] In addition, we should recall that once upon a time companies themselves paid for training.

A fourth possibility for evading the rules consists in providing land to firms at no cost or below market cost. This arrangement is quite common in the United States, but in the EU it is considered state aid and should therefore be reported to the Commission. One location consultant suggested that hiding aid in this form is relatively easy in the absence of a complaint.[40] As with other unnotified aids, there is still some chance of being caught. For example, Daimler-Benz had to pay back DM 33.8 million because the price it paid the Berlin government for land for a headquarters was too low. The Commission still allowed a DM 53 million subsidy on the sale.[41] Toyota was accused of receiving a below-market price for land in Derbyshire, England, and had to pay back 6.1 million ECU.[42] Most recently, the Commission has ordered Siemens to pay back 2.582 million ECU in aid it received in 1992 when it bought land from the German city of Mainz below market value.[43] Thus, this form of indirect aid clearly is not risk-free, though determining how much of it goes undetected is difficult.

Two further factors can increase the funds provided for the most desirable mobile investment projects, though neither of them involves creative financing. First, governments can become more selective: cutting the amount of aid they provide to projects they find less desirable, while raising the aid intensity for the investments they most want to attract. Thus, higher awards for some projects can be consistent with lower overall spending (as suggested above).[44] Moreover, this strategy can be construed to be part of a broader EU trend whereby policymakers—especially those in charge of regional development—have moved away from automatic forms of aid that were virtual entitlements (e.g., social security tax concessions for the Italian Mezzogiorno; a U.S. example would be accelerated depreciation) to more discretionary programs that allow them to keep a better lid on spending.[45] Overall, greater selectivity by government aid decision makers is difficult to evaluate. Although it may reduce the number of bidding wars, there is a danger that the ones that do occur may tend to favor the richer countries because they are better able to afford giving the maximum allowed than are the cohesion countries.[46] Furthermore, the largest firms probably will be the main beneficiaries of auctions for investment, to the detriment of SMEs.

Second, aid for mobile investment is affected by the increasing amount of Community funds that have been directed toward productive investment. The Structural Funds have been increasing as a proportion of the total EU budget (see Chapter 3); the first big increase took place in the 1989–93 round of Community Support Frameworks, and the increase was intensified in the 1994–99 round of Structural Funding. Moreover, the percentage of EU funds going toward investments, as opposed to infrastructure, was also increased beginning in 1989–93. For example, aid for the Ford/Volkswagen minivan plant in Portugal was half funded by the EU.[47]

Increased levels of Structural Funds going to investment can obviously offset the effect of decreased aid spending by national authorities. According to regional aid expert Fiona Wishlade, the only Structural Fund that contributes significantly to competition for investment is the ERDF—and it does so only in Objective 1 regions.[48] As Table 6-7 (which combines Table 6-6 with ERDF monies that are comparable to state aid, as defined in the *Surveys*) shows, this contribution increased with the reform of the Structural Funds. ERDF funding has increased consistently over the 1988–97 period, partially offsetting the decline in national aid potentially available to mobile firms through 1992–94, then combining with the increase in these categories of aid in 1995–97 to effect an overall increase, even compared with 1988–90. (This

Table 6-7 **ERDF and National Aid Available to Mobile Investment (excluding Germany) Annual Averages (millions of ECU, 1996 prices)**

	National	ERDF	Net	Percent Change
1988–90	15,085.3	694.4	15,779.7	
1990–92	14,819.0	952.3	15,771.3	–0.0
1992–94	13,047.7	1,351.4	14,399.1	–8.7
1995–97	13,889.2	1,991.8	15,881.0	+10.3

Sources: EC-11 national aid from Table 6-6; ERDF aid for 1988–90 from *Fourth Survey*, 87, Table C1; 1990–92 from *Fifth Survey*, 85, Table C1; 1992–94 from *Sixth Survey*, 95, Table C1; 1995–97 from *Seventh Survey*, 114, Table C2 (excluding Germany in all cases). Revised figures from the succeeding period's *Survey* used, except for 1995–97. Amounts converted to 1996 prices using EU-15 CPI, *Eurostat Yearbook '97*, 425.

analysis excludes Germany because of the effects associated with reunification.)

The addition of Community funds, then, has offset the decrease in national aid that is potentially available to mobile firms in eleven of the twelve original member states. Although the main increase in funding has been in the cohesion countries, several richer countries succeeded in having Objective 1 regions designated in their countries for the first time in the 1994–99 round of Structural Funds (see Chapter 4). The combined impact of these changes puts pressure on DG IV to successfully control aid for mobile investment.

We should not be surprised that the expansion of the EU to much poorer areas such as the cohesion countries and eastern Germany should expand competition for investment. As Stephen Gill and David Law presciently suggested on the eve of the collapse of communism:

> Recent changes in the policies pursued in communist states—notably in the Soviet Union, Eastern Europe, and China—towards a more liberal approach to private enterprise, markets, and international trade are major enhancements of the power of capital. They give more scope for foreign investment and increase the number of states competing to attract foreign capital.[49]

This analysis, of course, is precisely the point of the model of competition for investment in Chapter 2. Dampening such competition in the EU is difficult when new countries are joining—particularly when their standard of living is much lower than the EU average.

Beyond evasion of the state aid rules, there are two other unregulated ways to attract investment. First, a country can offer tax advantages that are available broadly enough that the Commission can be persuaded to consider them "general measures" rather than state aid. Ireland's 10 percent corporate income tax rate for manufacturing is the most important example of this approach (see Chapter 4); Belgium's "coordination centers" tax benefits for headquarters of multinational corporations are another example.[50] Finally, one consultant noted that Britain trumpeted its opt-out from the Social Charter and the Maastricht Social Chapter as a way of attracting investment.[51] Because this decision was part of the "high politics" of the Maastricht Treaty, there was nothing the Commission could do directly when the UK used this opt-out as part of its attraction package for an investment, as the French accused it of doing in the case of Hoover's relocation from France to Scotland.[52] With Tony Blair's election and the British signing of the Social Chapter as part of the Amsterdam Treaty in 1997, the playing field will become more level.[53]

We have seen, then, that the Commission's efforts to control aid to mobile investment have had only mixed success. On one hand, the amount of national aid in the categories that are most likely to be provided to mobile investment decreased during the period 1981–97 (excluding the effects of German reunification), though there was an increase from 1992–94 to 1995–97. On the other hand, increasing ERDF funds offset that overall decrease—though primarily in the cohesion countries. Combined with greater selectivity and indirect aids, investment attraction officials may well have been able to provide higher levels of aid than in the late 1980s.[54]

Yet there are limitations to each of these factors as a point against DG IV effectiveness. Greater selectivity means what it says: higher aid, though fewer firms get awards. This strategy can imply that lower amounts of aid are given out overall—and at the national level, it has meant just that. Indirect aid suffers from the same drawback as other non-notified aid: If discovered, it will probably have to be repaid, with interest. As the discussion below suggests, the number of complaints and other discoveries of non-notification are increasing. This trend provides a brake on the runaway use of indirect methods to support investment projects. Finally, although increased EU-funded aid has offset decreased national aid, the disbursement of such aid itself is under the purview of the Commission. Although projects are proposed by the national governments, DG XVI (regional policy) and DG IV must negotiate with the government over how much aid will be allowed for a mobile project and how much the EU will co-finance. As Yuill et al. write, "In most Member States the Structural Funds are playing a notably more central role in the policy formulation process, a reflection of the growing monetary flows with which they are associated."[55] In principle, this situation implies an increase in centralized control. The fact that the 1994–99 Structural Funds added new Objective 1 areas and increased the total population coverage of the Funds from 43 percent to 51.3 percent of EU population[56] does suggest, however, that the Commission succumbed to pressures for decentralization, which would increase the competition for investment.

Although the EU has had mixed success, its experience probably compares favorably with that of the United States and Canada. The qualifier "probably" is necessary because of the difficulty of establishing comparable estimates for state aid in North America, especially on a longitudinal basis (see Chapter 5). One useful type of evidence, however, can come from industry studies. For example, investment subsidies for the automobile industry in Canada and the United States have risen steadily since the early 1960s, whereas those in the UK have fallen from their highs of the late 1970s and early 1980s (see Chapter 2). As the data presented in Chapter 4 suggest, the Automotive Framework is probably an important part of the explanation, given the substantial decline in state aid to the automobile industry in 1989–96 compared to 1981–86. Although the framework covers only one industry, this result does suggest that, compared to the United States and Canada, the EU has had some success in reducing competition for mobile investment.

State Aid Policy in the Service of Cohesion?

Discussion of the use of Structural Funds to increase competition for investment leads to another critical issue: the extent to which the Commission has been able to use state aid policy to promote cohesion. The logic behind this activity (see Chapter 3) is that aid can be used to attract investment to the peripheral regions of the EU as a way to reduce regional disparities. Such efforts, however, depend on the differential between the aid intensity available in central areas and

Table 6-8 **Comparative Decline in State Aid to Manufacturing, Cohesion and Non-Cohesion Countries (MM 1996 ECU)**

	1992–94	1995–97	Percent Change
Cohesion Four[a]	2,806	4,061	+44.7
Six Rich[b]	8,913	8,305	−6.8
Old *Länder* (OL)	4,484	3,064	−31.7
New *Länder*	16,161	10,482	−35.1
Italy—Article 92(3)(a)	5,152	7,010	+36.1
Italy—all other	5,581	3,441	−38.3
Six Rich + OL + Italy—other	18,978	14,810	−22.0

[a]Ireland, Greece, Spain, Portugal.

[b]Belgium, Denmark, France, Luxembourg, The Netherlands, United Kingdom: None has large Article 92(3)(a) areas.

Sources: Calculated from *Fifth Survey*, 20, Table 6; *Sixth Survey*, 9, Table 3; *Seventh Survey*, 7, Table 3; Annex Table A4/10. Amounts converted to 1996 prices using the EU-15 CPI, *Eurostat Yearbook '97*, 425. Figures are for manufacturing only, excluding air transport and financial services.

that on offer in the periphery. To simultaneously maximize the differential and minimize distortions of competition, aid provided in central regions of the Community must be reduced as much as possible, both absolutely and relative to peripheral areas. After problems in this regard for several years, the Commission's efforts finally appear to be paying off here as well.

For example, until 1990–92, manufacturing aid decreased more rapidly in the cohesion countries than in more central areas of the Community; the picture was more mixed in 1992–94.[57] Since then, overall aid trends have been more supportive of cohesion: Aid has increased in the cohesion countries and the Mezzogiorno and declined in the rest of the EU, as Table 6-8 shows.

Table 6-8 shows that the poorer areas of the EU are the ones that now are increasing their aid to manufacturing. Germany is shown separately because of the effects of reunification; aid in the new *Länder* is now falling back from highs associated with the privatization of many firms that were state owned before reunification. Italy is also presented separately because of the presence of the Mezzogiorno, which is an Article 92(3)(a) region for state aid purposes and mostly an Objective 1 region for Structural Funds. The Mezzogiorno's economic

Table 6-9 **R&D Aid as a Share of Manufacturing Aid in 1995–97**

Country	R&D Percentage
Austria	25
Belgium	13
Denmark	25
Germany	9
Greece	0
Spain	7
Finland	35
France	28
Ireland	5
Italy	3
Luxembourg	7
The Netherlands	21
Portugal	3
Sweden	9
United Kingdom	9
EU Average	10

Source: Seventh Survey, 20, Table 9.

situation, therefore, is more similar to that of the cohesion countries than to the rest of the EU. Like them, the Italian Article 92(3)(a) areas also saw a substantial increase in aid to manufacturing in 1995–97; in earlier periods they had seen a considerably smaller decrease in aid to manufacturing than did the cohesion countries.[58] The six prosperous countries saw a small decrease in aid to manufacturing over this period—a divergence that is in line with the Commission's goal of supporting cohesion.

Not all state aid trends promote cohesion, however. Aid for R&D tends to be concentrated in the EU's central areas. None of the cohesion countries reaches the EU average in the share of manufacturing aid devoted to R&D, as Table 6-9 shows.

Moreover, as Jürgen Grote argues, EU technology policies "tend to widen already existing gaps in the technological factor endowment of regions."[59] Finally, if we look at actual spending per capita for R&D, not just state aid for R&D, we find that the cohesion countries spend only 50 percent of the EU average.[60] The combined effects of national and Community imbalances in spending for R&D do not

Table 6-10 **NGE Expenditure per Capita, Assisted Areas, Annual Average 1993–95 (pounds sterling, 1995 prices and PPP)**

Country	Expenditure
Italy	98.1 (1989–91)
Luxembourg	74.4
Ireland	73.4
Germany	58.2
Greece	47.1 (1986–88)
Sweden	46.4
Northern Ireland	39.9
Belgium	27.9 (1992–94)
Great Britain	18.4
Portugal	12.6
The Netherlands	12.3
Spain	8.7
France	2.3
Denmark	0.0

Source: Calculated from Yuill et al., *European Regional Incentives 1997–98*, 500, Table 5.6. No data provided for Austria or Finland. Figure is average for last three years of available data.

bode well for efforts to reduce the differences in living standards between the cohesion countries and the rest of the EU.

A second problem is the regional policy within the more prosperous countries. As noted in Chapter 3, states such as France and Germany have long been loath to abandon their long-established regional policies, despite the fact that their lagging regions are not nearly as poor as the cohesion countries (eastern Germany and the Mezzogiorno excepted). Moreover, in Britain and France, virtually all regional aid is used to provide investment incentives for individual firms.[61] As a result, some of the wealthier EU members provide regional aid that is competitive (on a per capita basis) with what is given in the cohesion countries. Table 6-10 shows regional spending per capita of assisted areas within the EU.

Table 6-10 highlights several aspects of EU members' regional policies. First, Italian regional spending (almost all of which goes to the Mezzogiorno) is 25 percent higher on a per capita assisted basis than anywhere else in the Community. Italian spending on the

Table 6-11 **Maximum and Average Grants (percent)**

Country	Maximum	Average
Luxembourg	17.5–25	18
Ireland	75	30
Spain	20–75	20
Great Britain	20–30	10

Source: John Siraut, "Exploding the grants myth," *Corporate Location* (February 1992), 2.

Mezzogiorno has been a fixture of national policy since before the Treaty of Rome, and it figured significantly in the negotiations for the Treaty (see Chapter 3). Second, Luxembourg spends more per person in assisted areas than any other cohesion country (though given its small size, of course, the absolute effect is rather small); Portugal and Spain both have very low regional spending on this basis. Indeed, Spain's state aid spending is more typical of non-cohesion countries in other important respects—most notably in that Spain devotes more to R&D aid (on an absolute and a proportional basis) than the other three cohesion countries. Although except for Luxembourg, the top seven spots all reflect spending in Objective 1 areas,[62] the trend is clear that even among poor regions, being part of a richer country generally means a greater intensity of regional aid spending. Yuill et al. conclude that the competitiveness of the richer countries in providing incentives for mobile investment is likely a problem: "Given the extent of the problems to be tackled in the designated areas of those countries with major Objective 1 areas, it may be of some concern that there are not bigger differences between countries in respect of *per capita* incentive support within the problem regions."[63]

There is a wide gap between the theoretical aid maxima that can be given in the Community's poorest regions and what is actually awarded for investment projects in practice (see Chapter 3) because of the limited budgetary resources of the cohesion countries as well as DG IV's considerations of competition policy.[64] The result is a reduction in the differential between aid offered in central areas and that offered in the cohesion countries or other Article 93(2)(a) areas. Table 6-11 lists several examples provided by plant location consultant John Siraut.[65]

As in the examples in Chapter 3, what appears to be as much as a 45 percentage point differential between Ireland and Great Britain, or between Spain and Great Britain, is in practice closer to 20 percent in the former case and only 10 in the latter. Table 6-11 highlights again the relatively large values given in Luxembourg, despite its standing among the more prosperous areas of the EU.

The data presented here present a mixed picture of state aid control policy's effect on cohesion. On one hand, after several years of faster aid cuts in the cohesion countries than the richer members, the 1995–97 period saw a sharp decrease in the former and a decrease in the latter. The earlier decline in the cohesion countries may well have occurred, as Martin and Steinen suggest, because the Maastricht convergence criteria required substantial budget cuts in these countries and "state aid is apparently a far greater burden for the public finances of lagging countries."[66] With the designation of countries for monetary union, this constraint has loosened, as the more recent state aid data show. On the other hand, although Objective 1 areas generally have had the highest aid intensity based on the population of the assisted region (especially in richer countries with Objective 1 regions), Spain and Portugal fall very close to the bottom on this measure—suggesting only partial success in terms of promoting cohesion. Finally, aid patterns may contribute to longer-term disparities insofar as the cohesion countries suffer from a sharp gap in aid to R&D, suggesting that the economic gulf between them and the other eleven member states will persist for the foreseeable future.

The Commission's concern about the previous aid trends undermining cohesion was an important factor motivating its overhaul of regional aid in 1997. Indeed, in the *Fifth Survey*, DG IV had even gone so far as to propose binding aid caps[67]—which was not acceptable to the member states. The regional aid framework lowered aid maxima throughout the Community, however, which should reduce the volume of regional aid while simultaneously enabling poorer countries to fund more projects at their aid maximum. Besides aid caps, some observers have suggested the complete takeover of state aid by the EU.[68] Either of these solutions would be very difficult to achieve politically, precisely for the reasons set forth in the model in Chapter 2.

Transparency

Transparency has long been an important goal of the Commission (see Chapter 3). DG IV has consistently urged countries to give aid in a transparent manner to help in the evaluation of its fairness and to reduce the problem of non-notified aids. The Commission has ranked different types of aid from most transparent to least transparent as follows: grants, tax reductions, soft loans or tax deferrals (i.e., accelerated depreciation), guarantees, and equity injections.[69] Overall, the Commission has been very successful in obtaining reductions in the portion of state aid provided through equity injections and loan guarantees;[70] the percentage of manufacturing aid given through the Commission's preferred methods of grants and tax reductions has increased or remained the same in almost all member states except Germany (a result of the transition in the new *Länder*).

The least transparent types of state aid are guarantees and state participation in equity because determining the aid element (i.e., the value of the guarantee or the amount received by a state-owned firm above what a private investor would do) is extremely difficult. As Table 6-12 shows, aid via equity as a percentage of total state aid has fallen from 1981–86 to 1995–97 in almost all member states—in many cases quite sharply. Only in France and Italy are equity injections still used significantly.

As Table 6-13 shows, several countries—particularly Germany, Greece, Ireland, The Netherlands, and the UK—have had substantial increases in the proportion of aid given through guarantees, although the overall trend is downward. Again, because these figures reflect guarantees that are actually called on,[71] the guarantees were made at some time in the past. This fact further illuminates the non-transparent nature of guarantees: We only see their value at a "lag," as it were. Nevertheless, the overall share of guarantees in total manufacturing aid is still quite small, and more recently it has started to fall again.

Turning to the preferred means of granting state aid, we find that the percentage of aid that takes the form of grants or tax reductions has increased or remained the same (at high levels) for all member states except Germany—the largest aid giver. The overall average has remained little changed in the past ten years, as Table 6-14 shows.

The share of grants and tax reductions is probably the broadest measure of the transparency of aid forms, and it shows that the Commission has succeeded in reducing the use of less-transparent forms of aid in most member states. The biggest increases in the grant/tax reduction share were in Denmark and France, both as a result of a dramatic cutback in soft loans. Belgium, Luxembourg, and the UK also had significant increases in these aid forms. Only in

Table 6-12 **Equity Participation as a Percentage of Manufacturing Aid (1981–86, 1986–88, excluding steel and shipbuilding)**[72]

Country	1981–86	86–88	88–90	90–92	92–94	94–96	95–97
Austria	N/A	N/A	N/A	N/A	N/A	0	0
Belgium	12	6	5	1	1	1	1
Denmark	0	0	0	0	0	0	0
Germany	0	0	0	0	0	1	1
Greece[73]	0	9	18	0	0	0	0
Spain	N/A	19	10	2	0	0	3
Finland	N/A	N/A	N/A	N/A	N/A	0	0
France	6	18	11	5	12	4	14
Ireland	9	6	2	5	8	0	0
Italy	19	7	5	5	14	9	5
Luxembourg	3	5	2	0	0	0	0
The Netherlands	0	0	0	0	0	0	0
Portugal	N/A	12	59[a]	0	0	0	0
Sweden	N/A	N/A	N/A	N/A	N/A	2	2
UK	7	16	8	0	0	0	0
Overall average (weighted)			7	3	6	3	4

N/A = not applicable

[a]This figure reflects a major restructuring of the steel industry. See *Third Survey*, 17.

Sources: Second Survey, Table VIII; *Third Survey*, Table 5; *Fourth Survey*, Table 5; *Fifth Survey*, Table 5; *Sixth Survey*, Table 7, *Seventh Survey*, Table 8.

Table 6-13 **Guarantees as a Percentage of Total Aid in Manufacturing (1981–86, 1986–88, excluding steel and shipbuilding)[74]**

Country	**1981–86**	**86–88**	**88–90**	**90–92**	**92–94**	**94–96**	**95–97**
Austria	N/A	N/A	N/A	N/A	N/A	7	7
Belgium	10	10	8	9	8	6	4
Denmark	1	1	0	8	1	2	1
Germany	1	1	1	8	11	5	5
Greece	5	3	11	13	13	18	0
Spain	N/A	1	1	3	2	0	0
Finland	N/A	N/A	N/A	N/A	N/A	1	1
France	7	19	28	25	15	10	5
Ireland	2	4	3	3	3	11	5
Italy	0	0	0	0	0	0	0
Luxembourg	0	0	1	0	0	0	0
The Netherlands	0	0	3	5	7	9	2
Portugal	N/A	0	1	10	5	8	0
Sweden	N/A	N/A	N/A	N/A	N/A	0	0
UK	1	2	1	1	4	4	4
Overall average (weighted)			6	7	8	4	3

Sources: Second Survey, Table VIII; *Third Survey*, Table 5; *Fourth Survey*, Table 5; *Fifth Survey*, Table 5; *Sixth Survey*, Table 7; Seventh Survey, Table 8.

Table 6-14 **Grants and Tax Reductions as a Percentage of Total Aid in Manufacturing (1981–86, 1986–88, excluding steel and shipbuilding)**[75]

Country	1981–86	86–88	88–90	90–92	92–94	94–96	95–97
Austria	N/A	N/A	N/A	N/A	N/A	79	79
Belgium	64	72	82	80	82	89	90
Denmark	44	70	62	87	96	93	93
Germany	86	85	89	83	66	70	67
Greece	95	88	61	74	74	79	96
Spain	N/A	78	78	79	86	93	88
Finland	N/A	N/A	N/A	N/A	N/A	84	86
France	31	45	44	59	65	82	70
Ireland	85	89	94	91	85	89	93
Italy	79	90	93	92	80	85	91
Luxembourg	78	77	80	87	93	96	98
The Netherlands	88	94	93	95	91	86	93
Portugal	N/A	86	37	84	93	90	97
Sweden	N/A	N/A	N/A	N/A	N/A	80	82
UK	83	72	82	95	93	93	94
Overall average (weighted)			79	84	74	80	80

Sources: Second Survey, Table VIII; *Third Survey*, Table 5; *Fourth Survey*, Table 5; *Fifth Survey*, Table 5; *Sixth Survey*, Table 7; *Seventh Survey*, Table 8.

Germany has there been a decrease in grants and tax reductions; these figures overstate this decrease, however, because of the Commission's use of *ex ante* calculations of the value of guarantees in eastern Germany, in contrast with its procedure for the rest of the EU (see note above). Overall, one can fairly conclude that transparency in EU state aid has improved substantially. Again, the German decline is a result of a historically unique circumstance; it therefore does not detract from the overall conclusion that these preferred aid forms have been far more widely adopted than in the past. Fiona Wishlade appears to share this conclusion, at least as far as regional aid is concerned:

> Commission insistence on transparency has been influential in shaping the regional incentive policies of the Member States over the last two decades, contributing to a situation in which virtually all (the one exception is Greece) offer a grant as the mainstay of their regional aid packages.[76]

The shift toward more transparent aid should make DG IV's monitoring job easier in the future. One example from the 1980s underlines this point. Ballantyne and Bachtler report several disputes between Germany and DG IV over non-notification in regional aid. Although these disputes also were related to disagreements over cumulation of aid, Ballantyne and Bachtler note, *inter alia*, that the transparency of German aid procedures made detecting non-notified aids easy.[77] If DG IV succeeds in channeling more aid into the most transparent forms, its ability to monitor will be further enhanced. At the same time, this shift will increase the EU's interest in having its trading partners increase the transparency of their subsidies and other state aid.

Commission Initiatives

General Aid

The Commission has noted on several occasions its criticism of "general" aid programs, which are not targeted sectorally, regionally, or to clearly permitted goals such as R&D or pollution abatement. As early as 1973, the Commission indicated the main problems with such programs:

- Their lack of regional or sectoral specificity meant they had no legal basis for approval under the exemptions of Article 92(3).
- They caused transparency problems because there was no way to assess in advance of individual cases the effect of the scheme on competition and trade.
- They could undermine approved aid programs.
- When they had the status of "existing" aid, they could be used to evade examination of aid given to particular firms even though competitor states would have to go through Commission scrutiny to accomplish the same purposes via new aid programs.

Recognizing, however, that states wanted flexible programs that could be used quickly, especially in the case of economic downturn, the Commission therefore preferred that general aid programs be converted to regional or sectoral programs, to ease the assessment of their competitive effects, or that member states reach agreement that all significant individual cases would be notified.[78] For more than twenty years, then, the Commission's policy has been to discourage the use of this sort of aid.

In 1990, however, the Commission intensified its efforts to eliminate general aid. As part of the policy review that took place under Sir Leon Brittan, DG IV focused new attention on existing aid programs, including general aid.[79] In the *Twentieth Report on Competition Policy*, the Commission wrote:

> Such assistance has repercussions contrary to economic and social cohesion and to Community regional development policy. Not only does it reduce the cost of investment by the recipient firms by comparison with their competitors in other Member States; it also attracts to the Member State concerned mobile investment which might have located elsewhere in the Community. In addition, a general aid scheme in one Member State can neutralize the attraction of regional aid available in other Member States and in the same Member State's own development areas.[80]

In the first round of this initiative, the Commission in 1990 secured the cessation of two general aid schemes: a Dutch program that had an annual budget of 26 million ECU and general investment aid under the Belgian Economic Expansion Law of 1959, which had a 1990 budget of 96 million ECU.[81] In 1991, Luxembourg agreed to terminate the general aid program under its Framework Economic

Table 6-15 **General Investment Aid Share in Manufacturing Aid**

Years	Percentage
1981–86	5
1986–88	5
1988–90	3
1990–92	2.1
1992–94	1.6
1994–96	0
1995–97	No longer listed

Note: Data for 1981–86 and 1986–88 exclude steel and shipbuilding.

Sources: 1981–88, *Second Survey*, Table IX; 1988–90, *Third Survey*, Table 6; 1990–94, *Fifth Survey*; 1994–96, *Sixth Survey*, Table 8; *Seventh Survey*, 18–21.

Expansion Law of 1986. In all, forty programs with total budgets of more than 5 billion ECU were examined, including at least one program from each member state.[82]

Over the course of the 1990s, general aid has been essentially wiped out, as Table 6-15 shows.

Intra-Community Export Aid

Export aid for intra-Community trade has been essentially wiped out (see Chapter 4). Since 1980, only relatively minor problems have cropped up from time to time—for example, the Greek system of export aid, which the Commission allowed to continue as a transitional measure from its 1981 accession until 1 January 1990, using a phased reduction beginning 1 January 1987.[83] The focus now is on aid to export insurance and aid to investment by EU firms in Central and Eastern Europe.[84]

Notification, Compliance, and Enforcement

To what extent has the Commission been able to enforce respect for the rules? This question is best assessed in the realm of notification and compliance (or, failing compliance, enforcement). These areas are at the heart of the characterization of the state aid regime as an example of cooperation among EU member states—or disconfirming that interpretation.

The Commission has complained about notification problems on numerous occasions.[85] In May 1989, the Commission demanded that five states institute specific programs to improve their compliance with the notification requirement, as a result of high proportions of aids that were not notified over the period 1985–87: France, 37 percent; Belgium, 32 percent; Greece, 28 percent; Spain, 23 percent; and Italy, 16 percent. At the same time, the increase in aid notifications beginning in 1987 was interpreted by the Commission as evidence of success in having the notification requirement of Article 93(3) obeyed.[86] Table 6-16 shows recent trends in notifications and non-notifications.

Table 6-16 is difficult to interpret. Does an increase in non-notifications mean that they are occurring more frequently (disrespect for the rules) or that a higher proportion are being caught (greater effectiveness in enforcement or a by-product of using more-transparent aid forms)? As usual, the aggregate data are sharply skewed by Germany (the largest aid giver), in which almost one-third of manufacturing aid cases were non-notified. By contrast, there has been improvement in four of the five previously identified non-notifiers, as an examination of cases decided in 1997 shows (Table 6-17).

As Table 6-17 indicates, France, Greece, and Belgium have dramatically reduced their non-notifications, Spain has improved moderately, whereas Italy has worsened slightly. The real problem now is Germany.

Over the years, state aid enforcement has been stepped up, as reflected in increasing numbers of cases in which the Commission opened the Article 93(2) "contentious" procedure, as well as the number of negative decisions issued (Table 6-18). From time to time the Commission has changed its method of aggregating cases, accounting for breaks in the series as noted.

As Tables 6-18a–c show, there were never more than four negative decisions in a year until 1981. With the exception of 1985 and 1987, every year from 1981 to 1990 had between ten and twenty-one negative decisions. The number then stayed in single digits until a sharp increase in 1996, followed by a new high again in 1998. In the 1980s, the Commission highlighted the rising number of negative decisions as a sign of the increasing stringency of enforcement.[87] Although the dip in the early 1990s is unlikely to mean decreased enforcement, the increase beginning in 1996 shows that it is still too early to believe

Table 6-16 **New State Aid Cases Before the Commission: Sectors Other Than Agriculture, Fisheries, Transport, or Coal**

Year	Total	Notified	Non-notified	Re-examined
1990[a]	547	429 (78.4 percent)	105 (19.2 percent) (19.7 percent of new)	13 (2.4 percent)
1991		No Information on Non-notification Given		
1992		No Information on Non-notification Given		
1993	561	475 (84.7 percent)	85 (15.2 percent) (15.2 percent of new)	1 (0.2 percent)
1994	594	510 (85.9 percent)	68 (11.4 percent) (11.8 percent of new)	16 (2.7 percent)
1995	803	680 (84.7 percent)	113 (14.1 percent) (14.2 percent of new)	10 (1.2 percent)
1996	644	550 (85.4 percent)	91 (14.1 percent) (14.2 percent of new)	3 (0.5 percent)
1997	656	515 (78.5 percent)	140 (21.3 percent) (21.4 percent of new)	1 (0.2 percent)
1998	444	342 (77.0 percent)	97 (21.8 percent) (22.1 percent of new)	5 (1.1 percent)

[a]Coal not noted as excluded in *Twentieth Report*.

Sources: Twenty-eighth Report on Competition Policy, Figure 6; *Twenty-seventh Report on Competition Policy*, point 320 and Figure 7; *Twenty-sixth Report on Competition Policy*, point 93 and Graph 1; *Twenty-fifth Report on Competition Policy*, 94, Graph 1; *Twenty-third Report on Competition Policy*, Annex III, Table e; *Twentieth Report on Competition Policy*, Table 2 and point 187.

that states have become so socialized to the rules that they rarely propose aids that are clearly at variance with them.[88]

Aid Repayment

Since 1982, the Commission has used aid recovery as a means of enforcing its decisions. Chapter 4 details the Commission's introduc-

Table 6-17 **Proportion of Aid Cases Decided That Were Not Notified Aid**[a]

	1997		Percent
	Notified	**Non-notified**	**Non-notified**
Belgium	10	1	9.1
Spain	38	6	13.6
France	25	7	21.9
Greece	3	0	0
Italy	45	11	19.6
Germany	135	64	32.2

[a]1985–87: France, 37 percent; Belgium, 32 percent; Greece, 28 percent; Spain, 23 percent; Italy, 16 percent.

Source: Tabulated from *Twenty-seventh Report on Competition Policy*, "List of state aid cases in sectors other than agriculture, fisheries, transport, and the coal industry," 261–87.

Table 6-18a **Commission Actions on State Aid Cases, 1970–80 (excluding agriculture and transport)**

Year	No. of Cases	No Objection	Contentious Procedure	Negative Decision
1970	21	15	6	1
1971	18	11	7	3
1972	35	24	11	3
1973	22	15	7	4
1974	35	20	15	—
1975	45	29	16	2
1976	47	33	14	2
1977	112	99	13	1
1978	137	118	19	—
1979	133	79	54	3
1980	105	72	33	2

Source: Thirteenth Report on Competition Policy, point 228.

Table 6-18b **Commission Actions on State Aid Cases, 1980–86 (excluding agriculture, fisheries, and transport)**

Year	No. of Cases	No Objection	Contentious Procedure	Terminate Procedure	Negative Decision	Withdraw
1981	92	79	30	19	14	—
1982	200	104	86	30	13	—
1983	174	101	55	18	21	9
1984	162	201	58	34	21	6
1985	133	102	38	31	7	11
1986	124	98	47	26	10	5

Source: Twentieth Report on Competition Policy, point 187.

Table 6-18c **Commission Actions on State Aid Cases, 1987–98 (excluding agriculture, fisheries, coal, and transport)**

Year	No. of Cases	No Objection	Contentious Procedure	Terminate Procedure	Negative Decision	Conditional Decision	Other
1987	294	188	28	30	7	6	35
1988	410	303	36	20	14	9	28
1989	343	259	36	21	16	0	11
1990	492	415	34	20	14	0	9
1991	597	493	54	28	7	2	13
1992	552	473	30	25	8	7	9
1993	467	399	32	19	6	1	10
1994	527	440	40	15	3	2	27
1995	619	504	57	22	9	5	22
1996	474	373	43	14	23	3	18
1997	502	385	68	18	9	5	17
1998	460	308	66	16	31	8	31

Note: "Other" decisions include Commission proposals of "appropriate measures" for modifying or abolishing an existing aid under Article 93(1) of the EEC Treaty and Council decisions under Article 95 of the ECSC Treaty. "Terminating" the Article 93(2) procedure means that the aid was approved after detailed examination (usually after modification).

Sources: Twenty-fourth Report on Competition Policy, Annex III, 638, Table 5; *Twenty-fifth Report on Competition Policy*, Part Two, 316, Table 4; *Twenty-eighth Report on Competition Policy*, 344, Table 4.

Table 6-19a **Commission Use of Aid Recovery Orders**

Year	No. of Cases[a]	Countries Involved[b]	Amount (millions of ECU)
1982	3	B, NL	67.59
1983	2	B	25.17
1984	6	B, F, NL, UK	177.51
1985	2	D	5.71
1986	3	B, D	6.90
1987	6	B, D, F	829.34
1988	5	F, I	214.18
1989	5	E, F, GR, I	403.90
1990	5	D, F, GR, I	15.399
1991	4	F, I, UK	42.79
1992	5	B, D, E	130.00
1993	3	D, F, UK	127.88
1994	1	D	8.3
1995	6	B, D, E, F, NL	116.87
1996	15	B, D, E, F, I	525.72
1997	10	D, DK, E, F, I	389.567
1998	24	D, NL, I, L, A, F, E	530.13

[a]Each decision listed in the sources is counted as a separate case.
[b]A = Austria, B = Belgium, D = Germany, E = Spain, F = France, DK = Denmark, GR = Greece, NL = The Netherlands, I = Italy, UK = United Kingdom, L = Luxembourg

Sources: Twenty-third Report on Competition Policy, Annex II, 450–52; *Twenty-seventh Report on Competition Policy*, Part Two, Section IV, 306–315, Table F, *Twenty-eighth Report on Competition Policy,* Part Two, 309–311, Table 2.

tion of this sanction and the many legal challenges against it. Table 6-19 shows the amount of recoveries ordered each year. Note that not all aid that is ordered repaid actually is recovered by the governments. In some cases, the firm went bankrupt. In others, such as *Leeuwarder* and *Intermills*, the ECJ annulled the decision.

Table 6-19 requires explanation. The data for Germany reflect the many non-notified aids at the *Länder* level (especially in the new *Länder*), and the low level of actual repayment stems from repeated use of appeals to national courts that drag cases out for years (according to one official, no German repayment case had required less than eight years to secure compliance).[89] In Italy, several large repayment cases dragged on for many years, and Commission action in the ECJ

Table 6-19b **Aid Repayments by Country (millions of ECU)**

Country	No. of Cases[a]	Amount Ordered	Amount Repaid as of 1997
Belgium	14	478.46	292.23[b]
Germany	24	729.819	34.069
Denmark	1	0.137	0.137
Spain	7	125.90	39.70
France	17	845.97	644.97
Greece	2	Not specified	—[c]
Italy	11	693.96	529.50
The Netherlands	4	147.79	0[d]
UK	3	67.64	66.14

[a]Each decision listed in the sources is counted as a separate case.
[b]A further grant of 5.6 million ECU has also been repaid, but the amount of interest to be repaid was in dispute.
[c]In one case, the ECJ ruled that the Greek government had not complied with its Treaty obligations; in the other, the Commission concluded that the sale of the firm to the highest bidder satisfied its original decision.
[d]Two older decisions were annulled by the ECJ; there was one bankruptcy, and repayment is pending in one recent decision.
Sources: Twenty-third Report on Competition Policy, Annex II, 450–52; *Twenty-seventh Report on Competition Policy*, Part Two, Section IV, 306–315, Table F.
Note: 1998 not included due to change in reporting.

against Italy was required; in recent years, however, Italy's compliance seems to have improved: One aid was partly repaid in less than a year. Although France had substantial repayments ordered, that country has been comparatively prompt in fulfilling repayment orders. Belgium—the other country with large repayment orders—has had aid repaid in several cases (most important, the huge case of Tubemeuse, a 292 million ECU capital injection); many of its cases ended with the bankruptcy of the aid recipient, however, making recovery impossible. (Recall from Chapter 4 that Belgium raised the bankruptcy issue in several of its appeals against repayment orders.)

Of 105 cases in which repayment had been ordered, the ECJ annulled the Commission's decision in eight cases (The Netherlands, one; Belgium, two; Spain, two; Italy, one; Germany, two; UK, one). In the British case (*Rover*) the Commission subsequently fixed its procedural errors and successfully obtained recovery. In *Bremer Vulkan* (Germany) and *Hytasa* (Spain), the Commission also prepared new repayment orders; the first became moot after the company's bankruptcy, however, and the second is pending. In the other six cases, the aid was not recovered because of the ECJ's decision.

The most recent case of government intransigence concerns state aid to Volkswagen by the *Land* of Saxony in eastern Germany. After a June 1996 Commission ruling allowing DM 539 million but blocking DM 241 million for VW investments in Mosel and Chemnitz, the company announced that it was suspending its investments. The following month, Saxony illegally paid the company DM 91 million of the banned aid. To the embarrassment of the German federal government, Saxony vowed to defy the Commission and refused to repay the aid. The Commission responded by refusing to approve other subsidies to Volkswagen until Germany secured the repayment of the Saxony aid. After legal skirmishing and more than a year of negotiations, Germany and Saxony agreed to repayment in November 1997, clearing the way for VW to receive already approved aid for a plant in Hesse in western Germany.[90]

These patterns provide important insight into compliance with Commission decisions. Table 6-19 shows that, when all appeals are exhausted, even an "ideological enemy" (Michelle Cini's term) of DG IV such as France complies with these orders. After years of intransigence, Italy also appears to be moving toward a higher degree of compliance. Germany's record is clearly the worst in the EU now. With the adoption of the Procedural Regulation, the constant delays there may be brought to an end as well.

Overall, although the long-running battles by member states against repayment orders undermine Lavdas and Mendrinou's view that such orders are "highly effective . . . in compelling state compliance,"[91] we can reasonably conclude that the use of aid repayment orders has strengthened the Commission's hand in securing compliance with its decisions. As Cini remarks, "The advent of . . . the required repayment of state aid has helped to close the enforcement gap by means of deterrence."[92] The gap is by no means fully closed, but most states comply if they lose at the ECJ, and the Procedural Regulation is likely to strengthen the sanction of repayment in the future.

Conclusion

The data presented here suggest that the Commission's efforts to control state aid have been successful—though by no means perfectly.

In particular, the overall volume of state aid has fallen in real terms over the period 1981–97, as has the amount of aid to manufacturing (excluding the extraordinary effect of German reunification). These results compare favorably with those of OECD members for aid to manufacturing.

The issue of whether state aid policy directly affects competition for investment is less clear. Although the amount of those types of aid that are most likely to go to mobile investment have fallen in real terms (eastern Germany is special case, however), there are contrary trends as well that make this aspect of policy difficult to assess overall. The increase in Structural Funds—which can be used to co-finance investment incentives—is one important example of this difficulty. Although the Commission in principle should have more control over these Funds than over national aids, adding to the pool of funding available should make it easier to increase the level of aid given to each investment. Plant location consultants generally believe that aid levels have been rising, at least for the most desirable projects. They point to several ways to evade the rules—often legally—that tend to increase overall aid levels for mobile projects. Moreover, there are ways of competing for investment that are not covered by the state aid rules (i.e., Britain's former opt-out from the Social Chapter of the Maastricht Agreement and Ireland's 10 percent corporate income tax for manufacturing firms) that tend to increase aid levels in other states. Given these mixed trends, we should not be surprised that the Commission introduced the Multisectoral Framework to directly address aid for mobile investment.

With regard to the issue of transparency, the Commission has had better success. Most member states increasingly give state aid in forms that are easiest to assess: grants and tax reductions. Similarly, the least transparent form of aid—capital injection—is now used by only six member states; in only two does it constitute 5 percent or more of manufacturing aid. Finally, guarantees (another relatively opaque aid form) have decreased in recent years after a slight increase through 1992–94. Given the centrality of monitoring in making cooperative arrangements work, the improvements in transparency augur well for the continued success of state aid policy.

The impact of state aid control on cohesion is also mixed. Although aid levels are now increasing in the cohesion countries, this trend follows several years in which they had a much more rapid decline than in richer member states—likely as a result of meeting the Maastricht convergence criteria. Moreover, in the key area of aid to R&D, the central countries are disproportionately the aid providers, a factor that should tend to promote their more rapid growth compared with the cohesion countries. The Commission's recognition of problems here was one motivating factor behind the December 1997 regional aid guidelines.

There seems to have been some improvement in the thorny areas of notification, compliance, and enforcement. The proportion of non-notified aids has decreased since 1990 for four of the five previously worst offenders, although non-notification has emerged as a substantial problem in reunified Germany. Higher rejection rates of aid proposals have not yet deterred proposals of incompatible aid, but these rejections continue to provide evidence of continuing Commission oversight. Moreover, as Mitchell Smith emphasizes, rejection rates are not the whole story: Negotiations between DG IV and member states often result in modification of aid proposals.[93] Furthermore, an analysis of repayment orders from 1982 through 1997 suggests that, despite strong initial resistance, the level of compliance with such orders is high—again, except in Germany. With the adoption of the Procedural Regulation, the Commission may now have the tool it needs to prevent the kind of multiple appeals to national courts that have led to delays in Germany.

Finally, two important Commission policy initiatives—against export aid for intra-European trade and against general investment aid—have met with high levels of success.

Taken together, these results suggest a moderately high level of Commission effectiveness in state aid control. Although the control mechanism is by no means perfect, it has been able to reach many of its goals. The analysis here provides many lessons for regulating competition for investment, in North America and more generally. I turn to these lessons in Chapter 7.

Notes

1. Edward M. Graham, *Global Corporations and National Governments* (Washington, D.C.: Institute for International Economics, 1996), 81. Stephen Thomsen and Stephen Woolcock also view the EU as relatively unsuccessful in controlling competition for inward investment; see *Direct Investment and European Integration: Competition among Firms and Governments* (London: Pinter, 1993), 76–77.

2. Damien Neven and Georges Siotis, "Foreign Direct Investment in the European Community: Some Policy Issues," *Oxford Review of Economic Policy* 9, no. 2 (summer 1993): 91.
3. Cini, "Policing the Internal Market," 262–65. She contrasts this with Commission "success" in having extended a set of rules and procedures for dealing with state aid cases.
4. See, for example, Cini, "Policing the Internal Market," 265.
5. *First Report on Competition Policy*, points 141–142.
6. *Fourth Survey on State Aid*, 46.
7. See also Cini, "Policing the Internal Market," 272–88.
8. Although some previous studies have offered such evaluations, none is as comprehensively based. Relatively favorable evaluations appear in Kostas A. Lavdas and Maria M. Mendrinou, *Politics, Subsidies and Competition: The New Politics of State Intervention in the European Union*; Mitchell Smith, "Integration in Small Steps: The Commission and Member-State Aid to Industry," *West European Politics* 19 (July 1996): 563–82; Keith Middlemas, *Orchestrating Europe: The Informal Politics of the European Union, 1973-95* (London: Fontana Press, 1995), 519–29. Mixed reviews include Stephen Wilks and Lee McGowan, "Competition Policy in the European Union: Creating a Federal Agency?" in *Comparative Competition Policy: National Institutions in a Global Market*, ed. G. Bruce Doern and Stephen Wilks (Oxford: Clarendon Press, 1996), 225–67; Thomsen and Woolcock, *Direct Investment and European Integration*; and Cini, "Policing the Internal Market." The most negative evaluation is that of Fiona Wishlade; see, for example, "The Policy Relevance of the EU State Aid Rules," paper presented at the European Community Studies Association, Seattle, 29 May 1997.
9. This figure excludes agriculture, fisheries, coal, and transport. With these sectors included, there were 40 negative decisions in 1998.
10. That amount was given in the manufacturing sector alone; see *Fifth Survey*, 7, Table 3. East Germany is not separated out in the relevant Annex Table of the *Fifth Survey*.
11. Agricultural aid represented 13.8 percent of total national state aid in 1995–97. *Seventh Survey*, 49, Table 18.
12. *Fourth Survey*, 45. On the likely rise of investment incentives during recessions, see Dennis P. Quinn, "Investment Incentives: A Five Country Test of the Lindblom Hypothesis," in *Research in Corporate Social Performance and Policy*, Vol. 10, ed. Lee E. Preston (Greenwich, Conn.: JAI Press, 1988), 87–111.
13. J. Knox, *Towards 1992: State Aids to Industry* (Trade and Tariffs Research, London, November 1989), 56–60.

14. Or more precisely, "manufacturing and certain other sectors"—the most important of which are the airline industry and, more recently, financial services. Railway transport, which receives high subsidies in every member state, is not, however, classified together with industry for statistical purposes.
15. Excluding those two industries, aid as a proportion of manufacturing value added fell only from 4.0 percent in 1981–86 to 3.8 percent in 1986–88. *Second Survey on State Aid*, 10, Table I.
16. Kenneth P. Thomas, "International Control and Discipline of Subsidies: The EU and WTO Surveillance Exercises," *STI Review* no. 21 (1998): 33–34.
17. Personal communication with Reinhard Walther, DG IV Inventory and Analysis Unit, 25 August 1999.
18. OECD, *Public Support to Industry* (Paris: OECD, 1996). This is based on data from 24 member states (excluding Luxembourg and Greece), the European Commission, and one country with observer status (the Slovak Republic).
19. For the record, reported industrial support fell by 36 percent in real terms over the 1986–89 period. Virtually all of the decline between 1986 and 1989, however, was the result of tax reform's impact on tax expenditures. The value of directly financed aid fell by only 2.8 percent in real terms in that period. OECD, *Industrial Support Policies in OECD Countries, 1986-1989* (Paris: OECD, 1992), 17, and 31, Table 12. Finally, the 1989 figure was revised downward by $14.1 billion from the 1992 to the 1996 report.
20. Note, too, that many aid projects are multi-year in nature, so there clearly is some arbitrariness in assigning aid to individual years. Hence the EU *Surveys* use multi-year averages. Moreover, a few bailouts or restructuring operations coinciding in a single year can cause a sharp increase even if the overall trend is downward. This is precisely what happened in Spain and Italy in 1990 (*Fourth Survey*, 8).
21. Excluding the new *Länder* alone would overstate the decline because aid fell in western Germany to partly compensate for the increase in the east. See Table 6-8.
22. See especially the discussion of the "First Framework on General Systems of Regional Aid" in *First Report on Competition Policy*, points 141–142.
23. *Twenty-fifth Report on Competition Policy*, point 151.
24. Interview in Brussels, 23 September 1993. One might also add Ireland's Export Sales Relief, which clearly functioned as a general investment program. It never exceeded ECU 150 million annually (on average), however, so it does not affect the results that follow. It has now been abolished, of course.

25. As the *Fourth Survey on State Aid*, 45, noted, the economic situation was not good in 1990–92, but EU-15 real GDP actually decreased in 1993. OECD, *National Accounts, Volume I (Main Aggregates) 1960-94*, 27.
26. Though it is not obvious from Table 6-6, this is true even including Germany, once privatization aid from the Treuhandanstalt (or its successor, the Bundesanstalt) is excluded. This is because an average of ECU 5 billion per year in 1995–97 comes from this source (see *Seventh Survey*, Table 10). Subtracting this figure from the 1995–97 total leaves aid in these categories more than ECU 2 billion below the pre-reunification 1988–90 figure.
27. Timothy J. Sinclair, "Passing Judgement: Credit Rating Processes as Regulatory Mechanisms of Governance in the Emerging World Order," *Review of International Political Economy* 1, no. 1 (spring 1994): 133–59.
28. Sinclair, "Passing Judgement," 144–45.
29. Timothy J. Sinclair, "Between State and Market: Hegemony and Institutions of Collective Action Under Conditions of International Capital Mobility," *Policy Sciences* 27, no. 4 (1994): 459–60.
30. Personal communication with European site location consultant, Brussels 23 September 1993.
31. Douglas Yuill et al., eds., *European Regional Incentives*, 10th edition (London: Bowker-Saur, 1990), 25–26.
32. Which defined initial investment as investment in *fixed assets*. See CEC, *Competition Law in the European Communities, Volume II*, 107–108. For changes in the December 1997 guidelines, see Fiona Wishlade, *RAGS and LIPS: New Weapons in the Commission's Regional Aid Control Armoury*, Regional and Industrial Research Paper Series, No. 31, European Policies Research Centre, February 1999, 25.
33. Richard E. Caves, *Multinational Enterprise and Economic Analysis*, 2nd edition (New York: Cambridge University Press, 1996), 208, 213. "Transfer prices" are prices charged in sales from one branch of a multinational corporation to another—for example, the price charged by Ford in France when it sells automatic transmissions to Ford U.K.
34. Personal communication with European plant location consultant, 3 November 1993. Another consultant mentioned that alternative financing mainly goes to smaller start-ups than to large multinationals (personal communication, 14 October 1993).
35. The quote is from European Information Service, "Official EU State Aid Inquiry into Dutch Technolease Scheme," *European Report* No. 2219, 26 April 1997. See also "Parliament Launches Inquiry into Techno-Lease," *ANP English News Bulletin* [The Netherlands], 2 May 1997; and European Information Service, "State Aid: Experts to Probe Dutch

'Technolease' Affair," *European Report* no. 2217, 19 April 1997. Aircraft maker Fokker, now bankrupt, benefited in 1994.

36. Technical Annex, point 14.
37. Yuill et al., *European Regional Incentives 1995-96*, 410, Table 1.4.
38. On these bans, see William C. Green, "Constitutional Dimensions of State Industrial Recruitment," in *The Politics of Industrial Recruitment: Japanese Automobile Investment and Economic Development in the American States*, ed. Ernest J. Yanarella and William C. Green (New York: Greenwood Press, 1990), 54.
39. Personal communication with European site selection consultant, 14 October 1993.
40. Personal communication with European site selection consultant, 3 November 1993. This consultant also mentioned other possibilities for indirect incentives, including warehouses rented by local governments (not necessarily below market price), training grants and facilities, and management housing.
41. Robert McDonald, "State Aids & the Effort to Ensure Fair Competition," *EIU European Trends*, no. 2 (1992): 62.
42. David Bowen, "Toyota Pays 4m Pounds After EC Ruling" *The Independent*, 3 October 1991, 26.
43. See Commission Press Release IP 96/670, 18 July 1996.
44. Personal communications with European plant location consultants, 14 October 1993 and 3 November 1993. The first of these interviewees also noted that the United Kingdom and Ireland operate on the basis of fixed budgets, which means that in recessionary years with fewer projects, more money is available per project.
45. Yuill et al., *European Regional Incentives 1994-95*, 10–11.
46. Yuill et al., *European Regional Incentives 1994-95*, 100–102.
47. Audrey Choi and Carlta Vitzthum, "Iberian Struggle: Big Auto Plant Sparks a Debate in Portugal Over How to Develop," *Wall Street Journal*, 30 June 1995, 1.
48. Personal communication, 5 September 1996.
49. Stephen R. Gill and David Law, "Global Hegemony and the Structural Power of Capital," *International Studies Quarterly*, December 1989, 491.
50. See Fiona Wishlade, "The Policy Relevance of the EU State Aid Rules," paper presented at 5th Biennial Conference of the European Community Studies Association, Seattle, 29 May 1997, 9.
51. Personal communication with European plant location consultant, 14 October 1993.

52. "Hoover Affirms Dijon Plant Move," Facts on File World News Digest, 15 July 1993, 529, F2. For an example of the criticism of Britain's highlighting the opt-out in its economic development advertising, see Robin Gedye, "British low-pay ads rile Germans," *Daily Telegraph*, 11 May 1993, 13.
53. Charles Bremner, "EU Will Extend Social Laws to Britain," *The Times* (London), 24 September 1997. Even before the Blair election, the EU was able to impose a 48-hour maximum working week on the U.K. via the use of Article 118A of the Single European Act to introduce Directives on working conditions via a majority vote of the Council of Ministers. This 1993 initiative was upheld by the ECJ in 1996. See "Shaky truce on social battlefield," *Financial Times*, 5 August 1996, 13; Suzanne Perry, "EU Court Rejects UK Work-Hours Challenge," Reuters World Service, 12 November 1996.
54. One site selection consultant suggested in 1993 that aid, measured by its impact on profitability, had increased by 30 to 100 percent over the previous five years, depending on the country.
55. Yuill et al., *European Regional Incentives 1995-96*, 6.
56. Yuill et al., *European Regional Incentives 1995-96*, 93.
57. For details, see *Fifth Survey*, 40; Kenneth P. Thomas, "International Control and Discipline of Subsidies," Table 3.
58. Again, see Thomas, "International Control and Discipline of Subsidies," Table 3.
59. Jürgen R. Grote, "Diseconomies in Space: Traditional Sectoral Policies of the EC, the European Technology Community and their Effects on Regional Disparities," in *The Regions and the European Community: The Regional Response to the Single Market in the Underdeveloped Areas*, ed. Robert Leonardi (London: Frank Cass, 1993), 27.
60. Reiner Martin and Mathias Schulze Steinen, "State Aid, Regional Policy and Locational Competition in the European Union," *European Urban and Regional Studies* 4 (1997): 21.
61. Personal communication with Fiona Wishlade, European Policies Research Centre, University of Strathclyde, Glasgow, May 1994.
62. See Yuill et al., *European Regional Incentives 1997-98*, 87. Note, however, that Northern Ireland and parts of the Republic of Ireland are being de-designated from Objective 1 beginning in 2000. The Swedish areas referred to were designated as Objective 6 in the 1994–99 round of Structural Funds but Objective 1 in 2000–2006.
63. Yuill et al., *European Regional Incentives 1995-96*, 34.
64. Tim Frazer, "The New Structural Funds, State Aids and Interventions on the Single Market," *European Law Review*, February 1995, 12.

65. John Siraut, "Exploding the grants myth," *Corporate Location*, February 1992, 2.
66. Martin and Steinen, "State Aid, Regional Policy and Locational Competition," 28–29.
67. *Fifth Survey*, 40.
68. Tim Frazer, "The New Structural Funds," 17–18.
69. *Second Survey*, 26–27.
70. This is largely related, however, to heavy use of guarantees by the Treuhandanstalt in privatizing industry in eastern Germany and the subsequent decline as the process was completed.
71. Except for guarantees issued by the Treuhandanstalt in eastern Germany, which the Commission considers substantially more likely to be called upon, and where the aid element is estimated at 20 percent of the amount guaranteed. See *Fifth Survey on State Aid*, 23–24. The fact that the German data therefore are not lagged explains why the German figure has fallen from highs in 1992–94.
72. Following the Commission's presentation, the 1981–86 data exclude steel and shipbuilding because of extremely high short-term spending on those sectors in that period. Without adjusting for steel and shipbuilding, the levels of equity participation are as follows: Belgium, 28 percent; Denmark, 1 percent; Germany, zero; Greece, zero; France, 26 percent; Ireland, 13 percent; Italy, 19 percent; Luxembourg, 35 percent; The Netherlands, 1 percent; United Kingdom, 18 percent. These data come from the *Second Survey on State Aids*, Annex I, 9, Table IX; this Annex consisted of revisions to data from the *First Survey* for Ireland and Italy.
73. The data for Greece in all tables, especially for 1981–86, are not as reliable as the statistics for other countries. Because of a lack of cooperation from the Greek government, the Commission used a consultant's study and its own extrapolations. In the *Fifth Survey*, 4, the Commission reports, "The contribution received from the Greek authorities has permitted improvement of the Greek data. Regrettably, however, as no comprehensive contribution is forthcoming from the Greek authorities, the figures still remain essentially estimates, and therefore the results for Greece should be treated with some caution."
74. Without adjusting for steel and shipbuilding, the 1981–86 levels of guarantees are as follows: Belgium, 13 percent; Denmark, 3 percent; Germany, 1 percent; Greece, 5 percent; France, 5 percent; Ireland, 2 percent; Italy, zero; Luxembourg, zero; The Netherlands, zero; United Kingdom, 1 percent. *Second Survey on State Aids*, Annex I, 9, Table IX.
75. Without adjusting for steel and shipbuilding, the 1981–86 levels of grants and loans are: Belgium, 49 percent; Denmark, 43 percent; Germany, 86

percent; Greece, 95 percent; France, 24 percent; Ireland, 81 percent; Italy, 79 percent; Luxembourg, 61 percent; The Netherlands, 85 percent; United Kingdom, 71 percent. *Second Survey on State Aids*, Annex I, 9, Table IX.

76. Fiona Wishlade, *EC Competition Policy and Regional Aid: An Agenda for the Year 2000?* Regional and Industrial Research Paper Series, No. 25, European Policies Research Centre, December 1997, 10–11.

77. Elaine Ballantyne and John Bachtler, "Regional Policy Under Scrutiny: The European Commission and Regional Aid," Research Paper no. 9, European Policies Research Center, University of Strathclyde, Regional and Industrial Policy Research Series, 1990, 42. Germany's procedures apparently remain transparent—as the high rate of discovery of non-notified aid in Germany attests.

78. CEC, *Second Report on Competition Policy*, points 116–117; see also CEC, *Competition Law in the European Communities,* Volume II: Rules applicable to State aids (situation at 31 December 1989) (Brussels-Luxembourg: CEC, 1990), 142–44.

79. Cini, "Policing the Internal Market," 254–56, 260–61.

80. CEC, *Twentieth Report on Competition Policy*, point 171.

81. CEC, *Twentieth Report on Competition Policy*, point 247; CEC, "Fair Competition in the internal market: Community State Aid Policy," *European Economy* no. 48 (September 1991): 71.

82. CEC, *Twenty-first Report on Competition Policy*, points 240–47.

83. *Sixteenth Report on Competition Policy*, point 258.

84. CEC, *Twenty-fourth Report on Competition Policy*, point 390; CEC, *Twenty-fifth Report on Competition Policy*, points 209–10.

85. See, for example, letter to all member states regarding notification, suggesting that non-notified aid was illegal and might be subject to a repayment requirement (*Tenth Report on Competition Policy*, point 162); letter of 3 November 1983 noting rising non-notification problems and announcing its intent to regularly use aid repayment as a sanction (CEC, *Competition Law in the European Communities, Vol. 2*, 1990, 35–36); comments on the problem in the *Fifteenth Report on Competition Policy*, where it announced measures to increase third-party involvement in aid cases (point 171); observations in the *Seventeenth Report on Competition Policy* notes that there were 41 more non-notifications in 1987 than in 1986 and that subnational governments were becoming a particular problem in this regard (points 173–74); letter to member states of 27 April 1989 (CEC, *Competition Law in the European Communities, Vol. 2*, 1990, 19); on new rules regarding aid repayment and bringing national courts into the enforcement process, see *Twenty-fourth Report on*

Competition Policy, point 394, and *Twenty-fifth Report on Competition Policy*, points 153–55.

86. *Nineteenth Report on Competition Policy*, point 132.
87. *Thirteenth Report on Competition Policy*, point 219.
88. This possibility is raised in the *Fifteenth Report on Competition Policy*, point 169. Developments after 1985 made the Commission's optimism appear premature, as does the spike in 1996–98. Economic difficulties may not only increase demands for state aid; they also may increase the likelihood that states will propose aid that ultimately is deemed incompatible with the common market. Given the drawn-out nature of many Article 93(2) proceedings, this phenomenon may well show up at a lag of several years—as with the eleven steel aids that were disallowed in 1996. Tabulated from DG IV's Web site, "Cas pour lesquels la Commission a pris une décision négative ou partiellement négative au titre de l'article 6, paragraphe 4, de la decision 3855/91 du traité CECA" (Cases in which the Commission has taken a negative or partially negative decision under Article 6, paragraph 4, of Decision 3855/91 of the ECSC Treaty), available at: <http://europa.eu.int/en/comm/dg04/aid/aid96/aidp47.htm>)
89. Emma Tucker, "Boost for Brussels Over Illegal State Aid," *Financial Times*, 16 November 1998, 4.
90. Wolfgang Munchau and Neil Buckley, "News: Europe: VW Halts Investment in East Germany," *Financial Times*, 27 June 1996, 2; European Information Service, "Volkswagen Row Escalates as Bonn Takes Commission to Court," *European Report* no. 2157, 14 September 1996; European Information Service, "VW Files Court Complaint Over State Subsidies Row," *European Report* no. 2158, 18 September 1996; "Deal Near on Illegal Aid to VW," *Financial Times*, 25 October 1997, 2; Emma Tucker, "Commission Resolves VW Row," *Financial Times*, 19 November 1997, 2. For an analysis of the legal issues involved, see Ben Perry, "State Aids to the Former East Germany: A Note on the VW/Saxony Case," *European Law Review* 22 (February 1997): 85–91.
91. Lavdas and Mendrinou, *Politics, Subsidies, and Competition*, 62.
92. Cini, "Policing the Internal Market," 137.
93. Mitchell P. Smith, "Integration in Small Steps: The European Commission and Member-State Aid to Industry," *West European Politics* 19 (July 1996), 576–77.

7

Lessons for Theory, Lessons for Policy

This book explores the phenomenon of competition for investment and methods for its control (or the lack thereof). As Chapter 2 shows, increasing capital mobility exacerbates governments' need for investment, resulting in more intense competition to attract and retain it. As a consequence, the corporate sector's tax burden has fallen for more than four decades, forcing governments to make up the difference by increasing individual tax burdens, increasing their budget deficits, or cutting services. Moreover, as a result of the subsidization of *capital*, returns on investment have been greater than they would have been without subsidies—implying a distribution of income away from labor and toward capital.

Controlling competition for investment takes the form of a prisoners' dilemma. The dominant solution has been the non-cooperative option of offering locational incentives; a state cannot make itself better off by unilaterally disarming. Because there is no individually accessible solution, states must find ways to effectively cooperate if they want to reduce the negative consequences of competition for investment. Two broad approaches to the cooperation problem are most relevant here: third-party enforcement of cooperative agreements, whereby a "superior" body can guarantee that actors will carry out their promises, and decentralized cooperation that uses "tit-for-tat" strategies, reciprocating positive and negative behavior. In general, we should expect the former to be more reliable than the latter.

The cases examined in this book present a continuum on the relationship between two (or more) levels of government: EU member states are sovereign but have given some powers to a supranational body; Canadian provinces are not independent but have great autonomy from the federal government in many areas; U.S. states are weaker still, having seen the federal government take over many of their prerogatives since the 1960s, using federal funding as the lever to achieve this aim. At first glance, then, U.S. states might appear to be most likely to achieve some sort of cooperative arrangement to reduce investment competition because of the presence of the federal government as a potential third-party enforcer; the independent EU states would seem least likely to achieve this cooperation, and Canadian provinces would likely fall somewhere in between. As we have seen in Chapters 5 and 6, however, exactly the opposite has been the case: The United States has achieved almost no control, Canada has achieved a small amount, and the EU has a reasonably successful system for controlling many kinds of subsidies. This chapter seeks to understand these surprising findings, to enhance our understanding of international cooperation, to assess the possibility of controlling investment competition in North America, to examine some related efforts at controlling subsidies in the WTO and the OECD, and to draw policy implications from these cases.

Lessons for Theory

Two theoretical conclusions stand out from this study. The first conclusion is that we cannot derive predictions about the likelihood of successful cooperation simply from the potential availability of third-party enforcement of agreements, as one might surmise the federal governments in the United States and Canada are capable of providing. The second conclusion is that attempts to regulate activity must be comprehensive, or states will circumvent them by engaging in unregulated activities that have similar effects.

Factors That Affect Cooperation

The relative lack of success among U.S. states and Canadian provinces in cooperatively controlling investment competition stands in contrast with the EU's moderate achievements in this area. This situation has consequences for our understanding of when cooperation is likely to be successful. Table 7-1 shows how the United States, Canada, and the EU compare on several important factors that affect the likelihood of achieving cooperation.

As Table 7-1 shows, the number of actors differs dramatically among the three cases: fifty states in the United States, ten provinces in Canada, and 6–15 member states of the EC/EU. As Mancur Olson has argued, cooperation becomes more difficult to achieve as the

Table 7-1 **Possible Factors Affecting Cooperation over Investment Competition in the United States, Canada, and EU**

Factor	**U.S.**	**Canada**	**EU**
Number of actors	50	10	6–15
Relative strength of central government	Highest	Medium	Lowest
Central monitoring	No	No	Yes
Enforcement	None	Complaints	Own Initiative

number of actors increases.[1] On this basis, we would expect to find difficulties for the United States compared with either Canada or the EU. We also would expect to find that the EU has had more difficulties implementing its state aid policy as its membership has expanded.

We have already discussed the relative strength of the central government. In no case can the central body dictate to the subordinate governments, but there is a clear difference between the United States and Canada, in that provinces have far more autonomy from their federal government than do U.S. states. In the EU, of course, the member states are sovereign, and only the poorest receive any significant net funding from the EU. On the basis of this factor, we would expect the United States to have the easiest time organizing cooperation via third-party enforcement, with Canada next and the EU last.

Charles Lipson has emphasized the importance of monitoring ability for the achievement of cooperation in prisoners' dilemma strategic situations.[2] Only the EU has a body charged with ongoing monitoring of investment subsidies (and other subsidies as well)—that is, DG IV of the European Commission. Only the EU has pre-implementation notification requirements for subsidies.[3] On this basis, we would expect that the EU would be better able to keep up with whether actors are abiding by agreements not to use prohibited methods of competing for investment, such as excessive state aid in the EU or relocation incentives in Canada and in the U.S. regional agreements.

Finally, the possibility of enforcement of agreements clearly is crucial for the likelihood of achieving lasting cooperation. In the United States, no mechanism existed to enforce regional "no raiding" agreements in the Midwest and Northeast. In Canada, enforcement with regard to violations of the Code of Conduct on Incentives are similar to GATT dispute resolution; such enforcement is based on complaints to the Internal Trade Secretariat followed by consultations. This procedure is relatively cumbersome, as the GATT experience and Canada's short experience under the Code of Conduct have shown. In the EU, by contrast, the Commission acts on its own initiative to oppose proposed aid that appears to be incompatible with the common market, and it has the power of the ECJ to support it. In the future, the Procedural Regulation should strengthen the Commission's hand further, and theoretically it could propose fines for governments that refuse to honor their Treaty obligations. On this basis, the EU would appear to be best placed to achieve cooperation on subsidy/state aid issues, with Canada a perhaps distant second and the United States dead last.

We know from the discussions in Chapters 5 and 6 that this ranking is an accurate description of the achievements in these three cases. Diagnosing the causes of the relative success or failure of the U.S., Canadian, and EU efforts is difficult, however; as Table 7-1 shows, the results are somewhat overdetermined. In particular, the U.S. situation is inhospitable to cooperation on three of the variables: it has a large number of actors, no monitoring, and no enforcement. If not for the occasional example of federal pressure forcing changes in state laws (e.g., civil rights, drinking age), we would not be surprised at all that so little action on investment competition has occurred in the United States.

The differences between Canada and the EU are narrower on the independent variables, in particular the number of actors. Yet a wide gulf separates the EU's relative success and the baby steps that have been taken in Canada. Again, the Canadian federal government claims far more resources as a proportion of GDP than does the EU, and provinces are not sovereign. This factor favoring Canadian success is overwhelmed, however, by those favoring EU accomplishments: the existence of centralized monitoring and specific enforcement powers in the Commission. On the basis of subsidy/state aid control, these factors would appear to be more important for obtaining durable cooperation than the general strength of the central government. Although a stronger central government is a potential source for third-party enforcement, that factor is not relevant unless it is actually mobilized via specific monitoring and enforcement mechanisms. In Canada, the creation of the Internal Trade Secretariat is the first, albeit small, step toward building such mechanisms. In the United States, although state preferences are no different (they want to avoid bidding wars for investments),[4] there is no agreement on the necessity for a centralized solution. I return to this issue below in discussing the likelihood of controls on competition for investment in North America.

Circumventing Regulation

This point should come as no surprise: Regulatory efforts are met by attempts by the regulated to move to less or unregulated ways of accomplishing the same ends. We must keep this point in mind, however, as we try to think of better ways to control competition for mobile investment. As the European experience has shown, there are numerous ways to compete for investment without being hampered by the state aid rules. The Irish have pioneered one approach: turn "state aid" into a "general macroeconomic measure" by making it widely available—in this case, the 10 percent corporate income tax for manufacturing (see discussion in Chapter 4). Although the European Commission long accepted the Irish government's argument that this tax rate is a general measure, it figured centrally in EU and OECD discussions of "unfair taxation" (see below). Another unregulated way to compete for investment is to tolerate abusive transfer pricing—as has been alleged, for example, in the case of Ireland and the UK.[5] This strategy increases a multinational corporation's after-tax profits, thereby providing an incentive to locate in countries that will allow it. A third, nonfinancial, approach is to construct labor laws that systematically reduce the cost of employment (e.g., the UK's decision to opt-out from the Social Chapter of the Maastricht Agreement from 1993 to 1997, which reduced labor protections and costs, or "right-to-work" laws in several southern and western U.S. states, which weaken unions and thereby reduce wages).[6] Finally, the EU has witnessed ploys such as the move to packaging more state aid as R&D aid, once the Commission expressed a favorable attitude toward it.[7] Overall, then, regulating competition for investment should be as comprehensive as possible if it is to succeed.[8]

Prospects for Controlling Investment Competition in North America

I have argued in Chapters 1 and 2 that controlling location subsidies is desirable, and the analysis in Chapter 6 of the EU experience concludes that such control is technically feasible. Whether it is *politi-*

cally feasible in North America, particularly in the United States, is more doubtful, however. The biggest obstacle appears to be U.S. state governments, which only grudgingly give up any power to the federal government. Despite their recognition of a problem, governors are not ready to cede their authority.[9] This situation is precisely what the prisoners' dilemma model of investment attraction would lead us to expect.

In addition, with the passage of NAFTA, the discussion of subsidy control as a Canada/U.S. problem is already anachronistic. Extending investment incentive limits to Mexico, however, could reopen the wounds of the NAFTA debate. For example, bringing the equivalent of EU regional aid policy into NAFTA (i.e., by allowing higher subsidy levels in Mexico and by creating a North American equivalent of the Structural Funds) would further encourage the gradual relocation of some production from Canada and the United States to Mexico. Although some opponents of NAFTA advocate this approach to regional integration, it is hard to imagine such a solution being adopted.

Nonetheless, some observers, such as Graham and Warner, argue that a North American state aid policy is necessary in the NAFTA context (as part of a broader competition policy, similar in many ways to that of DG IV).[10] Although one can disagree with their prescription in its details, there are reasons to believe that political support is growing for controls on location incentives, even in the United States. The problem itself is far more widely recognized than it has been in the past (witness the NGA statement), and Canada's move to ban relocation aids may well be a first baby step that U.S. governors can be persuaded to take on this side of the border.[11] At the same time, there is substantial pressure from below for controls, as the campaigns against corporate welfare and for subsidy accountability demonstrate. Moreover, several attorneys believe that most state locational incentives are open to legal challenge under the Commerce Clause of the U.S. Constitution, which prohibits individual states from interfering with interstate commerce.[12] Their reasoning is that by affecting the location of production, the programs are clearly affecting interstate commerce as well.

After many years of discussion, this theory is now being tested in court. A December 1999 lawsuit filed by citizens of Toledo, Ohio, and nearby Erie, Michigan, charges that a $185 million incentives package given to retain a Jeep plant in Toledo "discriminate[s] in favor of in-state business activity and against out-of-state investment, in violation of the restrictions imposed on discriminatory state and local taxation by the Commerce Clause ... of the United States Constitution." The action seeks to have the subsidy to Daimler-Chrysler declared unconstitutional. As Ralph Nader said of the case, "If it goes anywhere it's going to affect a lot of subsidies."[13]

Finally, there have been recent efforts to revive regional agreements. The Council of Great Lakes Governors has tried to revive no-raiding rules there (see Chapter 5), though ultimately without success.[14] One state, Maryland, took the prisoners' dilemma aspect of investment attraction seriously: The legislature asked the governor to seek a regional compact—but with the proviso that Maryland would *escalate* competition if agreement is not reached in two years.[15] Nothing came of this effort, however, and Maryland and Virginia continue to conduct major bidding wars—as demonstrated by Maryland's recent decision to offer a package worth more than $40 million to Marriott to keep it from relocating to Virginia.[16] Although both of these specific efforts met with failure, the increasing frequency of reform attempts nonetheless suggests that efforts to control location subsidies may soon reach critical mass.

Beyond the national or regional level, however, there are important international attempts at dealing with subsidies and competition for investment.

OECD and WTO Work on Subsidies

There are two international forums carrying out work that is relevant to the focus of this book. First, the OECD conducted surveys of industrial subsidies among its members—similar in coverage to the notion of "manufacturing aid" in the EU—from the late 1980s to 1998 (when the project was terminated under pressure from the United States and Canada). More recently, the OECD has established a Working Party on Tax Competition, which issued its first report in April 1998.[17] Second, the WTO has begun to require its members to make notifications of subsidies. The Uruguay Round negotiations also created detailed guidelines regarding which subsidies were generally permissible ("green light"), which were potentially actionable ("yellow light"), and which were definitely prohibited ("red light"). While these have now lapsed, the negotiations over their initiation and possible renewal tell us alot about global subsidy politics.

OECD: Studies on Public Support to Manufacturing

The OECD began surveying public support for manufacturing industry in OECD countries in the late 1980s. According to one U.S. Department of Commerce official, the OECD originally hoped that this project would affect the Uruguay Round subsidies negotiations.[18] A first report, covering 1982–86, was published in 1990; this report was deficient in its coverage in several respects, however, and I do not consider it here. The second study covered 1986–89 and included data on 879 aid programs in 22 countries plus the Commission of the European Communities (CEC).[19] The most recent full analysis, covering 1989–93, includes data on 1,552 programs in 24 member states, the European Commission, and the Slovak Republic, which has observer status in the relevant OECD Working Party.[20] This report was revised, updated, and expanded (but not for all countries) in 1998.

As Rauf Gönenc, the OECD administrator who formerly was in charge of the project, has said, achieving transparency in state subsidization of industry is itself a process of negotiation. Until all countries report equally, countries with full reporting may appear to be providing higher subsidies relative to less-complete reporters and may be subject to disapprobation as a result. The OECD's mandate for this project was to improve transparency and comparability of the data on public support to industry.[21] Although no enforcement mechanisms were involved, the Working Party utilized a "peer review" process in which each country could review every other country's submissions.[22] As noted above, each successive report had expanded coverage, and the final report, covering 1989–93, included individual country data for most participating members (though the United States and Canada were prominently absent),[23] in many cases updated beyond 1993. By comparison, the 1986–89 study only provided an index of real spending for each country and the European Commission. Even in the final report, however, there are still deficiencies in the coverage of subcentral government support to industry as well as the coverage of aid provided to firms via tax expenditures.[24] The most recent study suggests that industrial subsidies in non-EU OECD states are under less control than in the EU (see Chapter 6). Besides these reports, the project also generated an international standard for identifying and quantifying the value of a comprehensive list of subsidy tools.[25]

This project proved to be politically controversial. Although the effort was strongly supported by European OECD members (the EU, after all, produces similar data already—which it relied upon for its OECD submissions), the United States and Canada opposed the project. As another Commerce Department official told me, "We took issue with the ability to make comparisons across countries." Moreover, he said, "There were some attacks on us for incompleteness."[26] This latter point is hardly surprising because the two main shortcomings of the 1989–93 study—subcentral subsidies and tax subsidies—are strongly characteristic of the United States. Tax expenditures make up 70 percent of business support at the federal level and an even greater percentage at the state and local level (see Chapter 5). Among the 20 U.S. states that were sampled for the final phase of the OECD study,[27] financial information was provided for only 28 programs of 115 reported. The United States was showered with 3,000 questions on its submission; Commerce officials felt that the Europeans did not understand the difficulty in obtaining state-level data because subsidy usage is far more decentralized than in Europe.[28] Canada did not provide provincial data at all and did not give quantitative information on tax concessions.[29]

At the May 1998 meeting of the OECD Industry Committee, U.S. opposition (along with that of Canada and also Mexico) meant that a renewal of the Working Party's mandate was impossible. As a result, the OECD's data collection efforts in this area have ceased.[30] Because OECD subsidy reporting was more comprehensive than that obtained in the WTO (at least at the time of this writing),[31] this development is an unfortunate blow to subsidy transparency.

WTO: Notification Requirements after the Uruguay Round

The Agreement on Subsidies and Countervailing Measures annexed to the 1994 agreement that established the WTO provided, for the first time, a GATT definition of a subsidy; explicitly introduced the concept of specificity; and divided subsidies into three categories: prohibited, actionable, and nonactionable (popularly known as red, yellow, and green light subsidies). In the red-light (banned) category were export subsidies and those requiring minimum local content.[32] Green-light status could be accorded to subsidies for regional aid, subsidies designed to meet new environmental regulations, and subsidies for R&D purposes—strongly mirroring the types of aid toward which the European Commission is favorably disposed.[33] All other subsidies were considered actionable if they caused "adverse effects" to other WTO members.[34]

In addition, the SCM Agreement requires WTO members to report their subsidy programs to the Secretariat annually (a "new and full" notification every three years and updates in the intervening years).[35] Unlike EU practice, this is *ex post facto* notification rather than *ex ante* notification. Nonactionable subsidies were to be reported in advance of implementation, however.[36] Like the OECD exercise, WTO notification is best considered "a long-term confidence-building measure," as one U.S. official described it.[37] It also resembles the OECD effort in that it includes a peer-review process.

The first round of new and full notifications was due 30 June 1995, and the second was due 30 June 1998, with updating notifications due 30 June of each intervening year. Delays in submissions and in the peer-review process meant that the first round of peer reviews was not completed until summer 1997. Reviews of the 1998 full notifications were still underway as this book went to press. Outside the industrialized countries, compliance with the notification requirement has been uneven (forty members, all of which are developing countries, have submitted no notifications), and even industrialized nations often fail to meet the notification deadlines.[38] Other problems include sometimes implausible claims to have *no* subsidy programs as defined in the SCM Agreement or apparently incomplete notifications (e.g., by omitting agricultural subsidies, ad hoc subsidies not provided within the context of a formal program, or tax expenditure subsidies).[39]

In the first round of notifications, a major problem was that, outside of the EU, many countries, including federal states (e.g., the United States, Canada, Australia, and Switzerland), provided little or no subsidy information for subcentral levels of government. The EU was unhappy with the failure by the United States and other countries to notify subcentral subsidies. Staff members in DG I (External Relations) put together a list of about 400 state-level programs that they felt possibly should have been notified.[40] The United States was unwilling to notify state-level subsidies until it was satisfied that other WTO members would also notify subnational subsidies, and negotiations on this issue took more than a year. Much of the U.S. concern was directed toward Canada because of its status as the country's largest trade partner and because of the growing importance of provincial subsidies relative to federal subsidies there.[41] In August 1997, the EU counter-notified ten U.S. state programs to the WTO. According to one official in DG I, although the United States initially offered no response, it soon announced that it would notify its subfederal programs in the 1998 round of new and full notifications and confirmed four of the counter-notified programs.The EU has focused less on federal states other than the United States, though it has raised questions with Canada regarding several provincial programs.[42]

The second round of new and full notifications was still underway as this book went to press. As of July 1999, only 35 of the WTO's 119 members had submitted their notifications, compared with 70 for the first round.[43] The United States and other federal states notified subfederal programs that had not been included in the first round of notification. For the United States, this notification meant reporting all state programs for which the states provided information, as well as some local programs when information was provided by the states.[44]

U.S.–EU conflict on notification remains substantial. One important issue beneath some of the disputes concerns the definition of "specificity." In EU state aid policy, horizontal programs (such as aid for R&D or the environment) are considered specific. In the WTO, specificity appears to mean firm or sector specific, so an R&D program that is widely available among different sectors might not be specific and hence not a subsidy under the WTO definition, even though R&D fall in the "green light" category if the provisions of Article 8 were met. Thus, the EU raised questions about the U.S. failure to notify the Advanced Technology Program (see note 31)—which the United States defended on the grounds that it was not specific in law or in fact.[45] The EU also remains critical of the United States in its handling of state-level subsidies and aerospace, although it judges the quality of overall subsidy notification to have improved.[46] Conflict of this sort seems certain to continue.

In the long run, the notification process should contribute to the control of subsidies in general, including those used in investment competition. One promising sign is that these notifications are publicly available, rather than confidential. Moreover, the peer-review process and related efforts are improving the quality and completeness of notifications. Nevertheless, it will be some time before all WTO members are reporting equally—a subject of obvious concern to the more complete notifiers (compare the Gönenc statements above). Although the overall decline in notification rates in the 1998 round of new and full notifications is cause for concern, that concern does not extend to the major trading countries that are the subject of this book.[47]

As the WTO moves beyond notifications and begins to generate case law under the new SCM agreement, it will face several issues similar to those the European Commission sees in its enforcement role. For example, will dispute resolution panels be able to gather information from a potentially recalcitrant member against whom a complaint has been lodged? Can sanctions against an already-paid-out subsidy work? (Compare the problems raised in the *Boussac* case.) How these and similar issues are resolved will determine the effectiveness of the WTO's subsidy controls.

An early indication of how this might take place also reflects the influence of EU practice. On 11 February 2000, the WTO ruled in a U.S. complaint against an Australian export subsidy that the company receiving the funds must return them to the government in full. Aid repayment, of course, is the most powerful weapon in the Commission's armory, but its use in the WTO caused shock waves. Canada and Brazil, both of which recently were ruled to have provided illegal export subsidies for commuter aircraft, were concerned that the decision not set a precedent for their cases. The United States said the repayment order went "beyond that sought by the U.S." Even the EU, which uses such a tool, urged further study in the WTO context.[48] How this ruling plays out in the future will be an important sign of how WTO subsidy rulings will be enforced.

In addition, the rules themselves require the development of some case law before it is clear how they will work in practice. For example, how would the Mercedes Alabama case have been affected if the SCM Agreement had been in effect at the time? On one hand, the main incentives were generally available, seeming to make the package "nonspecific" and hence not subject to WTO subsidy discipline. On the other hand, some elements of the Mercedes package do appear to have been specific—such as the state's agreement to pay the salaries of the workers for the first year of operation, at a cost of $45 million.[49] At such a high level, that provision would appear to trigger the possibility of causing "serious prejudice" based on the standard established in Annex IV of the agreement—which specifies that "Where the recipient firm is in a start-up situation, the overall rate of subsidization shall not exceed 15 per cent of the total funds invested."[50] Whether the subsidies fell into the actionable or nonactionable category, however, would determine what type of action could be taken by a WTO member.

Complaints about actionable subsidies are heard by the WTO's Dispute Settlement Body, which must accept panel reports unless all members (including the complaining party) agree not to. Complaints about nonactionable subsidies, by contrast, go to the Committee on Subsidies and Countervailing Measures, which operates by consensus—meaning that the defendant could block any action. Finally, there is some question regarding who would lodge a complaint in these cases: The United States would not complain about its own subsidy (and other U.S. states do not have standing to do so); the EU presumably would not because an EU firm is the beneficiary; and Japan might not—even though the incentives surely affect Japanese exports of sport utility vehicles—because many Japanese firms have benefited from similar subsidies.

That the actual impact of the rules on such a situation is uncertain is nicely illustrated by the widely varying responses I have received from trade experts on whether the SCM Code would have applied to the Mercedes Alabama case had the Code been effect at that time: from "absolutely" (a Canadian who has served on bilateral dispute resolution panels), to all sorts of "it depends," to "almost certainly not" (a high EU official). This divergence of opinion is related, I suspect, to another problem: GATT has historically concerned itself with trade subsidies, and "it may well be that location subsidies aren't well handled by trade rules," as a U.S. official acknowledged. "Like research and development subsidies, it's something that is paid early on and then possibly has disproportionate effects." Again, growing familiarity with investment location incentives will improve how they are handled in the future.

One major area of contention—both during the Uruguay Round negotiations and since—has been the issue of green-light subsidies. While green-light provisions expired at the end of 1999, the debates continue to reverberate and will arise again in the next round of multilateral trade negotiations. The U.S. position under the Bush administration was very hostile to the concept of green-lighting subsidies at all, but the Clinton victory in 1992 changed that, at least in terms of subsidies for R&D. As Robert O'Brien notes, the new U.S. negotiating team proposed subsidy limits that exceeded what the EU allowed under its existing rules—whereas with the Bush administration negotiators, the EU was having difficulty getting agreement for limits that were *below* the EU maxima (the higher limits were in fact adopted, necessitating a new EU framework on R&D aid).[51] However, since the agreement was signed, the U.S. maintained its hostility to the idea of nonactionable subsidies, even in R&D. This situation led to a complicated game where the EU tried to find a clear-cut program to notify to the WTO and successfully defend as nonactionable. Given the certainty of a U.S. challenge, the Commission had difficulty finding a "volunteer" to take on the job.[52] Moreover, as Fiona Wishlade predicted in 1996, EU and national regional programs do not strictly fit the WTO criteria for nonactionability, which are even more inflexible than the Commission's criteria for designating maps of assistable areas (see Chapter 4). Thus, the most likely candidates for a program to be notified as green would have been the Commission's own, most likely in R&D. However, no subsidy was notified as nonactionable before the expiration of Article 8 at the end of 1999, so this will be a dead letter unless Article 8 is ultimately renewed (see further below).

Although no programs were notified as nonactionable, Article 10 of the Agreement provided for the defense of subsidies as *de facto* green, and this provision has been used.[53] The U.S. never accepted this claim in any countervail case; indeed, according to one EU official, the U.S. decided to rule a case *de minimis* rather than accept "*de facto* green." Other countries, however, have accepted the *de facto* green claim even where the U.S. did not—as with the "Italian Pasta" case, in which both New Zealand and Canada accepted this argument.[54]

One factor that impeded the notification of subsidies as nonactionable was the lack of a legal framework. The final elements of an arbitration process for disputes were adopted only in June 1998, after previous agreement had been reached on "formats for the initial notification of such programmes and for updating notifications."[55] However, this late adoption left little time to notify a subsidy as nonactionable before the green light provisions expired 31 December 1999.

The green-light provisions were subject to a mandatory renegotiation after five years.[56] According to a U.S. International Trade Administration document, most WTO members favored a limited extension of the green-light provisions to determine their effectiveness, but there were some objections among less-developed country members. This was also the recommendation of the U.S. Advisory Committee for Trade Policy and Negotiations, but some businesses suggested that there was nothing to be gained from green-light provisions. In the end, LDC objections proved decisive: they sought weaker discipline on export subsidies and others they were more likely to use in return for the renewal of green light, and developed countries refused to do this. The result was the automatic termination of the nonactionable categories at the end of 1999. This topic is sure to be revisited in the next round of global trade talks.[57]

The effect of the WTO agreement on subnational and regional aid is another area of uncertainty. Canada lobbied very hard (and successfully) to ensure that a subsidy offered throughout the territory of a subnational government "would not be automatically deemed specific," as it would have under the so-called "Dunkel draft" of the Uruguay Round that formed the basis for the final successful negotiations. This understanding was intended to avoid giving Québec separatists an argument that provincial industrial policy would be restricted under the SCM agreement, in a way that would not be true were Québec independent.[58]

Wishlade argues that this provision could give U.S. states and Canadian provinces advantages in competition for investment vis-a-vis the EU. First, although a generally available subsidy in a country with its own currency would affect its exchange rate, there would be no such negative impact for such a program in a U.S. state or Canadian province.[59] Second, European subnational governments must have Commission approval for subsidy programs, whereas states and provinces do not have a comparable requirement.[60] Moreover, Wishlade contends, "It seems likely that there will be considerable difficulty in demonstrating that the regional policy programmes of the Member States, as approved by the Commission, comply with the GATT Code." The main difficulty is that regional subsidies must be nonspecific to be green-lighted under the WTO rules, and many regional aid programs in the EU are highly discretionary in terms of sectoral emphasis, amount granted to each aid recipient, and so forth.[61] The question, then, is how much discretion is too much to be considered nonactionable under the SCM agreement? This issue will be key in determining the agreement's impact on regional aid policies. It seems reasonable to suggest, however, that the SCM emphasis on nonspecificity will collide with the EU's long experience showing that nonspecificity is expensive—which is why European regional aid programs have become increasingly more discretionary over the past decade and a half.[62]

Regarding the United States, Charles Colgan has speculated that "it seems likely that state and local development programs will be exposed not only in theory but also in practice to challenge under the newly expanded GATT rules on subsidies." Most likely, he argues, there will be occasional challenges to such programs, rather than wholesale attacks by other countries or voluntary compliance by the states.[63] Although this assessment seems quite plausible, again, more experience is needed.[64]

Although it is still too early to predict the exact effects, it seems clear that the WTO subsidy rules will be significant. In particular, the effectiveness of the WTO as an enforcement body in this area and the impact of the SCM rules on existing regional policies bear watching. Despite the nonrenewal of the key rules on the presumption of serious prejudice, nonactionable subsidies, and consultations over nonactionable subsidies, there will be no change in the notification requirement, which should strengthen subsidy transparency over time as the quality of notifications improves.

Multilateral Work on Tax Competition

As the discussions at numerous points in this book have emphasized, countries that face regulations on their ability to provide subsidies will often resort to policy tools that are similar in effect but unregulated. Ireland's 10 percent corporate income tax for manufacturing (now on its way out) has been a prominent example of this phenomenon, but many other countries have resorted to tax measures to attract investment. The OECD and the EU have recently addressed the issue of tax competition—largely in mutually reinforcing fashion, although there are differences in emphasis and in the political dynamics involved. Both of these efforts are noteworthy in that neither has been motivated as much by efficiency concerns as by the potential for the degradation of tax revenue that tax competition is perceived to have caused, as well as the potential for addressing the problem of competition for investment directly. In addition, the EU efforts have been motivated explicitly by equity issues, clearly documenting the shifting of tax burdens from capital to labor and the potential for substituting capital for labor as this tax incentive shifts.

OECD Report on Harmful Tax Practices

In April 1996, the OECD established a Forum on Harmful Tax Practices, "to examine how this competitive bidding [for mobile investment] may distort investment flows and undermine revenues."[65] This initiative followed an earlier attempt (in 1992–95) to study the issue that, for political reasons, never released a report. According to Jeffrey Owens, head of the OECD's Fiscal Affairs Directorate, the rapid increase in the use of tax havens "was depriving governments of legitimate tax revenues, undermining the integrity of their tax systems, and threatening their fiscal sovereignty."[66] Although some of the project's preliminary criteria appeared to include Ireland's 10 percent corporate tax rate for manufacturing within the purview of the project—and high-profile relocations such as Boston Scientific's moves from Belgium and Denmark to Ireland added fuel to the fire[67]—this politically sensitive issue ultimately was excluded from the first phase of the project in favor of a focus on tax competition for financial and other services. This narrowed focus was sharply criticized by Luxembourg and Switzerland, who both abstained on the report's approval.[68] In April 2000, however, both countries signed on to a process that may reduce bank secrecy in connection with taxation—though how far this will go is still being debated.[69]

The study identified several factors associated with tax havens and harmful preferential tax regimes, including no or very low taxes, lack of effective exchange of information (the perceived assault on bank secrecy laws was a major objection of Switzerland and Luxembourg), and non-transparent operation of the tax regime. In addition, tax havens are characterized by the absence of any requirement that substantial activities take place, and preferential tax regimes are commonly "ring-fenced": either unavailable to domestic taxpayers (that is, available only to foreigners) or requiring that firms that benefit from the tax regime not operate in the domestic market.[70] None of these criteria—particularly the question of zero or low tax rates—is necessarily decisive by itself. These criteria will be used to publish a list of tax havens and to designate OECD members' tax regimes as "harmful," which would require their abolition within three years (though benefits could be grandfathered until 2005). Because most, if not all, OECD members operate at least some "harmful" preferential tax programs, the impact should be substantial.[71]

The OECD Forum will also conduct outreach to persuade nonmembers to operate their tax systems in non-harmful fashion.[72] According to an OECD official, forty-seven potential tax havens were identified (on the basis of publications or information on the Internet) and asked to participate in the process.[73] Discussions are continuing with the forty-seven, while planned sanctions against harmful tax practices have been put off until 2001. The OECD still plans to publish the names of countries or territories with such practices in June 2000.[74] Although the Irish corporation tax was excluded from the first phase of the project, the Committee on Fiscal Affairs has indicated its intention to address such "tax incentives to attract plant, building and equipment" in future phases of its work.[75]

EU Tax Competition Code of Conduct

The European Commission foresaw the potential for revenue degradation when capital movements were liberalized; even in 1989 there was a proposal for an EU-wide minimum tax on savings.[76] Yet revenue degradation has not been the only motivation for EU policy to combat tax competition. The Commission also recognized that tax competition to attract mobile investment was contributing to a long-run shift of the tax burden from capital to labor. From 1980 to 1994, taxes on labor increased from 34.7 percent of total labor income to 40.5 percent; taxes on capital, the self-employed, energy, and natural resources fell from 44.1 percent of income to 35.2 percent.[77] The Commission suggested that this shifting tax burden was contributing to the EU's severe unemployment problem by providing tax incentives to substitute capital for labor.[78]

Starting with meetings of economic and finance (ECOFIN) ministers at Verona in 1996, the Commission gradually hammered out a Code of Conduct on business taxation that was adopted by the Council of Ministers on 1 December 1997. The agreement represents a political commitment by all fifteen member states to identify harmful tax measures, not introduce new ones, and roll back existing measures. The final hurdle was a battle between Ireland and France over the former's low corporation tax rates, which France regards as unfairly attracting investment; ultimately, Ireland received five years to phase out many of its programs.

A further contentious issue is how to craft a method to combat tax evasion by individual investors, via either tax withholding or information sharing with home country tax authorities. Luxembourg has long claimed that it will not compromise on this issue without an agreement on a minimum corporate income tax rate, which Ireland and the UK oppose. Because tax policy requires unanimity in the Council of Ministers, agreement may be difficult to achieve.[79] Luxembourg's recent movement on bank secrecy does make compromise more likely, however. The situation was further complicated by the forced resignation of the College of Commissioners in March 1999, as Single Market Commissioner Mario Monti's 1998 proposed directives on tax policy (to impose a 20 percent withholding tax or provide information to the recipient's home tax authorities) were put in question because his designated replacement, Frits Bolkenstein of The Netherlands, was thought to be less insistent on tax harmonization than Monti was.[80]

To follow up on the Code of Conduct, a monitoring group chaired by UK Treasury Secretary Dawn Primarolo began reviewing programs that were possibly in violation. Tax experts originally identified a total of about 80 such programs; the group was then flooded with complaints by governments, bringing the total to more than 200 altogether. The torrent of complaints began when the Dutch government, which operated many of the schemes targeted in the first round, released a report it commissioned on tax incentives in the EU. Then-Internal Market Commissioner Monti asked member states not to lodge further complaints to let the monitoring body report its findings in late 1999 as scheduled.[81]

Two differences in the political dynamics of these parallel processes stand out. First, the OECD's motivation is more narrowly cast, primarily relating to the problem of fiscal degradation, whereas the EU explicitly has taken equity issues into account (one might argue, however, that the issue of fiscal degradation is indirectly an equity issue, given the mechanism by which tax capacities have been undermined). Second, the presence of the United States within the OECD negotiations, but not those of the EU, has made the issue of bank secrecy more central in the OECD process because of strong U.S. opposition to bank secrecy.[82]

Policy Recommendations

Controlling competition for investment is a priority if governments are to avoid, or at least ameliorate, the three-pronged choice that results as the corporate share of taxation falls: increasing personal taxation, running higher deficits, or cutting services. What is the best way to control this competition?

The situation is most acute in the United States because federal controls are weak and state governments are unwilling to consider federal preemption of their powers to attract firms. Although a blanket ban on subnational location subsidies is desirable in the abstract, even better, as Barbara Jenkins has argued, would be for the states to negotiate an agreement on "what is an acceptable subsidy and what is not."[83] In a sense, the WTO Agreement on Subsidies already accomplishes this aim, with its specification of R&D, regional, and environmental subsidies as non-actionable. The U.S. situation is complicated, however, because poorer states such as Alabama or Mississippi might rightly object if richer states such as Connecticut also had regional subsidy programs—which they could accomplish not only by labeling a program as "regional" but also by making it generally available and hence not subject to WTO subsidy rules. In short, the United States needs a centralized regional program that would allow investment subsidies only for projects in poorer parts of the country. As the EU's experience has shown (see Chapter 6), decentralized regional aid in wealthier areas works against the reduction of regional economic disparities.

Of course, none of this is yet politically feasible, so what should we do now? First, the United States should compile periodic surveys of federal and subfederal subsidies *on an internationally comparable basis*. As the public becomes more aware of the magnitude of these subsidies, the pressure to reduce them is likely to grow. At present, we have only ad hoc reports by the CBO or by NGOs, which provide only partial answers (see Chapter 5). The U.S. WTO subsidy notification, which could meet this recommendation, is seriously flawed, as we saw above. Although the second new-and-full notification improves on the first with much greater inclusion of spending figures for federal subsidies and with notification of many subfederal programs, state and local subsidies only rarely include spending data, and many well-known programs are omitted from the notification. For example, the Advanced Technology Program is not notified (although it was reported in the OECD subsidy exercise) on the grounds that it is not specific—although R&D subsidies are certainly specific in the EU context and are designated as potentially green-light WTO subsidies. Instead of trying for advantage vis-a-vis its trading partners, the United States should build up its notification to something resembling the EU state aid *Surveys* (in part by devoting more staff to WTO notification than the current *one* professional) because ameliorating the efficiency and equity problems of domestic subsidy programs is in the country's own interest.[84]

Second, U.S. states should take a page from the Canadian book and negotiate a ban on *relocation* subsidies. This type of subsidy is the most objectionable of present practices, and this one delimited issue should be the easiest for finding consensus. The Canadian experience shows that making even this small step work takes time (and it is far from being consolidated in Canada, as we saw in Chapter 5), but success here is a precondition for moving to more ambitious steps.

Third, it would be useful if more states adopted the common Canadian position of banning local government use of investment incentives.[85] Even here, starting with a ban on relocation subsidies might be necessary.[86] This issue really is more usefully addressed at the national level, however, because a firm rarely threatens to move *only* to another locality within the same state; potential new sites in other states are mentioned, even if a firm only moves from a central city to the suburbs—as, for example, in the case of Sears, Roebuck, and Co.[87]

As noted above, a Commerce Clause legal challenge to state programs has now been launched. Obviously, if it is successful it will dramatically change the landscape for economic development efforts, perhaps necessitating the introduction of a national regional development program to replace decentralized location subsidies.

An even longer-term agenda, suggested by Schweke et al., "is to take some issues out of interstate competition."[88] By this they mean equalizing levels of partly state-funded transfer programs such as Aid for Families with Dependent Children (of course, the 1996 "welfare reform" went in exactly the opposite direction) and having shared federal-state taxes. Again, this proposal relies on the game-theoretic rationality of third-party enforcement but faces the usual problem that state policymakers are loath to give up their powers.

We should not assume that all proposals to end targeted business subsidies are created equal. Conservative and libertarian critics of business subsidies merely propose replacing firm-specific tax breaks with across-the-board business tax reductions.[89] There are two major problems with this approach. First, it completely ignores the equity issue contained in the cumulative shift in tax burden from mobile to nonmobile sectors. Second, European experience has shown that "automatic" tax breaks are far more expensive than discretionary incentives for investment, which is why the trend in Europe has been away from automatic incentives since at least 1980.[90]

In Canada, the effect of free-trade agreements on the welfare state interacts with issues of competition for investment in ways that are largely beyond the scope of this book. I therefore offer only two observations. First, insofar as investment competition is interprovincial, the agenda for Canada is to consolidate the relocation incentive ban and then move on to find ways of controlling location subsidies for new investments. Second, Canada faces the broader problem that provinces often find themselves in competition with U.S. states for investment. For this reason, Canada has a strong incentive to seek a North American solution to the problem of investment competition.

In the EU, the most critical problems are widely recognized—which does not mean there are easy solutions. As Chapter 6 shows, state aid policy has had only mixed effects on cohesion because of the continued existence of large regional aid programs in richer areas of the Community and because certain types of aid (most important, aid for R&D) are provided disproportionately in those areas. It is difficult to imagine the richer member states with active regional programs simply ending them (Denmark did end its small regional aid program in 1991),[91] although reunification led to a large cut in German regional spending in the old *Länder*.[92]

As in the United States, regional aid in the EU should be carried out at the "federal" level; this approach may already be the long-run trend as the Structural Funds rise relative to national subsidies.[93] "Federalizing" regional aid would respond to the concerns of Yuill et al. cited in Chapter 6 that the EU was itself contributing to competition for investment; indeed, federalization would make the largest part of such competition impossible. Moreover, it would equalize competition among eastern Germany and the Mezzogiorno on one hand—where being part of a far more prosperous state allows high levels of regional aid—and the cohesion countries on the other, which cannot afford to grant aid at levels they are legally entitled to give.

A second important failing concerns non-regulated means of competing for investment. Although the UK has now signed the Maastricht Social Chapter and Ireland's tax rate will become 12.5 percent for all corporations, many programs remain to be addressed under the new guidelines on fiscal aid, and the Irish tax is likely to come under renewed attack as being too low. Therefore, continuing the two-pronged approach on tax competition and fiscal aid is a high priority, in my view.

Third, notification and control of non-notified aid remains a problem. The real question is whether the Procedural Regulation has the teeth to make a dent in this problem. Until it is tested before the ECJ, we can only speculate.

Fourth, the extraordinary effect of German reunification must be more adequately reflected in Commission policy proposals on state aid. If we exclude the impact of reunification, the EU's record in reducing aid to manufacturing, lowering aid types most likely to go to mobile investment, and persuading states to use less transparent forms of aid improves dramatically (see Chapter 6). Nevertheless, the Commission's policy statements treat all member states as equally "guilty":

> The fact is that Commission action alone is not enough: Mr. Van Miert is proposing a genuine dialogue with all the Member States, with a view to establishing precise targets and a timetable for the reduction of aid budgets, alongside the action to be taken by the Commission itself.[94]

These far-reaching changes seem difficult to justify when the real "problem" is occurring in one country. Moreover, although scandals such as Bremer Vulkan highlight difficulties in the administration of aid in eastern Germany, those difficulties do not mean that large subsidies there are not justified (considering that it is poorer than any of the cohesion countries). Thus, sharing the Commission's view that dramatic measures are now needed to cut state aid further is difficult.

Finally, the Commission must be more sensitive to the fact that aid must have a countercyclical element. The Commission statement quoted above concerns 1992–94. Nowhere in this statement can one read that Europe went into recession in 1993—which would tend to increase subsidies, all other things equal.[95] Despite the decrease in aid once Germany is excluded from the calculation, the Commission focused on the failure of overall aid to fall and concluded that drastic action was needed. This performance is bad only if the goal is a reduction in state aid *regardless of external circumstances*. For the foregoing reasons, I would regard this conclusion as inappropriate, although the tone of the analysis in the *Fifth Survey* and in the press release quoted above suggest that that may now be DG IV's goal. Moreover, new Competition Commissioner Monti has announced a "zero target" for state aid and has indicated that he will investigate public broadcasting companies for hidden state aid during his tenure, both of which will be highly controversial.[96]

Conclusion

Competition for investment is not just any kind of competition. Unlike competition in goods markets, there can be no presumption that competition for investment is efficiency enhancing (on the contrary, it directs capital to less-efficient locations), and it clearly has the potential to result in "races to the bottom" in terms of wages, social protections, environmental standards, and tax base degradation via subsidies and lower tax rates on mobile actors. Conscious intervention in markets is necessary to prevent these negative outcomes.

Competition for investment does not come out of the blue sky. If capital were not mobile, governments and workers would merely negotiate (perhaps only implicitly) with domestic owners of capital concerning the conditions of investment and employment (see Chapter 2). Capital is mobile, however, and this factor strengthens capitalists in this bargaining situation. This circumstance raises serious equity problems that are exacerbated precisely by the competition of governments and groups of workers for investment.

The strength of early work on interdependence—in particular that of Richard Cooper—was that it recognized that investment competition gave states choices that Stephen Guisinger has since shown to be a prisoners' dilemma. This analysis implies that collective action by states can bring about satisfactory solutions, *if cooperation can be achieved*. A large literature in international relations as well as game theory testifies to the fact that such cooperation is difficult, but not impossible.

One crucial precondition, of course, is that states in fact must *want* to cooperate. As critics of location subsidies become more numerous on the Right and the Left, this desire to cooperate grows more likely. In present circumstances, most North American and EU states appear to be far more likely to see the need for subsidy control not for equity reasons directly but because of problems of tax base degradation, which have indirect links to equity concerns. Many observers have argued, for instance, that an important reason for the increased success of the European Commission's state aid control efforts is budget problems in the member states.[97] In the long run, however, budget problems also derive from competition from investment. If the corporate sector's tax burden falls, the only choices are to increase the burden on (non-mobile) individuals, to run bigger deficits, or to cut programs. Over the past twenty years, the limits of the first two strategies have been reached. With the move to smaller budget deficits in North America and western Europe, the emphasis has now shifted to cutting the programs of the welfare state. Citizens' reactions, in elections and in non-electoral politics, suggest that this strategy for dealing with the tax burden shift is rapidly reaching its limit as well. Something has to give.

One way or another, that something is capital mobility. Either international cooperation will be able to blunt all of its potential negative effects by controlling competition for investment or capital will be re-regulated—perhaps as part of a move to competing, even hostile, blocs of countries. The EU experience offers us some hope that the former can be achieved, but history gives us good reason to fear the latter.

Notes

1. Mancur Olson, *The Logic of Collective Action: Public Goods and the Theory of Groups* (Cambridge, Mass.: Harvard University Press, 1971), 35.
2. Charles Lipson, "International Cooperation in Economic and Security Affairs," *World Politics* 37, no. 1 (fall 1984), 7.
3. The World Trade Organization now oversees postimplementation notification of subsidies under the Uruguay Round Subsidies and Countervailing Measures code.
4. National Governors' Association Policy on Economic Growth and Development Incentives, in Jay Kayne and Molly Shonka, *Rethinking State Development Policies and Programs* (Washington, D.C.: National Governors' Association, 1994), 25–26.
5. Alex Rubner, *The Export Cult* (London: Maurice Temple Smith, 1987), 292–93; T. D. Breverton, "Effects of the Growth of Foreign Ownership of, and Penetration into, UK, Belgian and Irish Economic Sectors, 1978–1996," paper presented at 5th Biennial Conference of the European Community Studies Association, Seattle, 29 May–1 June 1997, 5, 8; P. Shirlow, "Transnational Corporations in the Republic of Ireland and the Illusion of Economic Well-Being," *Regional Studies* 29, no. 7 (1995): 688, 690.
6. Kenneth P. Thomas, " 'Corporate Welfare' Campaigns in North America," *New Political Economy* 2, no. 1 (1997): 118.
7. Konstantine Gatsios and Paul Seabright, "Regulation in the European Community," *Oxford Review of Economic Policy* 5, no. 2 (1989): 56.
8. William Schweke, Carl Rist, and Brian Dabson, *Bidding for Business: Are Cities and States Selling Themselves Short?* (Washington, D.C.: Corporation for Enterprise Development, 1994), 56, suggest that some public services and transfer programs be transferred to the federal government—precisely to prevent the possibility of "races to the bottom" in those areas substituting for financial competition for investment.
9. Kayne and Shonka, *Rethinking State Development Policies and Programs*, 25.
10. Edward M. Graham and Mark A. A. Warner, "Multinationals and Competition Policy in North America," in *Multinationals in North America,* ed. Lorraine Eden (Calgary: University of Calgary Press, 1994), 479–80.
11. Cooperation theory has identified the usefulness of dividing up large issues into smaller ones that make it easier to assess whether other parties

are cooperating without taking too great a risk from noncompliance. See Robert Axelrod, *The Evolution of Cooperation* (New York: Basic Books, 1984), 131–32.

12. Peter Enrich, "The Rise—And Perhaps Fall—of Business Tax Incentives," in *The Future of State Taxation,* ed. David Brunori (Washington, D.C.: Urban Institute Press, 1998); Schweke, Rist, and Dabson, *Bidding for Business*, 66.
13. Good Jobs First e-mail list, "Constitutional Lawsuite—Big News," 9 December 1999; John Seewer, "Group Challenges Tax Breaks that Kept Jeep in Toledo," Associated Press state and local wire, 8 December 1999.
14. Paul Souhrada, "Fewer Battles Urged," *Dayton Daily News*, 24 December 1996, 5B; personal communication with Jeff Edstrom, Council of Great Lakes Governors, 6 April 1999.
15. Peter Behr, "Battle to Attract Firms, Teams Hurting Some States, Experts Agree," *Washington Post*, 24 May 1996, F01.
16. Scott Wilson, "Marriott Takes Deal to Stay in Maryland," *Washington Post*, 12 March 1999, A1.
17. OECD, *Harmful Tax Competition: An Emerging Global Issue* (Paris: OECD, 1998).
18. Personal communication with Jane Corwin, Department of Commerce, 9 November 1998.
19. OECD, *Industrial Support Policies in OECD Countries, 1986-1989*, 11. Greece and Luxembourg did not participate. An interesting analysis using this data is Daniel Verdier, "The Politics of Public Aid to Private Industry: The Role of Policy Networks," *Comparative Political Studies* 28 (April 1995): 3-42.
20. OECD, *Public Support to Industry* (Paris: OECD, 1996), 7. Greece and Luxembourg did not participate, but Mexico and the Czech Republic had joined the OECD since the previous study.
21. Personal communication, Paris, 5 October 1993.
22. *Industrial Support in OECD Countries, 1986-1989*, 10.
23. However, according to one U.S. participant, the United States reported $9 billion in federal subsidies in the final phase of this project.
24. OECD, *Public Support to Industry*, 7.
25. OECD, *Industrial Subsidies: A Reporting Manual* (Paris: OECD, 1995).
26. Personal communication with Jonathon Menes, Director, Office of Trade and Economic Analysis, U.S. Department of Commerce, International Trade Administration, 4 October 1996.
27. For the list, see OECD, *Industrial Subsidies: A Reporting Manual*, 71–72.
28. Personal communication with Jane Corwin, Department of Commerce, 9 November 1998.

29. OECD, *Public Support to Industry in OECD Countries* (Paris: OECD, 1998), 17.
30. Personal communication with Udo Pretschker, OECD Directorate for Science, Technology, and Industry, Paris, 15 May 1998. Pretschker was the lead staff person for the Working Party.
31. For example, several federal technology subsidies, such as the Advanced Technology Program, were reported to the OECD but were deemed non-industry-specific and not notified to the WTO (personal communication with Jane Corwin, Department of Commerce, 9 November 1998).
32. Unless otherwise noted, the discussion in this paragraph draws on Robert O'Brien, *Subsidy Regulation and State Transformation in North America, the GATT and the EU* (London: Macmillan, 1997), 115–25.
33. Ironically, the Mexicans introduced environmental subsidies for green-light status, after the EU had previously abandoned the issue. See O'Brien, *Subsidy Regulation and State Transformation*, 122. Fiona Wishlade points out that the SCM criteria for "legitimate" regional subsidies were drawn directly from EU practice (employment at 110 percent of average, GDP per capita 85 percent of average or lower). See "Subsidies and State Aids: The Definition of Acceptable Measures Under the European Union and World Trade Organisation Rules," Regional and Industrial Research Paper Series, no. 21, September 1996, 37.
34. SCM Agreement, Article 5, "Trade Effects."
35. SCM Agreement, Article 25, "Notifications," paragraph 25.1.
36. SCM Agreement, Article 8, "Identification of Non-Actionable Subsidies," Paragraph 8.3.
37. Personal communication, Washington, D.C., 10 June 1996.
38. See WTO, Committee on Subsidies and Countervailing Measures, "Note by the Secretariat," document G/SCM/23, 30 July 1999.
39. Kenneth P. Thomas, "International Control and Discipline of Subsidies," *STI Review No. 21*, January 1998, 33–34.
40. Personal communication with Stephen Gospage, Section Head, Subsidies, DG I, Brussels, 19 May 1998.
41. Personal communication with Ronald Lorentzen, Director, WTO Industrial Issues, Office of the U.S. Trade Representative, 19 October 1998. For a concise history of the many U.S.-Canadian subsidy disputes, see Robert O'Brien, *Subsidy Regulation and State Transformation* (London: Macmillan, 1997).
42. Personal communication with Stephen Gospage, Section Head, Subsidies, DG I, Brussels, 19 May 1998.

43. WTO, "Note by the Secretariat," 1.
44. This might well occur when local subsidies are authorized by state law and reporting to the state is required by statute. Tax increment financing is an example in many states.
45. See WTO, "Questions from the European Community Regarding the New and Full Notification of the United States," 24 June 1996, G/SCM/Q2/USA/4; WTO, "Replies of the United States to Questions Posed by Korea, Norway, Japan, the European Community, Argentina, India, Canada, and Thailand," 3 July 1997, G/SCM/Q2/USA/10.
46. CEC, *1999 Report on United States Barriers to Trade and Investment* (Brussels: CEC, 1999), 39.
47. WTO, Committee on Subsidies and Countervailing Measures, "Note by the Secretariat."
48. Frances Williams, "WTO Calls for Illegal Subsidy to be Repaid," *Financial Times,* 12 February 2000, 6.
49. This subsidy is detailed in Douglas J. Watson, *The New Civil War: Government Competition for Economic Development* (Westport, Conn.: Praeger, 1995), 75–76.
50. Agreement on Subsidies and Countervailing Measures, Annex IV, "Calculation of the Total Ad Valorem Subsidization," paragraph 4.
51. O'Brien, *Subsidy Regulation and State Transformation*, 120–21.
52. Personal communication with Commission official, Brussels, 19 May 1998.
53. This defense is provided for in the Agreement on Subsidies and Countervailing Measures, Article 10, n. 33.
54. Department of Commerce, *Report to Congress: Review and Operation of the WTO Subsidies Agreement*, June 1999, n. 14.
55. "WTO Completes Framework for Environmental, Regional, and R&D Subsidies," available at: <http://www.wto.org/wto/new/subpr2.htm> (accessed 29 November 1998); personal communication with Ronald Lorentzen, Office of U.S. Trade Representative, 19 October 1998.
56. Agreement on SCM, Article 31, "Provisional Application."
57. Department of Commerce, *Report to the Congress: Review and Operation of the WTO Subsidies Agreement*, June 1999, available at the Electronic Subsidies Enforcement Library: <www.ita.doc.gov/import_admin/records/esel/scm-0699.htm>; personal communication from Commission official, 22 June 2000.
58. O'Brien, *Subsidy Regulation and State Transformation*, 121. He notes that although the United States supported this position, the issue was far more critical for Canada.

59. With the coming of the euro, this objection may no longer be germane for the members of the euro zone.
60. Wishlade, "Subsidies and State Aids," 45–46.
61. Wishlade, "Subsidies and State Aids," 47–48. The quote is from page 47. Wishlade also mentions that member state pressure has diluted Commission adherence to the letter of its published methodology and that regional aid approved for Sweden and Finland on the basis of low population density does not meet the SCM unemployment and GDP/ capita tests.
62. Yuill et al., *European Regional Incentives 1994-95*, 10–11.
63. Charles S. Colgan, "Brave New World: International Regulation of Subsidies and the Future of State and Local Economic Development Programs," *Economic Development Quarterly* 9, no. 2 (May 1995): 116. The U.S. law implementing the Uruguay Round agreement does not allow private parties to use it as a cause of action, so NGOs do not have an easy route to challenge state programs or the quality of any notifications they make under the SCM agreement.
64. The Corporation for Enterprise Development, which advises economic development officials, has recently begun a research project on the effect of international agreements on economic development activities. See CFED Web site at <www.cfed.org>.
65. OECD, Fiscal Affairs, "What's new: Tax Competition," OECD Web site: <http://www.oecd.org/daf/fa/taxcomp.htm>.
66. Guy de Jonquieres, "Drive to Stamp Out Tax Havens Hits Snag," *Financial Times*, 29 April 1998, 5.
67. Anthony Browne, "You Can Run Low Taxes But You Can't Hide; The OECD Has a Message for Cut-Price Nations," *The Observer*, 17 May 1998, 4.
68. OECD, *Harmful Tax Competition*, 8; for statements by Luxembourg and Switzerland, see pages 73–78. An OECD official described the Irish 10 percent tax rate as "the political limit to this study."
69. Michael Peel, "OECD Seeking Bank Openness to Beat Tax Evasion," *Financial Times,* 13 April 2000, 13; and "Soft Words on Secrecy: The OECD's Approach to the Banking Transparency Issue Is Too Cautious," *Financial Times,* 20 April 2000, 2.
70. OECD, *Harmful Tax Competition*, 23, 27.
71. Some examples of presumably targeted tax regimes are Belgium's "coordination center" law, for headquarters and financial and other services; Dutch advance tax rulings; and a wide variety of regimes for the banking sector in the United States, Canada, Australia, Japan, Luxembourg, and Switzerland. Other members have dependencies that may be categorized

tax havens, such as the U.K.'s Channel Islands or The Netherlands Antilles. See Browne, "You Can Run Low Taxes But You Can't Hide."

72. OECD, *Harmful Tax Competition*, Recommendations, 58–59.
73. Personal communication, 20 July 1999.
74. Mark Atkinson, "OECD Delays Crackdown on Tax Havens," *The Guardian,* 26 April 2000, 28.
75. OECD, *Harmful Tax Competition*, p. 8. This intention was reaffirmed at the last OECD Ministerial meeting in 1998.
76. Personal communication with European tax official, 22 May 1998.
77. Commission of the European Communities, *Taxation in the European Union: Report on the Development of Tax Systems*, COM(96) 546 final, 22 October 1996, 2.
78. Commission, *Taxation in the European Union*, 6.
79. Emma Tucker, "Deal Is Clinched on EU Tax Code," *Financial Times*, 3 December 1997, 2.
80. "Eurocrat Eases Threat to Meddle in Our Tax Rates," *Daily Mail*, 21 August 1999, 4; Joanne Hart, "Bonds Tax Battle Faces A New Delay," *Evening Standard*, 3 September 1999, 41. For details on the Monti proposal, see Lionel Barber, "Fighting Shy of the Full Monti," *Financial Times*, 2 October 1998.
81. Agence France Presse, "EU Puts Corporate Tax Breaks Under the Spotlight," 30 November 1998; Patrick Smyth, "EU Efforts to Eliminate Tax Conflict Get Bogged Down," *Irish Times*, 19 April 1999, 18; David Wighton, "Joint Group Launched to Consider EU Tax Reform," *Financial Times*, 8 June 1999, 12.
82. "OECD Says Switzerland Should Fix Tax System to Meet International Standards," *AFX News*, 5 August 1999.
83. Barbara Jenkins, *The Paradox of Continental Production: National Investment Policies in North America* (Ithaca, N.Y.: Cornell University Press, 1992), 205.
84. One might object that I ignore the claims of strategic trade theory in assuming the desirability of getting rid of most subsidy programs. To the contrary: Without more complete information on what is actually being offered in this country, it is impossible to know which subsidies, if any, can have strategic effects. Furthermore, I would argue that subnational location incentives have no strategic content—and this is precisely the area for which we have the least information at present.
85. A similarly motivated alternative, suggested by Schweke, Risk, and Dabson, *Bidding for Business*, 73–74, is to reduce the amount of state revenue-sharing going to localities with high tax abatements.

86. In Minnesota—the state with the best data on business assistance—subsidized relocations seem to be a particular problem with tax increment financing subsidies. See Greg LeRoy and Tyson Slocum, *Economic Development in Minnesota: High Subsidies, Low Wages, Absent Standards* (Washington, D.C.: Good Jobs First, 1999), 29–33.
87. In 1989, Sears threatened to move its headquarters operations from the Sears Tower in downtown Chicago to an out-of-state location unless it was given assistance for a move to the affluent suburb of Hoffman Estates. It received aid estimated at $240 million (approximately $43,000 per job) to do this. See Schweke, Risk, and Dabson, *Bidding for Business*, 27–28.
88. Schweke, Risk, and Dabson, *Bidding for Business*, 56–57.
89. See, for example, Lee Leonard, "Lawmaker Suggests Dropping Business Incentives," *Columbus Dispatch*, 21 September 1995, 7C, and compare the statement by Dean Stansel in Chapter 5.
90. Yuill et al., *European Regional Incentives 1994-95*, 10–11.
91. Douglas Yuill et al., *European Regional Incentives 1995-96*, 40.
92. In 1992–94, state aid in the new *Länder* constituted 76.1 percent of total German aid, compared to 47.2 percent in 1990–92; in both periods, regional aid was 80 percent of total aid. Calculated from *Fifth Survey on State Aid*, Table 3, 7.
93. F. Knox, *Towards 1992: State Aids to Industry* (Trade and Tariffs Research, London, November 1989), 61. Tim Frazer suggests coordinated caps on regional aid or centralized regional aid at the Community level. See "The New Structural Funds, State Aids and Interventions on the Single Market," *European Law Review*, February 1995, 17.
94. "State Aid: Worried Commission Proposes Stricter Rules," RAPID Press Release IP 97/308, 16 April 1997.
95. Again, see Quinn, "Investment Incentives: A Five Country Test of the Lindblom Hypothesis."
96. Alasdair Murray, "Monti Signals Intent to Attack All State Subsidies," *The Times* (London), 2 September 1999.
97. Cini, "Policing the Internal Market," 281; Stephen Thomsen and Stephen Woolcock, *Direct Investment and European Integration: Competition among Firms and Governments* (London: Pinter, 1993), 75.

Bibliography

Abedian, Julia. *Exposing Federal Sponsorship of Job Loss: The Whitehall Plant Closing Campaign and "Runaway Plant" Reform*. New York: Garland, 1995.

Abernathy, Pauline, Bob Greenstein, and Richard Kogan. "Will Corporate Welfare Be Reined In? Congressional Action Related to Business Subsidies." Washington, D.C.: Center on Budget and Policy Priorities, 7 November 1995.

Agence France Presse. "EU Commission Strengthens Arguments to Justify Rescue of Air France." 22 July 1998.

———. "EU Puts Corporate Tax Breaks Under the Spotlight." 30 November 1998.

"Airlines: The Sky's the Limit For Iberia Following Political Accord." *Transport Europe* 19 (January 1996).

"Alberta May Ban Business Investments by Government." Canadian Press Newswire, 17 August 1995.

Alterman, Simon. "Spanish Drive for Better EC Deal Poses Summit Threat." Reuter Library Report, 9 February 1988.

Andrews, David M. "Capital Mobility and State Autonomy: Toward a Structural Theory of International Monetary Relations." *International Studies Quarterly* 38, no. 2 (June 1994): 193–218.

Axelrod, Robert. *The Evolution of Cooperation*. New York: Basic Books, 1984.

Bache, Ian. *The Politics of European Union Regional Policy*. Sheffield, England: Sheffield Academic Press, 1998.

Bachtler, John. "Grants for Inward Investors: Giving Money Away?" *National Westminster Bank Quarterly Review* (May 1990), 15–24.

Ballantyne, Elaine, and John Bachtler, *Regional Policy Under Scrutiny: The European Commission and Regional Aid*. Glasgow: European Policies Research Centre, 1990.

Barber, Lionel. "Fighting Shy of the Full Monti." *Financial Times*, 2 October 1998.

Barber, Lionel, Andrew Baxter, and Michael Lindemann. "Steel Back in the Melting Pot: The Collapse of the EU Rescue Plan for the Industry." *Financial Times*, 26 October 1994, 22.

Barrett, William P. "Willis Carrier's Ghost," *Forbes,* 29 May 2000, 152.

Bartik, Timothy J. *Who Benefits from State and Local Economic Development Policies?* Kalamazoo, Mich.: W. E. Upjohn Institute for Employment Research, 1991.

Begg, Iain. "European Integration and Regional Policy." *Oxford Review of Economic Policy* 5, no. 2 (summer 1989): 90–104.

Behr, Peter. "Battle to Attract Firms, Teams Hurting Some States, Experts Agree." *Washington Post*, 24 May 1996, F01.

Belcredi, Massimo, Lorenzo Caprio, and Pippo Ranci. *The Aid Element in State Participation to Equity Capital*. Brussels: CEC, 1988.

"Berlin European Council—Presidency Conclusions." Press release, 25 March 1999.

Bhaskar, Krish, and the Motor Industry Research Unit. *The Effect of Different Aid Measures on Intra-Community Competition, Exemplified by the Case of the Automotive Industry*. CEC, March 1990.

Black, Dan A., and William H. Hoyt. "Bidding for Firms." *American Economic Review* (December 1989), 1249–56.

Blair, John P., and Robert Premus. "Location Theory." In *Theories of Local Economic Development: Perspectives from Across the Disciplines*, edited by Richard D. Bingham and Robert Mier. Newbury Park, Calif.: Sage, 1993.

Blair, Judy P., Carole Endres, and Rudy Fichtenbaum. "Japanese Automobile Investment in West Central Ohio: Economic Development and Labor-Management Issues." In *The Politics of Industrial Recruitment: Japanese Automobile Investment and Economic Development in the American States*, edited by Ernest J. Yanarella and William C. Green. New York: Greenwood Press, 1990.

Blais, André. *A Political Sociology of Public Aid to Industry*. Toronto: University of Toronto Press, 1986.

Blässer, Maria. "Implementing Rules for State Aid—Czech Republic." *Competition Policy Newsletter* (October 1998), 59–60.

Blum, Ken, with Robert Ginsburg. *The Mercedes Benz Subsidy Package: Whose Benefits? Whose Losses?* Chicago: Midwest Center for Labor Research, 1995.

"BMW's Site Selection in South Carolina." *Expansion Management* (January-February 1993), 24–25.

Boltho, Andrea, "European and United States Regional Differentials: A Note." *Oxford Review of Economic Policy* 5, no. 2 (summer 1989): 105–15.

Bowen, David. “Toyota Pays 4m Pounds After EC Ruling.” *The Independent*, 3 October 1991, 26.

Brasier, Mary, and Christopher Lockwood. “Commission attacked over Air France aid.” *The Daily Telegraph*, 28 July 1994, 20.

Bremner, Charles. “Regions Will Lose in EU Spending Reform.” *The Times* (London), 19 March 1998, 23.

Brennock, Mark. “Axe Will Not Fall Suddenly on All EU Funding.” *Irish Times*, 22 March 1999, 13.

Breverton, T. D. “Effects of the Growth of Foreign Ownership of, and Penetration into, UK, Belgian and Irish Economic Sectors, 1978–1996.” Paper presented at Fifth Biennial Conference of the European Community Studies Association, Seattle, Washington, 29 May–1 June 1997.

Brown, John Murray. “Dublin Ends Tax Dispute with EU.” *Financial Times*, 23 July 1998, 2.

Browne, Anthony. “You Can Run Low Taxes But You Can’t Hide: The OECD Has a Message for Cut-Price Nations.” *The Observer*, 17 May 1998, 4.

Buchan, David. “Brussels Threatens to Cut State Subsidies to European Industry.” *Financial Times*, 10 March 1989, 18.

Buchan, David, and Tim Dickson. “An End to the Nay-Saying.” *Financial Times*, 15 February 1988, 21.

Buchholz, David. “Competition and Corporate Incentives: Dilemmas in Economic Development.” Ph.D. diss., Duke University, 1998.

Buckley, Neil, and Judy Dempsey. “Brussels fury over cash for VW.” *Financial Times*, 31 July 1996, 2.

Buraff Publications. “State Aids: Brussels Faces Tough Task in Controlling State Subsidies.” *1992—The External Impact of European Unification* 1, no. 6, p. 5.

Bureau of National Affairs. “Sutherland Reflects on Success and Setbacks in EC Competition Policy.” *Antitrust and Trade Regulation Report* 56, no. 1403 (16 February 1989), 253.

“Business and the Law: Few Exceptions to Rules on Recovery of State Aid.” *Financial Times*, 28 February 1995, 16.

“Business and the Law: Decision on French Aid Annulled—European Court.” *Financial Times*, 3 October 1995, 13.

California Budget Project. *California Unified Economic Development Budget*. May 1999 (draft).

“Canada, Brazil Both Claim Win in WTO Aircraft Ruling.” *Vancouver Sun*, 3 August 1999, C8.

Canada. Department of Finance. *Tax Expenditures 1999.* Available at: http://www.fin.gc.ca/taxexp.

"Cas pour lesquels la Commission a pris une décision négative ou partiellement négative au titre de l'article 6, paragraphe 4, de la décision 3855/91 du traité CECA" [Cases in which the Commission has taken a negative or partially negative decision under Article 6, paragraph 4, of Decision 3855/91 of the ECSC Treaty]. Available at: http://europa.eu.int/en/comm/dg04/aid/aid96/aidp47.htm.

Caves, Richard E. *Multinational Enterprise and Economic Analysis*, 2nd ed. New York: Cambridge University Press, 1996.

Center for Community Change. "CDBG and Job Piracy." *Organizing* (December 1998). Available at: www.communitychange.org/organizing.cdbg11.htm.

Chase-Dunn, Christopher. "Interstate System and Capitalist World-Economy: One Logic or Two?" *International Studies Quarterly* 25, no. 1 (March 1981): 19–42.

Chi, Keon S., and Drew Leatherby. *State Business Incentives: Trends and Options for the Future*. Lexington, Ky.: Council of State Governments, 1997.

Choi, Audrey, and Carlta Vitzthum. "Iberian Struggle: Big Auto Plant Sparks a Debate in Portugal Over How to Develop." *Wall Street Journal*, 30 June 1995, 1.

Cini, Michelle. "Policing the Internal Market: The Regulation of Competition in the European Commission." Ph.D. diss., University of Exeter, 1994.

Citizens for Tax Justice. *The Hidden Entitlements*. Washington, D.C.: CTJ, 1996.

"City Comment: The Euro control tower believes a dodo can fly." *The Daily Telegraph*, 28 July 1994, 21.

Cohen, Karen J. "Wisconsin Democrats Reintroduce Briggs Bill." States News Service, 11 January 1995.

Colgan, Charles S. "Brave New World: International Regulation of Subsidies and the Future of State and Local Economic Development Programs." *Economic Development Quarterly* 9, no. 2 (May 1995): 107–18.

"Commission Addresses Recommendations to Ireland Regarding Corporate Tax," Commission Press Release IP/98/691, 23 July 1998.

"Commission Asks Italy to Suspend Aid to Restructuring of the Road Haulage Sector and Requests Further Information." RAPID press release IP/96-364, 30 April 1996.

"Commission Sets National Ceilings for Coverage of Regional Aid." RAPID Press Release IP/98/1133, 16 December 1998.

Commission of the European Communities (CEC). "Fair Competition in the Internal Market: Community State Aid Policy." *European Economy* no. 48 (September 1991), 7–114.

———. *Competition Law in the European Communities,* Volume II: Rules applicable to state aids (situation at 31 December 1989). Brussels-Luxembourg: CEC, 1990.

———. "Community State Aid Policy: An Overview." RAPID Press Release, 10 November 1994, 1.

———. *The Regions in the 1990s—Fourth Periodic Report on the Social and Economic Situation and Development of the Regions of the Community.* COM(90) 609 final, 9 January 1991.

———. *Competitiveness and cohesion: trends in the regions.* Luxembourg: Office for Official Publications of the European Communities, 1994.

———. *Industrial Policy in an Open and Competitive Environment: Guidelines for a Community Approach.* COM(90) 556 final, 16 November 1990, 8.

———. *Taxation in the European Union: Report on the Development of Tax Systems.* COM(96) 546 final, 22 October 1996.

———. *First Report on Competition Policy* through *Twenty-eighth Report on Competition Policy.* Brussels-Luxembourg: CEC, 1972–1999.

———. *First Survey on State Aid.* Brussels-Luxembourg: CEC, 1989.

———. *Second Survey on State Aid.* Brussels-Luxembourg: CEC, 1990.

———. *Third Survey on State Aid.* Brussels-Luxembourg: CEC, 1992.

———. *Fourth Survey on State Aid.* Brussels-Luxembourg: CEC, 1995.

———. *Fifth Survey on State Aid.* Brussels-Luxembourg: CEC, 1997.

———. *Sixth Survey on State Aid.* Brussels-Luxembourg: CEC, 1998.

———. *Seventh Survey on State Aid.* Brussels-Luxembourg: CEC, 1999.

———. *Competition Policy Newsletter,* October 1998: staff directory, 66.

———. "Guidelines on National Regional Aid." Downloaded from DG IV Web site (http://www.europa.eu.int/comm/dg04/lawaid/aid3.htm#F), adopted 15 December 1997.

———. "Multisectoral Framework on Regional Aid for Large Investment Projects." Downloaded from DG IV Web site (http://www.europa.eu.int/dg04/lawaid/en/98c107.htm), adopted 15 December 1997.

———. *Reform of the Structural Funds*. COM (1998) 131 final, 18 March 1998.

———. *1999 Report on United States Barriers to Trade and Investment*. Brussels: CEC, 1999.

"Commission letter and annex on textile and clothing industries," 4 February 1977. In *Competition Law in the European Communities*, Volume II: Rules applicable to state aids (situation at 31 December 1989), 50.

Commission Press Release IP 96/670, 18 July 1996.

"Commission's Duties on State Aid Clarified." *Financial Times*, 21 April 1998, 24.

"Community State Aid Policy: An Overview." RAPID Memo 94-67, 10 November 1994.

Congressional Budget Office (CBO). *Reducing the Deficit: Spending and Revenue Options*. Washington, D.C.: CBO, 1994.

———. *Federal Financial Support for Business*. Washington. D.C.: CBO, 1995.

Cooper, Richard N. "Economic Interdependence in the 1970s." *World Politics* 24, no. 2 (January 1972): 159–81.

Cope, Peter. "1992: The Anxieties of the Motor Sector," *European Trends* no. 4 (1988): 48–56.

Council Press Release Number 127 43/98, 16 November 1998.

Council of Ministers Press Release, PRES 98/129, 14 May 1998.

Council of Ministers Press Release, PRES 98/381, 22 January 1999, "2133rd Council meeting INDUSTRY Brussels, 16 November 1998."

"Court Dismisses Textilwerke Challenge to State Aid Decision." Reuter European Community Report, 15 May 1997.

Cownie, Fiona. "State Aids in the Eighties." *European Law Review* 11, no. 4 (1986): 247–67.

"Crown jobs to relocate to Regina as promised." *Toronto Star*, 28 May 1992, D1.

Dahl, Fredrik. "European Firms Get Tough on EU State Aid Policy." Reuter European Union Business Report, 6 June 1996.

Damme, Mieke, ed. *Perte Totale: La Fermeture de Renault-Vilvorde*. Antwerp: Hadewijch, 1997.

Damsell, Keith. "B.C. Files Objection to Loss of UPS to N.B." *Financial Post*, 27 April 1996, 14.

Daw, James. "GM-Suzuki plant includes $85 million aid packages." *Toronto Star*, 28 August 1986, A1.

Deacon, David. "Current state aid policy in the EC and the implications of 1992." In *Producer Subsidies*, edited by Ronald Gerritse. London: Pinter, 1990.

de Jonquieres, Guy. "Drive to Stamp Out Tax Havens Hits Snag." *Financial Times*, 29 April 1998, 5.

DeMont, John. "Fast Frank: How New Brunswick's Premier Turned His Province Into Canada's Social Laboratory." *Maclean's*, 11 April 1994, 22–29.

Depypere, Steffan, Thinam Jakob, Brona Carton, and Y. Scaramozzino. "Summary of the Most Important Recent Developments (International Dimensions of Competition Policy)." *Competition Policy Newsletter* (Spring 1996), 38–40.

Diaz, Kevin. "Minneapolis Aims for Compromise on Living-Wage Rule." *Star Tribune* (Minneapolis), 5 March 1997, 1B.

Dicken, Peter. *Global Shift*, 2nd ed. New York: Guilford Press, 1992.

"Disappearing Taxes: The Tap Runs Dry." *Economist*, 31 May 1997, 21–23.

Done, Kevin. "Chrysler to go to law against EC." *Financial Times*, 11 November 1992, 4.

DuBois, Martin. "EC Approves $7.66 Billion Aid Package in Bid to Revive Sluggish Steel Industry." *Wall Street Journal*, 20 December 1993, A9A.

"East, West—Home's Best." *Financial Times*, 20 December 1993, 13.

"E.C. Commission vs. France: Re Export Credits (Cases 6/69 and 11/69)." *Common Market Law Reports* [1970] Part 41, 43–76.

"EC Commissioner Outlines Areas of Aid Review." Reuters, 31 March 1989.

Economist Intelligence Unit. "German Labour Costs Continue to Cause Problems." *Business Europe*, 27 December 1993.

Eisinger, Peter K. *The Rise of the Entrepreneurial State*. Madison: University of Wisconsin Press, 1988.

Enrich, Peter. "The Rise—And Perhaps Fall—of Business Tax Incentives." In *The Future of State Taxation*, edited by David Brunori. Washington, D.C.: Urban Institute Press, 1998.

"EU Commission says German objections to regional aid rules are unacceptable." *AFX News*, 14 July 1998.

"EU Gives Germany Till Aug 10 to Fix VW Subsidies." Reuter European Community Report, 2 August 1996, BC Cycle.

"EU orders Spain to notify car sector state aid projects over 17 mln Ecu." *AFX News*, 20 December 1995.

"EU probes Spanish state aid for motor industry." *AFX News*, 21 September 1995.

"EU: Spain Attacks Commission Decision to Extend State Aid Framework to Car Sector." Reuter Textline, 21 September 1995.

"EU Summit Roundup: Talks Suspended but Agenda 2000 Deal Expected Tonight." *AFX News*, 25 March 1999.

"Eurocrat Eases Threat to Meddle in Our Tax Rates." *Daily Mail*, 21 August 1999, 4.

"European Commission and Germany Head for Clash Over Subsidies." Reuters, 7 April 1989, AM cycle.

"European Commission reestablishes right to monitor state automobile aid." *AFX News*, 5 July 1995.

"European Commission Rejects Austrian Aid Proposal." *Pharmaceutical Manufacturing Review* (June 1997), 38.

"European Community: Poorer than Thou." *Economist*, 10 July 1993, 41.

European Information Service. "State Aid: Commission to Bail Out East German Shipyards." *European Intelligence* No. 113, 7 March 1996.

———. "Commission Outlaws Italian Law on State Aid for Bankrupt Firms." *European Report*, 16 March 1996.

———. "Volkswagen Row Escalates as Bonn Takes Commission to Court." *European Report* No. 2157, 14 September 1996.

———. "VW Files Court Complaint Over State Subsidies Row." *European Report* No. 2158, 18 September 1996.

———. "State Aid: Commission Extends Bremer Vulkan Investigation." *European Report*, No. 2173, 13 November 1996.

———. "State Aid: Commission's Extension of Motor Industry Aid Code Not Justified." *European Report* No. 2216, 16 April 1997.

———. "State Aid: Experts to Probe Dutch 'Technolease' Affair." *European Report* No. 2217, 19 April 1997.

———. "Official EU State Aid Inquiry into Dutch Technolease Scheme." *European Report* No. 2219, 26 April 1997.

———. "State Aid: Commission and Council at Loggerheads Over Tighter Rules," *European Report* No. 2314, 9 May 1998.

———. "EU Approves Changes to Procedural Regulations." *European Report* No. 2393, 24 March 1999.

———. "Commission Tables Draft Regulations for State Aid Exemptions." *European Report* No. 2249, 30 July 1999.

Eurostat. *Eurostat Yearbook '95*. Luxembourg: Office for Official Publications of the European Communities, 1995.

———. *Eurostat Yearbook '97*. Luxembourg: Office for Official Publications of the European Communities, 1997.

"EU's Wolf-Mathies to look at ways of preventing plant transfers for subsidies." *AFX News*, 10 March 1997.

Evans, Andrew, and Stephen Martin. "Socially Acceptable Distortion of Competition: Community Policy on State Aid." *European Law Review* 16, no. 2 (1991): 79–111.

Faust, Fred. "The 'Air' in Nike Stays Here." *St. Louis Post-Dispatch*, 30 September 1994, E1, E7.

Field, David. "Healthy airlines are livid over billions in subsidies for weak European rivals." *Washington Times*, 9 August 1994, B8.

"Financing of Public TV in Portugal: No aid involved." *Competition Policy Newsletter* (Autumn/Winter 1996), 48.

Fisher, Peter S., and Alan H. Peters. *Industrial Incentives: Competition Among American States and Cities*. Kalamazoo, Mich.: Upjohn Institute, 1998.

Flynn, James. "State Aid and Self-Help." *European Law Review* 8 (1983): 297–312.

Ford, Robert, and Wim Suyker. "Industrial Subsidies in the OECD Economies." *OECD Economic Studies*, no. 15 (autumn 1990), 37–81.

Fowlie, Laura. "Canada: Cost of Wooing Carmakers Too Rich for Ontario's Blood." *Financial Post*, 19 February 1994, 8.

Frazer, Tim. "The New Structural Funds, State Aids and Interventions on the Single Market." *European Law Review* (February 1995), 3–19.

"French State Aid Lawful." *Financial Times*, 4 March 1997, 14.

Frieden, Jeffry A. "Capital Politics: Creditors and the International Economy." In *International Political Economy*, 2nd ed., edited by Jeffry A. Frieden and David A. Lake. New York: St. Martin's Press, 1991.

Friedman, David. "The New Civil War." *Inc. Special Issue: The State of Small Business* (21 May 1996), 99–106.

Friends of the Earth. *Green Scissors 1997*. Washington: FoE, 1997.

———. *Green Scissors 99.* Washington: FoE, 1999.

Fry, Earl H. *The Expanding Role of State and Local Governments in U.S. Foreign Affairs*. New York: Council on Foreign Relations Press, 1998.

Gardner, David. "The Edinburgh Summit: Spain 'first, first, first' but other members do well too—Budget," *Financial Times*, 14 December 1992, 2.

———. "EC loses state aid case: Court rules against closer public sector scrutiny." *Financial Times*, 17 June 1993, 2.

Garrett, Geoffrey. "Capital Mobility, Trade, and the Domestic Politics of Economic Policy." In *Internationalization and Domestic Politics*, edited by Robert O. Keohane and Helen V. Milner. Cambridge: Cambridge University Press, 1996.

Gatsios, Konstantine, and Paul Seabright. "Regulation in the European Community." *Oxford Review of Economic Policy* 5, no. 2 (1989): 37–60.

Gauf, Michael. "In the Midwest, It's Every State for Itself." *St. Louis Post-Dispatch*, 2 December 1992.

Gedye, Robin. "British low-pay ads rile Germans." *Daily Telegraph*, 11 May 1993, 13.

Geisel, Amy. "Federal Aid for Knox Plant's Illinois Move is Put on Hold." *Knoxville News-Sentinel*, 15 March 1995, A1, A3.

George, Vic. "The Future of the Welfare State." In *European Welfare Policy: Squaring the Welfare Circle*, edited by Vic George and Peter Taylor-Gooby. New York: St. Martin's, 1996.

Gilchrist, Joseph, and David Deacon. "Curbing Subsidies." In *European Competition Policy*, edited by Peter Montagnon. New York: Council on Foreign Relations Press, 1990.

Gill, Stephen R., and David Law. "Global Hegemony and the Structural Power of Capital." *International Studies Quarterly* (December 1989), 475–99.

Gilpin, Robert. *Political Economy of International Relations*. Princeton, N.J.: Princeton University Press, 1987.

Goodman, Robert. *The Last Entrepreneurs: America's Regional Wars for Jobs and Dollars*. New York: Simon and Schuster, 1979.

Gow, David. "Euro Eye: First Shots in a Long and Bloody Battle Over Jobs." *The Guardian*, 15 March 1997, 22.

Graham, Edward M. *Global Corporations and National Governments*. Washington, D.C.: Institute for International Economics, 1996.

Graham, Edward M., and Paul R. Krugman. *Foreign Direct Investment in the United States*, 2nd ed. Washington, D.C.: Institute for International Economics, 1991.

Graham, Edward M., and Mark A. A. Warner. "Multinationals and Competition Policy in North America." In *Multinationals in North America*, edited by Lorraine Eden. Calgary: University of Calgary Press, 1994.

Gray, Ian. "Alberta to Restrict Province's Investments." *Financial Post*, 4 April 1996, 8.

Green, William C. "Constitutional Dimensions of State Industrial Recruitment." In *The Politics of Industrial Recruitment: Japanese Automobile Investment and Economic Development in the American States*, edited by Ernest J. Yanarella and William C. Green. New York: Greenwood Press, 1990.

Greenwald, John. "A No-Win War Between the States." *Time*, 8 April 1996, 44–45.

Groom, Brian. "Minister Attacks Proposed Changes to EU Aid." *Financial Times*, 6 February 1998, 10.

Groom, Brian, and Michael Smith. "Spain and UK the Biggest Winners: Regional Aid." *Financial Times*, 27 March 1999, 2.

Grote, Jürgen R. "Diseconomies in Space: Traditional Sectoral Policies of the EC, the European Technology Community and their Effects on Regional Disparities." In *The Regions and the European Community: The Regional Response to the Single Market in the Underdeveloped Areas*, edited by Robert Leonardi. London: Frank Cass, 1993.

"Growing firm lured away from Ontario." *Calgary Herald*, 28 December 1992, C2.

Guisinger, Stephen E. "An Overview of Country Studies." In Stephen E. Guisinger and Associates, *Investment Incentives and Performance Requirements*. New York: Praeger, 1985.

———. "Rhetoric and Reality in International Business: A Note on the Effectiveness of Incentives." *Transnational Corporations* 1, no. 2 (August 1992): 111–23.

Gunter, Lorne. "Canada's Corporate Trough-Dippers Unmasked." *Ottawa Citizen*, 22 June 1998, A9.

Hall, R., and D. van der Wee. "Community Regional Policies for the 1990s." *Regional Studies* 26, no. 4 (1992): 399–404.

Hamburger, Henry. *Games As Models of Social Phenomena*. San Francisco: W. H. Freeman and Company, 1979.

Hancher, Leigh, Tom Ottervanger, and Piet Jan Slot. *EC State Aids*. London: Chancery Law Publishing, 1993.

Hancock, Jay. "S.C. Pays Dearly for Added Jobs." *Baltimore Sun*, 12 October 1999.

Handyside, Gillian. "MEPs Demand Explanation of Iberia Aid Decision." *The Reuter European Community Report*, 9 February 1996, BC Cycle.

Hanson, Monte. "Legislature Puts Clamps on Corporate Welfare." *Finance and Commerce* (Minneapolis), 20 May 1999, 1, 7.

Hardin, Russell. *Collective Action*. Baltimore: Johns Hopkins University Press for Resources for the Future, 1982.

Hart, Joanne. "Bonds Tax Battle Faces A New Delay." *Evening Standard*, 3 September 1999, 41.

Hermann, A. H. "The EEC power struggle." *Financial Times*, 13 July 1982, 2.

"Highest Bidder: Competition for New Firms Unfair" (editorial). *Cincinnati Enquirer*, 27 March 1997, A18.

Hill, Andrew. "Ruling on Italian Repayments." *Financial Times*, 5 April 1995, 2.

Holland, Kitty. "Regionalisation Has Shallow Roots in Our Traditions." *Irish Times*, 21 November 1998, 10.

"Hoover Affirms Dijon Plant Move." Facts on File World News Digest, 15 July 1993, 529 F2.

"How Will National Tax Systems Fare As Globalization Proceeds?" *IMF Survey*, 26 May 1997, 166.

Howard, Marcia. *A Corporate Welfare Reform Agenda*. Washington, D.C.: American Federation of State County and Municipal Employees Public Policy Department, 1994.

Hudson, Kellie. "Premier Rules Out 'Handouts' for NHL." *Toronto Star*, 8 April 1999.

Hufbauer, Gary Clyde, and Joanna Shelton Erb. *Subsidies in International Trade*. Washington, D.C.: Institute for International Economics, 1984.

Hullinger, Dana. "Risk Management in Local Economic Development Projects: Beginning the Transformation from Structure to Strategy to Process." Unpublished paper, University of Missouri-St. Louis, December 1998.

"Iberia Cash Infusion Shows European State Aid Still Flowing." *Airline Financial News* 5 (February 1996).

IDA Ireland. *Guide to Taxes and Tax Reliefs in Ireland*. Dublin: IDA Ireland, 1991.

———. *Ireland: Put Yourself in Our Hands in the 1990s*. Dublin: IDA Ireland, 1991.

Industrial Development Authority (IDA). *Annual Report 1979.* Dublin: IDA Ireland, 1980.

"Intel Given Tax Break." *Phoenix Gazette*, 21 September 1994, C1.

Internal Trade Secretariat. *Agreement on Internal Trade: A Guide.* Ottawa: Internal Trade Secretariat, 1994.

"The Invaders Are Welcome." *Economist*, 8 January 1994, 32.

Iskandar, Samer, and Michael Skapinker, "BA Angered at Outcome of Air France Subsidy Ruling." *Financial Times*, 23 July 1998, 26.

Jacobs, Jerry. *Bidding for Business: Corporate Auctions and the 50 Disunited States.* Washington, D.C.: Public Interest Research Group, 1979.

Jacobsen, John Kurt. *Chasing Progress in the Irish Republic: Ideology, Democracy and Dependent Development.* Cambridge: Cambridge University Press, 1994.

Jasper, Debra. "Horn Seeks End to Tax Breaks." *Dayton Daily News*, 21 September 1995, 7B.

Jenkins, Barbara. *The Paradox of Continental Production: National Investment Policies in North America.* Ithaca, N.Y.: Cornell University Press, 1992.

Johnson, Boris, and George Jones. "Europe: 'Poor four' still asking for more." *Daily Telegraph*, 12 December 1992, 9.

Joint Committee on Taxation. *Estimates of Federal Tax Expenditures for Fiscal Years 1996–2000.* Washington, D.C.: Government Printing Office, 1995.

Jones, Bryan D., and Lynn W. Bachelor. *The Sustaining Hand: Community Leadership and Corporate Power*, 2nd ed. Lawrence: University Press of Kansas, 1993.

Jordan, Steve. "Groups Attack States' Special Incentives for Firms." *Omaha World Herald*, 20 September 1995, 16.

Kapstein, Jonathan, with John Rossant. " 'Subsidy" Becomes a Dirty Word." *Business Week*, 19 June 1989, 48.

Karacs, Imre. "Bremer head detained in search for missing money." *The Independent*, 21 June 1996, 21.

Kayne, Jay, and Molly Shonka. *Rethinking State Development Policies and Programs.* Washington, D.C.: National Governors' Association, 1994.

Kershner, Vlae. "Legislators Warned to Allow Business Tax Breaks; Association Says State Should Attract Manufacture." *San Francisco Chronicle*, 17 March 1993, A11.

Khalil, Hany, and Theresa Gardella. "Reforming Alabama's 'Mercedes Law.' " In *Public Subsidies, Public Accountability: Holding Corpora-*

tions to Labor and Community Standards, edited by Sandra Hinson, Richard Healey, Jim Benn, and Kary L. Moss. Washington, D.C.: Grassroots Policy Project, 1998.

Kimmel, Bruce, Eric Rothman, and Alexis Thompson. *Increasing the Visibility and Accountability of Economic Development Spending: A Unified Development Budget for Massachusetts*. Cambridge, Mass.: Kennedy School of Government, 1997.

Kines, Lindsay. "Meat Plant Closure 'Job Poaching,' Union Says." *Vancouver Sun*, 2 December 1996, B4.

Knox, J. *Towards 1992: State Aids to Industry*. Trade and Tariffs Research, London, November 1989.

Krikorian, Greg. "Council Overrides Veto, OK's Wage Law." *Los Angeles Times*, 2 April 1997, Metro section, Part B, 1.

Kurzer, Paulette. *Business and Banking: Political Change and Economic Integration in Western Europe*. Ithaca, N.Y.: Cornell University Press, 1993.

Lamphier, Gary. "Suzuki set for auto plant: But it's Quebec vs. Ontario for location." *Financial Times of Canada*, 21 April 1986, 3.

"Large Investment Projects. New State aid framework approved for large investment projects." *Competition Policy Newsletter* (February 1998), 70–71.

Lasok, K. P. E. "The Commission's Powers Over Illegal State Aids." *European Competition Law Review* 11, no. 3 (1990): 125–27.

Lavdas, Kostas A., and Maria M. Mendrinou. *Politics, Subsidies and Competition: The New Politics of State Intervention in the European Union*. Cheltenham: Edward Elgar, 1999.

Leblanc, Daniel. "Corporate Welfare Costs Citizens Billions: Study." *Ottawa Citizen*, 17 April 1998, A12.

———. "Big Business's Best Friend: The Cash Cow on the Hill: 'Corporate Welfare' Recipients Evade Millions in Payments: Report." *Ottawa Citizen*, 5 June 1998, A1.

"Legislature Reins In Corporate Welfare." *MAPA Bulletin*, 18 May 1999.

Leonard, Lee. "Lawmaker Suggests Dropping Business Incentives." *Columbus Dispatch*, 21 September 1995, 7C.

LeRoy, Greg. *No More Candy Store: States and Cities Making Job Subsidies Accountable*. Chicago: Federation for Industrial Retention and Renewal, and Washington: Grassroots Policy Project, 1994.

———. "The Terrible Ten Candy Store Deals of 1998." *The Progressive*, May 1999, available at: http://www.progressive.org/leroy9905.htm.

LeRoy, Greg, and Tyson Slocum. *Economic Development in Minnesota: High Subsidies, Low Wages, Absent Standards*. Washington, D.C.: Good Jobs First, 1999.

Lillie, Nathan. "Transnational Labor Mobilization in Europe: The Case of Renault-Vilvoorde." Paper presented to European Community Studies Association annual meeting, Pittsburgh, June 1999.

Lind, Nancy S. "Economic Development and Diamond-Star Motors: Intergovernmental Competition and Cooperation." In *The Politics of Industrial Recruitment: Japanese Automobile Investment and Economic Development in the American States*, edited by Ernest J. Yanarella and William C. Green. New York: Greenwood Press, 1990.

Lindblom, Charles E. *Politics and Markets: The World's Political-Economic Systems*. New York: Basic Books, 1977.

Lipson, Charles. "The International Organization of Third World Debt." *International Organization* 34 (October 1981): 603–31.

———. "International Cooperation in Economic and Security Affairs." *World Politics* 37, no. 1 (October 1984): 1–23.

———. "Bankers' Dilemmas." In *Cooperation Under Anarchy*, edited by Kenneth Oye. Princeton, N.J.: Princeton University Press, 1986.

"Living Wage Movement Scores New Victories, Keeps Rolling." *The ACORN Report*, April 1999, 1–2.

Loveridge, Scott. "On the Continuing Popularity of Industrial Recruitment." *Economic Development Quarterly* 10, no. 2 (May 1996): 151–58.

Lynch, Robert G. *Do State & Local Tax Incentives Work?* Washington, D.C.: Economic Policy Institute, 1996.

Mac Carthaigh, John, and Eibhir Mulqueen. "EU Tax Policy Aimed at Reducing Overall Rates." *Irish Times*, 19 June 1999, 19.

Machlup, Fritz. "Introduction." In *International Mobility and Movement of Capital*, edited by Fritz Machlup, Walter S. Salant, and Lorie Tarshis. New York: National Bureau of Economic Research, 1972.

Mahtesian, Charles. "Romancing the Smokestack." *Governing* (November 1994), 36–40.

———. "Saving the States from Each Other." *Governing* (November 1996), 15.

Mariano, Ann. "Senate Votes to Cut Off Development Grants; Decade-Old Program for Troubled Areas Succumbs to Deficit Pressures." *Washington Post*, 14 July 14, A17.

Martin, Reiner, and Mathias Schulze Steinen. "State Aid, Regional Policy and Locational Competition in the European Union." *European Urban and Regional Studies* 4 (1997): 19–31.

Martin, Robert. "Nova Scotia wins bidding war for $18 million Litton plant." *Globe and Mail*, 26 July 1986, A3.

Marx, Karl. *Wage-Labor and Capital*. In *Karl Marx: Selected Writings*, edited by David McLellan. Oxford: Oxford University Press, 1977.

Matz, Kristin. "Economists Call for End to Incentive Packages." *Lafayette Business Digest*, 30 October 1995, Section C, 2.

McCulla, Don. Untitled. Paper presented at Special Session of the Industry Committee on Industrial Support in the OECD Area: The Future of Public Support, Paris, October 1996.

McDonald, Robert. "State Aids & the Effort to Ensure Fair Competition." *EIU European Trends* no. 2 (1992): 58–67.

"McDonough Details Program to Reduce GST." New Democrat Press Release, 30 May 1996.

McManus, John, and Fiona McHugh. "Irish Tax Strategy Blocked by EU." *Sunday Times*, 4 October 1998.

Mederer, Wolfgang. "The Future of State Aid Control." *Competition Policy Newsletter* (autumn/winter 1996), 12–14.

———. "State Aid: Summary of the most important recent developments." *Competition Policy Newsletter* (autumn/winter 1996), 46–51.

Mendrinou, Maria. "Non-Compliance and the European Commission's Role in Integration." *Journal of European Public Policy* (March 1996), 1–22.

"MEPs Split Over State Aid and Liberalization." Reuter European Community Report, 14 February 1996, BC Cycle.

Meyers, Mike. "Ban Urged on States' Financial Competing for Business; Regional Presidential Commission Urges Halt to Subsidies for Teams, Industries." *Minneapolis Star-Tribune*, 26 November 1996, 8D.

———. "Relocation Subsidies Target of Minge Bill." *Star Tribune*, 3 December 1997, 1D.

Middlemas, Keith. *Orchestrating Europe: The Informal Politics of the European Union*. London: Fontana Press, 1995.

Milward, H. Brinton, and Heidi Hosbach Newman. "State Incentive Packages and the Industrial Location Decision." In *The Politics of Industrial Recruitment: Japanese Automobile Investment and Economic Development in the American States*, edited by Ernest J. Yanarella and William C. Green. New York: Greenwood Press, 1990.

Moore, Stephen, and Dean Stansel. *Ending Corporate Welfare As We Know It*. Cato Institution, electronic edition (http://www.cato.org/main/pa225.html), 1995.

Moran, Theodore H. "Managing an Oligopoly of Would-Be Sovereigns: The Dynamics of Joint Control and Self-Control in the Oil Industry Past, Present, and Future." *International Organization* 41, no. 4 (autumn 1987): 575–607.

———. *Foreign Direct Investment and Development*. Washington, D.C.: Institute for International Economics, 1999.

Mørch, Henrik. "Summary of the most important recent developments (state aid)." *Competition Policy Newsletter* (summer 1995), 43–49.

———. "Summary of the most important recent developments (state aid)." *Competition Policy Newsletter* (autumn/winter 1994), 61–66.

———. "Summary of the most important recent developments (state aid)." *Competition Policy Newsletter* (spring 1996), 33–37.

Morris, Chris. "Province Offers $5.3M 'Loan' to Lure Air Canada Call Centre." *Ottawa Citizen*, 30 August 1996, D10.

Motor Industry Research Unit. *State Aid to the European Motor Industry: Disaster Aversion or Strategic Investment?* Norwich, England: University of East Anglia, 1987.

Mueller, Dennis. *Public Choice*. Cambridge: Cambridge University Press, 1979.

Mukherjee, Sougata. "Feds look to stop economic incentive wars between states." *Jacksonville Business Journal*, 14 June 1996, 1.

Munchau, Wolfgang, and Neil Buckley. "News: Europe: VW Halts Investment in East Germany." *Financial Times*, 27 June 1996, 2.

Murray, Alasdair. "Monti Signals Intent to Attack All State Subsidies." *The Times* (London), 2 September 1999.

Myers, Steven Lee. "Giuliani Says Connecticut Broke Truce." *New York Times*, 14 October 1994, B1.

Myerson, Allen R. "O Governor, Won't You Buy Me a Mercedes Plant?" *New York Times*, 1 September 1996, Section 3, 1.

National Association of State Development Agencies (NASDA). *State Economic Development Expenditure Survey/Summary: Analysis and Tables*. Washington: NASDA, n.d.

Neven, Damien, and Georges Siotis. "Foreign Direct Investment in the European Community: Some Policy Issues." *Oxford Review of Economic Policy* 9, no. 2 (summer 1993): 72–93.

"New Resolve to Control State Aids." *Financial Times Business Law Brief*, April 1989.

"Nine Provinces Trying to Woo Piper Aircraft." *Globe and Mail*, 10 December 1991, B6.

Norman, Peter. "Twenty-Hour Talk Marathon Ends in Compromise." *Financial Times*, 27 March 1999, 2.

North, Douglass. *Institutions, Institutional Change and Economic Performance*. Cambridge: Cambridge University Press, 1990.

O'Brien, Robert. *Subsidy Regulation and State Transformation in North America, the GATT and the EU*. London: Macmillan, 1997.

"OECD Says Switzerland Should Fix Tax System to Meet International Standards." *AFX News*, 5 August 1999.

Offe, Claus, and Helmut Wiesenthal. "Two Logics of Collective Action: Theoretical Notes on Social Class and Organizational Form." *Political Power and Social Theory* 1 (1980): 67–115.

Olson, Mancur. *The Logic of Collective Action: Public Goods and the Theory of Groups*. Cambridge, Mass.: Harvard University Press, 1971.

Ontario Coalition for Social Justice and Ontario Federation of Labor. *Unfair Shares: Corporations and Taxation in Canada*. Don Mills, Ontario: Ontario Coalition for Social Justice and Ontario Federation of Labor, 1996.

"Ontario Creates Jobs and Attracts Investments Without Hand-outs to Business—Palladini." Canada NewsWire, 19 February 1998.

Organization for Economic Cooperation and Development (OECD). *Industrial Support Policies in OECD Countries, 1986–1989*. Paris: OECD, 1992.

———. *Industrial Subsidies: A Reporting Manual*. Paris: OECD, 1995.

———. *National Accounts, Vol. I (1960-93)*. Paris: OECD, 1995.

———. *National Accounts, Volume II: 1981–1993*. Paris: OECD, 1995.

———. *National Accounts, Volume I (1960–94)*. Paris: OECD, 1996.

———. *National Accounts, Volume II: 1982–1994*. Paris: OECD, 1996.

———. *Public Support to Industry*. Paris: OECD, 1996.

———. *Tax Expenditures: Recent Experiences*. Paris: OECD, 1996.

———. *Revenue Statistics 1965–1997*. Paris: OECD, 1998.

———. *Harmful Tax Competition: An Emerging Global Issue*. Paris: OECD, 1998.

———. *Public Support to Industry in OECD Countries*. Paris: OECD, 1998.

OECD-DSTI-Shipbuilding. "The Agreement Respecting Normal Competitive Conditions in the Commercial Shipbuilding and

Repair Industry—Overview." OECD Web site (http://www.oecd.org/dsti/sid/sp7.html).

OECD, Fiscal Affairs. "What's New: Tax Competition." OECD Web site (http://www.oecd.org/daf/fa/taxcomp.htm).

Osterberg Consulting. "Corporate Welfare in Iowa." January 1997.

Oye, Kenneth A., ed. *Cooperation Under Anarchy*. Princeton, N.J.: Princeton University Press, 1986.

"Parliament Launches Inquiry into Techno-Lease." *ANP English News Bulletin* (Netherlands) 2 (May 1997).

Patterson, Eric. "Behind the Mercedes Move." *Expansion Management* (January/February 1994), 4.

Peirce, Neil R. "To Curb Tax Giveaways: Bring on the Feds." *Nation's Cities*, 25 December 1995, 14.

Pemberton, Max. *Europe's Motor Industry After 1992*. EIU Special Report No. 2090, January 1991.

Perry, Ben. "State Aids to the Former East Germany: A Note on the VW/Saxony Case." *European Law Review* 22 (February 1997): 85–91.

Perry, Suzanne. "EU Court Rejects UK Work-Hours Challenge." Reuters World Service, 12 November 1996.

"Piper Aircraft Corp to Investigate Location of all New Operations." *Financial Post*, 21 November 1991, 3.

"Piper Aircraft Ready for British Columbia Landing by Dancan Investments." *Financial Post*, 11 June 1992, 4.

"Piper Aircraft Rescue Deal in Sight." *Financial Post*, 6 March 1992, 4.

"Piper Bid Dead." *Financial Post*, 1 May 1993, 4.

"Piper May Locate to Canada if Funds Can Be Arranged." *Financial Post*, 18 December 1991, 7.

Pitt, William. *More Equal Than Others . . . A Director's Guide to EU Competition Policy*. Hemel Hempstead, U.K.: Director Books, 1995.

Porter, Chris. "Commission Loses Out in Bruising Regional Aid Battle." Reuter European Community Report, 20 July 1993.

Press release from Janice Shields, Corporate Welfare Project Coordinator, Essential Information, 29 January 1997.

Proctor, Paul. "Fear of New Taxes Dims Glow from Sales." *Aviation Week and Space Technology*, 25 September 1995, 45.

Prokesch, Steven. "Despite Pact, New York and Region Spar for Jobs." *New York Times*, 30 November 1992, Section C.

"Provincial Trade Agreement Doesn't Pass Crucial Test" (editorial). *Financial Post*, 19 September 1996, 10.

Przeworski, Adam, and Michael Wallerstein. "Structural Dependence of the State on Capital." *American Political Science Review* 82 (March 1988): 11–29.

Quinn, Dennis Patrick. *Restructuring the Automobile Industry: A Study of Firms and States in Modern Capitalism*. New York: Columbia University Press, 1988.

———. "Investment Incentives: A Five Country Test of the Lindblom Hypothesis." In *Research in Corporate Social Performance and Policy*, Vol. 10, edited by Lee E. Preston. Greenwich, Conn.: JAI Press, 1988.

———. "The Correlates of Change in International Financial Regulation." *American Political Science Review* 91, no. 3 (September 1997): 531–51.

Rakovsky, Claude, Stefaan Depypere, Thina Jakob, and Brona Carton. "Summary of the most important recent developments (International Dimension of Competition Policy)." *Competition Policy Newsletter* (autumn/winter 1995), 51–56.

Ranney, Nora, and Alexa Bradley. *1996 Corporate Welfare Handbook: A Comprehensive Handbook on Corporate Welfare in Minnesota*. St. Paul: Minnesota Alliance for Progressive Action, 1996.

Reese, Laura. "Local Economic Development Practices Across the Northern Border." *Urban Affairs Quarterly* 28, no. 4 (June 1993): 571–92.

———. "The Role of Counties in Local Economic Development." *Economic Development Quarterly* 8, no. 1 (February 1994): 28–42.

Reeves, Jay. "Honda Deal with Ala. Less Sweet Than 1993 Package to Mercedes." *Chattanooga Times*, 8 May 1999, C1.

Riker, William H., and Peter C. Ordeshook. *An Introduction to Positive Political Theory*. Englewood Cliffs, N.J.: Prentice-Hall, 1973.

Ritzler, Karl. "Alabama Proposal Attracts Honda: State Probably Will Use Tobacco Money to Fund Incentive-Laden Plan for Manufacturing Plant." *Atlanta Journal and Constitution*, 6 May 1999, 1A.

Robertson, David, and Dennis Judd. *The Development of American Public Policy: The Structure of Policy Restraint*. Glenview, Ill.: Scott, Foresman, 1989.

Robinson, Ian. *North American Trade As If Democracy Mattered*. Ottawa: Canadian Centre for Policy Alternatives, 1993.

Ronayne, Mark. "Disciplining Industrial Incentives to Promote Competitive and Efficient North American Markets." Industry and Science Canada discussion paper, August 1993.

Ross, David, and Benedict Brogan. "Sea Lochs the Key to Subsidy." *The Herald* (Glasgow), 24 March 1999, 7.

Ross, Malcolm. "A Review of Developments in State Aids 1987–88." *Common Market Law Review* 26 (1989): 167–92.

Rubenstein, James. "The Changing Distribution of Automobile Assembly Plants." *Focus* (fall 1988), 12–17.

———. *The Changing U.S. Auto Industry: A Geographical Analysis*. London: Routledge, 1992.

Rubin, Herbert J. "Shoot Anything That Flies; Claim Anything That Falls: Conversations With Economic Development Practitioners." *Economic Development Quarterly* 2, no. 3 (August 1998): 236–51.

Rubner, Alex. *The Export Cult*. London: Maurice Temple Smith, 1987.

Schina, Despina. *State Aids Under the EEC Treaty, Articles 92 to 94*. Oxford: ESC Publishing Limited, 1987.

Schweke, William, and Carl Rist. *Managing for Higher Returns: What Does North Carolina Actually Spend on Economic Development and How Can These Investments Be Better Managed?* Washington, D.C.: Corporation for Enterprise Development, 1997.

Schweke, William, Carl Rist, and Brian Dabson. *Bidding for Business: Are Cities and States Selling Themselves Short?* Washington, D.C.: Corporation for Enterprise Development, 1994.

"Shaky truce on social battlefield." *Financial Times*, 5 August 1996, 13.

Shapiro, Robert J. *Cut-and-Invest: A Budget Strategy for the New Economy*. Washington, D.C.: Progressive Policy Institute, 1995.

Shapiro, Robert J., and Chris Soares. *Cut-and-Invest to Grow: How to Expand Public Investment While Cutting the Deficit*. Washington, D.C.: Progressive Policy Institute, 1997.

Shields, Janice. *Aid for Dependent Corporation (AFDC) 1995*. Washington, D.C.: Essential Information, 1995.

———. "Ending (Corporate) Welfare As We Know It." Electronic version, available at: http://www.emf.net/~cr/govreform/corpwelf-012596. 1996.

Shirlow, P. "Transnational Corporations in the Republic of Ireland and the Illusion of Economic Well-Being." *Regional Studies* 29, no. 7 (1995): 688–91.

Sinclair, Timothy J. "Passing Judgement: Credit Rating Processes as Regulatory Mechanisms of Governance in the Emerging World Order." *Review of International Political Economy* 1, no. 1 (spring 1994): 133–59.

———. "Between State and Market: Hegemony and Institutions

of Collective Action Under Conditions of International Capital Mobility." *Policy Sciences* 27, no. 4 (1994): 447–66.

Siraut, John. "Exploding the grants myth." *Corporate Location* (February 1992), 2–3.

Slot, Piet Jan. "Facts, procedure and comments in Case C-301/87." *European Law Review* 16 (1991): 38–47.

———. "Procedural Aspects of State Aids: The Guardian of Competition Versus the Subsidy Villains?" *Common Market Law Review* 27 (1990): 741–60.

Smith, Mitchell. "Integration in Small Steps: The European Commission and Member-State Aid to Industry." *West European Politics* 19 (July 1996): 563–82.

———. "Autonomy by the Rules: The European Commission and the Development of State Aid Policy." *Journal of Common Market Studies* 36, no. 1 (March 1998): 55–78.

Smyth, Patrick. "Corporation Tax Deal Could Lose Us EU Goodwill." *Irish Times*, 30 November 1998, 16.

———. "Ireland Suffers Cut of More Than Half in Total Receipts from EU Funds." *Irish Times*, 27 March 1999, 14.

———. "EU Efforts to Eliminate Tax Conflict Get Bogged Down." *Irish Times*, 19 April 1999, 18.

Snidal, Duncan. "The Game *Theory* of International Politics." *World Politics*, (October 1985), 25–57.

Soames, Trevor, and Alan Ryan. "State Aid and Air Transport." *European Competition Law Review* 5 (1995): 290–305.

Souhrada, Paul. "Fewer Battles Urged." *Dayton Daily News*, 24 December 1996, 5B.

"South Carolina: What Does BMW Know that You Don't?" *Expansion Management* (September-October 1993), 76.

SouthWest Organizing Project (SWOP). *Intel Inside New Mexico*, revised ed. Albuquerque: SWOP, 1995.

"Spanish subsidies." *Financial Times*, 2 February 1996, 15.

Springer, Beverly. *The European Union and its Citizens: The Social Agenda*. Westport, Conn.: Greenwood Press, 1994.

"State Aid: Commission Extends Bremer Vulkan Investigation." European Report No. 2173, 13 November 1996.

"State Aid: Worried Commission Proposes Stricter Rules." RAPID Press Release IP 97/308, 16 April 1997.

"States Should Embrace Tax-Incentive Backlash" (editorial). *Dayton Daily News*, 28 September 1995, 10A.

Statistics Canada. *Canadian Economic Observer*, August 1993.

———. *Canadian Economic Observer, Statistical Summary*, August 1996.

———. *National Income and Expenditure Accounts*. Ottawa: Statistics Canada, 1996.

Steinmo, Sven. *Taxation and Democracy*. New Haven, Conn.: Yale University Press, 1993.

Straiger, Joos. "Competition Conference in Bratislava." *Competition Policy Newsletter* (October 1998), 59–60.

"The Aid Plague." *Economist* Survey of Business in Europe, 8 June 1991, 12–18.

Thomas, Kenneth P. "Auto Bargaining in Canada, 1965–87." In *Multinational Corporations in a Changing Global Political Economy*, edited by Steve Chan. London: Macmillan, 1995.

———. "EU Regulation of State Aid to Industry: Lessons for North America." In *Economic Integration in the Americas*, edited by Christos C. Paraskevopoulos, Ricardo Grinspun, and George E. Eaton. Cheltenham: Edward Elgar, 1996.

———. " 'Corporate Welfare' Campaigns in North America." *New Political Economy* 2 (March 1997): 117–26.

———. *Capital Beyond Borders: State and Firms in the Auto Industry, 1960–94*. London: Macmillan, 1997.

———. "International Control and Discipline of Subsidies: The EU and WTO Surveillance Exercises." *STI Review* no. 21 (1998), 25–42.

Thomsen, Stephen, and Stephen Woolcock. *Direct Investment and European Integration: Competition among Firms and Governments*. London: Pinter, 1993.

Tilmans, Madeleine. "The Commission decided that Germany must apply the multisectoral framework on regional aid to large investment projects." *Competition Policy Newsletter* (October 1998), 50.

———. "State Aid: Principaux développements du 1er mai au juillet 1998." *Competition Policy Newsletter* (October 1998), 57–58.

Toulin, Alan. "Canada: Provincial Trade Pact Starting to Crumble." *Financial Post*, 14 September 1996, 1.

"Toyota Investment Shows Confidence in Ontario Economy, Says Premier." Canada NewsWire, 3 November 1994.

Tucker, Emma. "Cresson Halts EU Block on State Aid to Chips Venture." *Financial Times*, 20 June 1997, 2.

———. "Commission Resolves VW Row." *Financial Times*, 19 November 1997, 2.

———. "Deal Is Clinched on EU Tax Code." *Financial Times*, 3 December 1997, 2.

———. "EU to Reconsider Regional Aid: Commission Plans to Focus Help on Areas Most in Need of Help." *Financial Times*, 19 December 1997, 2.

———. "Boost for Brussels Over Illegal State Aid." *Financial Times*, 16 November 1998, 4.

Tucker, Emma, and John Griffiths. "Aid deal for Jaguar could embarrass London." *Financial Times*, 2 February 1996, 2.

"UNICE Disappointed with Proposed State Aid Rules," *European Report* no. 2293, 21 February 1998.

United Nations Conference on Trade and Development, Division of Transnational Corporations and Investment. *World Investment Report 1994: Transnational Corporations, Employment and the Workplace*. New York: United Nations, 1994.

U.S. Department of Commerce (DOC). *Statistical Abstract of the United States*, 1995. Washington, D.C.: Government Printing Office, 1996.

———. *Statistical Abstract of the United States*, 1998. Washington, D.C.: Government Printing Office, 1999.

———. *Report to Congress: Review and Operation of the WTO Subsidies Agreement*. Washington, D.C.: Government Printing Office, 1999.

U.S. Trade Representative. "Agreement on Subsidies and Countervailing Measures." In *Final Act Embodying the Results of the Uruguay Round of Multilateral Trade Negotiations*, 15 December 1993.

Van Miert, Karel. "Karel Van Miert's Guidelines and Intentions Over State Aid." *Europe Documents*, English edition, no. 1848, 9 July 1993.

Verdier, Daniel. "The Politics of Public Aid to Private Industry: The Role of Policy Networks." *Comparative Political Studies* 28 (April 1995): 3–42.

Vernon, Raymond. *Sovereignty at Bay*. New York: Basic Books, 1971.

Vogel, David. *Trading Up: Consumer and Environmental Regulation in a Global Economy*. Cambridge, Mass.: Harvard University Press, 1995.

Waddell, Christopher. "Ontario to get $300 million Toyota plant." *Globe and Mail*, 19 October 1985, A1, A11.

Watson, Douglas J. *The New Civil War: Government Competition for Economic Development*. Westport, Conn.: Praeger, 1995.

Waltz, Kenneth N. *Theory of International Politics*. Reading, Mass.: Addison-Wesley, 1979.

Webb, Michael. "Taxing Transnational Capital: Transfer Prices in US Policy and the OECD." Paper prepared for workshop on capital mobility, Princeton University, Princeton, N.J., March 1996.

Whalen, Jessica, Jesse Bacon, and Alexa Bradley. *Minnesota Corporate Welfare Law . . . 2 Years Later*. St. Paul: Minnesota Alliance for Progressive Action, 1997.

Wighton, David. "Joint Group Launched to Consider EU Tax Reform." *Financial Times*, 8 June 1999, 12.

Wilks, Stephen, with Lee McGowan. "Competition Policy in the European Union: Creating a Federal Agency?" In *Comparative Competition Policy: National Institutions in a Global Market*, edited by G. Bruce Doern and Stephen Wilks. Oxford: Clarendon Press, 1996.

Wilson, Scott. "Marriott Takes Deal to Stay in Maryland." *Washington Post*, 12 March 1999, A1.

Winter, J. A. "Supervision of State Aid: Article 93 in the Court of Justice." *Common Market Law Review* 30 (1993): 311–29.

Winters, Jeffrey A. *Power in Motion: Capital Mobility and the Indonesian State*. Ithaca, N.Y.: Cornell University Press, 1996.

Wishlade, Fiona. "Competition Policy, Cohesion and Co-ordination of Regional Aids in the European Community." *European Competition Law Review* 14, no. 4 (1993): 143–50.

———. "Subsidies and State Aids: The Definition of Acceptable Measures Under the European Union and World Trade Organisation Rules." Regional and Industrial Research Paper Series no. 21, European Policies Research Centre, University of Strathclyde, September 1996.

———. "The Policy Relevance of the EU State Aid Rules." Paper presented at a meeting of the European Community Studies Association, Seattle, May 1997.

———. *When Are Tax Advantages State Aids and When Are They General Measures?* Regional and Industrial Policy Research Paper no. 20, European Policies Research Centre, University of Strathclyde, June 1997.

———. *EC Competition Policy and Regional Aid: An Agenda for the Year 2000?* Regional and Industrial Research Paper Series, No. 25, European Policies Research Centre, University of Strathclyde, December 1997.

———. *RAGS and LIPS: New Weapons in the Commission's Regional Aid Control Armoury*. Regional and Industrial Research Paper Series no. 31, European Policies Research Centre, University of Strathclyde, February 1999.

Woods, Jim. "City Doesn't Squander Abatements, Study Says." *Columbus Dispatch*, 13 March 1998, 1.

World Trade Organization (WTO). "Questions from the European Community Regarding the New and Full Notification of the United States," document G/SCM/Q2/USA/4. Geneva: WTO, 1996.

———. "Replies of the United States to Questions Posed by Korea, Norway, Japan, the European Community, Argentina, India, Canada, and Thailand," document G/SCM/Q2/USA/10. Geneva: WTO, 1997.

WTO, Committee on Subsidies and Countervailing Measures. "Note by the Secretariat," document G/SCM/23. Geneva: WTO, 1999.

"WTO Completes Framework for Environmental, Regional, and R&D Subsidies." WTO Web site (http://www.wto.org/wto/new/subpr2.htm).

Yuill, Douglas, Kevin Allen, John Bachtler, Keith Clement, and Fiona Wishlade. *European Regional Incentives*, 10th ed. Strathclyde, Scotland: European Policies Research Centre, 1990.

———. "European Regional Incentives (1992–93)." *Journal of Regional Policy* 12, nos. 3/4 (July/December 1992).

———. *European Regional Incentives 1993–94*, 13th ed. London: Bowker-Saur, 1993.

———. *European Regional Incentives 1994–95*. London: Bowker-Saur, 1994.

———. *European Regional Incentives 1995–96*. London: Bowker-Saur, 1995.

Zitner, Aaron. "Mass. Seeks Curb on States Job 'Poaching.' " *Boston Globe*, 3 June 1995, 59.

Web Sites

Corporation for Enterprise Development: www.cfed.org

Federal Reserve Bank of Minneapolis, "Economic War Among the States": http://woodrow.mpls.frb.fed.us/sylloge/econwar/index.html

U.S. Department of Commerce, Electronic Subsidies Enforcement Library: www.ita.doc.gov/import_admin/records/esel/

Interviews

Eric Berggren, UNICE, telephone interview, 23 March 1999.

Commission official, Brussels, 18 May 1998.

Jane Corwin, DOC, telephone interview, 9 November 1998.

Jeff Edstrom, Council of Great Lakes Governors, telephone interview, 6 April 1999.

European plant location consultant, Brussels, 23 September 1993.

European plant location consultant, telephone interview, 14 October 1993.

European plant location consultant, telephone interviews, 3 November and 5 November 1993.

Kimball Forrester, Alabama Arise, telephone interview, 5 August 1999.

Jeanne Gauna, SWOP, telephone interviews, 27 November 1996 and 18 February 1997.

Joseph Gilchrist, DG IV, Brussels, 14 September 1993.

Robert Ginsberg, Midwest Center for Labor Research, 6 January 1997.

Rauf Gönenc, OECD, Paris, 5 October 1993.

Jeff Goodman, Mancon Tax Incentive LLC, telephone interview, 7 January 1997.

Stephen Gospage, Section Head, Subsidies, DG I, Brussels, 19 May 1998.

Marcia Howard, Economic Policy Analyst, Public Policy Department, AFSCME, Washington, D.C., 6 June 1996.

Richard Jacques, office of the Permanent Representative of the UK to the EU, Brussels, 20 May 1998.

Jen Kern, ACORN, telephone interview, 28 May 1996.

Gawain Kripke, Friends of the Earth, telephone interview, 21 May 1996.

Iris Lav, CBPP, Washington, 7 June 1996.

Ronald Lorentzen, Director, WTO Industrial Issues, Office of U.S. Trade Representative, telephone interview, 19 October 1998.

Katherine McGuire, Ontario Ministry of Economic Development and Trade, telephone interview, 29 January 1997.

Cyrus Mehta, head of CBI's State Aid Working Group, telephone interview, 22 March 1999.

Jonathon Menes, Director, Office of Trade and Economic Analysis, U.S. Department of Commerce, International Trade Administration, telephone interview, 4 October 1996.

Municipal economic development director in Ontario, telephone interview, 26 November 1996.

OECD official, telephone interview, 20 July 1999.

Ken Poole, National Association of State Development Agencies, telephone interview, 31 May 1996.

Udo Pretschker, OECD Directorate for Science, Technology, and Industry, Paris, 15 May 1998.

Judy Randall, Canada's New Democrats, telephone interviews, 19 August 1996 and 11 September 1996.

Simon Reisman, Canadian negotiator for U.S.-Canada Auto Pact, telephone interview, 10 September 1991.

Walter Robinson, CTF, telephone interview, 23 July 1999.

Mark Ronayne, Industry, Science and Technology Canada, telephone interview, 5 August 1996.

Robert Shapiro, PPI, Washington, 7 June 1996.

Dean Stansel, Cato Institute, Washington, 11 June 1996.

Tax officials in Europe, May 1998.

Norm Treneman, British Columbia Ministry of Employment and Investment, telephone interview, 26 March 1999.

Jim Turk, Ontario Coalition for Social Justice, telephone interview, 5 September 1996.

U.S. trade official, Washington, D.C., 1 July 1996.

Emmy Verdun, Industry Canada, telephone interview, 19 July 1994.

Reinhard Walther, Unit Head, Inventory and Analysis, DG IV, Brussels, 23 September 1993.

Fiona Wishlade, European Policies Research Centre, University of Strathclyde, Glasgow, May 1994.

NOTE: Where no name is provided, the interviewee requested anonymity.

Appendix 1

Notes on Game Theory

This appendix addresses two issues in a more technical fashion than did Chapter 2. By using a more general model of strategic interaction than the Prisoners' Dilemma (though one that at most points *is* the Prisoners' Dilemma), I hope to tease out some further implications of the work here. First, I address whether very high levels of incentives transform the game from a Prisoners' Dilemma to something in which cooperation is more likely to arise. Second, I use a different set of payoffs to model a situation in which location incentives do *not* affect location decisions. The results require us to assume that policymakers are irrational to offer incentives—which is so implausible as to cast doubt on the view that subsidies do not affect location.

Very High Levels of Incentives

In this section, I modify the Prisoners' Dilemma model of Chapter 2 by collapsing its dual metric of jobs and money into a single money-based payoff matrix by specifying the value of jobs and the cost per job of incentives. Such numbers are arbitrary, of course, and I have made no attempt here to derive realistic figures. Instead, I try to highlight broader generalities.

One crucial assumption that has been modeled into the matrices below is that offering unanswered incentives shifts jobs to the jurisdiction that offers them (see Chapter 2 for discussion and point 2 below for the opposite assumption). All of the payoff matrices are characterized by the fact that universally refraining from incentives will be the Pareto optimal strategy, but the difficulty of achieving that strategy will vary. In particular, the greater the value of a job relative to the cost of incentives, the more likely the interaction is to be a Prisoners' Dilemma. As incentives increase relative to the value of a job, the game changes to a form of Assurance, then to what one might call Harmony (in which cooperation becomes a dominant strategy)—even maintaining the assumption that offering incentives shifts jobs to jurisdictions that offer them.

I start with my basic matrix, which assumes that offering incentives leaves the overall number of jobs created unchanged and specifies an arbitrary number of jobs that are shifted by unanswered incentives (250 out of a total of 1,000 jobs created). C is "not offer incentives," D is "offer incentives," *i* is incentive per job, numbers by themselves are the number of jobs, and MM is million. Thus, for CC or DD, each government creates 500 jobs, but in CD or DC 250 jobs are shifted to the unilateral defector.

	Player 2	
	C	D
Player 1		
C	500, 500	250, 750-750*i*
D	750-750*i*, 250	500-500*i*, 500-500*i*

Let the value of a job be $20,000 for all the following matrices; we will vary the cost of *i*.

i = $5,000

	Player 2	
	C	D
Player 1		
C	$10MM, $10MM	$5MM, $11.25MM
D	$11.25MM, $5MM	$7.5MM, $7.5MM

This matrix represents a Prisoners' Dilemma. Now let *i* = $8,000

	Player 2	
	C	D
Player 1		
C	$10MM, $10MM	$5MM, $9MM
D	$9MM, $5MM	$6MM, $6MM

Now we have a variant of Assurance. According to Michael Taylor, cooperation is unlikely to be a problem here because joint cooperation is an equilibrium, and both players prefer cooperation to joint defection.[1]

i = $20,000

	Player 2 C	Player 2 D
Player 1		
C	$10MM, $10MM	$5MM, 0
D	0, $5MM	0, 0

Now cooperation is the dominant strategy.

As we can see from these three matrices, cooperation theoretically can become easier as the cost of a job increases relative to its benefits. There are good reasons to believe that the more harmonious situations do not describe the real world, however. First, agreements to cooperate should be easy to maintain in both Assurance and Harmony, but the actual practice of investment attraction suggests that this cooperation hardly obtains in the real world. As we saw in Chapter 2, unconstrained competition for investment (as in the North American auto industry) has led to rising levels of subsidy—exactly the opposite of what would be the case if the underlying game were Assurance or Harmony. Even in the EU, constraints exist because the member states have delegated enforcement authority to the European Commission, not because investment promotion authorities have ceased activities.

Second, economic development officials or outside observers would have difficulty distinguishing empirically when the game has moved from Prisoners' Dilemma to Assurance (the more important of the two transformations). This difficulty exists because there are standpoint (should decisions be based on the value of a job to the government via tax revenue or to the economy?) and valuation problems that have no simple answer in theory—and in practice are constantly subject to manipulation to make an economic development project look better. Currently, investment promotion officials continue to try to persuade the public that their deals are cost-effective, which means that for them the underlying game is still Prisoners' Dilemma.

Third, the strategies in this game are not simply a choice of incentives or no incentives. Even if i reached $20,000 and the game were Harmony, nothing stops economic development officials from offering less in incentives—when the game would again become more like Prisoners' Dilemma. The result here may imply that there is some maximum level that incentives can reach, but empirically it is unlikely we have reached that point—and in any event, the Pareto optimal option remains not to use incentives.

Finally, as the level of subsidies rises but before the game changes from Prisoners' Dilemma to Assurance, incentives may cause capital to substitute for labor instead of employing labor. We may have reached this point already in the auto industry: Generally speaking, incentive/investment is falling but incentive/job is rising,[2] implying substitution of capital for labor.

What if Incentives Do *Not* Affect Location?

Using the foregoing notation, below we have a game in which incentives do not affect location. This factor is modeled in by assuming that each player receives the same number of jobs regardless of whether either player uses location incentives.

	Player 2 C	D
Player 1		
C	500, 500	500, 500-500i
D	500-500i, 500	500-500i, 500-500i

For any positive value of i, cooperation is the dominant strategy. Indeed, this is not really a game at all because there is no strategic interaction: Player 1's move does not affect Player 2's payoffs, and vice versa. In this scenario, a government is worse off if it uses incentives; therefore, officials would have to be irrational to use them if they did not affect location. Rather than starting from this position and trying to find some tenuous political rationality for this economically irrational behavior, I start with the more realistic assumption that location incentives do affect location, which does not require assuming that officials act irrationally.

Notes

1. See Michael Taylor, *The Possibility of Cooperation* (Cambridge: Cambridge University Press, 1987), 38–39. This particular game is Taylor's second variant in Figure 4 on page 38.
2. Kenneth P. Thomas, *Capital Beyond Borders: States and Firms in the Auto Industry, 1960–94* (London: Macmillan, 1997), 143.

APPENDIX 2

Text of Articles 87–89 EEC
(formerly Articles 92–94)

Article 87 (formerly Article 92)

1. Save as otherwise provided in this Treaty, any aid granted by a Member State or through State resources in any form whatsoever which distorts or threatens to distort competition by favouring certain undertakings or the production of certain goods shall, insofar as it affects trade between Member States, be incompatible with the common market.
2. The following shall be compatible with the common market:
   (a) aid having a social character granted to individual consumers, provided that such aid is granted without discrimination related to the origin of the products concerned;
   (b) aid to make good the damage caused by natural disasters or exceptional occurrences;
   (c) aid granted to the economy of certain areas of the Federal Republic of Germany affected by the division of Germany, insofar as such aid is required in order to compensate for the economic disadvantages caused by that division.
3. The following may be considered to be compatible with the common market:
   (a) aid to promote the economic development of areas where the standard of living is abnormally low or where there is serious underemployment;
   (b) aid to promote the execution of an important project of common European interest or to remedy a serious disturbance in the economy of a Member State;
   (c) aid to facilitate the development of certain economic activities or of certain economic areas, where such aid does not adversely affect trading conditions to an extent contrary to the common interest.

(d) aid to promote culture and heritage conservation where such aid does not affect trading conditions and competition in the Community to an extent that is contrary to the common interest;

(e) such other categories of aid as may be specified by decision of the Council acting by a qualified majority on a proposal from the Commission.

Article 88 (formerly Article 93)

1. The Commission shall, in co-operation with Member States, keep under constant review all systems of aid existing in those States. It shall propose to the latter any appropriate measures required by the progressive development or by the functioning of the common market.
2. If, after giving notice to the parties concerned to submit their comments, the Commission finds that aid granted by a State or through State resources is not compatible with the common market having regard to Article 87, or that such aid is being misused, it shall decide that the State concerned shall abolish or alter such aid within a period of time to be determined by the Commission.

   If the State concerned does not comply with this decision within the prescribed time, the Commission or any other interested State may, in derogation from the provisions of Articles 226 and 227, refer the matter to the Court of Justice direct.

   On application by a Member State, the Council may, acting unanimously, decide that aid which that State is granting or intends to grant shall be considered to be compatible with the common market, in derogation from the provisions of Article 87 or from the regulations provided for in Article 89, if such a decision is justified by exceptional circumstances. If, as regards the aid in question, the Commission has already initiated the procedure provided for in the first subparagraph of this paragraph, the fact that the State concerned has made its application to the Council shall have the effect of suspending that procedure until the Council has made its attitude known.

   If, however, the Council has not made its attitude known within three months of the said application being made, the Commission shall give its decision on the case.
3. The Commission shall be informed, in sufficient time to enable it to submit its comments, of any plans to grant or alter aid. If it

considers that any such plan is not compatible with the common market having regard to Article 87, it shall without delay initiate the procedure provided for in paragraph 2. The Member State concerned shall not put its proposed measures into effect until this procedure has resulted in a final decision.

Article 89 (formerly Article 94)

The Council, acting by a qualified majority on a proposal from the Commission and after consulting the European Parliament, may make any appropriate regulations for the application of Articles 87 and 88 and may in particular determine the conditions in which Article 88(3) shall apply and the categories of aid exempted from this procedure.

APPENDIX 3

A Portrait of State Aid

In 1995–97, state aid to manufacturing in the EU averaged 37.7 billion ECU, or 2.8 percent of value added in industry. Excluding new members Austria, Finland, and Sweden (which were not members for the entire 1993–95 statistical period), the 1995–97 average was 36.4 billion ECU—a 13.0 percent decrease in real terms from 41.8 billion ECU in 1993–95 (expressed in 1996 prices). The entire decrease was accounted for by Germany, largely in the new *Länder*, as Table X3-1 shows.

Table X3-1 **State Aid to Manufacturing (millions of 1996 ECU)**

Country	**1993–95**	**1995–97**	**1995–97 Percent**
Austria	N/A	537	1.4
Belgium	947	936	2.5
Denmark	623	725	1.9
Germany (total)	19,232	13,547	36.0
Old *Länder*	3,395	3,064	8.1
New *Länder*	15,836	10,482	27.8
Greece	619	657	1.7
Spain	1,665	2,472	6.6
Finland	N/A	383	1.0
France	4,401	4,284	11.4
Ireland	329	395	1.0
Italy	11,529	10,451	27.7
Luxembourg	45	46	0.1
The Netherlands	585	674	1.8
Portugal	495	537	1.4
Sweden	N/A	394	1.0
United Kingdom	1,339	1,640	4.4
Total	41,809	37,680	100

Source: Seventh Survey on State Aid, 7, Table 3.

Note: Totals may not sum because of rounding.

What does all this money go to? Aid in the *Surveys* is classified into three broad categories: horizontal, sectoral, and regional. Table X3-2 shows the breakdown among these categories during 1995–97.

Table X3-3 lists the totals for the various types of aid in the EU. The most important nonmanufacturing uses of aid are for transport (mostly railways) and coal mining. As Table X3-3 shows, transport and coal mining aid are a combined 41.3 billion ECU—higher than the 37.7 billion ECU in aid to industry.

Table X3-2 **Objectives of State Aid (percent)**

Objective	Percent
Horizontal	31
Research and development	10
Environment	1
Small/medium enterprise	7
Trade/export	2
Energy saving	3
Other horizontal objectives	8
Sectoral	12
Shipbuilding	4
Other sectors[a]	8
Regional	57
92(3)c	9
92(3)a	48

[a]Mainly includes rescue operations for individual firms.
Note: Totals may not sum because of rounding.
Source: Seventh Survey on State Aid, 20, Table 9.

Table X3-3 **Total National Aid, 1995–97 Annual Averages (millions of 1996 ECU)**

Type	Amount
Manufacturing	37,680
Agriculture	13,129
Fisheries	252
Coal Mining	7,646
Transport	33,655
Financial services	2,702
Total	95,065

Source: Seventh Survey on State Aid, 49, Table 18.

APPENDIX 4

NGOs Campaigning on Corporate Subsidies/Accountability

Numerous local NGOs are working on issues of banning corporate subsidies or making them more accountable (see Chapter 5). This listing is provided for researchers who may want to study these organizations in more depth than I was able to. This list is by no means exhaustive, but it provides a good beginning for those who wish to pursue these issues further. Further examples can be found in the text and notes of Chapter 5.

This list was compiled especially for this book by Sandra Hinson of the Grassroots Policy Project (GPP) in Washington, D.C., which provides training and technical assistance to a number of local NGOs. GPP is the copublisher of *No More Candy Store*—a useful sourcebook on local campaigns around subsidy issues. GPP can be reached at 202-387-2935.

Alabama Organizing Project
c/o Greater Birmingham Ministries
2304 12th Avenue North
Birmingham, AL 35234
205-326-6821
Contact: Scott Douglas
(This is one of the groups that campaigned for changes in the "Mercedes Law" in Alabama.)

Campaign for a Sustainable Milwaukee
1726 North First Street, Suite 202
Milwaukee, WI 53212
414-372-7175
Contact: Bill Dempsey

Carolina Alliance for Fair Employment
1 Chick Springs Road, #110-B
Greenville, SC 29609
864-235-2926
Contact: Carol Bishop or David Kennedy

Citizens Clearinghouse for Hazardous Wastes
P.O. Box 6806
Falls Church, VA 22040
703-237-2249
Contact: Charlotte Brody or Lois Gibbs

Connecticut Citizens Action Group
45 South Main
West Hartford, CT 06107
860-561-6013
Contact: Tom Swan

Community Family Alliance
311 Wilkinson Street
Frankfort, KY 40601
502-223-3655
Contact: Deborah Webb

Environmental Research Foundation
P.O. Box 5036
Annapolis, MD 21403
410-263-1584
Contact: Peter Montague

Food & Allied Service Trades
815 Sixteenth Street, NW, Suite 408
Washington, DC 20008
202-508-8205
Contact: Jeff Fiedler

Good Neighbor Project
P.O. Box 79225
Waverly, MA 02179
617-489-3686
Contact: Sanford Lewis

Grassroots Leadership
P.O. Box 36006
Charlotte, NC 28236
704-332-3090
Contact: Alfreda Barringer

Kentuckians for the Commonwealth
P.O. Box 1450
London, KY 40743
606-878-2161
Contact: Burt Lauderdale

Louisiana Injured Workers Union
926 Milan Street
New Orleans, LA 70115
504-899-4196
Contact: Allen Bernard

Minnesota Alliance for Progressive Action
1821 University Avenue, Suite S-307
St. Paul, MN 55104
612-641-4050
Contact: Mel Duncan

Missouri ACORN
4304 Manchester
St. Louis, MO 63110
314-531-7023
Contact: Craig Robbins

Missouri Rural Crisis Center
710 Rangeline Street
Columbia, MO 65201
573-449-1336
Contact: Rhonda Perry

Multnomah County Office of Community Action and Development
421 Southwest Sixth Avenue, Suite 500
Portland, OR 97204
503-248-3707
Contact: Janet Hawkins or Jill Bills

New Jersey Work Environment Council
452 East Third Street
Moorestown, NJ 08057
609-886-9405
Contact: Rick Engler

North East Citizen Action Resource Center
Progressive Policy Institute
186 Hampshire Street
Cambridge, MA 02139
617-547-4474
Contact: Cynthia Ward or Tim Costello

Northwest Federation of Community Organizations
Montana People's Action
208 East Main
Missoula, MT 59802
406-728-5297
Contact: James Fleischmann

Northwest Federation of Community Organizations
100 South King Street, Suite 240
Seattle, WA 98104
206-382-2082
Contact: Lee Ann Hall

Oregon Fair Share
702 Northeast Schuyler
Portland, OR 97212
503-280-1762
Contact: Kathy Donaldson

Pilchuck Audobon Society
9210 Market Place #H103
Everett, WA 98205
206-397-6056
Contact: Bonnie Phillips

Revisioning New Mexico
P.O. Box 4345
Albuquerque, NM 87196
505-255-4266
Contact: Santiago Juarez or Max Bartlett

Save Our Cumberland Mountains (SOCM)
P.O. Box 479
Lake City, TN 37769
423-426-9455
Contact: Steven Taylor

SouthWest Organizing Project
211 10th Street SW
Albuquerque, NM 87102
505-247-8832
Contact: Jeanne Gauna or Michael Guerrero
(This is the central organization fighting the subsidies to Intel discussed in Chapter 5.)

Tourism Industry Development Corporation
634 South Spring Street, Suite 1016
Los Angeles, CA 90014
213-486-9880
Contact: Madeline Janis-Aparicio
(This organization was key in the Los Angeles "living wage" campaign discussed in Chapter 5.)

Western Organization of Resource Councils
60584 Horizon Drive
Montrose, CO 81401
970-323-6849
Contact: Kevin Williams

Western States Center
Progressive Leadership Alliance of Nevada
428 Hill Street, Suite 204
Reno, NV 89501
702-348-7557
Contact: Jan Gilbert

Western States Center
P.O. Box 40305
Portland, OR 97240
503-228-8866
Contact: Dan Petegorsky or Kathy Howell

Western States Center/Institute for Washington's Future
3118 34th Avenue South
Seattle, WA 98144
206-324-7324
Contact: Rebecca Bauen

Working Partnerships, USA/South Bay Labor Council
2102 Almaden Road, Room 100
San Jose, CA 95125
408-266-3790
Contact: Amy Dean

Index

www.ingramcontent.com/pod-product-compliance
Lightning Source LLC
LaVergne TN
LVHW090144080826
844660LV00013B/670/J

* 9 7 8 0 8 7 8 4 0 8 0 8 5 *